Stanley Weintraub

IRON
TEARS

America's Battle for
Freedom, Britain's
Quagmire: 1775-1783

FREE PRESS
NEW YORK   LONDON   TORONTO   SYDNEY

*f*P

A Division of Simon & Schuster, Inc.
1230 Avenue of the Americas
New York, NY 10020

FREE PRESS and colophon are trademarks
of Simon & Schuster, Inc.

Designed by Karolina Harris

Manufactured in the United States of America

10 9 8 7 6 5 4 3 2 1

Library of Congress Cataloging-in-Publication
Control No. 1004056363

ISBN 0-7432-2687-9

For information regarding special discounts for bulk purchases, please contact Simon &
Schuster Special Sales at 1-800-456-6798 or business@simonandschuster.com

(FRONTISPIECE) American commisioners of the preliminary peace negotiations with Great
Britain, 1782 *Copyright Henry Francis du Pont Winterthur Museum. Courtesy of Winterthur
Museum*

for Major General (ret.) Bill Duncan,
great-great-great-great-great-great-great grandson
of the American Revolution

"*LOST. A large tract of land called AMERICA: whoever shall bring it back again to Mrs. Britannia, shall receive thirteen stripes reward.*"

—A MOCK CLASSIFIED ADVERTISEMENT IN A LONDON NEWSPAPER, REPRINTED IN THE *Boston Gazette and Country Journal* ON DECEMBER 22, 1783

"*Can Washington be called the conqueror of America? By no means. America was conquered in the British Parliament. Washington could never have conquered it. British Generals never did their duty.*"

—NEW YORK SUPREME COURT JUSTICE THOMAS JONES, IN POSTWAR EXILE IN LONDON, FROM HIS *A History of New York During the Revolutionary War*

Contents

A Note on the Text

SPELLINGS in the years 1775–1784 were not yet firm and formalized, nor were capitalization and punctuation. In the German manner, the English capitalized many nouns, but not always with any consistency. Punctuation relied more on semicolons, and some sentences with commas ran on into the sentence following, or were separated informally by a dash. Spellings were often idiosyncratic and even inconsistent when a word was repeated in the same text. Since it seems an abrupt break in continuity to call attention to such contemporary usages with a [*sic*], this device has been employed only in the most extraordinary circumstances.

Readers will recognize from the context that Washington's reference to "centinal" is to a sentinel, or that when Dean Josiah Tucker writes "Burthen" he is using the noun for burden. Certainly recognizable also are such usages as "sculk," "smoak," "takeing," "Chesapeak," "Pensilvania," "negociate," "publick," and "encreasing." In a few cases I have noted earlier usages of words we now employ differently.

Extracts from the colonial and British press, sometimes from the same sources, will often differ in spelling or be inventive in other ways. I have attempted to use what appears to be the most reliable text. Reported dates may vary slightly for the same reasons, and may differ also because there was as yet no formal global division into time zones, and communications then were slow and unreliable. Time and distance in the later eighteenth century create other problems of perception. Although it takes forty-eight hours for the rotation of the Earth to wheel a calendar date around the sun, time today is virtually simultaneous, although the hour and even the day (or night) might be different. Newspaper readers or readers of letters in England in 1775 would access news from America a month or more later than it happened, depending upon winds and waves. Since winds normally blew roughly from west to east, sailing ships from England to America, tacking against the wind and waves, might take as much as three months to cross the Atlantic. Thus, urgent news arriving in hours or days by courier on horseback might still be urgent news on arrival an ocean away—or moot because events had overtaken it. What happens on a particular day may, then, also be what happened months before but which only became known on the day in question. Every day, then, has two calendar faces.

Similarly, first-person accounts differ, just as they do when witnesses testify to a traffic accident. Some long postdate the events. There are many versions of the surrender of Earl Cornwallis at Yorktown, as to who tendered the symbolic sword of defeat to whom, and why it happened that way. In an age that preceded photography and television, there are also artist's conceptions of the event, all accomplished decades or more later. Some may be dramatic and some may be romantic, but none are any more accurate than the famous German canvas by an artist never near the Delaware of Washington's famous crossing in 1776. The historian must deal with reason rather than romance.

Some events have been recounted so often that to cite a source would be useless. I have detailed, rather, those sources that are original or unique, and multiple sources where there may be controversy. A bibliography of books and articles on the American war of Independence would take all the pages remaining, and more.

Preface
The Abandoned Canvas

There has been built in the port of Chatham [in Kent] a ship of war of 74 guns, called the Atlas. *The figurehead represents that gigantic fabulous personage with an enormous globe on his shoulders. The head carver having taking his measures badly, the globe was so high as to be in the way of the bowsprit, and it became necessary to take off part of the upper hemisphere. The part taken off was precisely North America.*

—*The Hague Gazette,* September 13, 1782, in a translation from the Dutch reprinted in a London newspaper

O N a summer morning in 1782 the energetic, fortyish Benjamin West, an expatriate Philadelphian and official history painter to George III, visited what was then Buckingham House to call upon Queen Charlotte. Expecting West, Charlotte asked him into her private sitting room, where he also found the king.

Realizing that the ongoing peace negotiations with the former colonies in America would lead to formal independence, the king asked West what he thought General Washington would now do. The godlike Washington, whom many Americans expected would be king if he wanted a throne, was more likely, West predicted, to return to his farm in Virginia.

If Washington did that, exclaimed His Majesty, who could not believe that anyone willingly relinquished supreme authority, he would be the greatest man in the world.

While General Washington still commanded the dwindling Continental army, and by strength of personality held the fractious colonies together, he had no authority over the peacemaking process three thousand miles away in Paris. Congress's appointees dealt with that, and West's immediate ambition was to paint the peace commissioners on both sides who were negotiating a draft of the peace treaty, a group portrait to be the first painting in a projected series on the long American war.

One of the most memorable paintings in American history, it achieves its dramatic resonance in part because a third of the canvas remains empty. Few great pictures better illustrate a wry later observation that "victory has a hundred fathers, but defeat is an orphan."

The seven persons West intended to represent as working on the preliminary treaty included Benjamin Franklin, John Adams, John Jay, Henry Laurens, and William Temple Franklin, the sage's grandson and secretary to the commission appointed by Congress.* The British had great difficulty naming appointees willing to negotiate openly for the losing side while being directed by bureaucrats in Whitehall who did not want to be associated with the national embarrassment. Only a single royal commissioner, Richard Oswald, a wealthy former army contractor and slave trader with American connections, who had the courage to put up the fifty thousand pounds to bail Henry Laurens, a former president of the Congress, out of the Tower of London after he was seized at sea en route to Holland, proved willing to serve. With his secretary, Caleb Whitefoord, a writer and wit who had been a neighbor of Franklin's in London, Oswald was to be remembered by history on West's canvas.

The Americans duly posed for West—all but Franklin, who at seventy-seven was too frail for the turbulent Channel crossing from Paris. With the good offices of Whitefoord he arranged to lend a portrait and a bust in his stead. Since Oswald was unwilling to pose in the ignominy of defeat and risk the ruin of his reputation (legend had it that he also felt too ugly to show his face), Whitefoord, his subordinate and the seventh intended subject, could hardly offer to sit himself. Then Oswald died suddenly in November 1784 on his estate in Scotland. The scene could no longer be completed from life.

West abandoned the canvas—and any plans to do other episodes for his abortive series. The indelicate venture might in any case have cost him his prestigious standing at court and his market in England for other pictures. The five abandoned Americans loom quietly over the partly open scroll of the draft treaty, while the blank third is dramatically unfinished, orphaned by defeat.

Some ghostly suggestions for carrying the picture further emerge

*Laurens and Temple Franklin were not at the formal signing in September 1783. West was painting what he called *The Signing of the Preliminary Treaty in 1782.*

on close examination—a building and a grid for a more extended structure that could be the new Somerset House on the Thames, or merely a symbolic evocation of London. A hint of another treaty scroll, held by Oswald, also surfaces faintly. (Each side needed to archive its own authentic, signed copy—thus, a likely duplicate.) John Jay's shoes remain unfinished; John Adams's breeches lack texture and his chair's legs are incomplete; and Henry Laurens's coat has an unfinished swath across his chest. Young Franklin's coat is only partially painted.

At the bicentennial of the 1783 Treaty of Paris ending the war the United States Post Office issued a twenty-cent stamp ostensibly reproducing West's painting, as if referring to the definitive event. A travesty of history and a mischievous misuse of West's canvas, it cut Jay and Laurens out and moved Adams, and in imagining how the gap which West had left would be filled, the anonymous postal artist inserted an unidentifiable Englishman in Laurens's place and a second colleague at his right. A large sheet of paper substitutes for the treaty scrolls. The grid of characteristic English buildings in the background is replaced by buildings and steeples that could be as much West's own Philadelphia as any venue in England.

History painting has often reimagined history, but the curious postal image, presumably issued with the imprimatur of the United States of America, then thirty-seven states beyond the original thirteen, is unique in its expunging and invention. With Benjamin West long dead there was no estate to bring suit for falsification and enjoin release of the stamp.

In the historical reality beyond commemorative postage Edmund Burke, MP for Bristol and an outspoken critic of colonial policy, had talked of "iron tears" being shed as America slipped away from imperial grasp. "Iron tears" suggests musket shot and cannonballs when fired as much in sadness as in anger. Was the inevitable separation worth a war? Frederick, Prince of Wales, who died before he could succeed his father, irascible old George II, had left "Instructions for my son George [III]" in which he had exhorted, "If you can be without war, let not your ambition draw you into it. . . . At the same time, never give up your honour nor that of the nation."

Was it honorable, if mistaken, to attempt to subdue rebels who no longer wanted to be the king's subjects? Could the exasperating and expensive long-distance conflict that West's painting recalled have possibly been won? How did relinquishing America look from the remote European side of the Atlantic? Were the admirals and the generals involved enthusiastically in the king's service, or only supplicants at, or beneficiaries of, his traditional reward system? How did the country gentlemen who held the decisive seats in the king's pliant House of Commons respond to the seemingly irrelevant war, which had become a quagmire? How did the divisive conflict appear to the prosperous London brokers, bankers, and traders who benefitted from the American trade?

Further, how did the Cabinet of the unhappy and flaccid Lord North, and his unpopular but forceful Secretary for America, Lord George Germain, a saturnine former general cashiered for alleged cowardice in an earlier war, cope with the increasingly distressing events, and—for better and for worse—help to shape them? Did they see the self-styled Americans as suffused with patriot zeal—or, with colonial irresponsibility, eager to escape their reasonable, even bargain-rate, burden of taxation? Or were there other reasons? The colorful and tumultuous background of that vacant third of Benjamin West's haunting canvas emerges in *Iron Tears,* in which the British empire loses its first jewel in the crown, America.

Stanley Weintraub
Beech Hill
Newark, Delaware

1

"Cousin America" 1775

"By the waters of Babylon we sit down and weep, when we think of thee O America!"

—*Sir Horace Walpole to the Reverend William Mason in 1775*

"COUSIN AMERICA has run off with a Presbyterian minister," Horace Walpole quipped to a friend in the summer of 1775. *The Daily Advertiser* had misidentified a militia leader at Bunker Hill as "a dissenting clergyman," but Walpole, youngest son of Britain's first actual prime minister, Sir Robert Walpole, was essentially correct. The cockpit of rebellion was Puritan Massachusetts. As Ambrose Serle, civilian secretary to Admiral Lord Richard Howe, would concede, "Republican Presbyterianism can never heartily coalesce with Monarchy & Episcopacy." Dissenting preachers, "firebrands to a man," he wrote, "inculcate War, Bloodshed & Massacres, as though all these were the express Injunctions of Jesus Christ, and they call for Destruction upon the loyal Subjects and Army of their rightful Sovereign, like so many Arbiters of the Vengeance of Heaven."

An embattled royal governor in South Carolina, James Simpson, claimed to the American Secretary in London that "there was nothing that conduced more to foment the disturbances and set the minds of the people in a flame than the exertions of some itinerant preachers who were sent throughout the country where they poisoned the minds of the people with groundless fears and false apprehensions." It remained convenient for Englishmen to blame colonial unrest on the mischief of outspoken Massachusetts clergy. Although disobedience existed also in more conservative Anglican Virginia, the resistance to imperial rule seemed stirred up primarily by a noisy but intimidating minority in the bleak North populated by dour self-exiles from an unsympathetic Britain.*

Despite their own, more phlegmatic homage paid to piety and worship, Englishmen found their cousins in America remote in more than distance. Without an acknowledged aristocracy a contrary "levelling principle" prevailed in the colonies, Sir Richard Sutton explained to the House of Commons in 1775. He knew a gentleman who asked a servant, at the residence of a merchant he visited in Boston, whether his master was at home. *"My Master!"* the servant declared; "I have no master but Jesus Christ." But, he added, the head of the household was indeed present. How, Sutton wondered, could English law and customs apply to such people?

To the baffled Establishment, frustrated by its own folly, burgeoning repudiation of colonial rule from across the Atlantic seemed still a trifling minority affair, the malefactions of willful political and religious radicals in a domestic climate of righteous misrule. Parliamentary authority exercised by the home authority was, to most Americans, hardly perceptible. Most colonial subjects of George III seemed at worst indifferent to change, far from eager for any disruption in their unexacting routines.

The cost of fighting the Seven Years' (French and Indian) War, which had ended in 1763, had doubled the English national debt and left the nation without major allies in Europe. American colonists, whose homes and farms had been protected from the French by the king's redcoats, who now occupied Canada, overtly contributed little toward reduction of that debt. Taxpaying Britons rued that distortion in revenue collection. A press report in London in 1774 enumerated the burden in England as

The land tax, poor tax, tavern and ale-house licences, &c., with taxes and duties on tea, coffee, leather, [silver]plate, soap, candles, beeswax, and wax-tapers; coney [rabbit] hair for the hatter's wife; starch, treacle, sugars, tobacco, snuff, glass, and house window lights; painters colours, wheels of carriages; wines of all kinds, that is, foreign and home made;

---

*A Hessian officer, Captain Johann Heinrichs, later in the war wrote to a friend in Germany that it was "nothing more or less than an Irish-Scotch Presbyterian Rebellion."

all sorts of spiritous liquors, and beer, cider, mum [Brunswick beer], metheglin [Welsh mead], perry [pear cider], and malt; hops, salt, paper, quills, printer's ink, and many other articles, which are too tedious to enumerate.

Merely the cost of garrisoning America approached £300,000 a year at a time when wages for a laborer in England were a shilling a day—a twentieth part of a pound. Yet across the Atlantic a patriot versifier in a New Hampshire gazette branded intrusive (but legal) English tax collectors and customs officers as "venal tools of power." Despite some customs seizures, the legitimate trade in taxable commodities in the colonies was reduced by blatant smuggling. Reports of criminal incidents abetting the evasions exasperated readers of London newspapers, especially since colonial juries rarely brought in convictions. One episode that caused grumbling in England occurred on June 10, 1772, when the revenue cutter *Gaspee* ran aground in Narragansett Bay, Rhode Island, while pursuing a smuggler. Eight boatloads of armed colonials led by a local merchant, John Brown, boarded the ship, overpowered the crew, injured the captain, and set the *Gaspee* afire. The culprits were never punished. Such episodes multiplied.

A navy accustomed to fighting textbook engagements had to begin dealing at sea with a Lilliputian guerrilla adversary. Little concerned now with external threats from France or Spain, colonists thriving on noncompliance had few ties of self-interest with distant Britain.

Because of its theatricality, the most notorious colonial outrage was the Boston "Tea Party" of December 16, 1773. Bank failures in London the year before had threatened even the prosperous East India Company, and to protect its major export as well as to symbolize Parliament's right to tax its subjects abroad, the life-enhancing leaf remained dutiable. The English press reported that some stubborn colonists, spurning the tax, were drinking "Labrador tea,"* or substituting coffee or chocolate "except in Case of Sickness." A monologue reaching England from America purported to have an affronted, cup-clutching fanatic exclaim,

*From a hardy brush in beds in Labrador with leaves of a distinctive aromatic taste and smell

A tax on my Tea?
Then why not a tax on my breath?
My daylight? My smoke? My everything?

At the infamous Party, 342 chests of cheap East India tea had been emptied and dumped into Boston Harbor by colonists transparently disguised as Mohawks. The actual tax to Americans, only threepence a pound, was a fourth of the impost paid in England, where illegal tea was purchased even by the otherwise upright. The parson at Weston Longeville in Norfolk, the Reverend James Woodforde, recorded without embarrassment in his diary, "Andrews the Smuggler brought me this night about eleven o'clock a bagg of Hyson Tea 6pd Weight. He frightnd us a little by whistling under the Parlour Window just as we were going to bed. I gave him some Geneva [gin] and paid him for the Tea at 10/6 Per Pd—[£]3.3.0." Smuggling had long been winked at on both sides of the ocean, but the crude vandalism at Boston, described as a patriotic protest against the principle of external taxation, enabled colonists to indulge in bargain, usually Dutch, tea. Evading lawful duties, American importers also smuggled molasses from the West Indies to be turned into rum. Puritan Massachusetts alone had more than sixty rum distilleries relying on contraband cargo.

Benjamin Franklin, agent in England for Massachusetts, Pennsylvania, and several other colonies, had long been an advocate for accommodation (as he put it in a ballad in 1765) with "an old mother that peevish is grown." Since "we know it must all be our own when she goes," and time was on America's side, he had advised that such acts of piracy were criminal and that compensation for the vandalized Boston tea should be paid. Extremists like Sam Adams made certain that would not happen. The government of Lord North, the prime minister, retaliated by proposing what would be called in America when put into force the Intolerable Acts. Just how intolerable they were was suggested by a cartoon sympathetic to the colonists, "The able Doctor, or America Swallowing the Bitter Draught," in *London Magazine* on May 1, 1774. A nubile young woman naked to the waist and wearing her hair Red Indian style is being held down while Lord North, fierce in face, with a bulging belly, pours the contents of a teapot down her throat. Chief Justice Mansfield pinions her arms. While gripping her ankles the randy

First Lord of the Admiralty, the Earl of Sandwich, peers up her skirts. Others look on, but a distraught, motherly woman, identified by Britannia's shield at her right arm, holds her left hand over her eyes. Poking out of the pocket of the prime minister's coat is a paper labeled Boston Port Bill.

Lord Chief Justice William Murray Mansfield, the abrasive peer who formulated the coercive legislation for parliamentary action, belligerently quoted one of Swedish warrior king Gustavus Adolphus's generals during the debate: "My lads, you see these men. If you do not kill them, they will kill us." Mansfield would never live down the remark.

The Declaratory Act of 1766 had asserted the right of Parliament to make laws binding the American colonies "in all cases whatsoever." Imperial overreach became an annual exercise. The act became the basis for the punitive Prohibitory Bill, which interdicted all trade with the thirteen colonies; legalized seizure, in harbor or at sea, of American property; and authorized royal commissioners to determine whether a colony might earn release to the king's "peace and protection" by returning to "a state of obedience." One clause specifically closed the port of Boston to all commerce. Fiery but failed opposition flared in the Commons, where a member asked, "Are we to find peace in a cruel, indiscriminate, and perpetual declaration of war, against all the people in our own colonies?" Concerns were raised that the prohibitions would impel Americans to convert their merchant ships into hostile privateers, and that the "abdication" from reasonable oversight would precipitate the colonies "headlong into the arms of some foreign power." Still, impolitic legislation always passed overwhelmingly.

American radicals had already summoned a Continental Congress to air mutual grievances across the colonies. At the time, the elder William Pitt, now Lord Chatham, had warned that the "unhappy business" of taunt and retaliation was "beset with dangers of the most complicated and lasting nature. . . . Perhaps a fatal desire to take advantage of this guilty tumult of the Bostonians, in order to crush the spirit of liberty among the Americans in general, has taken possession of the heart of government . . . but to consent quietly to have no right over their own purse, I conceive the people of America will never be brought to do."

In a heated House of Commons debate in 1774, the MP for Preston in Lancashire, Sir John Burgoyne, who had secured his seat through the influence of his powerful late father-in-law, the Earl of Derby, excoriated the American colonies as "our spoilt child, which we have already spoiled by too much indulgence." An ambitious major general who sought favor at Court and new military opportunities, Burgoyne attacked efforts to conciliate the colonies as "a misuse of time." It was their independence from taxation "which is contended for; but I am ready to resist that proposition, and to contend at any future time, against such independence." He would soon have his wish.

George III's harried Secretary for America, the diffident Earl of Dartmouth, instructed Major General Thomas Gage in Massachusetts on January 27, 1775, that order in Massachusetts was to be restored by law if possible, by force if necessary. Paradoxically, since the government in London had withdrawn local rule at every level, the Crown had little recourse but the redcoats to enforce its laws. Vice Admiral Samuel Graves, ordered to administer the Boston Port Bill as commander-in-chief of the American Station since July 1774, but for a few armed sloops had no coercive resources, as the Admiralty was muddling along on a parsimonious peace establishment.

The king had already warned Lord North (who as the son of the Earl of Guilford sat in the Commons) that "blows must decide whether they are to be subject to this country, or [be] independent." North always did as he was instructed, for which the king valued him as first minister. (The title prime minister was not yet in general use.) In his early fifties, portly with flabby cheeks and protruding eyes, he resembled, someone quipped, a "blind trumpeter." But he was efficient and resilient. He promised Gage experienced reinforcements from home. North offered Graves nothing, and when he was relieved for ineffectuality, he angrily refused further service. (In the British rewards tradition, however, he would be promoted to admiral in 1778.)

Orders to seize illegal colonial stores of armaments moved slowly through the corridors of Whitehall red tape and were not dispatched until February 27, 1775, arriving at Gage's headquarters in Boston on April 16. From sympathetic informers in England, the Provincial Congress had already learned on April 3 of the plans to suppress dis-

sent. Six or seven weeks sailing westward was good time, and bureau-
cratic lag in London had given rebels in Massachusetts an additional
head start.

Every parliamentary restraint only engendered political whiplash.
Every Cabinet response to what would become a litany of accumu-
lating overseas grievances helped to unite unreconciled colonies that
had seldom before considered anything but their own self-interests.
The unfraternal provinces even coveted each other's lands. With royal
charters vaguely guaranteeing borders that seemed to stretch indefinitely, Virginians had tried to seize southwestern Pennsylvania, and
Connecticut invaders had claimed by force of arms the Wyoming
Valley in Pennsylvania, on the east branch of the sinuous Susquehanna River. New Hampshire and New York disputed what would
become known as Vermont. Spurred by land speculators, including
George Washington and Benjamin Franklin, colonies claimed over-
lapping parcels of land across the Appalachians, much of it promised
by British treaty to Indian tribes but soon stolen by illegal settlers.

In his pamphlet *Taxation No Tyranny* (March 8, 1775), Dr. Samuel
Johnson objected impatiently that Americans who appealed to abstract human rights while exploiting fellow human beings were
guilty of profound sophistry. "How is it," he argued, "that we hear the
loudest *yelps* for liberty among the [slave] drivers of Negroes?" He
also insisted—rightly—that Americans were no more deprived of
"representation" in Parliament than most Englishmen, who lived in
increasingly populous districts entitled to no seats in the Commons.
South Carolina, he could have pointed out, had more plantation
slaves, considered property, than lawful people. The "rights of Englishmen" as voiced in colonial oratory were far more limited on the
western side of the Atlantic. "Sir," Johnson once growled to his friend
John Campbell, "they are a race of convicts, and ought to be thankful
for any thing we allow them short of hanging." Helpfully, Justice
Mansfield in 1772 had ruled in the case of a slave brought to England that James Somerset be discharged. Slavery, he declared, was too
"odious" to be acceptable under the laws of England. While his rul-
ing effectively ended further slavery in England, it did not affect any
of the colonies—or the lucrative slave trade.

However pro-American, and hoping at thirty-five to propel a lag-
ging career, Johnson's aspiring biographer James Boswell was careful

not to antagonize his hawkish hero. Claiming also to be a Tory, Boswell added, cautiously, "It is not clear to me that our colonies are completely our subjects. . . . At any rate, the measures of Administration [from London] seem to have been ill digested and violent."

On the eve of war, selfishness, sanctimoniousness, intrigue, and disunion among the colonies were far more evident than suggested by the resolutions of the early Continental Congresses. To the English in the mother country the sternly moral uprightness of the king's disobedient subjects who were their transatlantic cousins—allegedly shifty lawyers, conniving merchants, and patrician slave owners—was sheer hypocrisy. The king's subjects at home felt that they enjoyed more real liberties. The king himself began a memorandum in which he excoriated "gentlemen who pretend to be patriots" but acted contrary to their breeding in "avowing the unnatural doctrine of encouraging the American Colonies in their disputes with their Mother Country." Their behavior, he went on unhappily, "so plainly shows that men not measures decide their opinions, that it is not necessary to deduce the total lack of principle by which this motley tribe by their conduct . . ."—and there His Majesty left his musings unfinished.

Joseph Warren, thirty-four, was the alleged "Presbyterian Minister" sending the warning to Massachusetts minutemen (illegal local militias to be ready at a moment's notice) about Gage's plan to seize militants and munitions stores. Although no minister, like every student at Harvard College he had studied the only curriculum offered, theology. In civil life he was a physician, and as an outspoken patriot became president of the Provincial Congress. On the night of April 18, 1775, Warren had dispatched his friends Paul Revere and William Dawes to warn of approaching redcoats at Lexington and Concord.* Although the experienced redcoats were efficient in direct confrontations, their sixteen-mile retreat to Boston, under fire by rebels sniping from behind trees and walls and from the windows of houses along the road, was nearly a rout. While the militiamen suffered 49 dead and 46 wounded, the British counted 73 dead and 200 wounded and missing.

---

*Revere fell off his horse and was captured after warning John Hancock and John Adams, but Samuel Prescott, a young local doctor encountered en route, continued the mission and warned the minutemen at Concord.

Afterward, Warren propagandized about ruthless British aggression and purveyed atrocity stories intended for sympathetic papers in England. The end, independence, justified the means, even to possessors of degrees in divinity.

An organizer of the patriot militia, but not yet assigned a command, Warren had volunteered to fight as an ordinary soldier. At Breed's Hill, below Bunker's Hill on the Charlestown Peninsula, overlooking Boston across the Charles River to the south, militia colonel William Prescott, with fewer than 1,200 men, determined to hold both hills overlooking Boston Harbor. Understanding the exasperation in Whitehall, Gage responded. Covered by a bombardment from the Boston side, at noon on June 17, 1775, he sent out 28 barges with 1,500 troops under General Howe, and 12 guns. Although another 1,000 reserves followed, it took three assaults for the redcoats to prevail—and only at Bunker Hill. Breed's Hill held. The British suffered over 1,140 dead and wounded; the colonists lost 441, one of them Joseph Warren. In the confusion he was abandoned to an unmarked grave.

America's first civil war had begun. With the first encounters emerged, from local militias, the beginnings of a determined rebel army. Distances down the colonies were long and communications slow, but the spreading news of Bunker Hill would rally many Americans into a semblance of unity. Yet on both sides of the Atlantic, conditions still seemed amenable to conciliation. Parliament had only to relinquish its unenforceable colonial perquisites, which stressed that explosive word: obedience.

The act forbidding trade by the New England provinces and denying access to the Newfoundland fishing grounds had been attacked in the Commons by Edmund Burke, a member for Bristol, and also in the Lords by the Earl of Camden, who warned:

> To conquer a great continent of 1,800 miles, containing three millions of people, all indissolubly united on the great Whig bottom of liberty and justice, seems an undertaking not to be rashly engaged in.... It is obvious, my lords, that you cannot furnish armies, or treasure, competent to the mighty purpose of subduing America . . . but whether France and Spain will be tame, inactive spectators of your efforts and distractions, is well worthy the considerations of your lordships.

The punitive act would be approved, and a second, extending the restrictions to the other provinces, became law on April 13, 1775, before Lexington and Bunker Hill. When the expected confirmation reached America by mail packet many weeks later it exacerbated what resistance had already arisen. To his friend Horace Mann, long-time British representative in Florence, Walpole wrote anxiously on May 7, 1775, "Our stake [in America] is deep . . . , yet it is that kind of war, in which even victory may ruin us." Bunker Hill would be that kind of victory, for local commanders feared more such losses in direct confrontation.

In London an opposition cartoon broadside appeared, "The State Blacksmiths. Forging Fetters for the Americans." A black-and-white print usually sold for sixpence and one in color for a shilling—a heavy expense for the purchaser, which meant that engravers and printers, who worked for a profit, targeted issues likely to be marketable. The increasing predominance of antigovernment broadsides over loyal ones suggested the winds of change in popular feeling, at least among literate Englishmen with sixpences to spare.

A blizzard of opposition caricatures and cartoons would appear over the years of division, and predictions about the futility of suppression were not uncommon. In December 1774 David Murray, Viscount Stormont, the shrewd royal envoy to Versailles, had reported French opinion that Americans, when "conscious of their superior strength," which was seen as looming, "will shake off all dependency on their Mother-Country, and form an Empire of their own." All that could be done, he warned, was "to palliate what cannot be cured, and keep off, for a time, what must inevitably come at last." Force would only "retard" what could not be stopped. "By vainly attempting to subdue that unconquerable spirit, we shall of course increase it, . . . and accelerate that fatal period." As an Establishment worthy, Stormont was unusual in his realism.

The influential universities at Oxford and Cambridge were strongholds of anti-American sentiment, as was the Church of England hierarchy. So too was the legal system. Lawyers and judges had much to gain from siding with the Crown. "The Court"—the circle around George III—"now have at their devotion," Walpole wrote, "the three bodies of the clergy, army, and law."

The law also included the houses of Parliament, which made legislation. Even the Commons was dominated by the lesser nobility and affluent country squires. The Earl of Camden was "grieved to observe, before the first shots were fired, that the landed interest is almost altogether anti-American, though the common people hold the war in abhorrence, and the merchants and tradesmen, for obvious reasons, are likewise against it." In that age of difficult communication, before the advent of telegraphy and cable, when messages were dependent on hooves and sails, ministers of state and members of Parliament were making decisions that were already irrelevant across the Atlantic. Events in America, news of which had to cross an ocean, were outdating policies planned in London and plodding, against headwinds and heaving waves, westward by sea. When, before Bunker Hill, redcoats on May 10 seized the Virginia militia's store of gunpowder in Williamsburg, it was tantamount to its explosion; and when, the same day, rebels took Fort Ticonderoga on Lake Champlain, along the northward track from upper New York to Canada, a rebellion was spreading without anyone being able yet to connect such events as a single phenomenon.

The law of unanticipated outcomes was already in force. Colonial resentment of restraints legislated an ocean away was fueling the desire to turn virtual independence into formal freedom. Men militarized to fight the French and Indians in a frontier war concluded little more than a decade earlier had weapons and experience, if little discipline. What was axiomatic parliamentary supremacy on one side of the Atlantic seemed deliberate provocation on the other.

Also on May 10, 1775, the Continental Congress reassembled in Philadelphia, unaware of either incident. Yet on its agenda was an appeal for assistance by Massachusetts, and soon with news of conflict in three colonies, Congress recognized that the undeclared war was becoming, without its overt involvement, a national struggle. The more conservative delegates were appalled by the attack on a Crown fort, and a divided assembly, uncertain how to react, voted lamely to keep the Ticonderoga cannons temporarily and to return them "safely" after making an inventory. Few sought premature and open rebellion, but debate began anyway on what was described as defensive preparations, and George Washington, a Virginia planter, was appointed to chair a committee on military supply. The highest ranking former British officer with active military experience, he had been on the staff of General Braddock in the wars with the French in the early 1760s. (Some of the militia officers at Bunker Hill had also learned about breastworks and field fortifications in the French and Indian War.) On May 20, the delegates formalized their newly unified posture by adopting pious if weak Articles of Confederation, which unhelpfully kept all significant powers within each colony.

Dispatches arrived daily from England at the port of Philadelphia less than a mile from the red-brick state house on cobbled Chestnut Street. Both official documents and the newspapers brought reports of additional restrictions on the colonies and further military reinforcements. In London, readers of the plethora of papers (each at most only a few folded sheets) printed daily and weekly would learn that upstart rebels were barricading General Gage's redcoats inside Boston. The king impatiently cautioned the Secretary for America, Lord Dartmouth, on May 29, 1775, to place no reliance on accounts "exaggerated in American newspapers." Although "the die is cast," King George concluded, Dartmouth should not see the initial reverse "in a stronger light than it deserves."

Congress perceived the events differently. New England delegates moved with religious zeal to mandate a fast day on July 20, to focus attention on the alarming situation. Pragmatically, George Washington suggested that fasting would not expel the British, and urged the assembly of rifle companies from the middle colonies to come to the aid of Massachusetts "under the command of the chief officer in that army."

No one in Philadelphia could forget that during the opening week of the Congress and often afterward Washington had worn, dramatically, his red-and-blue British brigadier's uniform that dated back to 1758, when he had that brevet—largely honorary—rank in the French and Indian War. A young colonel in the Virginia Regiment, he had temporarily commanded additional troops from Maryland, Delaware, and North Carolina, and remained the only American seasoned in battle to have held, even briefly, general's rank.

Proud and ambitious, and realizing that Virginia, the richest and most populous colony, had to be recognized, as well as his own well-advertised military stature, Washington knew who the commander-in-chief had to be, but when his name was to be proposed, he was discreetly absent from the chamber. The red-and-blue regalia in any case would be immediately inappropriate.

Expecting the appointment while claiming that he wanted only to lead the Virginia militia, he had already asked his colleague from Williamsburg, the lawyer Edmund Pendleton, to help him draft an acceptance speech. John Adams and Thomas Johnson of Maryland formally placed Washington's name in nomination, and no other candidate was proposed "to command all the continental forces raised or to be raised." Some mumbling from Massachusetts quickly quieted, and the vote was recorded as unanimous. But often given to gloom, and hedging his bets, he would confide private misgivings to fellow Virginian Patrick Henry: "Remember, Mr. Henry, what I tell you: from the day I enter upon the command of the American armies, I date my fall and the ruin of my reputation."

Across the Atlantic the same day "The Humble Address" of the Lord Mayor of the City of London and his aldermen was presented to His Majesty, requesting his "benign attention" to the "grievous distractions" abroad: "Your American subjects, Royal Sire, descended from the same ancestors with ourselves, appear equally jealous of the prerogatives of freemen, without which they cannot deem themselves happy." To avoid "civil bloodshed," they asked, for their American brethren, freedom "from the clog of compulsory laws."

The king responded that "while the constitutional authority of this kingdom is openly resisted by a part of my American subjects, I owe it to the rest of my people . . . to continue and enforce those measures by which alone their rights and interests can be asserted and maintained." It was, he contended, purely a matter of principle. But, in upholding "the defense of American liberty," the Continental Congress was raising an army. The two principles would collide.

Washington, who at forty-three and six-feet-four had appeared majestic in his old uniform in Philadelphia, had a very different reputation across the Atlantic, where he was remembered for surviving General Edward Braddock's debacle and death, surrendering Fort Necessity, and a regiment, to the French, and failing to protect the Virginia frontier. As he and his new adversaries, the British, knew, his rather inglorious military repute was that he had never won a victory and was experienced only at retreats.

Since Washington had resigned his provincial commission a dozen years earlier, and received his new elevated rank from a body London considered illegal, the British would insist demeaningly on calling him "Mr. Washington," or, more respectably on occasion, "George Washington, Esquire." But reassuming his military persona, he sent his green gentleman's carriage back to Mount Vernon with a long letter for his wife, Martha, and bought five new horses and a light-weight phaeton for accompanying his troops. On June 22, as he packed saddlebags for Massachusetts, he learned, in Philadelphia, of the battle in Boston the week before, and of Bunker Hill and Breed's Hill. The British had driven the Continentals from only one of the hills, in an expensive victory, and an unfruitful one. In dispatching an account of the affair to Lord Dartmouth, Gage confessed, "The rebels are not the despicable rabble too many have supposed them to be, and I find it owing to a military spirit encouraged amongst them for a few years past, joined with an uncommon degree of zeal and en-thusiasm."

Uncomfortably holed up on the Charlestown Peninsula, Gage wrote urgently and unrealistically to Whitehall for thirty thousand fresh soldiers. Volunteers would be few. Weeks of shipboard life on a wallowing frigate across the often stormy North Atlantic, in all its closely herded order and chaos, was nothing troops looked forward to, although career officers saw it from a distance as an avenue to promotion in a quick war against rebel amateurs.

While Englishmen across the countryside at home were largely supportive of conciliation if possible, suppression if necessary, a ward election in London revealed a different outlook. In Aldgate on May 23, 1775, an American resident, William Lee, was chosen as alderman, and declared in his acceptance speech that "the friends of freedom here, would teach the Tories of this day . . . how vain a thing it is to attempt wresting their liberties from a people determined to defend them." He was the first product of a protest vote in England.

Four days later a ship from Salem, Massachusetts, docked at the Isle of Wight with copies of the *Essex Gazette* that included accounts of the fighting at Lexington and Concord. On May 30, the news was reprinted in a special edition of the London *Evening Post,* then in other newspapers. British soldiers, the dispatch claimed with a Mass-achusetts slant, initiated the hostilities, "with Circumstances of Cru-elty not less brutal than what our venerable Ancestors received from the vilest Savages of the Wilderness." Countering the official *London Gazette* in justifying General Gage's response as defensive, newspapers published pathetic affidavits from redcoats wounded at Lexington, such as one beginning, "I,. Edward Thoroton Gould of his Majesty's Regiment of Foot, being of lawful age, do testify and declare. . . ."

In the *Morning Post,* "Crito" (it was an age of pseudonyms) claimed that it would not be possible to keep by force a country as extended in size as America. All that Britain could do in futility "is to burn it and destroy it from one end to the other." In what would become an oft expressed theme, the *Morning Chronicle* worried, in terms that would be repeated often, that defeat in America would mean "the ruin of the British Empire." In the *Gazeteer,* "Politicus" scoffed that the report was a fiction, but Lord George Germain, aspiring for office to direct the American war, concluded hopefully the day after that "the many joyful faces" of the Whigs—who were mostly in opposition—suggested their expectation "that the rebellion will be the means of changing the Ministry."

The official dispatches from Boston arrived, belatedly, on June 10, giving pro-American Londoners a nearly two weeks' news monopoly to dominate discussion in the dozens of city coffeehouses where many patrons came to read their papers. Although a circulation of two thousand was considered good, at least a dozen newspapers flourished, and each copy had many readers who passed on what they perused to the less literate. The office of Lord Dartmouth vainly kept advising the public to disregard what they were reading in the daily press. Much alleged news, as the king had complained to the secretary for America, came from imported patriot newspapers.

To Dartmouth, General Gage had claimed that before the incident the "provincial congress breathed nothing but war," and that when "the essential prerogatives of the King, the levying of troops and disposing of the public monies, were wrested from him . . . by an assembly of men unknown to the constitution, for the declared purpose of levying war against the King, you must acknowledge it was my duty, as it was the dictate of humanity, to prevent the calamities of a civil war. . . . This, and this alone, I attempted." Parliament discussed sending him additional troops, and authorized two thousand more seamen "on account of the Dispute between Great Britain and her American Colonies." Members referred to civil war rather than revolution.

Walpole wrote to Sir Horace Mann on June 5 that asking people "to suspend their belief" was impossible—"their patience is out." While the public waited, an advertisement in London papers on behalf of the opposition Constitutional Society announced that one hundred pounds had already been raised for the relief of widows and orphans "of our BELOVED American Fellow Subjects, who, FAITHFUL to the character of Englishmen, preferring Death to Slavery, were, for that Reason only, inhuman[e]ly murdered by the KING'S troops at or near Lexington and Concord." Countering that, London loyalists opened a subscription "for such occasional Acts of Benevolence as may be useful to the Soldiers who are or may be employed in His Majesty's Service in America and for succouring the[ir] distressed Widows and Orphans." (By January 1776 the committee, largely enterprising suppliers to the Navy Board, had raised nearly fifteen thousand pounds for the fund.)

Newspaper editors who printed the obviously disloyal advertisement intended to embarrass the government were indicted by the attorney general for seditious libel and tried by special juries. Duly found guilty, each was sentenced lightly to pay a fine of one hundred pounds. John Horne of the Constitutional Society, the writer of the advertisement, was prosecuted separately. Arrogantly and wittily defending himself before Lord Mansfield at the Court of King's Bench, Horne knew he would be found guilty, and made his defense a long-running provocation even as enthusiasm for the American cause temporarily dwindled with its recognized hazards. Finally in November 1777 he was sentenced to a year in prison and a two-hundred-pound fine.

The power of the press had long vexed governments, whatever their persuasion. In 1712 the Stamp Act, in 1765 unsuccessfully applied to an outraged America, imposed a tax of a halfpenny on every periodical of half a sheet and one penny on every full sheet (folded into four pages), and added a tax on advertisements, to limit their revenue to publishers. The intent was to kill off newspapers. To further restrict press freedom editors were forbidden to quote from parliamentary debates, but in 1771 Parliament was forced to concede that right. Governments continued to subsidize friendly papers, issue their own, and to furnish secret handouts to pliable journalists, but whether Whigs or Tories were in power, the press could be scurrilous and venomous, and remained a brake on official excesses.

Undaunted by libel laws was an anonymous rhymester who, after news that Thomas Gardner, a Yankee wounded at Bunker Hill, had died, published "Gardner's Ghost, A Prophetic Ballad found in Merlin's Cave, Richmond," about "conscience gor'd." The colonel's ghost appears before the sleeping King George (his country seat, Kew Palace, was in Richmond) and predicts the rise of France and the fall of Britain, frightening the king to "attone his guilt" and bid General Gage to "butcher" no more. King George is also warned of the fate of Charles I. Somehow the poet and the paper's editor both escaped prosecution. Most protesters did.

When opponents remained uncowed, often because juries became reluctant to render guilty verdicts, the solicitor general lost enthusiasm for prosecutions of the press. A generation later, when the Prince of Wales had become Prince Regent, the Crown oversaw the stretching of libel liability to include any remarks that might bring the sovereign into "public hatred, contempt, and ridicule." The press was more free in the later 1770s than it would be in 1812.

Another report in London newspapers embarrassing to Whitehall and coming from Massachusetts described the fate of two ammunition wagons dispatched by General Gage. When their commanding officer was captured by militiamen, the six redcoats with him fled to a house occupied by an old woman, who turned them over to the irregulars. "If one old Yankee woman can take six grenadiers," a newspaper gibed, "how many soldiers would it require to conquer America?"

By then, Gates's proclamation of June 12, 1775, had reached England. It demanded the laying down of arms, and offered pardons—except to Samuel Adams and John Hancock, "whose offences are of so flagitious a nature to admit any other consideration than that of *condign punishment.*" *Gentleman's Magazine* described Gates's choice of words as "much admired." Ironically, Adams's incendiary speeches would be published in England without restriction, *The Monthly Review* referring to him as "the American Cicero."

English casualties at Bunker Hill "still in a very bad way from their Wounds" were landed in Plymouth on September 17. They were the fortunate ones. The quality of medicine, especially surgery, before anesthesia and antisepsis, neither yet discovered, ensured that many wounds were not only agonizingly painful, but fatal. Religion, of little use to most wounded soldiers unvisited by the few military chaplains, was not even available for the interment of the dead. A local clergyman usually could be found to officiate at a hanging. Strong drink sometimes helped a soldier get through an amputation; often he was urged to bite hard on a piece of a wood. With the modernization of firearms, "biting the bullet" became recommended.

Before the first casualties were disembarked, "several of the Widows and Orphans of those who were Slain," also evacuated, came onshore, "begging Charity, in the Streets," according to a dispatch published in London on September 26. Pensions to service widows, even when paid, were not enough to live on. "They have met," the dispatch went on, "with the greatest Tenderness & relief, for inhospitality is not of the growth of Plymouth." Penury came later.

A letter from Plymouth published in London as early as September 17, as the casualties were off-loaded, claimed, "We learn here, by the sick & wounded Soldiers who are landed that there is not above 2000 Soldiers, including Officers, at Boston fit to do Duty, and these are averse to the Service. They declare, that up to 60,000 Men would not be able to bring the Americans under Subjection."

The anxious reports were the beginning of awareness of the human cost of the rebellion, and the likely difficulties in suppressing it, but further wounded would be kept well away from public view—and parliamentary concern. Arriving in London from Scotland Boswell boned up on the news and confided to William Temple, "I am growing more and more an American. I see the unreasonableness of taxing them without the consent of their assemblies. I think our ministry are mad in undertaking this desperate war." He would unbridle his pro-American feelings (but without his name) in several periodical pieces, writing in the *Public Advertiser* that Parliament could not reduce the colonies "to *infantine dependence* on their mother."

Parliament, however, was in the king's pocket, literally. Temple Simon Luttrell, MP from Milborne Port in Somersetshire, excoriated his colleagues, in what would have been sedition in any other country, as "a prostitute senate at the feet of deluded majesty." The courts were also effectively the king's. George III had an annual civil list of almost a million pounds from which he disbursed funds to purchase elections, bail out insolvent politicians, offer patronage, dispense pensions, and influence justice. "The King's Friends" in the two Houses openly combined loyalty with self-interest and, together with merely passive seatholders, assured him supportive majorities.

Prompted by the siege of Boston, the king had issued a proclamation on August 23, 1775, which confirmed the uprising as a civil war, with all its legal consequences. Colonists in America were "traitorously preparing, ordering and levying war against us." The king's "loyal and obedient subjects" on both sides of the Atlantic were ordered to furnish "due and full information of all persons who shall be found carrying on correspondence with, or in any manner or degree aiding or abetting the persons now in open arms or rebellion."

Taking the opposite view, General Gage proposed from Boston that Parliament temporarily suspend the Coercive Acts restricting trade in order to encourage conciliation, while readying more troops to come to his aid should that fail. The king scoffed at the idea, calling it "the most absurd that can be suggested." Opinion in the English press was that Gage's days in command were numbered. When rumors flew that Mrs. Gage, who was American, was returning to London, the *St. James's Chronicle* claimed in its September 23, 1775, issue that it was really the general slipping past Washington's troops, disguised as his wife—who might have been more formidable anyway if left to confront the rebels.

The full cycle of the Intolerable Acts had not yet been completed. Further bills were being debated in the Commons, which sat again on October 26 as the news from New England was troubling the many country gentlemen and provincial bourgeois whose essentially nonparty but royalist seats held the leverage in the House. After the king spoke they learned from Lord North that to suppress the rebellion forcibly the land tax would have to rise to four shillings in the pound, and Opposition MP George Byng rose to congratulate his colleagues on the additional shilling as "the first happy fruits of the American measures." (American colonists objecting that they were being taxed without representation in Parliament were paying only about a twenty-fifth of the British burden.)

Through the lenses of their pocketbooks business interests perceived a consumer rebellion across the Atlantic more than a political one. Seeing their trade with America already declining, "the Gentlemen, Merchants, and Traders of the City of London" had already sent a protest deputation to St. James's Palace on October 11, 1775. Their earliest appeals to the king had even predated Lexington, a "humble Address" on April 10 warning that "Oppression of our Fellow-Subjects in America" was not without cost. "These Measures are big with all the Consequences which can alarm a free & commercial People."

Now they importuned His Majesty "to cast an eye on the general prosperity of this land, and to reflect what must be its fate when deprived of its American commerce." What they understood was that Americans purchasing imported goods were paying more taxes than it seemed, although indirectly. As a wholesaler trader who traveled as far as Liverpool, Birmingham, and Bristol had written to the London *Public Ledger,* he saw "Ruin and universal Misery" threatening if colonists stopped importing English goods. "The Taxes and Excises paid by the Manufacturers and Labourers in England are really paid by the Consumers of the Manufactures, & Produce of their Labours in whatever Country they are consumed. Therefore every Person who wears English Shoes in America pays the leather Tax in England; those who wear English Woolen Goods, or silks, pay the Excises charged upon the Manufactures in England for Beer, Window-Lights, Candles &c. In short, all the Charge of Living."

A shopkeeper's ballad, cautiously anonymous and sung to the popular tune of "A-begging We Will Go," referred to the petitions of merchants and the profiteering of the king's friends, and charged, with "A-begging" choruses between stanzas,

> Come hither, brother tradesmen,
> And hear the news I bring;
> 'Tis of a Tory Ministry,
> A Parliament and King. . . .

> The Jacobites and Tories,
> Dance round us hand in hand,
> Like locusts, they surround the throne,
> And fatten on the land.

Our brothers in America,
With tyranny they grieve;
And to make us praise their deeds,
With lies they us deceive.

Their ports and harbors they've blocked up,
And all their trade they stop,
So all the poor are left to starve,
And we must shut up shop. . . .

Then let us to the Palace
And Parliament repair,
And see who will deny us right,
Or tell us if they dare:

That a-begging we may go,
A-begging we may go,
A-begging we may go, go, go,
That a-begging we may go.

More to the Crown's taste were the views from the country. The justices of the peace in Devonshire had drawn up an address to the king on October 5 that promised their "unfeigned readiness to strengthen the hands of government" and deplored "the miseries which our deluded fellow subjects in America have brought upon themselves by that daring abuse which they have made of your parental tenderness." But readiness among the country squires to support additional new taxes to put down the war was hard to find.

Although the colonies had "many Friends here," America "must expect nothing" from the government, a concerned "Gentleman" warned in a letter published in another London paper, "for the Trade of this Kingdom has not [yet] felt any sufficient Check to open the Eyes of its Inhabitants." But the large potential electorate in the burgeoning new manufacturing cities was almost totally unrepresented in the anachronistic House of Commons. For all their voting leverage they could just as well have resided in Connecticut.

Another body of London "Merchants and Traders" bearing a petition with 941 signatures implicitly deploring the likely loss in overseas markets came to St. James's Palace the following Saturday. The king reportedly received their address "very graciously; and the Gentlemen of the Deputation had the Honour to kiss his Majesty's Hand." The businessmen loyally registered "regret and indignation" at the colonists who owed their "prosperous situation" to their "parent country," but they had become disaffected and asked that the king administer his "experienced clemency" to restore peace. No one could recall any relevant royal lenity

King George responded belligerently when opening Parliament, describing colonial resistance as a "desperate conspiracy" employing "vague expressions of attachment to the parent state [and] loyalty to me" while preparing for a "general revolt." He would not permit an "independent empire." He castigated the "gross misrepresentations" of American radicals, whose opinions were "repugnant to the true constitution of the colonies, and to their subordination to Great Britain. . . . They have raised troops, and are collecting a naval force; they have seized the public revenue, and assumed to themselves legislative, executive and judicial powers, which they already exercise, in the most arbitrary manner." Their "usurpation," he promised, would have "fatal consequence" for them. "I am unalterably determined at every hazard and at every risk of every consequence to compel the colonies to absolute submission. It would be better totally to abandon them than to admit a single shadow of their doctrines."

Echoing the king's hard line, the liverymen of London—retainers and stablemen who wore distinctive garb a cut above ordinary servants'—offered another loyal address on America to the sovereign, with 1,029 signatures. Seven official bearers were introduced by the lord of the Bedchamber, and all, according to the Palace, "had the honour to kiss his Majesty's hand." From "sense of duty to your Majesty," the liverymen began, they saw the colonies as in "open rebellion . . . which we firmly believe has been excited and encouraged by selfish men, who hope to derive private emolument from public calamities." They prayed that the "defiance of the laws" would be put down, and that the king's subjects in America "may be restored to the allegiance which they owe to the mother country and their sovereign." In proper form for the occasion they also implored "clemency toward those whose eyes may be opened to a full conviction of their offences."

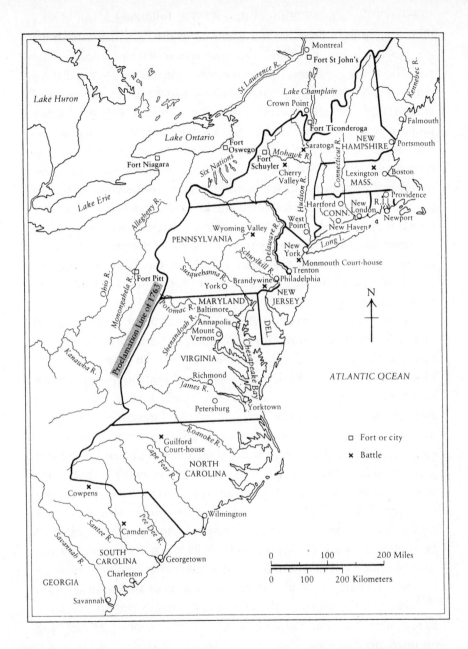

Where the war was fought (map). The Proclamation Act of 1763 forbade settlement to the west of the Appalachians, declaring the lands Indian Territory, but the line was violated by settlers, speculators, and provincial officialdom from the beginning. *From* The Search for Liberty. From Origins to Independence, *by Esmond Wright (Oxford: Blackwell Publishers, 1995). By permission of Blackwell Publishers.*

From 1775 into 1778 more than 44,000 Englishmen would affix their signatures to petitions and addresses to the Crown about America. Northern counties like Lancashire appeared enthusiastic for the war. The county's address included 6,500 names. A more conciliatory petition was signed by 4,000 inhabitants. More warlike, the town of Bolton alone offered a petition with 1,600 names. East Anglia, the point of origin of many of the early Puritan émigrés, seemed an antiwar stronghold. Even the gentry of Norfolk produced 5,400 signatures on an antiwar petition. Many worried about the economic cost of losing the colonies but saw military orders for the wherewithal to put them down as a replacement market. Edmund Burke, who saw no good coming from the conflict, claimed that merchants supported the government's hard line because "They all, or the greater Number of them, begin to snuff the cadaverous Haut Goût"—spicy seasoning—"of a Lucrative War. War indeed is become a sort of substitute for Commerce."

Prominent among the conciliators in the Commons was General Henry Seymour Conway, Horace Walpole's cousin, who in the debate on the king's Address described the war in America to the House sweepingly as cruel, unnecessary, and unnatural—a butchery of fellow Englishmen. His conscience quailed at it. Conquering America, he claimed, was as immoral as it was impossible. He questioned the causes of the impasse, and a government spokesman acknowledged that there were faults somewhere, but that he did not know which department was responsible. He knew only that adoption of more vigorously coercive measures was necessary. Echoing Conway, Colonel Isaac Barré reminded the House that the king's forces were isolated "on a wen, or little excrescence of land, blocked up within the walls of Boston, and the fleet not even master of the river in which it lies." No amount of soldiery that could be committed, on this example, would "effect the capture of all America."

At four in the morning the House divided. For the Address were 278; against, 108. The numbers would be typical of other balloting on the American war.

To thwart the colonial "authors and promoters of this desperate conspiracy," as the king had vowed to the City merchants, a Cabinet dove like Lord Dartmouth would no longer do. It was clear to the sovereign, he told his ministers, that his British subjects were becoming impatient. Someone with more iron in him was necessary, and indeed had been lobbying less than quietly for the American secretaryship. His Majesty asked Lord North to offer the impossible assignment as Secretary for America to the aspirant with the most iron—the hawkish Lord George Sackville Germain.

2
The Secretary for America 1775–1776

Good unexpected, evil unforeseen,
Appear by turns, as fortune shifts the scene:
Some rais'd aloft, some tumbling down amain,
And fall so hard, they bound and rise again.

> —*George Granville, Baron Lansdowne, from his cell in the Tower of London,*
> *circa 1715, as recalled by Horace Walpole*

MORE than eyebrows were raised when the dishonored former general Lord George Germain, fifty-nine, was named Secretary for America, succeeding the Earl of Dartmouth. The appointment became effective on November 10, 1775, with the king's warrant to authorize "Lord George Sackville Germaine" to countersign commissions. Signing also was the Earl of Suffolk, secretary of state for the Northern Department. The news took so long to reach overseas stations that Sir James Wright, royal governor of Georgia, was still writing to the Earl of Dartmouth as late as March 21, 1776, as was General Howe from Halifax.

The Cabinet, originally divided into "Southern" and "Northern" responsibilities for the interior of Great Britain, had been supplemented in 1768 by a third "principal," secretary of state for the colonies, generally known as the American secretaryship because it was the most visible aspect of the office. Secretaries of state were governments in themselves, able to instruct generals and ambassadors, appoint civil servants and arrest malefactors, and employ the purses

(Opposite) The country estates of English military and government figures in the period of the American rebellion (map). *From The Howe Brothers and the American Revolution, by Ira Gruber (Chapel Hill: University of North Carolina Press, 1974). Courtesy of the University of North Carolina Press*

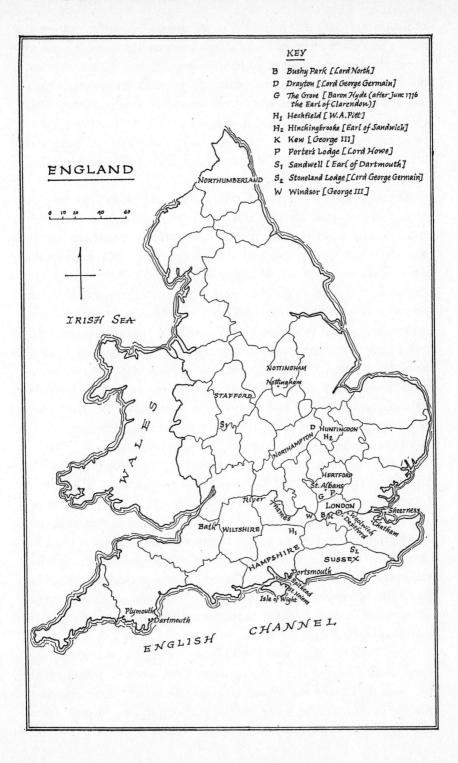

KEY

B   Bushy Park [Lord North]

D   Drayton [Lord George Germain]

G   The Grove [Baron Hyde (after June 1776 the Earl of Clarendon)]

H_1 Hechfield [W.A.Pitt]

H_2 Hinchingbrooke [Earl of Sandwich]

K   Kew [George III]

P   Porter's Lodge [Lord Howe]

S_1 Sandwell [Earl of Dartmouth]

S_2 Stoneland Lodge [Lord George Germain]

W   Windsor [George III]

ENGLAND

0 10 20 40 60

IRISH SEA

NORTHUMBERLAND

WALES

NOTTINGHAM
Nottingham

STAFFORD

S_1

D HUNTINGDON
H_2

NORTHAMPTON

HERTFORD
St. Albans
G P
LONDON
W B K Woolwich Sheerness
Deptford Chatham
Bath
WILTSHIRE
H_1
River Thames

S_2
HAMPSHIRE SUSSEX

Portsmouth
Spithead
St. Helens
Isle of Wight

Plymouth
Dartmouth

ENGLISH CHANNEL

of patronage. Only slowly did the new ministry acquire the inherent power that accrued to its agenda. Two years earlier, in the House of Lords, the Earl of Chesterfield had remarked that if the government did not soon create a position with full powers over America, "in a few years we may as well have no America." Its first occupant, Wills Hill, Viscount Hillsborough, finding resistance to his prerogatives from the two "ancient" secretaries, failed to dominate his post, and his successor, the diffident William Legge, Earl of Dartmouth, chose to operate within safely narrow confines.

Although Lord George Germain was an activist, he inherited an administrative structure that was ludicrously inadequate and often amateur. Placeholders on his payroll were often political appointees who expected to be salaried but not necessarily to appear for work. An assistant wrote of the drudgery of "circumlocutory reports and inefficient forms," for only the rustle of papers and the scratching of pens competed with the outside clatter of hooves and wagon wheels across the cobbled Whitehall promenade kept broad for ceremonial processions. From the few rooms occupied by the staffs of each ministry the business of government, foreign and domestic, went on placidly, recorded in large ledgers and communicated in leisurely fashion, through letters and memoranda, by a handful of clerks who wrote in a copperplate script that was close to calligraphic art.

Exempted from Lord George's purview was much of British India, run by the private East India Company, a trading organization and instrument of imperial supremacy that even maintained an army. Other overseas forces and a colonial bureaucracy, however, had to be supervised by the ministry in the Caribbean, North America, the Mediterranean, and even beyond, as remote from England as the settlements in Australia, halfway round the world. Until challenged by the upstart American colonies, the empire was a closed and highly profitable economic system, protected by its own tariffs, that produced what its own markets shipped and consumed. Or at least that was its lawful outward aspect.

From Paris two days after Lord George's elevation, reluctantly retired admiral Sir George Rodney wrote (very likely in self-interest) to congratulate the incoming American Secretary, observing that such recognition of the noble lord's merit "will in some degree make amends for the 'gross, cruel, base, unjustifiable persecution' in the late reign [of George II]." In Lord George Germain's new post he could command the forces already ordered abroad by his predecessor to reverse the expanding and unlawful rebellion of the American provinces.

The London press echoed public outrage at the appointment of the alleged "coward of Minden." One of his undersecretaries, Richard Cumberland, would remark that Germain took office with "all the requisites of a great minister, unless popularity and good luck are to be numbered amongst them." Horace Walpole was reminded of Baron Lansdowne's lines written hopefully under his cell window when he was imprisoned in the Tower of London in 1715:

> Some rais'd aloft, some tumbling down amain,
> And fall so hard, they bound and rise again.★

Lord George had indeed bounded and risen.

On August 1, 1759, during the Seven Years' War, he was successor to the deceased 3rd Duke of Marlborough as commanding general of British forces in Europe. Despite orders from Prince Ferdinand of Brunswick commanding the united armies, Lord George Sackville (as he then was) had not moved his cavalry near Minden (in Westphalia, northeast of Münster) against the reeling French until the battle was nearly decided. Haughty and proud, at forty-three he had attained the highest position in the British army short of commander-in-chief, and had accomplished that not on his patrician lineage but on his military abilities. The young heir apparent who would soon be George III even suggested privately that Sackville looked like a future prime minister.

Sensitive about his subordinate command under Ferdinand, Lord George was serving under a German who was merely a Serene Highness, a reigning prince or duke rather than an authentic sovereign. The pair shared both snobbishness and a mutual dislike, and second-guessed each other's strategies. The Englishman wanted no glory to go to someone whom even Prince George, the future English king, considered only "a little German prince." Yet Ferdinand had written diplomatically to General Sackville when he had returned to

★Lansdowne (1667–1735) was released to renewed favor in 1717, two years later.

England to urge, at Ferdinand's behest (in the royal third person), augmentation of the allied "light horse"—that "talent and zeal will do much, and he knows no one so capable as his Lordship of vanquishing even greater difficulties."

By the time that the British cavalry belatedly joined the battle at Minden, the retreating French had escaped disaster. The enemy artillery had stilled, and Lord George's missing horsemen (delayed only eight minutes, he claimed) suffered not a single wound. Yet Sackville himself would be the major casualty of the engagement. The noble lord was rebuked in writing by Ferdinand for not joining the battle in time, and the prince also wrote of his displeasure to the English king. Rejecting any blame, Sackville claimed that the orders to his horsemen were confusing as to the direction of attack, and seeking their clarification had caused only minutes to be lost.

Charging that Lord George's disobedience was deliberate, Prince Ferdinand asked King George II of Hanover and Britain to replace his general—who then demanded a court-martial for vindication. Sackville had already resigned his commission, hoping to prompt the king to refuse to accept it—but His Majesty had ignored the hint, leaving Lord George a civilian, and technically ineligible to face a military tribunal. He faced it nonetheless, conducting his own defense with overbearing pride and contempt for his accusers, as befit the near royalty of the venerable Sackvilles. He rebutted charges that his claimed confusion in interpreting orders relayed by several messengers masked cowardice. His judges were unpersuaded. Lord George remained unrepentant. After twenty days of sittings at the Horse-Guards, the army headquarters opposite Whitehall, beginning on March 7, 1760, and continued with several adjournments, the unusual and possibly illegal trial concluded on April 5, 1760.

A guilty verdict under the Mutiny Act might have meant the death penalty. Already cashiered before the trial, Sackville was also, by the king's displeasure, struck from the Privy Council. Shorn of his rank as lieutenant general, he was "hereby adjudged, unfit to serve his Majesty in any military capacity whatever." Insultingly, the king demanded that the sentence be published in army orders and read out at regimental parades.

By 1775, Lord George had endured, unbowed, a decade and a half of public disgrace. He knew he was no coward. In 1745, as a lieutenant colonel only in his late twenties, he was seriously wounded at the Battle of Fontenoy, where he had led his regiment so deep into the enemy lines that when he fell he was carried into the tent of the king of France. He preserved the bloody tunic the rest of his life.

The youngest son of the Duke of Dorset, Lord High Steward of England, a Sackville of the fabled, sprawling Knole House in Kent, with its 52 staircases and 365 rooms, one for each day in the year, he was born into a family of royal favorites, with more ambition than his elder brothers but little chance to inherit the dukedom. His godfather George I had attended Lord George's christening, where the infant was honored with the sovereign's name. He had acquired degrees from Trinity College, Dublin, and from Oxford by the time he was nineteen. He courted people who counted. In Dublin at seventeen he made friends with Jonathan Swift, and wrote to his father that the dean "has shewn himself more mad and absurd than ever," and that the Duke of Devonshire, then Lord Lieutenant of Ireland, "dined yesterday at Howth, and tho' he came away at six o'clock contrived to be as drunk as any of his predecessors have been at that place."

As private secretary to his father when the duke was Lord Lieutenant, George Sackville quickly involved himself in politics and the army. He acquired a family seat in Parliament, taking leave from it to fight on the Continent. His military vision seemed more pragmatic than enthusiastic, once writing (in 1743) to his father from Germany that if English forces attacked "and [were] not able to carry our point we shall be in a very disagreeable way." Later, also from Worms, he wrote that he disagreed with an Austrian plan of attack, "For supposing the best, that we should force their lines with little loss on our side, the only advantage arising from it besides the honour . . . , would be that we should be masters of five or six miles more of a country which is so destroyed that it would not produce subsistence for a hundred men, and the French would retire into some other strong camp where you would have the same difficulty to get at them." He seemed a prudent, coming man.

His reputation—and connections—soon earned him an appointment as chief of army ordnance under Viscount Ligonier, who knew him from Dublin days. Then he was assisted by the political intervention of the influential Duke of Newcastle, who felt it "would be cruel to send Lord George," now a major general, to America in 1754 to replace Lord Loudon. Instead, the undesirable and remote command fell to General Edward Braddock, who would be ambushed and killed by a party of French and Indians in July 1755 near Fort Dusquesne. The only one of Braddock's staff—which might have been Lord George's—to escape unwounded was a tall, ruddy young colonial officer from a tobacco plantation in Virginia, George Washington.

Lord George kept both his political and military careers going without thoughts of marriage until at thirty-eight he wooed Diana Sambrooke, who was well born and "good-tempered," but without the substantial dowry a duke's son might have expected from a family about to link itself to the haughty Sackvilles. His older brother, Lord John (the sons all had courtesy titles because of their father's dukedom), wrote his less than enthusiastic congratulations on September 4, 1754, sending an obscene Latin epigram by Marcus Valerius Martial. The betrothal was possibly a love match, which Lord George could then afford, as the marriage of his aunt, Lady Betty Germain, had produced no heirs. He was her designate—if at her death he took her surname.

The marriage may have also been cover, although the first of his five children was born within two years of the wedding, and Lord George remained a devoted husband. Gossips suggested on occasion that he was a covert homosexual—the reason for his late marriage and his circle of loyal young male associates. Sodomy was a capital crime, and a scurrilous pamphlet published soon after his court-martial claimed that his promotion of a "beautiful warrior" he had met on duty in Ireland had a dark side. Such unproved malice was another burden he would continue to endure, as there seemed always someone of the wrong sort—at the least a young social inferior—in his entourage.

Having outlived her husband by fifty years, Lady Betty Germain died late in 1769, bequeathing Drayton, her grand estate in Northamptonshire, and its income, to Lord George. In 1770 an Act of Parliament formally granted him her surname, which he hoped would assist him out of obloquy. Besides, he needed the long-withheld good opinion of George III, who had succeeded his grandfather in October 1760. But Minden had continued to burden the ambitious Lord George Germain, making any mark of the Crown's favor awkward to bestow. There was even talk among members of denying him his seat in the House of Commons.

Six days after his sentence was published, he made an appearance in Parliament. "None of the great men chose to look towards me," he wrote in seeming unconcern; "others in general [were] very civil and attentive." To prove beyond doubt that he was no coward he soon took on an additional dimension of aggressiveness. Once, when he referred in debate to the honor of his country, Captain George Johnstone, a former royal governor and naval commander, rose to question "that the noble Lord should interest himself so deeply in the honour of his country, when he had hitherto been so regardless of his own."

Lord George delayed for several days before issuing a challenge, ostensibly to arrange his affairs. Johnstone was known to be an experienced duelist and, according to Walpole, "meant mischief." In the climate of the time, shirking a public insult would have meant the destruction of what reputation remained. When a retraction was demanded and refused, Germain sought an immediate confrontation in the ring in Hyde Park, a course for riding and carriage driving where a crowd would have been drawn to the scene.

Johnstone, then attending a committee meeting in the Commons, returned a message that he hoped to be available within the hour. And he suggested that only one second, the bearer of the challenge, Thomas Townshend, later Lord Sydney, serve them both. Further, as Johnstone had an open but dressed surgical incision in an arm, and his legs were swelled by gout, he asked to employ pistols. Lord George acceded.

In Piccadilly on the way to the park, the governor unexpectedly encountered his friend Sir James Lowther, Tory MP for Cumberland, who then came with Johnstone as an informal second. On the dueling ground Lord George invited Johnstone to take any distance he pleased. Johnstone moved twenty short paces away. Then Lord George called on his adversary to fire, which he refused to do, declaring that since his lordship had brought him there, he was to shoot first. Both then fired to no effect, but a second shot from Johnstone shattered the pistol in Lord George's hand, a fragment from it drawing blood. The seconds intervened, and the governor avowed afterward that he had never met a man who exhibited more courage.

Dueling was still decades away from its decline as an institution. It was part of the honor code of gentlemen. Unimpressed, however, by Lord George's apparent delay in issuing the challenge, the king sneered that it "does not give much an idea of his resolution but that he has at length been persuaded by his Friends to take the step." His friends contended that his behavior validated his coolness under fire. When Lord George became Secretary for America, Johnstone defended him in the House of Commons and worked in his behalf. Eight years later, in a parliamentary debate after Germain took office, Colonel Temple Luttrell would make a provocative reference to Minden and the court-martial, suggesting that if the only safety for the royal army in America lay in flight, Lord George was the fittest man to lead it. Germain answered that as old as he was, he would demand his revenge. Members of the House quieted the affair. Minden would not go away.

The best that the king would offer in rehabilitation before the Sackville name disappeared into Germain was, late in 1765, the post of joint vice treasurer for Ireland, a minor but lucrative office possible because in many ways Ireland was exempt from English regulations. The position required little if any residence in Ireland. Appointees to distant places often hired a deputy at a fraction of the emolument, a practice also employed in assignments to the American colonies. Germain stayed in the Commons, where he had retained a family seat, and increasingly focused his attention on American affairs.

When the hated Stamp Act was repealed in 1766, Sackville—as he still was—spoke uncompromisingly for the companion Declaratory Bill, which asserted, contrary to the effect of the repeal, the power of Parliament to legislate for the colonies. Ironically, one of the tiny band of five peers to vote against the bill on February 10, 1766, in sympathy with colonial grievances, was a young veteran of Minden, Lord Charles Cornwallis, twenty-seven, and a colonel of the 33rd Foot, who would change his mind when the colonists took to arms, and whose name would later be associated with an obscure Virginia port on Chesapeake Bay, Yorktown.

When Germain's friends were in power he was a vigorous government ally on American policy, supporting the use of military force, then unpopular, to coerce the colonies. On January 29, 1775, he spoke in the Commons in support of restricting American flouting of colonial subordination to the Crown and Parliament. Lord George favored enforcing precedent "with a Roman severity." Speculation arose that he would soon be offered a ministerial role. To General Sir John Irwin, commander of British forces in Ireland and MP for East Grinstead, a Sackville "pocket borough," Germain confided—it was in effect an announcement of his candidacy—that Parliament had to persuade the "mob of Boston" to choose "between ruin and submission."

Boston was the cockpit of rebellion and the establishment metaphor for colonial misrule. The Tea Party could only have happened in radicalized Boston. Events in England while he acted as agent for Massachusetts (as well as Pennsylvania, New Jersey, and Georgia) had even radicalized the once conciliatory Benjamin Franklin. The ministry claimed that it was Dr. Franklin, almost a Londoner by long residence, who had publicly exposed letters from the unpopular but native-born Massachusetts royal governor, Thomas Hutchinson, revealing colonial policy for what it was. Franklin had sent copies to Thomas Cushing, an old friend in Boston, asking that they not be reproduced, but Cushing had shown them to the incendiary Sam Adams. Soon the correspondence appeared in the *Boston Gazette*. Franklin would never concede that he had intended that outcome.

Hutchinson had written to Thomas Whately, an MP and confidant of Lord North, of "the licentiousness of those who call themselves sons of liberty," and declared that "there must be an abridgment of what are called English liberties. I doubt whether it is possible to project a system of government in which a colony 3,000 miles distant shall enjoy all of the liberty of the parent state." Bostonians would be outraged.

On January 29, 1774, Franklin, sixty-eight, had appeared before the Privy Council in the Cockpit at Whitehall, a hearing chamber still recalling Henry VIII's uses for it. While Franklin's appalled friends in the gallery, including Edmund Burke, Joseph Priestley, and Richard Price, listened, Franklin—ordered to stand for an hour and a half while being interrogated—was subjected to a torrent of invective from Solicitor General Alexander Wedderburn. The private letters, Wedderburn claimed, pounding his fist for emphasis into the cushion on the council table, "must have been stolen by Dr. Franklin, whose . . . motive was to become governor of Massachusetts." The colony, after all, was the sink of criminality and sin.

Whatever his excuses were to be, the councillors wanted him disgraced and removed. Impassive in his suit of brown Manchester velvet, his grey locks tumbling over his collar, Franklin remained silent and unmoving. He conceded nothing.

"I hope, my Lords, you will mark and brand this man," said Wedderburn, exasperated. Dr. Franklin, he had claimed earlier, was not really a man of letters, as was his reputation in England.★ "This was a man of three letters." His listeners knew their Latin. In Rome, a robber could be branded on the forehead with the letters "FVR" (*furor*), for thief. Franklin was deprived of his chief source of income, his deputy postmaster generalship for America. His appointments by the colonies also became worthless. He would go home—but hardly to become governor of a rebellious Massachusetts. Hearing, in Philadelphia, of Franklin's public humiliation, patriot and physician Benjamin Rush wrote that Franklin "will be received and carried in triumph to his house when he arrives among us. It is to be hoped that he will not consent to hold any more [Crown] offices." There was no likelihood that he would be offered any. Further, Dr. Rush forecast, Franklin's defiance and return would cause him to be "handed down to posterity among the first and greatest characters in the world."

It would take Franklin some months to wind up his affairs in England, where his very person now dramatized the divide. He would go ashore from Market Street Wharf in Philadelphia on the evening of May 5, 1775. He learned that while he was at sea the affair at Lexington had erupted, and there seemed no turning back. In England, no one yet knew of it.

By 1774, the year of the Cockpit, Lord George was already accepted as an authority on American affairs, although like most such experts he had never set foot on its soil. He was strong in debate, admired for his grasp of detail. Saturnine and six feet tall (although with a belly going to pot), he seemed a striking figure in the Commons. When Thomas Hutchinson had left Boston after the embar-

---

★Franklin, whose schooling in Boston had ended at twelve, possessed honorary doctorates from Edinburgh and Oxford.

rassment of the Tea Party, and reported to the king, he had also visited Germain. Approving of Lord George's hawkishness, he noted in his diary, "He has a great knowledge in American affairs." Hearing rumors in America of the imminent appointment, Ben Franklin wrote to Joseph Priestley, "When Lord Germain is at the head of affairs, it cannot be expected that anything like reason or moderation could be attended to. Everything breathes rancour and desperation, and nothing but absolute impotence will stop their proceedings [against us]. We therefore look on final separation from you as a certain and speedy event."

Franklin also suggested that Priestley try out a question on their friend Richard Price, a nonconformist Welsh preacher who had a pulpit in the village of Hackney, east of London, and who enjoyed exploiting statistics. "Britain, at the expence of three millions," Franklin posited, "has killed 150 Yankies this campaign, which is £20,000 a head; and at Bunker's Hill she gained a mile of ground. . . . During the same time 60,000 children have been born in America. From these data his mathematical head will easily calculate the time and expence necessary to kill us all, and conquer our whole territory." Price, who was sympathetic to American aspirations, would have understood, but his parishioners were not Whitehall's policy makers.

When the disturbing news of Lexington and Concord arrived in London nearly two months later the Earl of Suffolk, Secretary for the North, wrote to Lord George on June 15, as if he were already a Cabinet colleague, that reports from Boston "don't do much credit to the discipline of our troops. The impression made at New York (that neglected place) by what has happened in Massachusetts is disagreeable." The reference to the city would be meaningful. He quoted a Colonel Maunsell, just arrived from there, who hinted that the way to "separate and divide the colonies" was to fortify New York. Boston was expendable.

Lord Suffolk saw no reason for alarm in London. "The stocks are unaffected, and the respectable part of the city is in very proper sentiments. Everything is right at *this end of the town*." He saw—from the St. James's district, then the center of aristocratic residence—no "disinclination to persevere."

Germain responded as if already at the secretary's desk in Whitehall, voicing his concern that General Gage in Boston would have to go: "I often lamented Mr. Gage's drawing thence all his forces to Boston." If New York were held, as Suffolk maintained, "The continent is divided; at present there is free communication between all the disaffected." Germain also agreed that blocking trade from the port of Boston, hitting at Puritan profits, would "shake off the power of those factious leaders who have been the authors of the present confusion." However, as others predicted, restrictions on legal trade would lead to more smuggling, and to the beginnings of privateering, by which some Yankee fortunes were made

Anticipating Germain's accepting office, Admiral Lord Howe sent from his estate in Barnet, just north of London, a copy of a letter from his ambitious brother, Major General William Howe, then encamped with his corps unhappily under siege on the Charlestown Heights above Boston. "I much doubt whether we shall get much farther this Campaign," Richard Howe deplored, "the rebels, on this side, having entrenched themselves very judiciously, about two miles in our front. On the Roxbury side they have done the same." He suspected that "a languid idea of withdrawing the troops from Boston may prevail"—a surprising state of affairs given the professionalism of British troops and the patchwork amateurism of the rebels.

Following the letter on August 7 was Admiral Howe's advice to Lord George (who as yet held no office) that though British sea power might "greatly distress the rebellious provinces in their trade," it would require "a considerable increase of land forces" the following spring "to cut off their mutual intercourse." The frustrations of supply and reinforcement at transoceanic distance already made it distressingly clear that in putting the rebellion down one had to plan in terms of future seasons—and the North Atlantic in winter was no season for sailing ships.

Also embattled on the outskirts of Boston was Sir John Burgoyne, who wrote to Germain on August 20, 1775, realizing that Lord George would not read the letter until October at best. It was "fatal procrastination" on the part of "all parties in England," the general charged, that had led to their plight. Now a crisis existed because, despite lack of preparation, "we took a step as decisive as the passage of the Rubicon, and . . . find ourselves plunged at once into a most serious war. . . . The rebels though undisciplined are expert in the use of firearms, and are led by some very able men."

Burgoyne quoted an intercepted letter that he mistakenly thought was written by the lawyerly John Adams but actually was the work of the firebrand Sam Adams, projecting an ambitious "constitution to form a great empire," with future "millions to arm and train." Burgoyne saw, with pessimism, "an aspiring and vigorous mind" that soars too high to be allured by any offer Great Britain can make. . . . America, if his counsels continue in force, must be subdued or relinquished; she will not be reconciled." Meanwhile, "British thunder is diverted or controlled by pitiful attentions and Quaker-like scruples." That would not be Germain's way, the Secretary assured General Irwin in September. "As there is not common sense in protracting a war of this sort," he wrote, "I should be for exerting the utmost force of this Kingdom to finish the rebellion in one campaign."

The British believed in their military superiority, which was genuine. They were better equipped, better trained, better fed, more numerous, and more professional in every way. Yet the realities would include other factors, like miles from home and muskets in householder use. Lord George received a long and detailed letter from Boston, written before he had taken office in Whitehall, on the allegedly poor state of the rebel army. The young informant, Benjamin Thompson, would become a prized confidant. Their cannon were "excessively bad" and their firearms "very indifferent, and . . . destitute of bayonets." Their "boasted riflemen" with legendary backwoods marksmanship were unable to pick off redcoat regulars, and "waste their ammunition." They were inexpert at engineering but "their works in general are very extensive, and as strong as labour alone can make them." (A smug cartoon published in London graphically confirmed redcoat potency. "The Yankee Doodles Intrenchments near Boston" sardonically depicted a "hypocritic parson" and ragged soldiers wearing caps labeled "Death or Liberty.")

Because of the "neglect of Congress," Thompson added, the rebels were "most wretchedly clothed, and as dirty a set of mortals as ever disgraced the name of soldier." They had no women in camp to do their washing, and preferred "to let their linen, &c., rot upon their backs." Short in "milk, vegetables, &c.," they lived "almost intirely upon flesh." The men were "most heartily sick of the service, and I

believe it would be with the utmost difficulty that they could be prevailed upon to serve another campaign." Germain appreciated the
roseate point of view, which also was his own.

Despite the efforts of "Mr. Washington" and his generals to
"arrange and discipline the army," Thompson claimed that no "tolerable degree of order and subordination" existed, largely because of
"the great degree of equality as to birth, fortune, and education. . . .
For men cannot bear to be commanded by others that are their superiors in nothing." Surely, he thought, wishful thinking overwhelming reality, "there was never a more mutinous and undisciplined set of
villains that bred disturbance in any camp." Further, there were "dis-
agreement[s] and jealousies between the different troops from the
different Colonies," which would breed division. And their leaders
"(with their usual art and cunning) have been indefatigable in their
endeavours to conceal the real state of the army." Yet these were the
rabble who had successfully besieged General Gage's disciplined regulars north of Boston. As Helmuth von Moltke would write in the
next century, no strategy survives the first contact with the enemy.

The secretaryship was nearly in hand as William Eden, the enterprising "confidential counsellor" to Lord Suffolk (and the future
Baron Auckland), wrote to Germain to inform him that a timid admiral in command of Atlantic forces off New England was being replaced, and that General Gage was being reinforced. "There has,
however, been one good effect in our inefficiency (if it deserves so
hard a name)," Eden claimed. "It has fully shown to the people of
Great Britain that the quarrel does not arise from any wish of the
Minister to oppress the Colonies, but from a determined purpose in
the New England Colonies to seek independence at all hazards."
Speaking her husband's mind, Lady North wrote to the Earl of Guilford, her father-in-law, that "Ld. N. thinks it lucky" to have "Ld.
G.G." in Whitehall "as it will be a great ease to him to have a respon-
sable person in the House of Commons for the three Secretaries [of
State] being all in the House of Lords made his Situation in the
House of Commons the more disagreeable." Germain could represent the Cabinet for North in the lower house.

The official *Gazette* had announced the appointment on November 11. As head of the ministry charged with suppressing the American rebellion, Lord George, a civilian since his cashiering after

Minden, could now commission, promote, and command generals, and even order armies. An agreeable ministerial salary of fifty-two hundred pounds a year was his, which made the upkeep of both a grand London residence and the late Lady Betty's mansion at Drayton, with its handsome stands of beech trees, affordable. To the Earl of Guilford, his son the Bishop of Worcester, who also sat in the Lords, complained the same day that Lord George might turn out to be "an unpleasant partner" for the prime minister, for the new American Secretary "is not a popular Man, & is reckoned impracticable and ambitious."

Germain did not expect conciliation of the colonies to work, and had already refused Lord North's proposal (through Eden) that he become royal commissioner to America, to negotiate an end to controversy and rebellion. "There never perhaps was a commission of such importance for any individual in the annals of mankind," Eden had cajoled him on October 3. He was "the fittest man in the Kingdom [for] so large a Vice-Royalty." But Germain wanted to be in the Cabinet, not in remote America entreating submission, and when Parliament reconvened on October 26, 1775, the speech from the throne suggested several other peace commissioners to placate the opposition, while advocating with the other hand a resolute policy to put down the colonies. After rancorous debate in the Commons the Address was approved at four in the morning, 279 to 108. "Pity me, encourage me," Germain wrote to Irwin, "and I will do my best."

Immediately the hawk of the Cabinet, Lord George would not sound that timid note again. The strident tone of the king had to be matched in Whitehall. (From Massachusetts, Sam Adams wrote, with some accuracy, "I have heard that [George III] is his own minister; why, then, should we cast the odium . . . upon his minions?") Also, the Secretary for America had to maintain his equivalency with the two "ancient" ministries. In the Commons on November 16 he declared that he would always be "decisive, direct, and firm." But none of that would be easy when dispatches to America usually took two months or more to send by sail, as—anticipating an unknown future that often, given distances and time, had already happened—he responded to messages that were already long obsolete when he read them. Being Secretary for America almost required the services of an astrologer.

Presenting his views on mediation, in which he did not believe, he told the House of Commons that the colonies could not be permitted to negotiate "with arms in their hands." The Crown could only offer "a door to retreat," as the two sides were not legal equals. If the colonies, he explained, "persist in their appeal to force, the force of this country must be exerted. The spirit of this country will go along with me."

Germain had wanted the rebellion crushed in one campaign, but his plans for crossing the Atlantic had to be laid many months in advance. He also had the ambitions of his generals in the field to deal with, and the ambitions of politicians in Parliament and entrepreneurs in the City who were suppliers to the government. Even the Established Church had its vested interests, for competing and nonconformist religious factions in America were in the way of an Anglican episcopacy. By English law, no deacon, priest, or bishop could be ordained or consecrated into the Anglican communion without taking an oath of allegiance to the king, who since Henry VIII included among his titles Defender of the Faith. The church was in danger of disestablishment in colony after colony.

Politics was even more labyrinthine than that. Anglican bishops (like Germain's own brother) sat in the House of Lords. And not only could the king blatantly purchase votes in both houses; businessmen purveying supplies to the army and navy often sat in Parliament, and Lord George's generals and admirals, like Lord George himself, sometimes held seats from family districts, even while serving in America.

The Secretary's decisions, he realized at the beginning of every working day, would always have more than military consequences. Funds for reinforcements that the generals requested required additional outlays, possible only with increased taxes, which had a political price. Domestic recruiting required enticing into service Catholic Irishmen, who were considered untrustworthy at best; Scots, bitter after uprisings in decades not long past, might be unsafe to employ; and Englishmen of the lowest classes, whom to arm in large numbers might abet revolution. One could not assure loyalty on sixpence a day in salary. (Sailors, who presumably lived a life of greater hardship, received ninepence.)

Urgently, the king sought German, Dutch, even Russian, mercenaries, although shipping them to the colonies would be a problem. He had warned Lord North on August 1, 1775, that "though brave on shore, Continental forces fear the sea." In debate in the Commons early in 1776 Lord George looked to history and pointed out that in every war or rebellion within memory England had to employ foreign troops "to fight our battles and to support our government." And to have them on the ground in America in time for a new season of campaigning meant soliciting impecunious European dukes and princes without delay, and organizing the transport as well as projecting a half year or more in advance where they would go and under whom they would serve. The king was willing to spend tens of thousands of pounds on mercenaries. One satirical paper suggested recruiting apes rather than Russians as less costly in rental and maintenance.

Lord George was warned astutely (by Jonathan Boucher on November 27, 1775) that George Washington would be a formidable opponent "although in the military line it is not possible [that] his merit can be considerable." He had "little personal experience [of war], and less reading," but he would "atone for many demerits by the extraordinary coolness and caution which distinguish his character." His best attributes were "steadiness and extreme care." The solution proposed was that "he should be perplexed and confounded by stratagems. . . . Against the manoeuvres of [military] art, I am satisfied he is defenceless."

One of Lord George's first acts was to replace Washington's adversary Thomas Gage. "General Gage, with all his good qualitys," the Secretary wrote, "finds himself in a situation of too great importance for his talents. The conduct of such a war requires more than common abilities. The distance from the seat of government leaves much to the discretion and resources of the general, and I doubt whether Mr. Gage will venture to take a single step beyond the letter of his instructions, and whether the troops will . . . march with confidence of success under his command." As Gage's successors would discover, Germain's increasing micromanaging of the distant war would inhibit such flexibility, however praiseworthy the American Secretary claimed, at the beginning of his tenure, was independent, on-the-scene judgment.

The last news from across the Atlantic to arrive before Christmas was that Quebec was being besieged, Boston was surrounded, and the rebels were fortifying New York. Although reasons for pessimism arose early, home front morale was dutifully propped up. A song, "The Loyal Briton," began hopefully, "Come, chear up your hearts, boys, our country commands," suggesting that loyal Englishmen would reconquer America. Yet it was not possible to defeat the Americans, the *General Evening Post* conceded, as they win by running away. It was almost true. Without a professional army or up-to-date equipment, and dependent on short-term recruits, Americans realized, confrontations with redcoats were hazardous. Fading away and rematerializing kept colonial armies alive and the war unwinnable by the enemy.

Although they did not know it yet, by New Year's Eve 1775 events nevertheless suddenly seemed promising for the British. The remnant of an American invasion force was being driven from the frontiers of Quebec City and retreating southward. Their most able general on the scene, Richard Montgomery, an Irishman of thirty-seven who had settled in New York only three years before and had become a delegate to the first Continental Congress, had been killed on the last day of the year, attacking rather than waiting because he worried that troops whose recruitments expired with the year might walk away. (The British would regularly count on expiring enlistments to deplete Continental forces. It seemed an index to faltering rebel zeal.) A second young general who had demonstrated both vigor and ingenuity, Benedict Arnold, thirty-four, had been seriously wounded and carried off. The winter of 1776 would be nearly over before the encouraging news reached Lord George's chambers in venerable Whitehall.

3

"A most unaccountable madness"
January 1776–June 1776

"A most unaccountable madness seemed to have seized both countries, urging them blindly on in pursuit of phantoms, the attainment of which could not greatly benefit either; and numberless political and domestic evils were likely to be the destructive consequences of not only their failure but [their] success."

—*General Sir Henry Clinton musing, in old age, about the war*

BEFORE Lord George Germain had moved into Whitehall the government had been forced into decisions that handicapped the new Secretary for America. Many influential soldiers and statesmen were either lukewarm about suppressing the rebellion or not among the "King's Friends." Even some generals who had accepted commands across the Atlantic had done so more in the interests of personal ambition than parliamentary supremacy. Conciliation on likely rebel terms would mean relinquishing not only colonial revenues but control of the colonies. Yet a winnable war across three thousand miles of turbulent ocean presented a financial and logistical nightmare. The hazardous voyage westward took twenty times longer than the trips taken by astronauts two centuries later to reach the Moon, about 240,000 miles from Earth.

Raising domestic taxes to pay for a war was likely to be even more unpopular than the war itself. Army chief Lord Jeffrey Amherst, victorious years before against the French in Canada, and Admiral Lord Augustus Keppel, second son of the Earl of Albemarle and the most distinguished naval commander, both refused to fight in America. Their status remained unimpaired, but when Kenneth Howard, Earl of Effingham, a career junior officer for nine years and an MP, refused to serve in America and deny countrymen he claimed were his cousins their liberties, he was ousted from his captaincy. "I have come to you with fair arguments," he declared in Parliament; "you have refused to hear them." The Americans, he charged, "have made the most respectful remonstrances, you answer them with bills of pains and penalties; they know they ought to be free, you tell them they shall be slaves. . . . Ever since I was of an age to have any ambition at all, my highest has been to serve my country in a military capacity. . . . It is not [a] small sacrifice a man makes, who gives up his profession."

The City of London under feisty Lord Mayor John Wilkes passed a resolution of public thanks to Effingham for having upheld "the principles of a true Englishman." In Dublin, the Guild of Merchants also offered him an address of thanks. The press predictably took both sides.

Professions of support for the American cause were both public and private. The aristocratic rake William Hickey, an Anglo-Irishman then twenty-seven and an attorney in London, had assembled with other gentlemen at the home of William Cane, who owned the cutter *Marguerite,* for a cruise down the Thames to Margate and Boulogne. Among the company was Lord George Gordon, to become notorious four years later,* but then a "volatile and elegant young man of the most affable and engaging manners." Also present was George Dempster, MP, secretary to the Order of the Thistle, the badge of which he wore suspended to a large green ribbon round his neck; Sir Charles Bingham, later the Earl of Lacan; and John Stephenson, "who[se father] had made a large fortune in the East India Company." To Hickey, the six, a cross section of upper-class Britain, were "exactly of the same political way of thinking, condemning the folly and injustice of the Government in endeavouring to dragoon the Americans into unconditional submission, [and] in no danger of arguments or difference upon that head. Upon Mrs. Cane and her mother leaving the table after dinner, our host desired each guest to fill a bumper of champagne, which being complied with, he gave 'Success to the Americans,' a toast that was applauded by all present with enthusiasm, and which we daily did due honour all the time we were out." Cane and his companions even renamed the cutter *Congress.*

---

*See Chapter 11.

The London gentlemen were hardly alone in toasting the success of the rebellion. Thomas Coke of Holkham, then a young MP, donned a broad-brimmed hat, shooting jacket, and long boots to carry a petition to the king from the county of Norfolk asking His Majesty to recognize the independence of the colonies. "Every night during the American War," he recalled as an old man—he lived into his ninety-first year—"did I drink to the health of General Washington as the greatest man on earth."

Interest in the remote provinces that few subjects of George III would ever see lay mostly in the revenues they returned across the Atlantic, or in a few imports like tobacco. To raise and pay for an army substantial enough for the job could not be accomplished on appeals to patriotism or national pride. But it might be done on appeals to recent national memory. Most remembered the Seven Years' War, which had only ended in 1763. The Continental nations then the enemy had been Russia, Austria, and France, and the French were still an invasion threat if war revived. American posturing about freedom seemed at first only an excuse to cut loose from Britain, but if the rebellion dragged on, the opportunity for French intervention—to recover lost colonies and wreak revenge—would increase.

King George hoped for a short war. Yet reinforcements to General Gage's troops beleaguered near Boston could only be inadequate, and slow to sail. The government, however, had a surplus of major generals. Already shipped out, on the *Cerberus,* months earlier, were William Howe, John Burgoyne, and Henry Clinton. When they disembarked on May 25, 1775, the fateful march to Lexington had already occurred, and Bunker Hill was only three weeks away. By the time that Lord George took office in London all three generals had appealed for more troops; Germain had relieved Gage and sent him home. Howe had replaced him.

Clinton, now Howe's deputy, disparaged the poorly dressed and equipped Americans as "ragamuffins," but conceded they were good at entrenchments. In rain turning to snow the British had bleakly looked forward to sitting out the dreary, gusty winter in the Boston area, and then evacuating to a location better situated for the slow and uncertain grinding down of the rebellion. No reinforcements were likely to arrive in time for a late-1775 campaign

Lord Dartmouth, Germain's predecessor, had informed Gage that the twenty thousand additional men he sought could not be extracted from England, but that he would try to hire Russian mercenaries, who, helpfully, spoke a language uncommon in America. (That failing would inhibit their desertion.) Frustratingly, as Dartmouth was giving way to Lord George, France and Prussia used their contrary influence in St. Petersburg to derail the negotiations, and smaller scale contracts had to be concluded instead with Brunswick and Hesse.

Employing mercenaries is as old as history. Even as North and Germain negotiated with foreign rulers, a Scots brigade recruited by the Dutch served the Hague. Earlier, Scots served the Hapsburgs in Austria. After the American Civil War, former Confederate officers hired themselves out to South American states; and in China early in World War II the "Flying Tigers," ostensibly a private air force, was a thinly covert American operation—mercenaries in that the pilots were equipped and paid to fight for a foreign nation. In the twenty-first century profit-seeking military entrepreneurs support democracies and dictators, rebels and nabobs, drug lords and terrorists.

Germain had to wait for Parliament, where there was outspoken opposition to using foreigners to suppress Englishmen (as they considered the colonists), to reconvene on January 25, 1776, following the Christmas recess, for ratification of the German treaties. Beginning on the sixth, blizzards swept across the countryside and continued intermittently through January. Braving the drifts, Germain struggled to his town house in Pall Mall from his estate at Stoneland Park, a sardonic epigram in the *London Evening Post* observing on January 18, "through hills of snow (such now's his patriot flame)." Supplies of provisions to towns in England ceased; in London, playhouses were deserted and the Court canceled its functions; newspapers reported people buried alive in snowdrifts.

Work on the complex logistics of the war burgeoned for Lord George at snowbound, nearly empty Whitehall, which harbored the ministries. He wanted the war to remake his reputation. That meant cultivating recognition for firmness while making no strategic mistakes. The press, however, was more interested in the complaint of a country neighbor about the secretary's allegedly barbaric behavior at home. Her hunting dogs had strayed into Stoneland Park and he had ordered them shot. Perhaps he aspired to a reputation for toughness, but the *Evening Post* scoffed that he did not fear American riflemen as long as they remained an ocean away.

Unable to reach Parliament from Bristol, Edmund Burke wrote to an Irish colleague that the government's response to America was "natural wickedness and folly," and that the colonists, with few facilities for manufacturing, were "under every disadvantage (except the distance of her Enemy), that can be imagined." He saw them as "alienated for ever," despite initial military weakness. "The greatest difficulty the Provincials labour under is the Want of Gunpowder. Habituated as they have always been to supplies from abroad of every thing—they have not been as diligent in establishing manufactures of military Stores as their situation necessarily requires."They would accommodate to that, he thought, and he saw Englishmen as already "begin[ning] somewhat to feel the loss of America."

Long after the snows had melted away, the House of Commons, lacking war enthusiasm, remained poorly attended—"a remarkable neglect of attendance," the *Annual Register* conceded in reviewing sessions of mid-March. Freed from duties as spokesman for the government in the nearly empty House, Lord George could work, in the interim, on troop deployment to more useful bases—southward from Halifax in Nova Scotia, to inhibit the New England trade; to Long Island and New York City, to divide quarrelsome New England from the more diffident middle colonies; and possibly to a point on the Chesapeake, or Cape Fear in North Carolina, from which to control the southern colonies. (The king guessed hopefully that Scottish settlers in North Carolina would be loyal to the Crown.) But twenty thousand professional soldiers, if they duly materialized, would be spread thin over more than a thousand miles of coastal America, little of it likely to be friendly to Hessians.

A Berkshire by-election resulting from the death of a county MP suggested what the mood of the populace beyond London was like. Neither of the candidates, Winchcombe Henry Hartley and Richard Aldworth Neville, made any reference to the rebellion in their election addresses, but in a letter canvassing support for Hartley the colonies became the issue. Neville, who was only trying to shift his seat from distant Grampound in Cornwall, was attacked with the prediction, "His Vote is always given for carrying on a ruinous War against his fellow subjects in America." Hartley was described as "an

Enemy to these Measures." At Abingdon on February 14 "the Gentlemen of the Vale" resolved to support Neville. Three days later a
meeting in Reading backed Hartley, and in Abingdon on February
21 another, led by Captain Peregrine Bertie, MP, an opponent of the
war, also supported Hartley. Since Lord North pressed Neville not to
lose both seats, he decided not to stand for Abingdon, and Hartley
was returned without a contest. The ministry began to worry that
other by-elections might further erode its majority, but the King's
Friends were still preponderant.

With hope for an easy passage, on the leap day of February 29,
1776, Lord North presented to Parliament the treaties with the
dukedoms of Brunswick, Hesse-Cassel, and Hesse-Hanau for the
employment of 17,000 mercenaries. In debate in the Lords, the opposition Duke of Richmond, although recognizing that he lacked
the votes, moved their rejection and called for an immediate end to
hostilities in America. (Eventually 29,867 soldiers would be hired,
with a commission of 30 thalers—a little more than £7—per man to
each Landgrave, who would also receive half more per wound, and
an additional third more for each soldier who was maimed.) In the
nearby suburb of Richmond, where Richard Penn represented the
commercial interests in England of the colony founded by his grandfather, and delivered a petition to the king from his "faithful
colonists" to negotiate a reconciliation, he told friends invited for
dinner that he hoped the Hessians would go to America. "The more
the better, as they might all be persuaded to join the Germans already in Pennsylvania, and so the back Parts of that Province [would]
be filled & settled with People." He would not be one of them. Remaining in the kingdom, with his Pennsylvanian wealth no handicap,
he became MP in 1784 for the borough of Appleby in Westmorland.

In the Commons, by 242 to 88, the opposition to mercenaries, led
by Charles Fox, who claimed that they would not be cost-effective,
was easily defeated. Anticipating that, Germain continued assembling
what would be the most massive and complex military expedition up
to then in British history. Rifles, artillery, and ammunition were a trifling part of his budget. Most went for horses, fodder (a third of it
consumed at sea), wagons, uniforms, ceremonial swords, traditional
pikes and bayonets, foodstuffs (each man ate his way through a third
of a ton annually), beer and rum, and hard currency—very little of

the coinage for the ranks. Sailors aboard were entitled to little pay, but it was supplemented by a gallon of beer daily, their thirst in the sea air alleviated by hundreds of hogsheads below that further limited carrying capacity for war matériel.

Lord George's generals in Massachusetts wanted more horsemen, allegedly for mobility, and on March 29, 1776, a London paper scoffed, "It is astonishing how any man could ever dream of sending cavalry to America. Only let us for a moment conceive [of] a dragoon, with his bags, his bucket, his boots, his belts, his havre sack, his cloak, his cantine, his broad sword and his carbine, galloping round a tree to catch a rifle-man . . . ! It is a cow catching a hare!"

A paragraph the day before reported, "Yesterday morning four waggons laden with money were sent off from the bank, under a proper escort, for Portsmouth, for payment of His Majesty's ships, and the transports lying there, for America." Senior officers were paid as well as members of the Cabinet, and garnered additional perquisites—stipends for supplementary unperformed appointments at home, and income from the sale of commissions. When Burgoyne left for America the second time—he had returned to visit his mortally ill wife—he was given a bonus of five additional cornetcies to sell. (A cornet was a fifth-level rank in a cavalry troop, the officer who carried the colors.) An ensign, a cut above, cost the applicant four hundred pounds, a dozen years' wages for a clerk. The accoutrements of appropriate lifestyle would cost an officer far more.

Enthusiasm at home for the war was as low as the supply of volunteers. It had to be cultivated by newspapers in the pay of the King's Friends. An anonymous versifier having it both ways published, in quatrains, "The Complaint: Or Britannia Lamenting the Loss of Her Children," deploring that "The King's War" had already cost the lives of Warren and Montgomery among others on both sides, and hoping for the return of the colonies to Britain's "bosom." The London Chronicle suggested that it would be better to let the colonies go rather than pay a heavy price to keep them, employing the analogy of freeing runaway horses from the harness of a chaise in order to save the lives of the passengers.

Purportedly an ode to Christopher Pinchbeck, an unsigned satire "Upon His Newly-Invented Patent Candle Snuffers" warned that snuffing out the rebellion would be self-defeating. In devastating

America, Britain would only gain the right to tax "a barren plain" and boast "a firmness in the wrong." Rather, Pinchbeck should "trim old England's candle" of "every Tory Chief." Soon another incendiary epigram would surface in "A Great Personage to Mr. Hartley, on his Experiment." Purportedly it was an appeal from Germain to David Hartley the younger, an MP who called the cause of freed America "the cause of the British nation." Also the inventor of a fireproofing material, he was urged in jocular fashion to teach the American Secretary the technique of putting out fires.

Much more publicity was gained by *An Essay on Civil Liberty and the Justice and Policy of the War with America,* published in February 1776 by Franklin's friend, the Reverend Dr. Richard Price, a persuasive and tireless pamphleteer. Americans could not be subdued, he contended, and the real losers would be holders of government bonds. Several thousand copies were sold in the first days after publication, and a popular cheap edition followed. Abuse and praise soon made Price one of the best known names in England. The City of London, where officialdom deplored the war, made him a Freeman. Thereafter, whenever the Crown proclaimed a day of fasting and prayer to the Almighty for a blessing on their arms—a propaganda device often exploited to build popular support—Parson Price, from his pulpit, and to crowded congregations, outspokenly decried its mischief and folly.

In America, Price was echoed by the impulsive General Charles Lee of the Continentals, who ridiculed the fast day with "Give me ten thousand more good fighting Fellows; and God Almighty may take which Side he pleases."

Undeterred by opposition criticism about the drain on the national debt, Germain assembled his deterrent forces, including Hessians uniformed smartly in green, with red facings and cuffs. No convoys could sail until the North Atlantic winter had abated. Still, he fretted over confusion and delays, and complained of endemic incompetence. His armadas, with wallowing troop transports, at best might arrive two months later, battered by wind and waves, with seasick soldiers and half-dead horses, possibly at ports no longer theirs. It was the chances one took when bound by weather and water.

Germain had to bargain energetically for shipping wherever he could find vessels, and he would instruct a general about Hessian mercenaries to arrive on ponderously sailing Dutch ships that "as soon as the troops are landed, you will give orders to the [sea captains] for their being discharged; and as from the behaviour of the masters there is good ground to suspect that they have stores of different kinds concealed on board, it will be very proper that their holds be carefully examined." Smuggling was as common as legal commerce.

A distant campaign would usually begin later than planned, and if success failed to materialize quickly in direct confrontations, winter encampments would come early and little movement would occur again until the snows melted and forage for beasts of burden and for cavalry again filled the fields. Nevertheless, on February 22, 1776, just as Dr. Price's pamphlet was making its sensation, Germain's relief force for Quebec sailed, riskily early for the season. It would be of no urgent use. Nearly two months earlier General Guy Carleton had brilliantly managed what he described to General Howe as his "wretched garrison," leaving the nearly leaderless Americans, without Montgomery or Arnold, in ragged retreat. High above the St. Lawrence River, and heavily fortified, Quebec could only be assaulted under cover of a snowstorm. On the last day of 1775 the depleted invading forces from New England, reduced to fewer than a thousand men, with their muskets useless in the cold and snow, had failed to breach the twelve-foot walls of the city, and retreated to the treacherous ice of the river, where many were taken prisoner the next day.

Later, Germain would quarrel (at a distance) with Carleton for not following up the enemy withdrawal, but Carleton understood northern winters better than could Lord George from the occasional snowdrifts at Knole or Stoneland Lodge. In England, although newspapers had reported in January that the ministry had abandoned hope that Quebec could be held, word of Carleton's surprising successes, and the gallantry of his eighteen hundred troops, failed to elevate him into a hero. Somehow his dour personality seeped into his dispatches, while the "bold" but dead Montgomery of the other side became the equivalent of the apotheosized General James Wolfe, of Quebec fame in 1759. John Almon's *Evening Post* bordered its March 12 edition, which reported the Irish-born Montgomery's death, "with virtue and honour" in black; the *Scot's Magazine* compared him to General Wolfe. The opposition *Morning Post* eulogized that he would have wanted no tears; rather, "Weep for my country's sake!"

Among the people, predictably, the ranks fared better. Redcoats were professional and plucky. Yankees were amateurs, and often unwilling besides. A popular ballad claimed,

> Brother Ephraim sold his Cow
> And bought him a Commission,
> Then he went to Canada,
> To fight for the nation:
> But when Ephraim he came home,
> He prov'd an errant Coward,
> He wouldn't fight the Englishmen,
> For fear of being devoured.

Associated with General Montgomery in the English press was Ethan Allen, hero of Ticonderoga, whose "Green Mountain Boys" had been an informal militia in the disputed region that became Vermont. He had operated in Canada in advance of Montgomery's forces, and was captured in a failed attack on Montreal in September 1775. Sent in irons to England on the frigate *Solebay* with ninety other prisoners, he was treated especially brutally, but when the frigate docked in Cork, he discovered that he was a local hero. Irish "Friends of the Cause" took up a subscription and sent him a hamper of wine, fruit, sugar, and chocolate, and raised fifty guineas for clothes and other necessaries for his men. On January 24, 1776, from Cove (now Cobh) Allen sent his sponsors a note thanking the people of Cork for their "feelings of humanity . . . towards those of your bone and flesh, who, through misfortune from the present broils in the empire, are needy prisoners."

Lodged in Pendennis Castle in Wales, still in irons, he remained a problem hostage. The government feared reprisals against its own commanders if captured. Rather than hanging him as an irregular, the ministry returned Allen via Halifax, paroling him in loyalist New York. After being exchanged months later for a Scots officer, he reported to Washington at Valley Forge and was breveted a colonel. Such exchanges were common. Each side valued its limited stockpile of officers, and most British officers were also from families of rank and influence. The ordinary soldier expected only to molder, at best, in bleak captivity.

From Halifax, Howe boasted to Lord George about evacuating Boston "without the least molestation by the rebels." Actually, Washington's artillery, much of it captured cannon hauled three hundred miles through the snows and over streams from Ticonderoga by Colonel Henry Knox's men, had been moved up to unoccupied Dorchester Heights looking down into Boston. Although the Congress after Lexington had timidly resolved only to tally the seized guns, in November 1775 Washington dispatched Knox and a party of cannoneers from Boston to haul them eastward. The patriots had almost no artillery, as for years Whitehall had forbidden domestic arms production. Despite Knox's weight and girth and legendary bookishness he was an effective commander, and he managed to load forty-four guns, fourteen mortars, and a howitzer on flat-bottomed boats and take them across Lake George. In the increasing snow and ice they fashioned sleds and drew the enemy's cannon across the mountains of Vermont and New Hampshire, losing only one gun in a water crossing. By mid-February the enemy's cannon was positioned against them. An epic trek, it demonstrated to the British that the Continentals were indeed serious—and dangerous.

Opposition newspapers in London were not taken in by the charade of empty successes concealing obvious disaster. A writer in the *St. James's Chronicle* charged,

> Last year the Ministers promised every Thing and performed nothing; nothing fell out as they had foretold; all their Measures were ill taken and worse executed; the Provincials proved as brave as they had been proclaimed Cowards. . . . The indulgent Nation, duped by such shallow Artifices and disappointed by such weak Councils, still persisted in believing in those who had nothing but Falsehood to varnish over Blunders.

Already the focus of discontent, Germain was blamed, although nothing he had done or directed, given the communications lag, had yet to be activated. Still, "the hero of Minden" was identified as the one who had "lulled" the public "with Visions and Victories." As in wars to follow, the dovish opposition recognized that it could only prevail by influencing publishers of newspapers and the purveyors of broadsides, and—through them—shifting public opinion.

When firing into the British lines from its own guns began, Howe saw no choice but to scuttle before his transports—still untargeted—were shelled. A London paper would publish, many weeks later, a letter from an officer who had embarked for Nova Scotia on March 6 but because of violent winds did not sail from Boston Harbor until the next day. His men had been left, he wrote on March 7, "void of both provisions and forage. . . . Never were troops in so disgraceful a situation, and that not in the last our own fault, or owing to any want of skill or discretion in our commanders, but entirely owing to Great Britain being fast asleep. I pity General Howe from my soul."

All Howe's troops, with whatever panicked civilian sympathizers could be crowded aboard, weighed anchor for Halifax by March 17. While the British had torched other towns, Boston was spared, as were the ships, perhaps in an unwritten deal that encouraged Howe's departure. Then, with drums beating and colors flying, Washington's Continentals marched in while Howe's rear guard was embarking. That Washington had not molested Howe further raised questions in Congress by some less inclined to join in the jubilation. On grounds of his excessive caution, rivals for Washington's command began to materialize. Yet for the moment, as even the English at home would realize, not a redcoat was in arms in any of the rebel colonies.

A letter from an officer serving under Howe, penned from Nantasket Beach, south of Boston, just before he sailed from Massachusetts, was later published in the London *Evening Post*. According to the unnamed writer, Howe's "council of war" had decided that had the British remained any longer, Boston "would have been laid in ashes, and the English army put to the sword. . . . Leave was humanely given by General Washington, who declared that too much blood had already been spilt in America." The rebels, he felt, with the excess of relief from hazard, were "regardless of danger, and will sooner die than part with their liberties. . . . We are fighting against our friends, and against the clearest conviction, and against heaven, which manifestly frowns on us."

One of the reluctant emigrants was Peter Oliver, loyalist chief justice of Massachusetts, sixty-three, whose ancestors had settled in the colony in 1632. Adjacent to his family's prosperous ironworks in

Middleboro, southwest of Plymouth, was elegant Oliver Hall, which would be burned down by rebels in 1782. Newly named lieutenant governor, he was accosted by an impatient mob in Cambridge and offered to resign the post to another appointee, but no one wanted yet another Tory. "We don't want a better man than you," he recalled an onlooker jeering. From Halifax he would sail to England, settling, with a royal pension and a D.C.L. from Oxford, in Birmingham, where he began writing "The Origin and Progress of the American War to 1776," a manuscript so embittered by antirebel bias as to remain unpublishable.

When the news of the evacuation to Nova Scotia, hastened by the winds, reached England early in May, six weeks after, Lord George Germain described the abandonment of Boston as if a victory, but in the Commons Colonel Isaac Barré held up a cutting from the ministry's *London Gazette,* calling the misleading claim "a disgrace to the nation," and moved that funding "for carrying on the said war" cease. Lord North responded unpersuasively that Howe's troops had not been "compelled" to embark but did so "with all possible coolness and regularity, . . . perfectly at their ease."

In advance of the Hessian reinforcements Howe and his major generals—Henry Clinton, John Burgoyne, Hugh Percy, and Charles Cornwallis—as well as all colonels in the command, were to be promoted a step. As Germain explained, they could not be "inconveniently"outranked "in America" by mercenary generals—but the higher English rank would be valid only in America, the only place the anomaly would exist. Further, since the situation on their arrival in American waters would almost certainly be different from that at their embarkation, Howe was given authorization to change troop destinations by posting "cruisers" along the coast to watch for the fleet's arrival "and to proceed with it to such other place as you shall appoint."

Of the foreign "auxiliaries," 12,200 Hessians—all Germans were loosely referred to as Hessians—were to serve under Howe. Waldeckers, Brunswickers, and the Prince of Hesse's personal regiment were assigned to Canada. A corps of 1,098 Guards and 3,466 Highlanders were also to sail—in all, with arms, tents, horses, and provisions the largest British deployment by sea until then. Recruiting at home, Lord George confided to Howe, had gone "very slowly"—"and the men raised in Ireland will be of little use to you." Responding to relentless enlistment drives, a nearly seditious cartoon published by William Humphrey in October 1775, "Six-Pence a Day. Exposed to the Horrors of War, Pestilence and Famine for a Farthing a Day," unfavorably compared the low wages of coachmen and even chimney sweeps to that of a recruit. Gaunt and sad-faced, the enlistee stands forlornly in ill-fitting uniform while his starving children and pregnant wife implore him not to go. To his right, a plump recruiting officer cradles a whip. A banner on a pole exhorts, "COURAGE BOYS!" To the left, two Yankee soldiers aim a volley. The watchword on their caps reads "Death or Liberty." Clearly the recruit will be at risk for much less.

Decades later, in *Barnaby Rudge,* Charles Dickens described in fiction very close to fact a recruiting scene in a tavern in the late 1770s, in which the publican comments cynically, "It's much the same thing, whatever regiment he's recruiting for. I'm told there an't a deal of difference between a fine man and another one, when they're shot through and through."

"Ah!" he is reminded, "but you don't care for glory."

"Glory's arms," the publican observes with "supreme indifference," referring to a hypothetical tavern signboard as much as to muskets, "wouldn't do a very strong business." Overheard is the recruiting sergeant in the next room describing army life once one accepted the king's shilling. "It was all drinking," he cajoled, "except that there were frequent intervals of eating and love-making. A battle was the finest thing in the world—when your side won it—and Englishmen always did that."

"Supposing you should be killed, sir," questioned a timid voice in a dim corner of the room.

"Well, sir, supposing you should be," said the sergeant confidently, "what then? Your country loves you, sir; his Majesty King George the Third loves you; your memory is honoured, revered, respected; everybody's fond of you, and grateful to you; your name's wrote down at full length in a book in the War Office. Damme, gentlemen, we must all die some time or other, eh!"

On March 18, 1776, with all the ceremony and publicity the Secretary for America could generate, a thousand royal guardsmen in three divisions marched jauntily off the parade in St. James's Park, presumably within easy view—or hearing—of the king, en route to Portsmouth to embark for America. A throng of tearful women watched. However melancholy to them, as a recruiting device the panoply was essential. In Cork, fifty sail of transports was assembling, to take on marines, foot regiments, and companies of artillery and dragoons—who earned their name from their short, large-bore muskets, known as dragons.

As in all wars, some fearful soldiers did violence to themselves to avoid exposure to violence abroad, one—emboldened by strong drink at a public house in Chelsea—chopping off his left thumb and two forefingers with a carving knife. Very likely he went to prison instead, from which potential recruits were tempted to enlist—as in many wars—by reprieves. In Salisbury, seven felons sentenced to lifetime transportation to Australia were permitted by the trial judge to serve instead in the 27th Regiment of Foot, embarking for America, where convicts could no longer be sent to do penal time. With seaworthy vessels no longer available to dispose of convicts sentenced to the Antipodes, an act in May 1776 established hard labor on pestilential hulks in the Thames as a temporary alternative for wrongdoers whom even desperate recruiting officers deigned to accept. The practice would be renewed in 1778 and again in 1779.

Although struggling where he could to remain ahead of events, Lord George had no idea how desperate the situation had been for Howe's troops north of Boston before they shipped out on March 17. (Howe, knowing nothing yet about Germain, was still reporting to the departed Earl of Dartmouth.) A cartoon in the English press, "Bunker's Hill, or America's Head Dress," showed a buxom Yankee lady with a hillock of a coiffure that hid cannons and Continental soldiers. In the harbor below her, redcoats leave in boats heading out to a fleet of transports under sail.

Few supplies from the southern colonies or from the West Indies had come in for the redcoats through the winter, but Halifax, General Howe understood, though "stripped of provisions . . . [and] affording few conveniences to so numerous a body," was the only place in North America his army could remain, although it had doubled the port's population, until stores arrived from Britain. A sardonic anonymous pamphlet appeared in London once the news arrived: "A Congratulatory Poem on the Late Successes of the British Arms, Particularly the Triumphant Evacuation of Boston." Prudently naming no names, it began, "While temper'd wisdom at the helm presides."

The same day that Howe wrote, March 21, royal governor Josiah Martin of North Carolina reported to Germain that he had only just received Lord George's circular letter of November 10, 1775, to officials in America notifying them of his appointment. The ejected governor was responding from the *Peggy,* in the Cape Fear River. Several other royal governors had also taken refuge at sea, as their lives were at hazard ashore. (Governor Sir William Tryon of New York fled to *The Duchess of Gordon,* in the North River, now often called the Hudson, and John Murray, fourth Earl of Dunmore, governor of Virginia, retreated to the *Dunmore,* modestly christened for him, on the Elizabeth River. His situation, he confessed to Germain, was "wretched," with "not a hope of gaining either honour, credit, pleasure or profit.") The Secretary's announcement had taken four months to reach Martin—a duplicate, as most messages were sent in several copies in hopes that one would evade sinking or seizure. Martin was dismayed that armaments and supplies he expected to be shipped from Cork at the beginning of December were still delayed. When reinforcements arrived, Cape Fear would earn its name.

Again on March 22, the aldermen and Common Council of the City of London, the economic heart of the kingdom, came to St. James's Palace to address the king—the text was read aloud by the City Recorder—about the likely "dismemberment of the empire," with its inevitable "increase in the national debt and burdensome taxes," and the "distress of our merchants and manufacturers." They sought the concession of "rightful liberties" to the colonists in America rather than "the dreadful operations of your armament." Obstinately, the king offered in return "mercy and clemency [to] my subjects in North America" whenever royal authority was reestablished "and the now existing rebellion is at an end." George III was the most hawkish of the hawks.

Although communications were slow, intelligence on both sides was quick and efficient, with the more affluent British able to buy informers, spies, and even double agents easily and cheaply. The rebels also hemorrhaged deserters from the ranks, who were poorly paid, if at all. Some traffic in information came from captured couriers and from packets seized at sail—and they in turn also provided commands with opportunities to convey disinformation. Both sides benefited, yet weighed such messages with skepticism. In early April, as Howe arrived in dreary Halifax, Governor Tryon reported to Lord George from *The Duchess of Gordon* that rebel Americans in New York and Long Island expected a British landing, and had already burned hay and killed flocks of poultry to keep them from Howe's troops. In London, an informant with access to Lord George reported on April 7 that he was preparing sufficient force for New York "to ensure an unconditional submission, of which he is secure. You may depend upon this language [as] coming immediately from his lips."

Rumors seemed to fly at more advanced speed than sails. On April 13, 1776, the *Morning Post* reported "betts of three to one" that either France or Spain, each with something to gain from the mother country's distraction with America, would be at war with Britain before May 1777. On April 18, another newspaper noted mischievously that "to morrow, the 19th," would be "SAINT YANKEY'S day (as tutelar Saint of North America) and also anniversary of the famous battle of Lexington." In the observance in London, "There will be a grand procession from the Crown and Anchor, the place of rendezvous in the Strand, to St. Dunstan's, where a sermon suitable to the occasion will be preached by the Rev. Mr. CORIOLANUS, from New York." (Shakespeare's Roman patrician, freely adapted from Roman history, was allegedly deaf to every entreaty.) The "Reverend Band of Martyrs" from St. Paul's would join, and various drummed-out colonial governors would appear, as well as the American commissioners of the revenue "in Harlequin dress." A "Doctor of Music from Rhode Island, with his newly raised band of Highland bagpipers," would quickstep to the tune of "YANKIE DOODLE." After the sermon "an elegant entertainment" would be ready at four o'clock, back in the Strand.

By May 2, 1776, as debate was already under way in the colonies about a common declaration of what the British referred to scornfully as "independency," General Clinton's troop transports from Halifax, awaiting reinforcements at Cape Fear off the Carolinas, joined with a fleet captained by Commodore Sir Peter Parker. The mission was to exploit what had been assumed to be popular disaffection with the rebels in the Carolinas. After weighing anchor in Cork, the convoy, crowded with two thousand additional troops commanded by Lord Cornwallis, many long seasick, had been eighty days at sea.

Germain's information months before had been that the local loyalists were few and weak, and he had sent a belated packet at the king's request, urging Clinton to forget Charleston, and to join Howe in taking New York, where the King's Friends were numerous and influential. After lying about in bad weather off Sullivan's Island, where a substantial log fort protected Charleston, Clinton made his assault on June 28 following nine hours of Parker's cannonade, which included mortar shelling by the lead ship, the vaunted *Thunderbomb.* Most shells fell into the boggy terrain; others failed to penetrate the thick palmetto walls of Colonel William Moultrie's fortifications. No local loyalists surfaced onshore. The attack failed. American coast artillery damaged three ships and destroyed another; three frigates ran aground. The remainder retreated northward to New York Harbor, or south to the Caribbean.

From his refuge on the damaged *Bristol,* off Five Fathom Hole near Charleston, the South Carolina governor, Lord William Campbell, reported by packet on July 8 to Germain that no one on the frigate's quarterdeck had escaped death or injury. Its captain lost his right arm, while Commodore Parker was only "severely bruised." But when the news arrived in London late in August, it was Sir Peter Parker who received the press's sardonic attention. The *London Chronicle* and the *Evening Post* had published earlier a surly complaint, as if by Parker, and to the tune of "Well Met, Brother Tar," that the British would retake the entire continent "if the cowardly Yankies will let us." Now, "Bold as a Turk," he was retreating to New York, for newspaper readers learned that an exploding Yankee shell had torn off Parker's breeches, injuring his thigh, and spurring an epigram beginning, "If honour in the breech is lodged . . ."

By July the commander in North American waters was another Howe, Richard Howe, elder brother of the general. Lord Howe was more interested in conciliation than coercion, but had made demands in his own interest that the jobbing Earl of Sandwich, 1st Lord of the Admiralty, found inconvenient to meet. It meant removing the elderly and ineffective Admiral Molyneux Shuldham and buying him off with a promotion, a peerage, and another command. Howe's own payoff was a promotion to vice admiral and the lieutenant generalcy of marines (with its additional emolument). The admiral originally promised that perquisite would receive an alternative plum. Howe was to command the fleet gathering to land on Long Island and seize New York City. The army chief would be his brother; jointly they were to be Germain's appointees (ostensibly North's, and the king's) as a conciliation commission to persuade the colonies to return allegiance to the Crown.

Approval of a useless conciliation mechanism was as inevitable as continued war once the Lords, on March 14, 1776, rejected the Duke of Grafton's proposed proclamation, which offered to suspend hostilities if the colonies would submit a petition of rights and grievances to the Crown. The futile joint assignment to the Howes was as logical as it was curious. Neither brother expected that a military solution would work, but both were willing to attempt it for their own greater glory (and fortune), and their loyalty to the king. Both also felt that colonial grievances were negotiable if somehow the unwritten constitution (a bundle of cumulative legislation and judicial decisions) and the supremacy of Parliament could be finessed. And both had the inherent authority of their seats in Parliament in an age when serving officers with nearly hereditary places in the Commons, from constituencies purchased with a handful of votes, mixed politics with military careers.

Lord Sandwich, whose gaming-table edible would immortalize his name, considered the brothers as too inexperienced to conduct diplomacy, however expert they were at war. "Who does not know," he deplored to Germain, "that when the two Brothers are partners in deep play at whist they are not an over match for two rustics who have never played at any games beyond Putt or Loo."* Most Englishmen assumed from the newspapers that the brothers had wide powers and vast discretion.

For the bellicose Lord George, the peace commission was a sop to the doves. To ensure that its authority to make concessions was so limited as to be ineffective, he arranged, as he prepared for massive coercion, to leave almost nothing to the Howes' discretion. Alexander Wedderburn, now the lord chancellor and key drafter

*Putt was a card game dating back to the Elizabethans, favored by sharks and cheats; loo was a simple card game in which a player failing to take a trick or violating any of the rules had to pay a sum to the pool.

with Edward Thurlow, the solicitor general, agreed with Germain that "to end the war without [formally] finishing the dispute" was a poor solution, yet that a declaration of submission to Parliament by the colonies—which would be resisted—need not be a prerequisite to all actions by the commission. Germain, Wedderburn conceded, "having now collected a vast Force and having a fair prospect of subduing the colonies . . . wished to reduce them before he treated [with them] at all."

The king wanted the commission to proceed, and insisted on a compromise with the more passive North. All Germain would agree to was that an acknowledgment of parliamentary supremacy could come after settlement of preliminary issues. Only then would the colonies be declared as "at the King's peace." When Lord Howe, on the verge of sailing, protested that the emotional issue would preclude conciliation, Germain agreed that compliance might be made informally. On Howe's refusing to embark without more leeway— after all, the back-and-forth across the Atlantic might take half a year—the admiral was offered some useless cosmetic changes. He could offer pardons to anyone who took an oath of allegiance, but not until a colony had been declared at peace, and had restored all royal and parliamentary prerogatives, would coercion laws and military action be suspended.

The taxation issue was evaded in the proposal by an offer permitting the colonies to make "contributions" for imperial defense. Lord Howe realized that such grudging concessions were useless, and that all he could hope for was a recognition by influential colonials that his intentions were benevolent. What the ministry really wanted was a sweeping victory in New York that would divide the colonies geographically and emotionally and spur sectional defections. The haggling in London dragged on until April 27, well into what should have been a campaign season across the Atlantic, and it took two further weeks until ministerial clerks copied out the rerevised instructions and messengers took them through the many offices of the Whitehall bureaucracy. In Halifax, his brother's last dispatch from Germain was dated January 5. It was increasingly obvious to Admiral Howe that only a vigorous prosecution of the war on land and at sea could alter the attitude of the Americans, but geography precluded that.

Forty-one warships were already in North American waters. Thirty-two more were en route or under orders. Howe knew that Parker had taken some of the forty-two to the southern colonies, but he would not know for months about their failure at Charleston. Ten thousand Hessians awaited sailing from Spithead, where they had been ferried across the North Sea. (In his diary, kept for his children, Lieutenant Heinrich Karl Philipp von Feilitzsch would write of the surprise of his men as a loyalist pilot came aboard his ship at "Staaten Island" on June 3, 1776, and the troops discovered he was white: "All our People had been of the opinion that the inhabitants of America were black.")

Parker's 73 ships were to blockade the inlet-riddled 1,800-mile coastline, convoy soldiers and supplies, and carry on the war. Germain expected to have nearly 24,000 troops, including mercenaries, sail for New York, with 10,000 others in Canada awaiting deployment south. By eighteenth-century standards, and within the limits of topography and technology, it was a very formidable force. "I cannot take my leave of your Lordship," Richard Howe wrote flatteringly to Germain despite their differences, "without expressing my utter amazement at the decisive and masterly Strokes for carrying such extensive Plans into immediate Execution as have been effected since your Lordship has assumed the conducting of this War."

At sunrise on May 11, 1776, the sixty-four-gun *Eagle* with Admiral Lord Howe on board weighed anchor from the Isle of Wight to join his fleet, stopping first at Guernsey to load wine, a cow, "and other necessaries." He set his course for Halifax, and despite squalls and ice made the westward voyage in six weeks. Off Nova Scotia on June 23 he learned, more than six months late, that Quebec had been relieved, and that his brother, with Admiral Shuldham, had embarked on June 10, on the slow, misnamed frigate *Greyhound,* for Long Island. Setting sail for New York he found himself pitching in rough seas off Nantucket. Three more weeks had passed before the *Eagle* slipped the bar at Sandy Hook and on July 12 reached the Narrows, off Staten Island, where British forces, unopposed, had landed on June 25. It was a fair day, and the pines and green hills were as welcome as the cheers of the redcoats onshore. A cannonade of greeting followed; then General Howe and Admiral Shuldham were received aboard "with a guard and a march."

In London, Lord George had just received a letter from General Howe dated April 25, responding to the secretary's letters of November 18, 1775, and January 5, 1776, outlining his plans for a new American campaign and the prospects for a peace commission. "The scene here at present," Howe wrote from wintry Halifax, "wears a lowering aspect, there not being the least prospect of conciliating this Continent until its armies shall have been roughly dealt with; and I confess my apprehensions that such an event will not be readily brought about." Two weeks later he wrote again, to acknowledge "your Lordship's indefatigable pains and resources in the prosecution of this complicated war," and he hoped the "foreigners" hired would help "produce the success to his Majesty's arms."

Intelligence gathered by spies, deserters, and loyalists, William Howe reported to his brother, estimated the American troop strength on Long Island and in New York, well entrenched, it seemed, at more than twenty thousand men, with Washington in command. More disturbing was Howe's unwelcome dispatch, just received, that the Congress in Philadelphia had declared the colonies to be free and independent. From the British camp on Staten Island and ships of the Royal Navy offshore, the British saw celebratory bonfires on Long Island and in New York City, and heard the booming of cannon. It would take many weeks by sail for the news from Congress to unsettle England.

4

A Most Precarious Independence
July 1776–December 1776

"I can hardly believe, by the Tranquility about me, that we are a people who have lost an Empire."

—*Edmund Burke to Richard Champion, May 30, 1776*

"The American Rope of Sand is beginning to fall in Pieces."

—*Ambrose Serle (secretary to Admiral Lord Howe), diary, October 1, 1776*

LONDON learned of the Declaration of Independence on August 11, 1776. Writing to Horace Mann, Walpole conceded that the Americans were determined on "this savage kind of war," which seemed a "melancholy prospect," but he had already glimpsed what foreshadowed to him the inevitable future. "This little island will be ridiculously proud some ages hence of its former brave days, and swear its capital was once as big as Paris, or—what is to be the name of the city that will then give laws to Europe—perhaps New York or Philadelphia."

As early as 1701 the board of trade in London had registered concern about an American thirst for independence, yet even after Bunker Hill, on July 6, 1775, the Continental Congress claimed, while recognizing a state of war with the mother country, "We have not raised armies with the ambitious design of separating from Great Britain and establishing independent states." Two days short of a year later its delegates in Philadelphia had done exactly that. North Carolina's representatives had been instructed by its assembly on April 12, 1776, to join any movement toward independence. On May 15, Virginia's delegates were authorized to initiate steps toward independence, and on June 7, at the State House on Chestnut Street, Richard Henry Lee of Virginia moved a resolution "that these United Colonies are, and of right ought to be, free and independent States." John Adams of Massachusetts seconded the motion, and on June 11, members were selected to draw up a draft document. On July 4, twelve states adopted a declaration largely composed by Thomas Jefferson, a rising politician of thirty-three who based it upon the preamble he had written for the Virginia constitution. Although it was printed for distribution on July 5, formal copies were not signed until August 2, by which time a mail packet with the text was nearing England.

Before General Howe, on Staten Island, now sprawling with troop cantonments and supply depots, had learned of "Independency," he had written frankly and unhopefully to Germain, "I am still of opinion that peace will not be restored in America until the rebel army is defeated." The confirmation in mid-August of the arrival of Admiral Howe's armada in New York harbor seemed to cancel out the news of the rebellious Declaration [of Independence] in Philadelphia, which quickly seemed to be only an empty piece of colonial posturing. The stock market in London rose, and the *Morning Chronicle* on August 19 published "The Bellman's Cantata. As it Was Sung or Said at the Royal Exchange." A bellman cried the news as well as the hours, and in the *Chronicle's* version of events, "Bulls, Bears and Jews" all reacted happily to the prospect of peace. Not only the stock market registered optimism, the verses suggested, for London Assurance and the Royal Exchange monopolized marine insurance in England. If shipping became safe from sinking and seizure, all investments were more secure.

The "Jews" in the verse, whatever the implications, was also a recognition that although their numbers in England were few, their financial energy (most occupations were closed to them) made them so influential on the Exchange that they were limited to twelve brokers. And there were already nearly traditional Jewish military connections. The broker Solomon de Medina, knighted in 1700, had organized the commissariat of Marlborough's army; Joseph Mendes da Costa supplied the English army in Flanders in 1710; Abraham da Prado and David Mendes da Costa supplied the European front in the Seven Years' War; while David Franks was responsible for the

American colonies and Aaron Hart was with Lord Amherst in Canada. The Rothschilds would later help finance Wellington's army.

Once the Howes acquired a printed copy of the Declaration of Independence, they had rushed it by packet to Whitehall, observing that they saw in its language "no prospect of a disposition in those who now hold the supreme authority over the colonies to make any advances towards a reconciliation." The Howe brothers also included a copy of their own offer of conciliation, sent by flag of truce to Washington, but reported that it had been refused. The Continental officers who came from New York City to meet the signal flag for safe passage off Governor's Island "asserted that they were under orders not to convey any papers to that gentleman unless the superscription specified his military titles." Since Britain refused to recognize rebel ranks, the packet had been addressed to "George Washington, Esq." There was no such person among them, his officers explained to Lieutenant Philip Brown. "All the world knew who General Washington was," Colonel Joseph Reed said impatiently, "since the Transactions of last Summer." Brown read the address to them aloud anyway.

Ambrose Serle, Lord Howe's civilian secretary, was outraged both by the "vanity and insolence" of Washington's claim to legitimate rank and the manifesto of July 4. "A more impudent, false and atrocious Proclamation was never fabricated by the Hands of Man. Hitherto they had thrown all the Blame and Insult upon the Parliament and ministry. Now they have the Audacity to calumniate the King and People of Great Britain." He read "this Paper" with "Horror at the daring Hypocrisy of these Men, who call GOD to witness the uprightness of their Proceedings," and with "Indignation at the low and scurrilous Pretences by w[hi]ch they attempt to justify themselves."

Many Englishmen would echo Serle's reaction. The heated rhetoric of the declaration struck newspaper readers across the Atlantic as excessive. Even more intemperate had been the unseen opening of Jefferson's unseen first draft, which began, legalistically, "Whereas George Guelf king of Great Britain and Ireland and Elector of Hanover, heretofore entrusted with the exercise of the kingly office in this government[,] hath endeavored to pervert the same into a detestable and insupportable tyranny." A broadside cartoon on sale in

London pictured an insufferable and unreasonable colonist being warned by an elderly lady, "Brother Patriot, you will choak yourself with Passion."

"Did you ever know a Patriot that could give a Reason?" he replies. "I hate every thing that's done by any body that could or would do good to their Country."

Support of the colonists in Britain suddenly seemed muted, especially after the press reported that New Yorkers "came down to welcome the arrival of their deliverers"—Howe's redcoats. Another cartoon, "News from America, or the Patriots in the Dumps," showed a spectrum of English leaders, from an unhappy Wilkes to a very pleased king. Another, in the *Westminster Magazine,* "The Parricide. A Sketch of Modern Patriotism," depicted a helpless Britannia, nude to the waist, held down by men directed by Wilkes, while a murderous young woman with Indian feathers in her hair, daughter America, attacks her with a tomahawk in one hand, a rapier in the other. Mother Britannia's broken spear and trampled shield lie on the ground, and a British lion at her side is being restrained by a kindly Anglican clergyman. "With effrontery without example in any other age or nation," the caption reads, "these men assume the name of Patriots."

Beyond the Declaration of Independence, perhaps the most outrageous rebel effrontery was the beheading, and tearing down, of William Wilton's statue of George III in Bowling Green by patriot Manhattanites calling themselves Sons of Liberty. As early as 1771, the year after the gilded equestrian figure arrived from England, the already anxious Common Council appropriated eight hundred pounds for a tall fence to protect it from becoming "a receptacle of all of the filth & dirt of the Neighbourhood." Even the fence post finials, six feet high, resembled crowns, and seemed a tempting target. On the evening of July 9, learning of formal independence from Philadelphia, New Yorkers gathered in the park and after a public reading of the Declaration, beheaded the statue, then pulled it down, along with the fence-post ornaments. The metal was hauled to Litchfield, Connecticut, where an armaments factory employing women now that local men were in the militia, turned the king into 42,088 cartridges for muskets—"to assimilate with the brains" of the enemy, the *Freeman's Journal* of New Hampshire crowed on July 20. The redcoats, Ebenezer Howard wrote to General Gates, "will probably have melted Majesty fired at them."

As the news reached other colonies, statues of imperial worthies were dismantled, and effigies of the king were either burned or exploded—or were buried, as in Savannah. There, Georgians listened to a reading of the Declaration at the courthouse steps, after which a spokesman declared, "We, therefore, commit his political existence to the ground—corruption to corruption—tyranny to the grave."

For some, discarding tradition was more difficult than compromising with change. The Reverend Philip Reading of St. Anne's parish in Middletown, Delaware, had come from England in 1746, overseeing the replacement of the original wooden church of 1705 by a Georgian structure of English bricks brought over as ship's ballast. Parishioners built their own box pews or brought stools—or stood. Above was a slaves' balcony. On Sunday, July 28, 1776, as light streamed through its Palladian window from the east, he ascended his three-tiered pulpit, seemingly as usual. Unable to resist independence but unwilling to breach his duty to the 1662 *Book of Common Prayer* and mandatory devotion to the Crown, Parson Reading exhorted the congregation to keep the faith, then shut up the emptying church, never to return.★

In England, the belligerent idealism of Jefferson's rhetoric was ridiculed. *Gentleman's Magazine* in September 1776 scoffed at the professedly "self-evident" truth that all men are created equal, which implied to an unrealistic Congress equality before the law. "In what are they created equal? Is it size, strength, understanding, figure, moral or civil accomplishments, or situation of life? Every plough-man knows that they are not equal in any of these." The July manifesto was either "ignorant" or "a self-evident falsehood." American papers reaching the British seemed as extreme as the declaration. One boasted, "Be assured, the Sun, Moon & Stars shall fall, the Ocean cease to roll, and all nature change its Course, before a few English, Scotch & German *Slaves* shall conquer this vast Country."

When the American press printed the Howes' conciliation statement, Serle complained, it was preceded by congressional criticism

---

★St. Anne's remained padlocked until the war ended. As Old St. Anne's it continues into its fourth century.

"to render its humane Intentions of no Effect." Some papers also published extracts from Parson Price's pamphlet referring to British slavery of the American people, noting that the colonists nevertheless worked hundreds of thousands of unmentioned slaves. "Nothing," Amrose Serle wrote from Admiral Howe's flagship, "can be a stronger Contradiction to the Fact, than this; the Book [by Price] has never been burnt, nor the author hanged; which would have been the certain Consequence in any State but G. Britain." The "Parent State" of the Americans enabled them to live "under the mildest & most relaxed Government in the World."

Working to end the war, Germain's ministry was anything but relaxed, managing to amass 325 ships with 10,000 seamen to carry 32,000 soldiers, most of them experienced and fully equipped professionals, to invade Long Island from Staten Island as prelude to taking New York City. Uneasily awaiting them were 19,000 scrappily equipped and trained Continentals, most on short-term enlistments, and led by mostly amateur officers who were often political appointees to keep the colonies in line. One was Major General John Sullivan, a self-taught and self-important lawyer in civilian life and a former major in the New Hampshire militia. Following service in the siege of Boston and the Canadian fiasco, he achieved a local command after threatening Congress that he would resign. Washington often had generals imposed on him by Congress.

Somehow Sullivan had Washington's trust—the general had limited alternatives. Sullivan fortified the Jamaica Road approaches on Long Island with all of five militiamen. Howe sent ten thousand redcoats. Captured easily on August 27, 1776, Sullivan was exchanged for a British general on September 25 and was back at Washington's headquarters on Manhattan Island two days later, continuing an up-and-down career.

In the interim, as the British occupied, to little further resistance, all of Long Island westward to "Brookland," the Howes dealt from strength by proposing a meeting with members of the Continental Congress, sending Sullivan to Philadelphia on parole to arrange it. On September 11, a committee consisting of Benjamin Franklin, John Adams, and Edward Rutledge were met by a barge at Perth Amboy and conveyed to Lord Howe on Staten Island. He could not receive them, the admiral explained affably at lunch, as representatives of a Congress he was not permitted to recognize, but only as private gentlemen. The delegates accepted the subterfuge, so long as they were not referred to as British subjects. After that, the conference on conciliation faltered. Howe could offer any number of pardons and discussions of grievances. But the colonies would not take up any issues prior to recognition of their independence. Ambrose Serle conceded in his diary, "They met, they talked, they parted. And now nothing remains but to fight it out." An English cartoon of a mother and daughter in argument, with the daughter bare-breasted to emphasize her radicalism, suggested the mutually closed minds. "I'll force you to obedience, you rebellious slut," warns the mother. "Liberty, liberty, Mother, while I exist," the rebellious daughter shouts back.

The battle for New York City, beginning on September 14 at Kip's Bay, was just short of a catastrophe for Washington's inexperienced, shattered, and quickly demoralized forces, which lost heavily in dead and wounded and in abandoned weapons, especially precious cannons. Galloping hastily from his headquarters in Harlem, he realized to his "surprise and mortification" that his troops were not falling back, but fleeing "in every direction and in the utmost confusion." In his fury he lost his composure, striking at several officers and flinging his hat to the ground. "Good God," one heard him shout, "have I got such troops as these?" Another recalled his raging, "Are these the men with whom I am to defend America?" Paralyzed by the debacle, he lingered until an aide clutched at the bridle of the general's horse and pulled him away.

Before the British landed, Congress in Philadelphia had muddied matters by passing resolutions about his defending the city or evacuating it. Spread over sixteen miles from north to south, his forces were too thin to repel the British. Henry Clinton wanted to cut off and destroy Washington's army, while Howe wanted to avoid a direct assault in order to protect the city as winter quarters and keep his casualties minimal. Later he claimed, "Even a victory, attended by a heavy loss of men on our part, would have given a fatal shock to the progress of the war, and might have proved irreparable." He was managing his operation with one ear cocked to London opinion.

Humiliated by the incompetence of his surviving officers and the panic of their troops, but rescued by Howe's caution about following up his successes, Washington withdrew to higher ground along the Hudson north of the city. His shrunken and shaken army was barely intact. On the eighteenth an angry message from Washington to some of his officers was seized, with its bearer, and soon transmitted to a pleased Secretary for America. Ambrose Serle described it happily as "upbraiding them with Want of Courage and Want of Discipline, and reproaching them that a Band of mercenary Hirelings . . . should so far excel them in both."

The next morning Serle went to the bookshop near the Battery where *Rivington's New York Loyal Gazette* was published, and to his dismay found James Rivington's shelves, despite his paper's masthead, "filled with the inflammatory Publications of the Faction in England, which, in great measure, have promoted, if not excited, the Troubles here." The kind of pro-Yankee provocation he alluded to suggests a September 14 London account in which an opposition paper "directly contradict[ed] Lord Sandwich's assertion in calling the Americans 'Cowards.'" In the year-old report, a Major John Pitcairn "echoes his Lordship's opinion" and boasts, before he embarks for America at Portsmouth, "that if he drew his sword but half out of the scabbard, the whole banditti (as he termed them) . . . would flee from him. Behold he is slain, on the first time he appears in the field against them." The account was only half-true. Pitcairn, who had fought with courage at Concord, had been killed at Bunker Hill.

Rivington had just returned from England, having been appointed King's Printer, and had apparently brought papers and pamphlets with him from both factions. "Nothing else would go down," the shifty proprietor explained, "as every Man has a Stoop or Seat at his Door, his neighbours would gather round and ventilate both Politics and the Air together." Whenever he could, Rivington profitably played both sides.

As was the practice with news worth exulting about, Howe sent an aide by fast packet to England with a full report of the victory, including a draft of his new offer dated from New York City to "misguided Americans" who had mistakenly accepted an "extravagant and inadmissable claim of Independence." *Gentleman's Magazine* celebrated Howe—a rare testimonial to him—with an ode, "The Genius of Britain to Gen. Howe, the Night before the Battle of Long Island."

Germain responded to Howe on October 18, 1776, via the returning Major Cuyler, "The glorious success of his Majesty's arms gave universal satisfaction to every good subject." Until then the London press had found little cause for confidence about putting down the rebellion. Only later did grumbling surface that Howe had not exploited his opportunities more rapidly and crushed what was left of Washington's forces. The general, by then back in London, explained that losses of career professionals would be difficult to replace from across an ocean, while the rebels could recruit marginally trained militiamen close at hand. He would "never expose the troops . . . where the object is inadequate." The object, however, had been more than adequate. That September, Howe may have saved the American revolution.

When the packet *Harriot* arrived in New York from England on October 21 with English newspapers two months old, and more, Serle complained to his diary that they "teem with Falsehoods respecting American Affairs; and I fear my dear Family has been frightened by some of them. . . . They freely killed Lord Howe at Rhode Island, while he was labouring to get over the Banks of Newfoundland. A very trifling Difference between the Plot and Action of a Lye!"

Many in England now assumed that the rebellion was effectively over, as reoccupation of the middle colonies, anchored by rather unmilitant New York, appeared to split the northern and southern provinces into two nearly disconnected fragments. Rebel forces could only communicate through upper New York, at Albany, or by contested sea routes, and the British had plans to cut off the Albany connection from Canada as well by reaching down the Hudson River. "The Declaration of Independency," Lord George wrote smugly to General Howe, "has staggered many of the former advocates for America. Among others I hear Lord Camden says there is no supporting the Americans [now] upon their present ground. Indeed the leaders of the rebellion have acted as I could have wished, and I trust that the deluded people will soon have recourse to your lordship for mercy and protection, leaving their chiefs to receive the punishment they deserve."

Distance and time kept Whitehall at several removes from events in America, and by the time Lord George had planned sequels to what seemed a continuation of victories, the situation on the ground had moved beyond his expectations. Time had also left many Englishmen still unnerved by the evacuation of Boston, and before the upbeat news from New York had reached London, a sardonic letter signed "Judaeus Apella" had appeared in the *St. James's Gazette* "to congratulate my dear Countrymen on the implicit Confidence, which they so reasonably place in the present unparalleled Administration; and which neither Rashness, Waste, Negligence, Miscarriages, nor Disgrace can shake. Last year the Ministers promised every Thing, and performed Nothing; nothing fell out as they had foretold.... All their Measures were equally bad and worse executed; the Provincials proved as brave as they had been proclaimed Cowards; and all the Steps taken from hence but tended to cement Union between those who had been represented as unilaterally disunited." Yet New York made a short war seem likely.

Germain counted upon the seizure of New York and the rout of the Continentals, even from Fort Lee across the Hudson in the Jerseys, to squelch opposition carping. Yet he realized that without the destruction of Washington's capacity to continue, the war would go on into another year. The seasons conspired against him more than did the beleaguered patriots. The onset of winter across much of provincial America could require yet another campaigning year.

The American Secretary did not want troops to hibernate, and was pleased by another dispatch from General Howe that arrived via Captain Balfour, his second aide-de-camp, in the last days of October. Howe was planning to send troops under Clinton by sea, which the British commanded, to Rhode Island to establish a base with an ice-free harbor to replace Halifax for supply, and from which to harass Continental commerce. But Howe had also learned, he wrote, of plans to send troops south from Canada, and confided his timidity about moving north to link up with Carleton or Burgoyne. Carleton reported in mid-October (it would be winter before the news reached Whitehall) that he had retaken Crown Point in upper New York, north of Ticonderoga, and captured a Continental brigadier general, but he had added, "The season is so far advanced that I cannot yet pretend to inform your lordship whether anything further can be done this year." The campaign season just below the Canadian border was short, and the distances long. Half a year of inaction was necessary north of Albany.

To the south, Howe remained hesitant about taking on what was left of Washington's army, and Germain knew when he received the dispatch that Howe's further ventures beyond Rhode Island in what remained of 1776 would be small ones. "I presume I must not risk, as a check at this time would be of infinite detriment to us," he explained. Although Howe had performed brilliantly in occupying Long Island and in taking New York, he had little flair for exploiting his momentum. Rather, he rationalized to London, "The enemy is too strongly posted to be attacked in front and innumerable difficulties are in our way of turning him on either side. Though his army is much dispirited . . . , yet have I not the smallest prospect of finishing the contest this campaign, nor until the rebels see [our] preparations in the spring that may preclude all thoughts of further resistance."

The key word was "preparations," for which he wanted massive supplements from Whitehall. Yet Parliament was unwilling to approve increased military expenditures (requiring new revenues), which would sit badly with the public and erode its already uncertain confidence in the cost-effectiveness of continuing the war. Lost to Germain in Howe's pleas was the bald statement that the king's adherents in America—the green-clad★ Provincials armed in New York—were disappointingly few and unwilling to fight. As Howe put it on September 25, and Germain would not read until mid-November, "We must also have [more] recruits from Europe, not finding the Americans disposed to serve with arms, notwithstanding the hopes held out to me upon my arrival at this post."

Lord George would never give up his belief that redcoat successes would unleash zealous volunteers to the colors. Loyalists remained numerous but quiet, intimidated almost everywhere by rebel outspokenness and aggressiveness. The king's American friends did not want their houses and hayricks burned, their domestic animals stolen or killed, or a personal tar-and-feathering. Howe would receive other Hessians al-

---

★By 1778, to encourage recruitment of loyalist volunteers, Provincials were offered uniforms of green coat with yellow trim and tan breeches. Full uniform also validated claims of prisoner of war status should they be captured.

ready authorized and at sea, but Lord George would not venture to ask Parliament to fund more mercenaries other than replacements.

Further Hessians and Waldeckers did disembark at Staten Island late in October, having sailed from Bremen months earlier. Not entirely welcome, they had a reputation not only for professionalism as soldiers but also for marauding and plunder. As Sir John Osborn wrote to Germain just after they landed, the first Hessians to arrive had already confirmed forebodings, believing "that they were come to America to establish their private fortunes and hitherto they have certainly acted with that principle." Even loyalist New Jerseyites would soon lock their doors when German troops were in the vicinity. Paradoxically, Washington was hopeful that they would like America enough to refrain from ransacking it, and desert to become settlers in existing German communities. A Hessian who, after arrival, straggled beyond his lines and was taken prisoner, Osborn reported, "was taken up to Mr. Washington, who released him immediately with a present, assuring him by a German officer in the rebel service that the Americans intended no hurt to the Hessian troops." (Washington's interpreter, like other Poles, Lithuanians, Frenchmen, and Germans, had come as volunteers, either out of idealism, adventure, or to chance a career in the promising new nation.)

Other useful auxiliaries from Germany were regiments loyal to George III in his capacity as Elector of Hanover, the title of his great-grandfather when he was translated to England. The closest royal relative to the heirless Queen Anne, George I spoke no English. The Hanoverians would see no action in America but released English troops on garrison duty. In Parliament, Lord John Cavendish criticized such expedients as "mortifying" and "humiliating"—and "an alarming consequence of the American war"—but Englishmen who remained comfortably at home found no fault with the practice.

Another expedient, however, would cause alarm whenever activated through the war. Although slavery in England was now illegal, the "pressing" of males into naval service—its equivalent—was lawful, and press gangs roamed the streets on orders of the Board of Admiralty whenever ship complements were needed. In October 1776, London's Lord Mayor asked for the exemption of John Tubbs and thirty other watermen plying the Thames for the City. Lord Mansfield issued an opinion denying it. Pressing, he wrote, has been a custom "established [since] time immemorial, for many ages past, and justifiable . . . on the safety of the state; upon this principle, that individuals must suffer some mischief rather than the public safety be endangered." Mr. Justice Ashhurst upheld the argument. "If pressing was supported by usage [from] time immemorial," he contended, "it established a general power to press, unless where an exception was created by statute."

In London, Lady Mary Coke wrote in her journal for October 30, 1776, that "last night . . . seventeen hundred [were] taken." Many would never see their homes and families again. Usually the rank of the employer was a guarantee, but the next day the Marquess of Hertford appealed to Lord Sandwich for an exemption for one of the king's watermen, and was told that a petition had to be lodged. "I suppose I am to imagine that he never does such things," Hertford wrote to Horace Walpole, "as the trade for granting protections at the Admiralty is a very lucrative one to some of the parties there." He saw the affair as representing the "gloomy . . . general prospect" of the war.

Reports from America were in sharp contrast. Howe wrote to London that with New York City in hand, Earl Cornwallis and his forces had crossed the Hudson to Fort Lee and penetrated into New Jersey easily with infantry, grenadiers, chasseurs, and dragoons, accompanied by tough, eager Hessians. Routed, the marginally trained Americans abandoned irreplaceable artillery and everything else they could not carry. The late autumn weather was still warm and dry, making both flight and pursuit possible. The remnants of the Continentals hastily regrouped southward, retreating across the Delaware to Pennsylvania and westward across the Hudson into upper New York. As Howe knew, Washington's demoralized army had dwindled rapidly through desertions, always a problem at harvest time, and might disappear altogether as yearlong enlistments ended while troops saw little hope and less pay. The Congress's Board of War on September 16, 1776, had approved giving every soldier who signed on for the duration of the war a bonus of twenty dollars and one hundred acres of land somewhere, but takers were few.

East Jersey was occupied by redcoats with few shots fired and, according to Howe, enthusiastic requests for royal pardons followed. Encouraged, he looked for potential winter quarters there. He understood from his informants, he told Germain, that Dr. Franklin (now nearly seventy-one) "is gone to France to solicit aid from that Court," and Howe suggested that the French be warned to stay away from a war they would lose. In the next and final campaign, in 1777, "little resistance would be made to the progress of His Majesty's arms in the provinces of New England, New York, the Jerseys and Pennsylvania, after the junction of the northern and southern armies." Even Philadelphia, Howe predicted, would fall easily. The crumbling colonies could be a poor investment for the French.

As prospects looked good for both Howes, a broadside cartoon, "The Catch Singers," was on sale in Fleet Street, the center of the printing and bookselling trade. (A "catch" was a round sung by three or more participants.) Four men with moneybags are singing and drinking, raising their glasses to toast each other. At the head of the table is a plump Lord North. His bag is inscribed *Treasury £100,000.* On the right of the First Lord of the Treasury (North's formal title) is a jovial man with a worthless bag labeled *£000,001 Minden*—obviously Lord George Germain. Their dialogue appears in balloon fashion, and the American Secretary sings (to rhyme with "gold"), "With their hearts so strong and bold." The other two are the Howe brothers, likely to be further enriched for their successes. Each holds a large moneybag and a glass, and toasts the other. Behind the quartet is a map of Europe and the Americas, the Atlantic Ocean between them. Curiously, the positions of the continents are reversed—if not an error, perhaps a code, like that of flying a flag upside down, signaling serious trouble.

Britain's unhidden troubles emerged in the proceedings of the House of Commons for November 18, 1776, during which Lord Barrington successfully moved resolutions for payment of British and mercenary military expenses through the end of the year, and for authorization of projected costs for 1777. War always exceeded preliminary financial estimates. Among the costs were £56,777.19.4—and a ha'penny—"for the pay of five Battalions of Hanoverians serving at Gibraltar and Minorca," and their provisions.★ Also authorized was £336,932.1.6—and three farthings—for the services of 12,667 Hessians, £18,181.15.6 (and 3 farthings) for a regiment of foot★★ from Hanau, £17,370.82 for a regiment of Waldecks, and £93,947.15.8

★The king's Hanoverians replaced redcoats for service in America.

★★Foot soldiers, infantry.

for 4,300 Brunswickers. For the Secretary at War to refer to the payments as "pay" masked the reality that the fees went to the Landgraves of each state, and only a little of it trickled down. A further £150,000 went to provisioning troops. In addition, more than two million pounds had to be authorized for British forces in 1777, and everyone in both houses knew that supplementary funding would be called for. Such appropriations meant a burden on the economy only new revenues could maintain, and which would not even end with victory.

Admiral Howe's aide, Ambrose Serle, had already predicted confidently that Washington would find it "rather difficult (and particularly after the ensuing Winter) to form any Army at all." And even if he could, he could not "maintain" his soldiery, whatever their numbers. "H[is] majesty's Troops need be in no great Concern about them." General Richard Prescott, who had been exchanged for the erratic John Sullivan, and then sailed off as third in command of the force seizing Newport, Rhode Island, had reported from his observations as a former prisoner "that if we make a Winter's Campaign, their Army must be destroyed, as they have neither Flannel nor warm cloth to put on their backs. They are also equally distressed for Salt, and many other Comforts, if not Necessaries of Life."

Gratified by the open loyalist sentiment in New Jersey, where its royalist governor had been (until seized, and jailed in Connecticut) Franklin's estranged illegitimate son William, General Howe reported to Germain that "a very considerable number of persons who had been active in the rebellion . . . have already subscribed [to] the declaration of allegiance," and that he was pardoning New Jerseyites as fast as he could get the certificates printed. The British press claimed that "vast numbers" were volunteering, and that two-thirds of tiny Rhode Island was already pacified. Less sanguine, his brother Richard believed that such turncoats were worthless, as "almost all the People of Parts & Spirit were in the Rebellion." Unlike Germain, who was remote from the realities, Admiral Howe believed that only persuasive conciliation would keep the empire together, for Americans resentful and dissatisfied in defeat would revolt again, and the painful cycle would continue until they succeeded.

In London, however, the events restored faith in the seemingly inevitable return to accommodation, if not loyalty, of those Americans who saw disintegration and disaster looming for the union. With renewed optimism, restored New York governor William Tryon wrote to Germain on Christmas Eve from festive, although partially destroyed, New York City that the successes in Rhode Island and New Jersey "will assuredly open considerable resources of provisions and forage for the army, which with the plentiful and abundant supplies from the mother country will enable this high-spirited and victorious army to take the field early next spring." As unifying sop to the Continentals, Tryon suggested to Lord George that after their defeat a battalion of Americans be added to His Majesty's guardsmen, as Swiss Guards were then in the French service.

Now sharing the buoyant prospects, the Howes as peace commissioners as well as senior commanders concluded that they had "the most sanguine hopes" that even the operations just winding down, once their dimensions became clear to the Americans, "will effectually crush the rebellion." Such wishful thinking was based upon soundings from loyalists, and in some dimension it was legitimate. A groundswell for independence did not yet exist, except perhaps in Massachusetts. There seemed, still, what a later generation would call a "silent majority" for the status quo. New York and New Jersey were relatively quiescent, as was Pennsylvania, with its peaceable German farmers and Quaker merchants. The outspoken patriot leadership of Virginia hardly reflected the ordinary people and the country squires of the middle South. So William Allen of Philadelphia, who spoke for the prosperous elite and knew little of the lower orders, contended to the admiral's secretary, claiming, "that three-fourths of the People are against Independency; that the Continent is under the Dominion of a desperate Faction, formed by the worst Characters upon it; that the Inhabitants in general begin to have their Eyes open relative to the Nature & Consequences of the Dispute."

With the holiday season approaching the king called for a day of "public Fast and Humiliation" to be observed on December 13, a Friday, "throughout that part of our Kingdom of Great Britain called England, our Dominion of Wales, and town of Berwick upon Tweed," to supplicate the Almighty to deliver the contrary provinces of North America "from the violence, injustice, and tyranny of those daring rebels who have assumed to themselves the exercise of Arbitrary Power." He called upon the archbishops to create a form of prayer for the occasion.

When Parliament recessed for the holiday season to enjoy Christmas pies at home, Whitehall had not yet learned that Cornwallis had overrun the Jerseys, and that the boastful Charles Lee had been captured at Basking Ridge on December 13. Three weeks earlier Washington had discovered a letter from Lee, a major general who was ambitious for the commander-in-chief's job, to Congressman Joseph Reed calling "a certain great man"—clearly Washington—"damnably deficient." Germain would order Lee returned to England for trial as a deserter, as he had once been a British lieutenant colonel, but General Howe ignored the demand. As a turncoat in trouble, Lee was working to save his neck by offering advice on how to defeat what seemed a faltering rebellion.★

After reaching the Jersey bankside of the icy Delaware, near Trenton and Princeton, Howe and Cornwallis left their deputies at advanced posts and began returning toward New York. The weather had turned too frigid to probe further for rebel weakness. Could they have crushed the beaten Continentals before taking to winter quarters? The season itself might do their work for them. Hazarding losses of irreplaceable professionals at the hands of desperate militiamen could ruin promising careers and prejudice support at home. Instead, large cantonments were thrown up near towns and villages from (New) Brunswick on the Raritan River southward to the Delaware at Trenton to await, if necessary, the spring thaws.

In a message written late in 1776 that reached London in February 1777, General Howe described to Germain changes in long-range strategy dictated by the unpromising outlook for further reinforcements. He would leave a force to occupy coastal Rhode Island, maintain New York and nearby Hudson River outposts, and occupy Philadelphia with ten thousand men, less than half his army. "We must not look for the northern army to reach Albany before the middle of September," he explained, justifying his disinterest in coordination of forces so far off in distance and time. Residents of comfortable Philadelphia, he had learned from informants, were "dis-

★Lee would be exchanged in 1778, and would run into more trouble with Washington.

posed to peace" despite the presence of the militant Continental Congress, and he could get at "the enemy's chief strength" collected there while dispersing the Congress. By the time that the American Secretary could react, much had changed—but not Howe's mind.

With remnants of his inadequately clad army in tents across the Delaware in the northern and western outskirts of Philadelphia, Washington had already written disconsolately on December 18, 1776, "The game is pretty near up." Had Howe known, he would have confirmed that assessment. Two days later, Washington, often prone to depression, worried, realizing how many enlistments terminated at year's end, that "10 days more will put an end to the existence of our Army."

With leave to return to England on family business, Earl Cornwallis had turned over his command in New Brunswick to Major General James Grant. Inheriting spies with access to Washington's headquarters, Grant would report, apparently to Howe (only the unaddressed draft exists), "Mr. Wharton is gone to Philadelphia for Intelligence, will be at Washington's tomorrow. Lowrie is to meet him there, will be in the Jerseys next [day] & I shall hear from him immediately." He also recorded information "given by Genl. Mercer's deputy." Hugh Mercer was a trusted subordinate of Washington, but obviously an aide had been suborned. An informant also reported that Washington was planning—however unlikely it seemed in the circumstances—to cross the Delaware to surprise the Hessian garrison at Trenton on Christmas night. At 5:00 P.M. on Christmas Day the message was relayed to Colonel Johann Rall, the post's commander.

From one of Washington's tents a young Irish officer, John Fitzgerald, wrote in his diary, "Christmas morning. They make a great deal of Christmas in Germany, and no doubt the Hessians will drink a great deal of beer and have a dance tonight. They will be sleepy tomorrow morning. Washington will set the tune for them about daybreak. The rations are cooked. New flints and ammunition have been distributed."

Why Rall took no serious heed of his warning is unknown. He had information—some of it misinformation—that Washington's dwindling troops were in a bad way. Overconfidence may also have accompanied easy success. Had he looked at the worsening weather he may have been tempted to enjoy a German Christmas. Bad weather might inhibit Jersey militiamen who lay low and ambushed his patrols. "We have not slept one night in peace since we came to this place," a Hessian officer wrote in his diary on Christmas Eve.

The warning of an improbable attack, Grant wrote, ruefully, later, "was better intelligence than I could be expected to have so soon after I was appointed to this command. No man in America knows the channel through which it came except the Genl. who I let into the secret before this cursed affair happen'd." Washington may have had an accomplice—John Honeyman, who posed as a cattle dealer and butcher in Griggstown, near Princeton, has been suggested*— who supplied food and liquor to the Hessians for a fatal holiday party, and information to the Continentals. The spying was double-edged, but the Hessians were quite capable of organizing a *Weihnachtsfest* without any covert assistance, and Rall, whether heady with Christmas cheer, or fatigue, or merely skeptical about a hazardous night crossing by the enemy through choking ice, gave the warning little credence. As sleet fell, most of his men slept into the morning.

Washington was relying on less than six thousand troops, their numbers soon to diminish. Dividing them into three columns, he assigned the 1,800 Philadelphia militiamen to Colonel John Cadwalader, kept 2,400 men for himself, and gave the remainder to Brigadier General James Ewing, who was to cross to the south to cut off any Hessian withdrawal in that direction.

The Continentals were experiencing a bleak Christmas, with little to eat but uncured beef from which the hides had been stripped to repair their shoes. Some had only their blankets for capes. Despite wind-driven snow and pelting hail, they pushed off at twilight from Dunker's Ferry in prudently collected ore barges. The high-walled boats had no benches and soldiers stood in several inches of slush. Concerned about the visibility across the Delaware, and the floating ice, Washington, stepping into the slush in his barge, called out, "Is any one here who is well acquainted with the river?"

"Here is Captain Blunt," someone ventured, "who is familiar with the navigation." John Blunt had coasted regularly between Portsmouth, New Hampshire, and the Delaware. He stepped forward

---

*Washington is recorded as paying Honeyman for spying.

and Washington directed, "Captain Blunt, please take the helm."

Only the barges carrying Washington's column got through the drifting ice to the Jersey bankside: It took ten grueling hours to reach the river from their cantonment and to paddle across. Wet and cold, the last men across made it ashore at three in the morning. (Some did not get over, Captain Thomas Rodney of Delaware wrote.) After that it was eight more miles to the village of Trenton and the improvised Hessian barracks on King Street.

According to Howe's account to Germain dated December 31, Colonel Rall, suddenly warned about a patriot force moving toward him in the lifting darkness, sent out his sleepy pickets to investigate. Surprised by what they found, they fell back in confusion. Gathering what men he could awaken, Rall rushed forward—and was shot down. At least 100 other Hessians were killed or wounded. Despite their reputation for hardiness and discipline, a further 919 were captured, including 20 drummers and 9 musicians with their "Trumpets and Clarionets," while 412 escaped to nearby Bordentown, where Colonel Carl von Donop garrisoned a battalion, and to Princeton.

Both Burgoyne and Clinton had returned to England to warm their parliamentary seats briefly and to promote themselves for larger roles in America. Burgoyne also had to deal with circumstances created by his wife's death earlier in the year. After an audience with the king, he reported to Germain, "I humbly laid myself at His Majesty's feet for such active employment as he might think me worthy of." On Christmas Day Burgoyne was marking a gentleman's Christmas, and boasting to Charles James Fox of the opposition at their favorite gambling haunt that he would be back next Christmas after quashing the rebellion in America. "Be not over-sanguine," said Fox. "I believe when you return to England you will be a prisoner on parole."

Recorded that date in the betting book at fashionable Brooks Club was "General Burgoyne wagers Charles Fox one pony* that he will be home victorious from America by Christmas Day, 1777." Then Burgoyne repaired to Bath, to take the steamy mineral waters, and to prepare a memorandum on how he saw his future role.

There he found another opposition leader, John Wilkes, MP for

*A pony equaled fifty guineas, or fifty-five pounds, a year's wages for a clerk or skilled laborer.

Middlesex, also enjoying the medicinal baths. Wilkes asked whether "next summer" the general proposed to return to Canada and push through "the Lakes" to Albany.

"Certainly," Burgoyne said, wondering how his bathing companion knew. But in gossipy London politics there were few secrets.

"Why then," said Wilkes, "you will certainly be taken prisoner by [Benedict] Arnold. Therefore, pray accept a letter from me to [John] Hancock."

"Sir," snapped Burgoyne, "no man's recommendation would be more acceptable to me on all occasions; but I am well assured that I shall have no use for your friendship at this time."

When the Continentals prudently recrossed the icy Delaware on December 27 Burgoyne's wager was already in jeopardy. Only four casualties were counted on the American side, one of them a future president, Lieutenant James Monroe. Unaware yet of the unexpected success, which might have suggested second thoughts, Congress on the same day gave Washington near dictatorial emergency powers, including the authority to raise 104 infantry battalions for terms of 3 years or the duration of the war. Recruiting 76,000 men was unrealistic, even fantasy—and no money had been voted to do it. Enlistments were expiring wholesale. The entire Delaware Regiment was scheduled to disappear on December 31.

Even extending enlistments required money, and—even more than that—hope. At least, now, there was hope.

Alerted at New Brunswick to the post-Christmas debacle, Cornwallis canceled his sailing and with hastily recalled infantry and grenadiers rushed to the aid of the remaining Hessians at Bordentown, and a rear guard of 1,200 redcoats at Princeton. The British could no longer take the loyalist New Jersey countryside for granted. While ministerial rejoicing over earlier victories enlivened New Year's Eve celebrations in London, Cornwallis was rushing south with the 17th and 55th Foot. Successes were as symbolic as they were strategic. Confidence revived. A small engagement had shifted control of a crucial contested space.

Ambrose Serle, who had remained under roof that day in New York City because of "tempestuous" lashings of "Rain, Frost, Wind & Snow," learned the "very unpleasant News" the day after the debacle. In his diary he regretted that it would "tend to revive the drooping

Spirits of the Rebels and increase their Force." Like the Howes, he had not anticipated that with one day now remaining before most enlistments expired with the old year, Washington, struggling to maintain his army, could build upon an unexpected turnabout.

Very likely the risky operation had rescued the rebellion for the winter. With only two days left for some enlistments, however, Washington wanted to re-cross the Delaware and follow up his sudden advantage. Encouraged but still desperate, and without any authorization from Congress, he offered a ten-dollar bonus for reenlistments of only "one month longer," appealing from horseback to soldiers who preferred to return to their safer, if humdrum, lives, mostly in Massachusetts and Virginia. Ten dollars was two months' pay for a private. "You will render that service to the cause of liberty," he cajoled, "and to your country, which you can probably never do under any other circumstance." After much hesitation, 1,600 men unlikely to be paid on time, if at all, stepped forward: 1,100 had extended their enlistments. Returning to their barges, they began pushing through the ice, now thicker than before, on the night of December 30. Following Washington across the Delaware was a dispatch confirming that Congress had voted him new powers.

"Rall's defeat," General Howe understated to Germain on December 31, 1776, "has put us much out of our way. His misconduct is amazing; had he remained to defend the village, he could not have been forced, nor could the attack have been pushed to any length. . . . Col. Donop's conduct upon this occasion is by no means commendable." (He had not hurried to Rall's aid.) "The rebels," Howe deplored, "have taken fresh courage upon this event . . . and their success will probably produce another campaign."

When Lord George learned of the reverse and assessed its implications months later, he mourned, "All our hopes were blasted by the unhappy affair at Trenton." The war would drag on. Yet there was no way that it was won or lost at the Delaware. As Franklin had noted sagely, it was a matter of simple arithmetic. There would never be enough Englishmen available to subdue, and hold on to, a burgeoning America.

5

The Best Laid Schemes
January 1777–July 1777

"Their Distresses are hourly increasing, & without any Hope of a Remedy, but in the Destruction of the King's Fleet, which is out of their Power, and in the Expulsion of the King's Army, to which they are altogether unequal in Point both of numbers & Strength."

—*Ambrose Serle, Admiral Howe's secretary, personal journal, January 30, 1777*

IN an "Ode for the New Year" of 1777, written by the hack poet laureate, William Whitehead, set to music by the notable William Boyce, and published in a dozen London papers, American rebels—both "wayward children" and "parricides"—were implored to stop the war and seek, with the mother country, the "Public Good, the blessings of peace." Hinting, perhaps, at Washington and his like, Whitehead did not believe that freedom "can e'er be found where many a tyrant reigns," but "true liberty" was assured by "Britain's well-mixed state."

Doing his laureate duty, Whitehead would pen loyal odes for every new year even as other bards deserted Toryism. It was not a great age for poet laureates. Whitehead would be succeeded by Thomas Warton and Henry James Pye.

In an opposing view, the unsigned verses "Mark the Train around Attending" in the *Evening Post* would satirize the king's fawning courtiers at St. James's Palace, contending that the rich and powerful supported tyranny at home. In the plethora of London papers there was something for everyone's fancy. And if the papers were insufficient, printers turned out pamphlets, mostly anonymous and usually sold for a shilling, exhorting some kind of accommodation with America. A few taking one side or another were shrill. "A Landed Proprietor" offered "Reflections on our present critical Situation," predicting "nothing but rue to this nation," while in defense of the government appeared "A Letter from an Officer retired to his Son in Parliament." Placing the blame on the colonists, "The American Crisis," "By a Citizen of the World," suggested, hopefully, "a general pardon," followed by "a day of Thanksgiving." "A Political Paradox" attacked the ministry sardonically for its "desire of restoring to America the blessings of law and liberty" by sending "40,000 lawgivers from Britain and Germany."

News of the Hessian embarrassment at Trenton had hardly been dispatched across the Atlantic when a second surprise arrived from supposedly loyalist New Jersey. Gathering his forces, augmented now by Cadwalader's troops and some additional Pennsylvania and Jersey militia, Washington waited for the muddy, rutted roads to ice over. Then, leaving some decoy campfires burning to mislead enemy watchers, he led the Continentals in early morning darkness on January 3, 1777, toward Princeton. Missing opportunities to outflank Washington, Cornwallis settled on a rearguard action, taking 200 casualties and losing 230 men as prisoners, but the action was not cheap for the rebels. Washington lost experienced officers he could not spare, including Hugh Mercer, educated as a doctor in Scotland but at fifty-two an infantry brigadier general from the Virginia militia.

Cornwallis had expected to be at sea en route to London. He had once boasted that he would "bag the fox." Instead, his redcoats withdrew northward toward Brunswick and Amboy, leaving much of New Jersey, which Howe had envisioned as winter quarters and sources of forage, to Washington. Even while conceding that its earlier reports of "naked Americans" wintering with difficulty west of the Delaware proved exaggerated, the *Morning Post* on February 5, 1777, quoted from what it identified as Washington's order book allegedly captured months earlier in New York, to demonstrate that the Continentals were in wretched shape and could not resupply themselves. That the evidence was more than six months old and may no longer have been valid was ignored. The rebellion continued.

The first report of the shocking rout at Trenton arrived in England on Captain Wallace's packet *Experiment*. Hardly believing it, *Lloyd's Evening Post* for February 7–10, 1777, observed somewhat cautiously, "A New York paper is said to be received, from which the following paragraph is taken, dated the 30th of December, 1776: 'Wednesday morning last one of the Hessian brigades stationed at Trenton, was surprised by a large body of rebels, and after an engagement which lasted for a little time, between 300 and 400 [Hessians] made good their retreat, and the whole loss is about 900 men.' The matter, however, is little credited." That the embarrassment followed claims of the success of the Howes' pardon scheme in New Jersey, Cornwallis's sweep to the Delaware, and the seizure of Rhode Island harbors, and was very likely worse than conceded, brought gloom to what had been an expectant London.

In sardonic amusement, Horace Walpole wrote to William Mason, "The Court denies being certain of the discomfit of the Hessians, yet their runners pretend that the Hessian prisoners have been retaken." Later he added to Mason, recognizing that the mercenaries, aside from their splendid uniforms, received little of the fees that the English paid for their services, that the Hessians apparently "laid down their arms as if they liked lands in America better than the wretched pittance they are to receive out of the Landgrave's dole." Confirmation of the losses came when Admiral Molyneux Shuldham on February 24 personally brought Germain the acknowledgment by General Howe that the event would prolong the war by another campaign, which meant at least a year. Then came the blunt acknowledgment to the American Secretary from Governor Tryon, "The moment was Critical and I believe the Rebel Chiefs were conscious if some stroke was not struck that would give life to their sinking cause, they should not raise another Army."

Although the stroke (and its sequel at Princeton, in gloomy news yet to arrive) meant that rebel resistance in the middle colonies would revive, the king told Lord North casually that he was still "most comfortable" with the way the war was going. The losses in men were mostly among the mercenaries. Brushing off Trenton and Princeton as trivial and temporary setbacks, the king deplored the "want of spirit in the Hessian officers as well as soldiers" as "not much to their credit." It would "undoubtedly elate the rebels, who were then in a great state of despondency . . . but I am certain by a letter I have seen from Lord Cornwallis that the rebels will soon have sufficient reason to fall into their former dejection."

A favorite of the king, Earl Cornwallis, not yet forty, born into the nobility and with a great career assuredly ahead of him, was the royal oracle, and unaffected by what seemed the mishandling of the response to Trenton. From (New) Brunswick, to which he had fallen back with his dragoons and infantry, Cornwallis wrote to London, confidently, of Washington, "He cannot subsist long where he is. I should imagine that he means to repass the Delaware [back into Pennsylvania]. . . . The season of the year would make it difficult for us to follow him; the march alone will destroy his army."

Almost from his succession in 1760 at twenty-two, George III proved to be no ceremonial sovereign content to sign papers and receive perquisites and homage. He examined detailed maps, resorted to his growing library of military histories, revised his ministers' strategies, read their mail, pored over the newspapers, micromanaged deployments, and developed grand plans. When Germain would write to a general that His Majesty had approved a proposal or had one of his own, Lord George meant it. The king knew that his army in America, all that Whitehall could send, was spread thin over extensive spaces, and in many parts of the provinces had no presence whatever. Hugh Percy, a wealthy lieutenant general with a courtesy earldom who had fought well on Long Island and helped take Rhode Island in December 1776, commented ruefully on returning to England, "Our army is so small that we cannot even afford a victory." Victories required maintaining what one seized, and space and time—and taxes—were as much the enemy as was "Mr." Washington.

Following several indecisive skirmishes with the Continentals, Cornwallis had relinquished much of the Jerseys, keeping posts in Brunswick and Amboy, and a sort of line at the Raritan River, to protect Staten Island and New York City. As he held little land from which to draw forage, food, and fuel, appeals to Whitehall would follow for thousands of additional tons of merchant shipping from across the Atlantic, a process likely to consume half a year. Urgently, four large vessels in the Thames already being loaded with live bullocks, hogs, and sheep for New York were rushed into readiness for embarkation, although the animals, if they survived the crossing, would eat their way through tons of fodder while at sea.

Largely abandoned, the anxious Jersey royalists had rebel retribution to anticipate rather than redcoat protection. Property owners who had tacked red ribbons on their doors and gates to mark their loyalty now prudently removed them. Others who had considered accepting the king's peace offered by the Howes cautiously took note.

As the surprising turn was likely to exacerbate criticism of the war, which had never quite ceased through the New York successes, a pending bill aimed at stifling dissent in the colonies by revoking the right to habeas corpus, a safeguard to liberty cherished by Englishmen, took on new parliamentary support. Part of common law until codified in 1679, it required a judicial hearing to legitimate a person's detention. The bill was presented in the Commons on February 7, 1777, and to obfuscate its intentions it was formally titled as legislation "to empower his Majesty to secure and detain persons charged with, or suspected of, the crime of high treason committed in North America, or on the high seas, or the crime of piracy."

At first, longtime opponents of the war like Lord Rockingham, Charles Fox, Edmund Burke, the Duke of Grafton, and the Earl of Camden stayed away from the debate on the grounds that attacking the bill would be futile. Rockingham's Whigs had been absenting themselves from Parliament since November as a protest against the North ministry's policies. Some now returned to oppose the suspension of a crucial liberty that could be extended at home. One returnee protested that a bill of such "dark and dangerous" import should be laid before the House when so many seats remained empty. Another minority MP described the legislation as mischievous, and was answered brusquely that the intent was to forestall mischief.

Burke wrote to the sheriffs of his constituency of Bristol, defending his opposition. "I am charged with being an American," he began. "If warm affection towards those over whom [as an MP] I claim any share of authority, be a crime, I am guilty of this charge." He contended that there were constitutional rights that it was sometimes inexpedient to exercise, and one of them was Parliament's overwhelming authority over the colonies. If one fact in the situation were perfectly clear, he explained, it was that Americans were "wholly averse to any other than a free government." If he were asked what a free government was, "I answer that, for any practical purpose, it is what the people think so; and that they, not I, are the natural, lawful, and competent judges of this matter." But his political philosophy was less persuasive than the news from Trenton, which sustained a majority for the bill. It passed in the depleted Commons, 195 to 43.

In the Lords there was no debate or amendment. Almost all opposition peers absented themselves from the division. Only the Earl of Abingdon voted "nay." With the new act, however unenforced, hopes for conciliation in America had effectively died.

Before Trenton, Henry Clinton had determined to return home to make his case for more independent authority. Second in command to General Howe, he agreed with little of Howe's caution, and was blamed for the Sullivan's Island fiasco preceding Howe's successes in New York. Small and paunchy, he radiated no air of command, but he felt he could bring boldness to the war effort where Howe seemed languidly content to wait out the Americans. A reluctant subordinate discontented with peripheral roles like the South Carolina adventure in which Commodore Parker had lost his breeches, Clinton had been sent off again to take Newport, Rhode Island, where he learned of the turnabout in the Jerseys. From Newport he intended to return to London to seek his own command, or be excused from further service in America.

In the usual practice, Clinton sent a fast packet ahead with his aide-de-camp, Captain Duncan Drummond, ostensibly to announce to the American Secretary the capture of Rhode Island. Germain did not want to lose Clinton, as few general officers were eager for what looked to realistic professionals as the likely graveyard of military reputations. South Carolina had almost been that, and Clinton felt that Lord George's report of the affair in the official *Gazette* did him an injustice. Made aware of the general's sensitivities, Germain was effusively cordial to Drummond, who reported ungrammatically to Clinton that Lord George "perceived by your laconic way of writing that you was hurt at what had happened at Charleston. Upon that I took the liberty of informing his Lordship that you was, very much so, as only an extract of your letter being published [in the *Gazette*]. The conversation upon this immediately dropped." Germain also gave Drummond as *douceur* a very substantial five hundred pounds when he would have preferred a promotion instead. A career officer, he felt, unhappily, "the oldest captain in the world." Clinton would consider the Drummond matter as an additional personal slight.

Drummond, nevertheless, was further honored by an audience

with the king, an indirect compliment to Clinton and His Majesty's way of sending the general a message. "Why does he plague himself so much," the king asked Drummond of Clinton, "when it was impossible for him to do more? I am thoroughly well satisfied with every part of his conduct; I have as high an opinion of him as any officer in my service."

When Clinton reached London on February 28, and reported to Whitehall himself, he found that Lord George appeared far more dissatisfied with Howe and Carleton, which awakened unexpected hopes. But Germain only promised that Clinton could inherit Howe's command if something happened to the general. Clinton was offered the thanks of Parliament—an empty gesture—and the Order of the Bath for his taking of Rhode Island. The red ribbon of knighthood, however, would be difficult to arrange, as membership in the order was full. Lord George managed an extra place in advance of the next vacancy, and a promotion to lieutenant general—on the understanding that Clinton would return to his former role, and possibly receive more responsibility as the 1777 campaign developed.

Although he told friends in London that Cornwallis, who had responsibility for the Jerseys, had shown "the most consummate ignorance I ever heard of [in] any officer above a corporal," Clinton wrote a letter to *The Public Advertiser* that made light of the setbacks at Trenton and Princeton and predicted the end of the rebellion. He knew nothing of Germain's dispatch to Howe of January 14, written before learning of the Jerseys debacle, congratulating each other that "under the command of Lord Cornwallis, the men have been brought into such a state of perfection while they were under your eye . . . as induces me to flatter myself that his Lordship's progress in East Jersey, notwithstanding the advanced season, will be considerable," and that they had gained "so fair a prospect of extensive and good winter cantonments" in the Jerseys. When Lord George registered that enthusiasm he did not yet know that the British were hastily evacuating most of the Jerseys.

On the same day that Clinton arrived in England General Burgoyne was visiting theaters in London (he was a playwright himself) and promoting his "Thoughts for Conducting the War on the Side of Canada," an ambitious plan for a junction along the Hudson with forces from New York City. Although Lord George (and the king) had first thought of putting Burgoyne under Howe, and giving the command of the planned offensive from Canada to Clinton, the memorandum persuaded the Cabinet that Burgoyne was their man. Seeing much risk in it, Clinton was not disappointed, claiming that Burgoyne understood the area and "knew better what to do and how to do it." Clinton also declined the command of forces in Canada, which would have demoted Sir Guy Carleton to civilian governor. Before returning to America Burgoyne and Clinton dined together on friendly terms, and discussed coordinating their future operations. Sir John then left for Plymouth with his aide-de-camp to sail to Quebec on the man-of-war *Apollo*. Two thousand recruits had already embarked on March 26, the day before Burgoyne arrived, and forty sail of transports were scheduled to load at Cork by April 20.

On April 7, Clinton was again at Whitehall, where Lord George confirmed the red ribbon of the Bath, explaining with self-satisfaction that he had persuaded the king "that an officer he approved of should receive such a mark, besides which Mr. H[owe] had no right to monopolize all the red ribbons nor anything else." The conversation moved to Clinton's implied threat to publish his own account of the Sullivan's Island fiasco, and Germain as part of the implied bargain ventured that it would be needlessly embarrassing. "Your Lordship," said Clinton, realizing how much the American Secretary feared controversy affecting him, "must permit me to be the best judge of my own affair."

"He argued; I bowed," Clinton remembered thirteen years later. The matter was dropped, and they turned to the military outlook. Germain wondered whether the rebels could raise and maintain an army, and assumed that the effort was beyond their resources. "Was, is, or will their inability be greater than ours?" he asked.

"Certainly no," said Clinton, closing all the alternatives.

Would Washington risk committing troops to a general action, Germain wondered, as the American commander could ill afford a costly defeat in which his army would evaporate.

"Knowing we wished it," said Clinton confidently, "he was a fool if he did; but *chicane*"—trickery—"might draw him to it."

Lord George turned to the question of Philadelphia. Howe wanted to take the city, ninety-odd miles and several formidable rivers south of New York City, for reasons beyond its strategic value. The Continental Congress met there; it was the seat of rebel government and the origin of the detestable Declaration of Independence. (It also promised to be a very comfortable place to wait out the war.) Neither knew that Howe had sent a message by packet on April 2, which would reach London on May 8, that he had decided to advance on Philadelphia by sea, rather than risk crossing the now dangerous Jerseys. Pennsylvania was the only colony without a seacoast (Maryland was on the expansive Chesapeake approaches to the Atlantic), but was accessible from the sea up the wide Delaware Bay.

Clinton dismissed Philadelphia as of no military consequence. Despite Trenton and Princeton, he thought, the war was nearly over—unless the French intervened. As early as January 19, 1777, long before news of the turnaround at Trenton had reached the Continent, stories from Paris, reported in the London press on February 3, were that it was "generally believed here, that a war with England will soon take place and great preparations are certainly making for it, particularly in the marine department. . . . It is no secret here, that this Court has furnished large quantities of military stores . . . to the Americans."

Unaware of the increasingly bold French designs, Clinton would explain to Germain in a later meeting that holding so large a city as Philadelphia, with its adjacent towns and villages, would immobilize much of the army in America. In any case, there was little to fear from them. He had little idea how much gunpowder, and even brass cannon and mortars, was crossing the Atlantic to them. The colonies had been forbidden to manufacture military weaponry, and aside from captured ordnance, they were supposedly an army of amateurs armed with fowling pieces and homemade muskets.

Benjamin Franklin and an associate appointed by Congress, Connecticut lawyer Silas Deane (who would turn out to be a double-dealing intriguer), Germain observed with concern, were already in Paris as American emissaries. Franklin was meeting openly with new friends in convivial coffeehouses and almost certainly in secret with others. French sympathies for American independence were less idealistic than pragmatic.

"Whether Franklin and Deane deceive the rebels or the French us, time will discover," Clinton said enigmatically.

There would be further conversations with Lord George before Clinton was invested with the Order of the Bath and at the end of April left reluctantly for New York, dreading, as he put it to intimates, "a very mortifying command." This time Germain and Clinton concluded with a litany of courteous formalities: "His Lordship said a thousand civil one, two, threes, and I as many polite four, five, sixes." Then Germain confided as they parted that "If any accident happened to Sir William Howe, he should think everything was safe with me."

Sailing from Plymouth in a sluggish convoy of supply ships was not to Sir Henry's liking. "The wind is coming fair, and to sea we must go; but very sulkily will I go." He would not arrive until early July. A few days after Clinton's departure Howe's revised, misguided, and later ignored plan of campaign arrived at Whitehall.

Two stories about General Washington kept the English public at their unreliable newspapers. In the dark, late days of 1776, the Continental Congress, then desperate, had given Washington new war powers that led Tory papers to refer to him as a dictator and tyrant. To Sir Horace Mann, Walpole amused himself by referring to "Washington the dictator, who has shown himself both a Fabius and a Camillus. His march through our lines [in the Jerseys] is accounted a prodigy of generalship." The Roman consul Quintus Fabius Maximus, elected dictator in 217, was known by his cautious tactics in the Second Punic War as *Cunctator,* or Delayer, for avoiding battle while Rome mustered its forces. Centuries earlier, the patrician Marcus Furius Camillus, appointed dictator circa 396 B.C., had driven invading Etruscans, Gauls, and others from Rome. Debates in the Commons soon referred to Washington disparagingly as a dictator, prompting Colonel Barré to rebut the charge on the floor of the House.

Wishful thinking among royalists after Trenton also led to reports of Washington's illness and death. An obituary editorial in the *Morning Post* recalled that he had served with distinction in the Seven Years' War, and eulogized him as a humane, brave, and skillful officer who had done more toward keeping the "provincial banditti" under arms than "all the hypocritical inventions of the whole Republican Congress put together." On discovering that he was alive after all, the *Morning Post* alleged, without retracting its earlier claims, that he had made himself dictator of America. Soon the London *Packet* and the *General Evening Post* were alleging that Washington had been taken prisoner by the British.

In further fantasy, the *St. James's Chronicle* had already declared, on March 27, 1777, crediting a pre-Trenton letter from New York, that Philadelphia was about to fall to forces moving in from New Jersey, after which the collapse of the rebellion was expected. "All Philadelphia is in the utmost consternation," the *Chronicle* claimed. Its inhabitants were fleeing the city with all the belongings they could carry. All trade, commerce, and industry had ceased. "The poor Wretches who have returned to Philadelphia from the Rebel Army [following the end of their enlistments] are in a calamitous Situation under the Oppression of many Diseases, and Want of common Necessaries." However, the *Packet* also contended that the ministry had bungled the transfer of supplies across the Atlantic so badly that the victorious redcoats were in "absolute want" of everything.

Even that assertion was erroneous, as most commodities were moving efficiently, although "victuallers" were notoriously ponderous and slow afloat. "Contrary winds" were blamed by Lord George for the delay of tons of dried "pease" for 8,000 men, but "four months provision for 20,000 men" were now packed aboard transports at Portsmouth, three weeks late, to arrive three months later. Much was still shipped via Halifax, from which frigates could protect victuallers from Yankee commerce raiders. Evacuees from Boston a year earlier had overtaxed Halifax, but it was now the major entrepôt in North America. In March 1777, about 35,000 troops and civilian employees of army departments were being serviced, despite endemic corruption among English suppliers and commissaries. Only in Rhode Island did Clinton's soldiers complain loudly about the poor quality of rations, in a travesty of the "Lord's Prayer":

> Our Commander who art in Newport,
> Honoured be thy name
> May thy work be done in Newport
> As it is in [New] York.
> Give us each day our dayly bread,
> And forgive us our not eating it. . . .

Howe's campaign strategy, revised after Trenton and accepted without enthusiasm at Whitehall and St. James's Palace, was to send a field army to occupy Philadelphia, avoiding a possibly treacherous but short land route from New York by sailing the troops around New Jersey into Delaware Bay and landing to the south of the city. He would leave a garrison under Clinton to maintain New York City and possibly send small units up the Hudson to link with Burgoyne, moving south from Canada. Realizing hopelessly that his instructions would be ignored and might even arrive too late anyway, Lord George wrote to Howe on March 3, while Burgoyne and Clinton were in London, "I am now commanded to acquaint you that the King entirely approves of your proposed deviation from the plan you formerly suggested, being of opinion that the reasons which have induced you to recommend this change in your operations are solid and decisive."

Howe would continue to deviate from the expected, and would claim sanction from London in each case; however, as his revisions crossed the Atlantic in the opposite direction from Germain's responses to earlier messages, one from Lord George, suggesting shameful neglect, later took on a mythic dimension. On the basis of Burgoyne's plan, on March 26, as Sir John left London, Germain had his undersecretary, William Knox, prepare orders to General Carleton in Quebec, ostensibly Burgoyne's superior in Canada, stressing that it was "highly necessary that the most speedy junction of the two armies be effected." But Burgoyne's command was to be independent of Sir Guy, who at Quebec had saved Canada from the Continentals. Carleton, who had been at Minden, had yet another reason to dislike Germain.

"I shall write to Sir William Howe from hence by the first packet; but you will endeavour," Lord George ordered Carleton shabbily, although he had no military responsibility for the colonies, "to give him the earliest intelligence of this measure and also direct Lieutenant General Burgoyne," so that neither would "lose view of the intended junction" with each other.

As Knox was comparing the office draft to the copy to go to Carleton, he recalled, Lord George, on his way to Stoneland Lodge for a Kentish weekend, came in to sign letters. Knox reminded him that no message directly to Howe had yet been prepared "to ac-

quaint him with the plan or what was expected of him in consequence."

As if the wish substituted for the deed, Lord George reacted in
surprise. His deputy secretary, Christopher D'Oyley, was also startled
by the inadvertent omission, and Lord George offered to "write a
few lines" to accompany a copy to Howe. Only a few lines, the secretary insisted impatiently, as "my poor horses must stand in the street
all the time, and I shan't be to my time anywhere."

According to Knox, D'Oyley said that "he would write from himself to Howe, and enclose copies of Burgoyne's Instructions, which
would tell him all that he would want to know, and with this his
Lordship was satisfied, . . . for he could never bear delay or disappointment, and D'Oyley sat down and writ a letter to Howe, . . . and
if Howe had not acknowledged the receipt of it, with the copy of the
Instructions to Burgoyne, we could not have proved he ever saw
them."

The dispatch was endorsed as "No. 6" to Howe, and went off on
the man-of-war *Somerset,* arriving on May 24 in New York. Howe
would not register its receipt until July 5, and he would ignore the
"intended junction," accepting it as pious wish rather than outright
command, for only Burgoyne was explicitly commanded. Sir William
was intent upon Philadelphia. Sir John could wait.★

When Burgoyne left Plymouth for Canada on March 27, 1777,
missing, in England, by a day the message for him sent via Carleton
an ocean away, he understood that Germain's objective was to cut off
New England from the lower colonies. (Burgoyne would arrive in
Quebec, in an unusually fast westward passage, on May 6.) Howe was
so focused upon Philadelphia, which he expected to be easy and
quick to take, that he remained totally unconcerned about Burgoyne,
who was expected to move south without much hindrance from the
depleted American troops along the upper Hudson.

★Despite the evidence, Germain would be blamed ever after for Howe's neglect. In 1933,
Bernard Shaw wrote a new scene for a film script of his play *The Devil's Disciple* (1897) in
which Lord George fails to send Howe instructions to link with Burgoyne (who appears in
Shaw's last act expecting to be defeated) because the secretary's carriage horses are champ-
ing at the bit. Shaw's source was Albany de Fonblanque's admiring biography of Burgoyne
(1876).

Administrative foot dragging in London slowed preparations for Burgoyne's campaign. Supplies were inadequate and sent late, and one crucial transport would be captured by a rebel raider. Lord George complained to a sympathetic MP, James Harris, on May 1 that he wished there had not been "such a delay." The king, Germain would learn from a strong message from the admiralty that suggested he was to blame, "was extremely chagrined to find that there was any delay whatsoever in a business of such national importance." George III had his eye on everything, however helpless he was about winds, weather, and whims of generals two or three months away across the Atlantic.

Lord George had to concede to Howe in his message "No. 11" on May 18, 1777, that "As you must, from your situation and military skill, be a competent judge of the propriety of every plan, his Majesty does not hesitate to approve the alterations which you propose, trusting however that whatever you may meditate it will be executed in time for you to cooperate with the army ordered to proceed from Canada and put itself [when the armies linked] under your command." Howe would evade such orders, as they were prefaced by apparent license to evade them. "Meditate" was hardly a strong injunction.

Always assuming more loyalists than would identify themselves in any colony, Germain saw, in his message to Howe, "every reason to expect that your success in Pennsylvania will enable you to raise from among them such a force as may be sufficient for the interior defence of the province and leave the army at liberty to proceed to offensive operations." Since that seemed more prayer than prescription, Howe would pay no more attention to it than to the ostensible royal command.

From Montreal, on his way southward into New York, Burgoyne wrote confidently to Lord George on May 19 that he hoped "to gain a start that may much expedite and facilitate my progress to Albany. Your lordship may rest assured that whatever demonstrations I may endeavour to impose upon the enemy, I shall *really* make no movement that can procrastinate the great object of my orders." Germain and the king had scrutinized his plans written while in England and turned them into formal instructions.

The trouble to come was that only one of the two commanders

who were supposed to coordinate forces in the proposed pincers movement to win the war thought he was subject to anything but suggestions from Whitehall. On July 2 Burgoyne would write confidently to Howe from his encampment just above Ticonderoga that his army was "in the fullest powers of health and spirit. . . . The enemy do not appear to have the least suspicion of the King's real instructions relative to the campaign after the reduction of Ticonderoga." As far as Burgoyne and Howe seemed concerned, the only substantial American army in the field was Washington's in the Jerseys, which could not confront Burgoyne.

Although Howe knew the king's intentions for him, he continued to complain to Germain of the weakness of his forces, preparing excuses in advance for noncompliance. In an office memorandum to William Knox on June 24, Germain wondered in frustration, "I cannot guess by Sir Wm. Howe's [last] letter when he will begin his operations, or where he proposes to carry them on." To Lord George, Howe wrote on July 7 from New York, compounding the muddle and still unready to initiate his summer offensive, which he already expected to be indecisive, "A corps of Russians of 10,000 effective fighting men I think would ensure the success of the war to Great Britain in another campaign." He knew there would be no Russians.

Between March 3 and April 19, while Burgoyne and Clinton were enjoying the pleasures of London and meeting with Germain in Whitehall, Lord George had continued to send long preparatory dispatches to Howe. The delights of London were largely lost on Lord George himself, who preferred long country weekends with his family, yet it was a canard that at Stoneland Lodge he was out of touch with events. Although couriers from Whitehall inevitably brought news of events beyond his intervention, they arrived daily with the latest messages from America. Unfortunately for him, the secretary was in the position of an astronomer who sees in his own moment of vision occurrences on distant objects that happened eons before.

Distance also kept the leisured elite unfocused on remote and joyless America. Writing to Sir Horace Mann in Italy that season, Walpole observed, "One effect the American war has not had, that it ought to have had; it has not brought us to our senses. Silly dissipation rather increases, and without an object. The present folly is late hours. Everybody tries to be particular* by being too late; and as everybody tries it, nobody is so. It is the fashion now to go Ranelagh [pleasure gardens on the Thames] two hours after it is over. You may not believe this, but it is literal. The music ends at ten; the company goes at twelve."

Howe himself did not need the dissipations of London. Since 1775 in Boston he had amused himself with Elizabeth Loring, the blonde, blue-eyed wife of his complaisant and well-rewarded commissary of prisoners. Howe had hibernated with her in New York in the winter of 1776 and fully intended to do so again in Philadelphia in 1777. Overly cautious in battle, he was less so in the bedroom. What Lord George knew about the sources of Howe's lack of militancy and chronic neglect cannot be gleaned from his messages as American Secretary, but London was well aware that Howe had other preoccupations than ruthlessly suppressing rebellion. Baron Friedrich von Riedesel, the Hessian general whose green-clad troops would be with Burgoyne's army, apparently learned in an audience with George III that the king knew the "scandalous stories . . . going the rounds in the army" about Howe. (Riedesel's grandmother had been one of the mistresses of George I, imported from Hanover.) In March 1778 a scurrilous handbill would be sent anonymously to members of both houses of Parliament condemning Howe's indiscretions, alleging that prior to the Trenton debacle, when Washington's "wretched" troops seemed helpless across the Delaware, the commanding general remained in New York City "in the lap of Ease; or, rather, amusing himself in the lap of a Mrs. L_____g."

None of Germain's first ten messages to Howe, voluminously detailed, referred to Burgoyne's thrust south, or to a junction with Howe's troops. That would only come with the eleventh message, on May 18, which arrived much too late to matter. Burgoyne remained low in Howe's priorities, which began with his own narrow vision of his mission and seemed to end with his amenities. While Germain took a long time to get to the point, the linkage with Burgoyne might have made the rebellion unwinnable by the Continentals. Howe preferred to end his war without undue strain. In his view, the attrition of Washington's forces and retrieval of easily won territory for the Crown would lead eventually and more comfortably to compromise.

*Specially attentive to details

Among other recommendations to which Howe was not listening were Lord George's repeated entreaties to arrange, presumably through his nautical brother, for harassment of the New England coast, both to deter commerce raiders and to bring a sense of some immediate danger home to a broad swath of the colonies that had become a wartime backwater. The American Secretary even dispatched an aide, Major Nisbet Balfour, by sea to New York to urge punitive raids, as the opening of Howe's summer campaign seemed increasingly remote. He stalled by requesting more horses, and forage for them. His repeated requests for more men were evaded with offers of some who were only replacements but were fudged numerically by Whitehall as supplements.

Quietly irked, Sir William finally responded for Admiral Howe as well as himself about harassing New England harbors. With labored politeness he wrote, "I have the honour to inform your lordship we have been ever sensible of the advantages of that mode of distressing the enemy, but we agree in opinion it is not practicable without interfering materially with the more important operations of the campaign that have received the royal approbation and are already much too curtailed by the want of land force to admit of a further reduction." Additional troops were unavailable because of the dearth of enlistments and the drying up of funds for mercenaries. The brothers Howe were uninterested in merely belaboring the colonial shoreline to show there was war on. With conciliation all but formally written off, both merely wanted to go home to enjoy their perquisites already in hand.

"In the next campaign," Germain had written John Stuart, the British supervisor for Indian affairs in the South, on April 2, "every possible effort will be made to reduce the rebel colonies to obedience." And he noted—and expected—"Sir William Howe's operations to the northward during the summer." But General Howe had no such intentions. He was running his own war. On the same day he wrote to Lord George, "From the difficulties and delay that would attend the passage of the River Delaware by a march through Jersey, I propose to invade Pennsylvania by sea; and from this arrangement we must probably abandon the Jerseys." On April 5, he informed General Sir Guy Carleton—ostensibly the liaison with John Burgoyne—that he had "little expectation . . . , from the want of sufficient strength in this army, to detach a corps . . . to act up Hudson's River, consistent with the operations already determined upon." He dutifully sent a copy by packet to Germain in London. By the time it arrived it was clear at home that the war was not being won. Even the hard-line *Morning Post* conceded that "preparations must be made for another campaign. . . . It being confessed on all hands, that the force under General Howe is not equal to operations which, in the course of the present summer, can be decisive."

Readers of newspapers in the coffeehouses saw a different war than most members of Parliament. For the upper echelons of English life the remote war, as Walpole had noted, only added to their possible diversions as the social season began, coordinate with the usual winding down of Parliament. "Oh! My dear Sir," he wrote to Horace Mann in Italy, "do you think a capital as enormous as London has its nerves affected by what happens across the Atlantic? . . . Wisdom forms empires, but folly dissolves them; and a great capital, that dictates to the rest of the community, is always the last to perceive the decays of the whole, because it takes its own greatness for health." Rockingham had told Burke, in seeing no audience for further agitation unless the course of the war altered, "Men's minds in the country are hung up, in the suspense of expectation. The end of the campaign is the settling day." But Burke already perceived a shift in sensibility. "Many things have been long operating towards a gradual change in our principles," he wrote. " . . . This American war has done more in a few years than all the other causes could have effected in a century."

Parliament would not be prorogued lengthily, as usual, for the summer and early autumn, but would have only short adjournments "at a time of such public alarm" (so went David Hartley's motion in the Commons on June 9, 1777). The king then spoke briefly to both Houses from the throne, having given his assent to all bills that had passed, and his thanks for "the unquestionable proofs you have given me, and to all the world, of the continuance of your attachment to my person and government." He trusted to Divine Providence that the military operations they had supported "will be blessed by such success as may most effectually tend to the suppression of the rebellion in America, and to the re-establishment of that constitutional obedience which all the subjects of a free state owe to the authority of law."

Since Parliament would resume on July 21, many of the gentry did not depart to their country seats. Some played soldier. "Our senators, instead of retiring to horse-races," Walpole wrote, ". . . are all turned soldiers, and [are] disciplining militia. Camps everywhere, and the ladies in the uniform of their husbands. In short, if the dose is not too strong, a little adversity would not be quite unseasonable." The wives of the smartly attired officers who had paid high prices for their commissions, dressed in feminine equivalents to the uniform of their regiments, complete to gaiters. The war had turned fashionable.

When Lady Louisa Lennox's husband was with his troops encamped at Romsey, north of Southampton, diarist John Marsh wrote, she was "the principal feature of the Show, at the Evening Parades," in a riding dress patterned after the regimental uniform. Georgiana, Duchess of Devonshire, wore an equivalent to the militia uniform when the Duke was encamped at Warley, and organized the wives of his officers into a pseudo-military unit. Soon Elizabeth Montagu noted disapprovingly that young women taking the waters at Tunbridge Wells were "striding about the walks . . . with their arms akimbo dressed in martial uniform." A cartoon, "An Officer of the Light infantry driven by his Lady to Cox-Heath," shows a woman in military-styled dress standing as she drives her chaise to the camp south of Maidstone in Kent. Her husband is sprawled asleep at her side. War—from the distance of an ocean—could be entertaining.

When Sir Henry Clinton returned to New York he discovered that although July had come, Howe's campaign was going nowhere. He had been skirmishing lightly with Washington's troops in upper Jersey, trying to mislead the American command about his ultimate purpose, while loading supplies, munitions, and horses aboard 260 of his brother's ships—and in stifling heat crowding 13,799 restless men into their holds. The preparations, lasting weeks, would have been hard to hide. He would not be marching. But where was he going?

In Howe's absence, Clinton was to command a New York garrison of seven thousand—"a damned starved defensive," he judged. He cautioned Howe that Washington might consider Philadelphia expendable, and either go north to head off Burgoyne or cross the Hudson to "murder us" in Manhattan. But Howe claimed that Philadelphia was the symbolic heart of the rebellion rather than merely a convenient locale for Congress to meet. If Washington could be tempted into fighting for it unsuccessfully, as Sir William hoped, the war would be over, whatever Burgoyne accomplished in unpopulated upper New York. Howe's belated messages to Lord George remained a tangle of unhelpful suppositions and alternatives. On July 9, having read the latest dispatches, Christopher D'Oyley wrote to a friend in India that "if the Howes do not drub the Americans this summer, that dispute, I shall begin to fear, will not end well for this country." Since Washington was in the Jerseys, Howe worried in a message to London on July 16, not to be received until September, that the Continentals might be emboldened to attack New York City when British forces there were depleted to go elsewhere. If Washington "should march to the defence of Pensilvania," Howe offered, he would send Clinton's reserves to confront him. "On the other hand," he added complacently, "if General Washington should march with the determination to force General Burgoyne, the strength of General Burgoyne's army is such as to leave me no room to dread the event." Washington "would find it difficult to escape." Given all the possibilities, Howe proposed—meaning that he intended, as no four months' delayed-message back-and-forth could stop him—"going up the Delaware [Bay] in order to be nearer [to] this place"—Philadelphia—"than I should be by taking the course of the Chesapeak[e] . . . , which I once intended and preferred to that of the Delaware provided the enemy had discovered a disposition to defend Pensilvania." It was exasperating and bewildering to hapless Whitehall—and Howe would yet again change his mind.

On July 23, with more than a month of the summer gone, the armada left New York harbor, straggling southward along the Atlantic coast toward Delaware Bay. By land Sir William would have been only a few days' march from Philadelphia.

6
Saratoga Trumps Philadelphia
July 1777–December 1777

"General Howe having received some articles much wanted, intends to go somewhere, to do somewhat, with somebody or other, and will let us know some time hence something more of the matter."

—*Howe's dispatch of June 3, 1777, to Lord George Germain as summarized sardonically in the* London Chronicle *six weeks later.*

"HAVE you read General Burgoyne's rodomontade, in which he almost promises to cross America in a hop, step and a jump?" Horace Walpole asked Lady Ossory early in August 1777. "I thought we were cured of hyperboles. I own I prefer General Howe's taciturnity, who at least if he does nothing, does not break his word." Reporting to London for the moribund peace commission, which was largely the brothers Howe, its secretary, Henry Strachey, conceded that an honorable peace was unlikely as long as Washington refused to be drawn into a decisive battle, and because the colonies occupied such a vast expanse that there would never be enough troops to subdue all of them.

Burgoyne had marched south from Montreal into upper New York, issuing from his base at Skenesboro (ironically since renamed Whitehall) on Lake George a bombastic manifesto warning citizens within his alleged reach against assisting the enemy and the likely "vengeance of the state." He threatened "hardened enemies" with the "stretch" he could give "to the Indian forces under my direction." However, it was all "in consciousness of Christianity, my royal master's clemency, and the honour of soldiership."

The text appeared in the press on both sides of the Atlantic, and was taken seriously nowhere. Robert Troup, an aide to American general Horatio Gates, wrote to John Jay, a young lawyer who was chief justice of patriot New York, that losing Ticonderoga was more a psychological than a strategic blow. "What vexes me, most," he confessed, "is the Disgrace which the Evacuation of such a strong Post will fix upon our Arms, in Europe." For loans and other assistance, colonial credibility abroad counted for much.

Swaggering even on paper, Burgoyne had sent Germain a copy of his decree on June 22, and added a duplicate on July 11, contending, "It has had a good effect where the country is not in the power of the rebels"—rather unconvincing evidence of his rhetorical flair. Wryly, Troup wrote to Jay, "I wish I could see Burgoyne's letter to Ld. Germaine on this Subject. His Proclamation shews more Profound Depth, in the Knowledge of Composition, that I ever discovered in the Works of the celebrated Martinus Scriblerus." (The famous "Scriblerus" was John Arbuthnot, a Scots physician and satirist, who had ridiculed "all the false tastes in learning.") According to Walpole, Burgoyne's declaration "did not want eloquence, but [lacked] judgment extremely. The Ministers . . . laughed at his pomp."

No one in England, however, derided Sir John's initial successes, achieved despite utter lack of support from Sir Guy Carleton in Canada, who behaved like a jilted bride. Burgoyne took Ticonderoga with ease after moving artillery onto Sugar Loaf Hill and rendering the rebel fort indefensible. "They have no men of military science," he reported smugly to England. He shared a fine dinner and celebratory bottles of claret and port brought from Canada with his current mistress, the wife of one of his officers accordingly expecting promotion.

When the news came to London many weeks later, the king was ecstatic, rushing into Queen Charlotte's apartments shouting, as if the rebellion had been quashed, "I have beaten them! I have beaten them!" In the House of Commons the American Secretary announced the capture of Ticonderoga as portending total victory. Yet, while Tory England toasted Burgoyne, he was already deeply in trouble, pushing farther south with unanticipated difficulty. The stubborn Continentals made his redcoats and greencoats struggle across every mile of march for every gain, sinking boats to clog streams and lakes and felling thousands of trees, tangling them lengthwise and crosswise, Sir John complained to Germain.

Burgoyne would continue to be ignored by Carleton, who wrote in pique to Lord George that "since you have taken the conduct of the war entirely out of my hands, even within the strict limits of my commission," he had no troops to spare to garrison Ticonderoga and relieve redcoats detached to the fort so that they could rejoin their forces. Although Sir John was shedding troops and provisions with every mile, Carleton hinted darkly at unidentified "evils" he might have to face with diminished forces of his own. He then asked to resign the Canadian governorship, "which, indeed, it could hardly be supposed that he ever meant to hold," North told the king on July 2, "when he wrote Lord George Germain the [vituperative] letters which are brought by the same conveyance." Always reluctant to accept a resignation, George III kept Carleton on, contending that Sir Guy had to preserve his dignity.

With Howe's army likely to be encountering the rebels elsewhere than in Burgoyne's direction, newspaper readers held their collective breath for belated news from both borders of New York. Although Howe controlled Burgoyne's destiny, he sailed obdurately in the opposite direction, for Philadelphia. First he feinted at Washington in the Jerseys, then countermarched to Perth Amboy, his troops looting vigorously along the way. (Hessians were always blamed.)

The road not taken, little more than ninety miles, would metamorphose after two weeks of loading provisions into a prolonged oceanic voyage. Sampling "every Variety of good & bad Weather," according to the exasperated Ambrose Serle, the sprawling fleet was "tossed about exceedingly, & exposed at times to much Danger in running foul of each other." Whitehall had no idea where Howe was heading, although he had mentioned Philadelphia earlier. Some reports in London suggested Rhode Island or Boston.

Rhode Island had just been the scene of a British humiliation made more of in the London press than its actual impact on the war was worth. General Richard Prescott, notorious for his insolence and his philandering, had been exchanged for John Sullivan late in 1776 and appointed commander of the Newport garrison. On the night of July 9 he was seized in a daring waterborne raid on his quarters and taken prisoner. When it became widely known that under the sheets with him had been a local doxy, he was lampooned mercilessly in English newspapers. "The Handcock trap'd the Fox upon the deep,"★ the *London Post* wrote none too subtly on August 20, 1777, in "On the Provincials stealing General Prescott out of his Bed, and Carrying him, Spite of Tears and Intreaties, Naked, to General Arnold." The *London Chronicle* on September 27 observed that there were "various lures . . . to ruin a man," such as the recent case where "A Nymph . . . spoiled a General's mighty plan" and "gave him to the foe—without his breeches"—which the *Chronicle* rhymed with "bewitches." Voluble American general Charles Lee had been captured earlier, at Basking Ridge, New Jersey, seized "as he was reconnoitering the field of *Mars,*" while Prescott had been caught in "the Field of *Venus.*"

In 1778 the two were exchanged—the British general had been targeted for his exchange value—and the officially unchastened Prescott (already twice a prisoner of war) resumed his command in Newport. By 1782, influence having more clout than incompetence, he was a lieutenant general.

Recognizing a dearth of good news, the English public in the summer of 1777 sensed bad news to come. The pessimism about the war was not restricted to London. "My father," Abigail Frost of Nottingham wrote, "had a dispute with Mr. Robert Denison at the Exchange hall [dinner] about giving 'General Washington' for a toast." The taunt was too provocative for Frost. He "got upon the table, crossed it, and leaned on Mr. R. Denison's shoulder and crushed him to the floor." Later in the year a clothier in Leeds was tarred and feathered "for drinking Gen. Washington's health in a public company."

Howe's whereabouts were still unknown in England, but by July 29, Howe's armada was in Delaware Bay, where the ships "lay on & off all the day" until Howe decided against all advice not to disembark, as Washington, although nowhere in sight, might contest the landing. On July 30, Burgoyne wrote to Germain with increasing anxiety, "I have employed the most enterprising characters and offered very promising rewards but of ten messengers sent at different times and by different routes [to Howe], not one is returned to me."

Penned and seasick soldiers impatient for dry land were dumb-

★The HMS *Fox* was a man-of-war; the rebel *Hancock* that had captured it was later taken by Commodore Sir George Collier. Sexual innuendo was a commonplace in the London press.

struck, as the complex turnabout of the heavily laden ships back into the Atlantic proceeded "without the Loss or Risque of a Battel" ashore. "What will my dear Country think & say too, when this News is carried Home? *Horreo,*" Serle complained to his diary. From a few defecting Continentals approaching the convoy in a small boat they were informed, mistakenly, of the opportunities to the north they seemed to be discarding. The Americans in upper New York were allegedly "being routed, above Albany, by Burgoyne, with the Loss of their Baggage & every thing." Howe nevertheless directed the dozens of sail round the long Delmarva Peninsula southwestward into Chesapeake Bay, the ships wallowing in calms and late summer heat while horses aboard sickened and died (and had to be heaved overboard), and campaign rations were depleted.

Washington wondered as much about the whereabouts of the British as Howe did about the Continentals. The armada had skirted the shoreline out of sight of coast watchers, but returning fishermen realized that they had encountered something big, and reported what they had seen. First lured north in the Jerseys, toward Amboy, Washington moved his forces south toward the Delaware approaches to Philadelphia.

"If [Washington] goes to the northward," Howe had claimed to Burgoyne in a message that arrived on August 3, ". . . be assured I will soon be after him to relieve you. . . . Success be ever with you." Whitehall assumed much the same, but Sir William had no intentions of deviating from his Philadelphia plan. Much of the Chesapeake Bay shoreland appeared to be "Dismal Swamp" and sandy beach, behind which spread pine forests; and as the sun-bleached days stretched out, Serle lamented the waste of "Fuel, Wine, Rum, Forage, Horses, & many a long *etcetera* aggravate[d] Charges, which my dear native Country will never be repaid, even if it had been the Sum total of the Produce of these ungrateful Colonies for a Century to come." At home, Germain was resorting to unconcealed irony to provoke the indecisive and unlocated Howe into meaningful action, observing on August 6 while the general was aboard ship that the London public, however devoid of strategic insight, was still "looking for bold and enterprizing Measures, and I shall be happy in seeing you meet with the Applause and Admiration of the Ignorant, as well as the abler judges of military merit."

When Howe anchored far up the Chesapeake Bay on August 17, well above the mouth of the Potomac, his army had traveled nearly 800 unproductive miles, often in teasing sight of land, taking 42 days. Chasing after him toward the close had been the *Eagle,* which anchored nearby after an eight weeks' passage from England. It took on mail and dispatches, brought Howe months' old messages from Lord George that were obviously now moot, turned sail and made for Plymouth. The immense fleet again weighed anchor and continued farther north to Turkey Point, between the rivers Elk and Susquehanna, arriving on August 22. There they took on an informant who told them that rebels onshore had observed their progress, and that Washington, marching southward to Philadelphia, was encamped on the banks of the Schuylkill, and likely to head farther south. Philadelphia was still seventy miles away, nearly as far as if Howe were in New York harbor.

By the twenty-fifth Howe's nearly fourteen thousand men were released from their stifling holds and were staggering ashore. Shortly thereafter two were hanged and five whipped for looting. A few days later forty-seven Grenadiers and a party of Hessians, all seeking plunder, were surprised by a forward party of Continentals and became the first casualties of the delayed campaign. While he regrouped his men and watered his emaciated horses, Howe ordered many of his victuallers turned round more hundreds of miles to unload supplies at New Castle, in northernmost Delaware. Washington, he learned from the disappointingly few loyalists in the area, seemed to be moving toward the village of Wilmington rather than toward the Elk River. Howe would have to find him to fight him.

By then Burgoyne was reporting to Lord George from "nearly opposite to Saratoga," and on August 20, in two long messages, described "sinister events." A Hessian force sent to sequester corn and cattle from nearby Vermont had been ambushed by watchful militiamen four miles from Bennington "and overpowered by numbers." A litany of accidents and errors that led to a rout followed. Burgoyne contended to Whitehall nevertheless that the disaster was "counterbalanced by spirit." Continual rains had washed away a pontoonlike bridge of boats he was constructing across the upper Hudson opposite Saratoga, but new efforts were being made. "I hope circumstances will be such," he closed with foreboding, "that my endeavours may be in some degree be assisted by cooperation of the army under Sir William Howe."

Burgoyne had no communication with Howe. "Of the messengers I have sent [to him], I know of two being hanged [on capture] and am ignorant whether any of the rest arrived. . . . But my orders being positive to 'force a junction with Sir Wm. Howe,' I apprehend I am not at liberty to remain inactive longer than shall be necessary. . . . I yet do not despond. . . ." Nevertheless, dejection was obvious from his messages, which he sent off in several copies north and south with hope that at least one of his couriers would not be captured. His situation was increasingly grim. A group of hungry soldiers on short rations were shot while foraging for potatoes in an open field, and Burgoyne warned, "The life of the soldier is the property of the King"—and that any redcoat caught venturing beyond British lines would be "instantly hanged."

Ten days later, from Head of Elk, Maryland, on August 30, Howe wrote candidly to Germain, sending his message off by fast packet to London. (It would arrive in mid-autumn.) In effect he was writing off Burgoyne. Lord George and the king had been forced by distance and time and future events still unforeseen to give the dilatory general whose goal was Philadelphia ex post facto flexibility. Howe regretted that "his Majesty trusts the operations of this army intended for the recovery of the province of Pennsylvania will be finished in time for me to cooperate with the northern army. . . . I cannot flatter myself I shall be able to act up to the King's expectations in this particular, as my progress independent of opposition from the enemy's principal army must be greatly impeded by the prevailing disposition of the inhabitants, who I am sorry to observe seem to be, excepting a few individuals, strongly in enmity against us, many having taken up arms and by far the greater number deserted their dwellings, driving off at the same time their stock of cattle and horses."

Rather than achieve a junction with Howe, Burgoyne would earn a consolation prize—the red ribbon of the Bath, an irony given the locale of his conversation at Christmas with Wilkes. The Earl of Derby, Burgoyne's brother-in-law, wrote to Germain on August 31 that he knew that the general had "a strong objection to that particular honour." Howe already had it.

Cautiously protecting his seat in the Commons while the American cause seemed in serious danger, Edmund Burke suggested to his constituents in Bristol that the principles of liberty for the people and supremacy for Parliament might still be reconciled. When the Earl of Abingdon, an aristocratic radical, published a pamphlet that August (it was a great age of pamphleteering), "Thoughts on Mr. Burke's Letter to the Sheriffs of Bristol on the Affairs of America," admonishing his fellow Whig for slackening in his liberal energy, Burke was embarrassed. He had met earlier with Abingdon after seeing the pamphlet advertised as forthcoming, and appealed to the author to suppress it, but the earl did not believe in halfway measures. Walpole was gleeful at the exposure of middle-of-the-road "sophistries." George III had declared before the war began that either the colonies were free, or they were not. They had to "submit or triumph."

The *Evening Post* claimed the last laugh on Lord Abingdon. On August 12 it published an epigram, "On Hearing that Lord Abingdon's Horse Washington was beat by Mr. O'Kelly's Filly Venus, at [the] Lewes Races." At Lewes, "Washington was beat." The American general was "famous for retreat," but unlike him, the horse "ne'er will run."

Washington would soon retreat, but not run, as Howe pushed to the northeast from Elk into Newark and on to Chadd's Ford, through the edges of three colonies, to find the Continentals entrenched behind Brandywine Creek. On September 9, pressed by General Knyphausen's Hessians and Earl Cornwallis's redcoats, Washington's troops fell back, rescued by late summer nightfall. "The enemy's army escaped a total overthrow," Howe reported ruefully to Whitehall, "that must have been the consequence of an hour's more daylight."

English towns and villages learned more from letters home brought by a returning packet or frigate than from skimpy newspapers and official reports that seldom reached far from London and the Channel ports. Captain William Dansey wrote exuberantly to his mother in Brinsop, Herefordshire, from his encampment near Brandywine that a "flanking party" of his 33rd Regiment of Foot "took the horse, arms, colours, and drums belonging to a rebel colonel of the Delaware Militia. Made his brother prisoner and caused all his baggage to be taken, which the General very politely sent back again. But the horse, arms, and colours came to my share." Very likely everyone in Brinsop shared the exciting news. Not until 1927 did the silk five-feet-by-four-feet flag, with seven red and six white stripes on the top corner of a green field, return to Delaware.

Howe dithered about following up his advantage at daybreak, claiming his troops now across the Brandywine Creek were sleepless and tired. So were Washington's. Although Howe knew that England, starved for victories, would delight in one, he delayed his dispatches to London in hopes of more definitive successes, and there were doubts at home about how decisive any Howe achievement was. "You will have seen in the papers . . . such accounts of a total defeat of Washington," Walpole wrote to Horace Mann on November 7, ". . . that you might wonder at my silence, if I did not say a word: that word must be that I very much doubt the fact; and if it was known at New York so long ago as the supposed gazette thence [from New York] says, it would be wonderful indeed that General Howe should keep it a profound secret from the government here, whom he might suppose a little interested to hear some good news."

By the time London knew of Howe's successes at Christiana in upper Delaware and "Chad-Ford" just to the north, Sir William had pushed the Continentals out of Philadelphia. Redcoats circled to the west to keep Washington from the road to Lancaster and York, toward which Congress had fled, then turned back to Norristown and Germantown, where in another engagement, in the last days of September, Howe managed to turn what could have been defeat into a marginal victory. Eight thousand of his troops, outnumbered by the Americans, fought a predawn battle ending in confusion when fog blanketed the field just after sunrise. Two of Washington's divisions, poorly guided, overlapped into "friendly fire." Then the reeling Americans faced British bayonets. Howe wrote to Germain of yet another victory, and indeed he had secured Philadelphia, but he had been frustrated by the inability of his victualling ships to pass beyond New Castle, as Washington had fortified and mined the Delaware.

Passage for Howe's supply vessels would not be possible until late November, after hard fighting to reduce the river fortifications. Rather than bringing all of Pennsylvania under the "King's Peace," Howe hung on only to the southeastern corner. As in Maryland and Delaware, many buildings and businesses were deserted. He had marched his men into Philadelphia to the acclamation of thousands, mostly women and children. Males likely to be pressed into military service had fled. There would be few recruits into loyalist green.

Since the rebels controlled the countryside, comfortable Philadelphia actually became a liability even as winter quarters. Both its internal ease, and the external hazards, diminished the appetite for further adventure. But not other appetites. Howe could settle in with Mrs. Loring, and many of his officers would soon find willing ladies from the socialite set.

Washington's apologetic letter of September 11 to John Hancock, for Congress, also on the run, about the missed opportunities at Brandywine was published in the American press and reached London in early November. "We have been obliged," he conceded, "to leave the enemy masters of the field." He blamed "uncertain and contradictory" intelligence, and "disadvantages" in disposition of troops. The English public soon heard further, from Howe's perspective, about the indecisive skirmish at Germantown, which came after. A letter they would not see was more realistic than either. Washington's "Condition," the acerbic John Adams wrote to his wife, Abigail, on September 30 from York, was only "tolerably respectable." Washington still had an army in being. Further, Howe's march from Elk to Philadelphia passed through "Regions of Passive Obedience," largely inhabited by Quakers. "There is not such another Body of Quakers in all America, perhaps not in all the World," Adams contended. "I am still of Opinion that Philadelphia will be no Loss to Us."

From the vantage of London the capture of the rebel capital looked positive indeed. A cartoon engraved by William Hitchcock of Birch Lane, "The Flight of the Congress," showed its members as frightened animals, largely petty creatures like squirrels, each with a rebel name, fleeing from a tree inscribed "Liberty," with a roaring British lion in pursuit. Washington is a startled armadillo. In the air a Hessian eagle circles, clutching in its claws a rattlesnake labeled "Independence." Since Benjamin Franklin was on his mission to France to seek aid, an owl holds a paper describing King Louis XVI as a baboon. The caption closes,

Lo! Midst broken Oaths and Curses,
The Rebel rout at once disperses.

The most difficult rebel strongpoint to take had been Mud Island in the Delaware, between Red Bank on the Jersey side and Fort Mifflin, across a swamp on the other shore. The Americans had blockaded the river with gun entrenchments and below-water obstructions, and a stubborn Hessian attack cost the life of the German commander, Colonel Carl von Donop, who had been embarrassed earlier at Princeton. Howe's engineers spent three weeks building causeways and artillery platforms, and at dawn on November 10 began a bombardment that in six days reduced Mud Island to rubble. Supply ships could now sail up to Philadelphia. In London the news came too late to mean much, but a salacious cartoon, "The Takeing of Miss Mud I'land," depicted the enemy defenses as a woman with a sardonic smile and flags in her hair, corseted only up to her bulging bare breasts, with a cannonade pouring forth toward British warships from between her legs under lifted skirts.

The mixed blessings from Philadelphia were soon blighted by the distresses of Burgoyne. His troubles, beginning in August, became known in England just as the King's Friends were rejoicing over Howe's successes. Conceding Burgoyne's burgeoning difficulties, the *London Gazette* noted the rout of his provisions seekers at Bennington, and the general's diminishing supplies, and seemed to be preparing the public for the worst. Yet, since most of the foragers mauled on crossing into Vermont were Hessian, several newspaper reports suggested that, as with the debacle at Trenton, Englishmen would have performed more spiritedly than hired foreigners.

Walpole wrote to Horace Mann of the *"check"* received by Burgoyne and added darkly, "There have been accounts of his recovering [from] the blow, but I cannot find one person who believes that." Even more gloomily, and he was hardly alone in his predictions, Walpole added, "I see no prospect of an end to this American war, but from our inability to carry it on—and what can that produce but a war *from* France." A broader conflict might last, he wrote to Lady Ossory, "to the end of the century; and then it is so inconvenient to have all letters [with delayed war news] come by the post of the ocean! People should never go to war above ten miles off, as the Grecian states used to do."

Writing on November 5 to the Whig leader in the Lords, the Marquis of Rockingham, Edmund Burke dismissed "the wild tumult of Joy that the News of Sunday"—Washington's defeat at Brandy-wine—"caused in the Minds of all sorts of people." It indicated "nothing right in their Character and disposition." He thought that since people taking up the rebel cause craved "comfort" about the possibilities, it would be necessary "not to carry the appearance of too much despondency." Burke refused to be impulsively pessimistic about American chances. The happy throngs in the London streets knew nothing of strategy and less of geography. He worried more about "jealousies and uneasiness" in the pro-American minority. (Lord Rockingham had urged a "bridle" on overt dissent.) And he wondered about what the still admired elder William Pitt, now the Earl of Chatham, would do, as however much he was looked up to, he was ill and feeble and unpredictable. The former prime minister's increasingly rare appearances in Parliament were the stuff of melo-drama, as he covered himself in layers of flannel to ease his gout. "The blood of St Januarius," Burke observed sardonically, referring to the third-century Naples martyr whose alleged blood created mira-cles when it decoagulated, begins "to Liquefie."

Chatham "was perfectly alive; very full of conversation; . . . and full resolved to go down to the house of Lords on the first day of the Session. But I am afraid, that the present American News will put as many folds of Flannel about him, as there are linnen Fillets round an Aegptian Mummy." Burke need not have worried about Chatham, who would rise dramatically in the Lords when Burgoyne appeared to be, from newspaper accounts, in desperate trouble and prospects seemed bleak.

Outmaneuvered and out of supplies, Burgoyne remained thwarted and nearly surrounded at Saratoga, above Albany. If he was tempted to go back while he could, he was too proud to acknowledge it. He had written to Germain on August 20 about obeying orders to join Howe; however, the instructions included authority to "Act as Exi-gencies may require." While Howe boasted on October 21 of his own "very important and brilliant success," he acknowledged that he had heard from General Clinton in New York City "of the very crit-ical situation of General Burgoyne's army." Still, he professed confi-dence that reports from the enemy about the plight of Burgoyne's trapped troops remained "extremely doubtful," as the Americans "are ever ready to propagate the most direct falsehoods upon every occasion." Howe knew better, as while he was elaborately preparing to attack Mud Island, jubilant salvos from American guns were celebrating Burgoyne's surrender. Burgoyne had sent officers to negotiate terms on the fourteenth, and by the eighteenth the news had reached the Americans along the Delaware.

At Saratoga, Horatio Gates had succeeded Philip Schuyler, a political major general and Hudson Valley patroon, and settled on a defensive position along the Albany road between the Hudson and steeply rising woods. There a volunteer Polish artilleryman and engineer, Tadeusz Kosciuszko, thirty-one and a colonel, built barricades. He had already planned the river defenses on the Delaware that had helped Washington hold up Howe. Gates also had the help of Brigadier General Benedict Arnold, an impetuous strategist who had survived Canada but nursed an unhealed leg wound, and Colonel Daniel Morgan, a Pennsylvania frontiersman who led five hundred sharpshooters. While Burgoyne was hemorrhaging soldiery, and complaining to Germain that he had found only four hundred loyalist recruits in all of upper New York, the cautious Gates was accruing men—and numerical superiority. Nearly cut off, the increasingly desperate British and Hessians, running out of everything from rations to gunpowder, had nowhere, themselves, to run.

Across the Atlantic, however, optimistic falsehoods arose on the thinnest morsels of hopeful evidence. On November 4, 1777, alone, both the *Chronicle* and the *Daily Advertiser* published intelligence of Howe's defeat of the "rebel army" at Christiana in Delaware, and Burgoyne's supposed victory along the Hudson. Burgoyne's only success, later thwarted by the Continental Congress, was to win a clause in the surrender agreement that his troops would be placed on parole and receive passage home, but he was an instinctive dramatist and reacted to the draft articles of capitulation with rhetorical excesses more appropriate for the London stage than for the realities of defeat. Replying to the instructions that his soldiers give up their weapons, he replied loftily to Gates, whom he had called privately an old midwife, "Sooner than this army will consent to ground their arms . . . , they will rush on the enemy determined to take no quarter. . . . If General Gates does not mean to recede from the 6th article, the treaty ends at once: the army will to a man proceed to any act of desperation sooner than submit to that article." He was playing to the gallery at home. There would be no dramatic acts of any sort.

Also on November 4, the *Public Advertiser* reported, "The *Isis* man of war, with the dispatches from New York . . . is not yet arrived at any port, and it is said the ministers are uneasy on her account. . . . A ship is arrived at Dartmouth, the master of which . . . spoke with her [at sea]; but that he could learn no other particulars of their dispatches than they contained 'Glorious news for Old England, and that Gen. Washington was completely beat.'" Also, the master of the *Charlotte* brought a report from New York, from which it departed on September 23, "of Gen. Burgoyne's having totally defeated the rebel army under Generals Schuyler and Arnold, and taken and killed about 7,000 men, and that Gen. Burgoyne was then at Albany." Even later, a frigate from New York commanded by a Captain Blackbourne arrived at Margate, where he reported fancifully that Burgoyne had reached Albany, and that since Howe's absence, three rebel attempts had been made on New York and Long Island, all repulsed by General Clinton, and that Howe had landed at Elk and burned a huge rebel supply magazine.

Horace Walpole characterized such newsprint certainties as "manifest lies." Understanding geography, he saw no likelihood of "resuscitation and victory" for Burgoyne, but confirmation of his surrender at Saratoga to Gates on October 18, 1777, would not arrive in England for six more weeks. Flanked by his aides and followed by his generals, Burgoyne had reined up for the formal capitulation opposite the stocky Gates, godson of Walpole, who thirty-two years before had been a lieutenant in the same redcoat regiment. "I am glad to see you," said Gates earnestly.

"I am not glad to see you," said Burgoyne. "It is my fortune, sir, and not my fault, that I am here." He offered his sword; it was returned.

Few in Britain in late autumn expected much glory from the northern operation they did not yet know was over, and badly, yet which offered opportunity to lampoon Burgoyne—and Germain—in advance. A column in the *Public Advertiser* on November 12, in the guise of a letter from Lieutenant General Swagger to Sir Matthew Minden, parodied the boastful style of Burgoyne's campaign rhetoric. Amused, Walpole snipped out and preserved the page.

Anticipating the worst from messages received by General Clinton, and attempting to cover his posterior, Howe, who had contributed to Burgoyne's catastrophe, emphasized over and over again to Germain that the Philadelphia operation was one "which his Majesty was pleased to approve," and that he—General Howe—had "positively mentioned that no direct assistance could be given by the southern army." On October 22, recognizing that there was "no prospect of terminating the war to the advantage of Great Britain without another campaign," and without "ample" reinforcements he had no expectation of receiving, Howe sourly asked to be replaced. "From the little attention, my Lord, given to my recommendations since the commencement of my command, I am led to hope I may be relieved from this very painful service, wherein I have not the good fortune to enjoy the necessary confidence and support of my superiors." By the return of the mail packet he applied for "his Majesty's permission to resign the command." (On November 23, in fraternal loyalty, Admiral Lord Howe would also ask to be relieved.)

Joseph Stansbury, a British agent in Philadelphia, derided Sir William as a "Carpet Knight" who would even reject Venus for Elizabeth Loring, but Howe realized that his exit from the colonies, when approved, would mean jettisoning Mrs. Loring. There were prices to pay for making war and for making love. But she had already become notorious in lyrics sung to "Yankee Doodle":

Sir William he, snug as a flea,
Lay all this time a-snoring,
Nor dreamed of harm as he lay warm
In bed with Mrs. Loring.

When Parliament sat again, on November 20, the king's opening address expressed "great satisfaction" in having popular support for the war. "The Powers with which the Parliament has entrusted the Crown for the Suppression of the Revolt have been faithfully exerted." Members assumed otherwise, as at his morning levee at St. James's Palace he had been so unnaturally merry that suspicions were aroused that His Majesty was concealing dire news. He had already written to North, who was preparing a text to satisfy the king, that "it has been a certain position with Me that Firmness is the Characteristick of an Englishman . . . and Ministers in their speeches [must]

shew that they will never consent to Independence of America."
Now, offering no details, he expressed his concern about the "heavy
charge" that carrying on the war "must bring on the people," but he
remained convinced that it was "in the essential interest of these
kingdoms."

Crowds clamoring to hear the king and the debates to follow
were large, and Edward Oxnard, a wealthy émigré loyalist from
Boston, bribed an usher with three shillings to obtain a seat in the
Strangers Gallery. Immediately, the traditional motion for the acceptance of the Address became subject to opposition amendments deploring the war and seeking unlikely accommodation. Even the
"country gentlemen," according to Lord John Cavendish, knew that
"every hope of obtaining a revenue from America" was now a "fran-
tic idea." The usual aspersions on "the noble Lord who presides at the
American Department" and had to find funds to pay for the war
changed few minds. The first amendment lost, 243 to 86, and the
next went down by an even larger majority. With majorities that preponderant, King George scorned North's suggestion that token
members of the opposition be brought into the government. Nothing would make him "stoop" to that. "Whilst ten men in the Kingdom will stand by me, I will not give up myself into bondage." He
had been sovereign for seventeen years and intended to rule rather
than merely reign.

Germain's deputies would endorse Howe's petulant resignation
letter as received December 1, the same day as Lord George received
Lieutenant Colonel Cornelius Cuyler, Howe's aide-de-camp, its
bearer. Lord George forwarded it to the king with the observation,
"Sir William Howe's complaint of want of support is very unjust; but
his desire of being recalled does not come unexpected."

News of Burgoyne's surrender had already come from Carleton in
Canada, thanks to two deserters who had turned up at Ticonderoga.
Then came a letter from France, according to press accounts, from a
gentleman who had learned that Burgoyne had "suffered a severe defeat, and was wounded in several parts of his body, and that the reflection of the disgrace of a conquest obtained by the rebels, together
with the anguish of his wounds, had brought him to his grave." The
Chronicle's story was poignant (the general actually took a shot
through his hat and another through his waistcoat), but the wounds

were fantasy, as was a report, also in the *Chronicle,* supported by the *Public Advertiser,* that Major General Benedict Arnold had been wounded in the thigh near Saratoga on October 7, and had died of "almost instantaneous mortification." The *General Evening Post* would carry a long account of Saratoga, softening the embarrassment by describing a "small but gallant handful whose numbers hourly diminished in the unequal contest," and speaking of "honourable surrender."

Whitehall conceded the capitulation on December 2 (nine days before Burgoyne's formal dispatch arrived). The First Lord of the Admiralty wrote that Tuesday evening to St. James's Palace, "It is with much concern that Ld. Sandwich sends to your Majesty the unpleasant account that has just been received by Captain Mountray of the *Warwick.*" The London press would publish the Articles of Convention stipulating the surrender terms, and even the minutes of Burgoyne's council of war preceding it. Whatever was not furnished by Whitehall came from American papers never censored by the ministry. Later, Burgoyne would write, shifting the onus of defeat to London, "I imagine I am reserved [by fate] to stand a war with ministers who will always lay the blame upon the employed who miscarries. . . . I expect ministerial ingratitude will be displayed, as in all countries and at all times as usual, to remove the blame from the orders to the execution."

Germain—the target of Burgoyne's reproach—acknowledged the "melancholy" event in the Commons the next day, challenged by Colonel Barré, who referred to "expresses from Quebec," to "declare upon your honour what has become of General Burgoyne and his brave troops."

"Though the recital must give me pain," Lord George rose to confess, "I know it is my duty to inform the House that I have indeed received expresses from Quebec." But the news that Carleton received had come from unreliable sources. He pleaded for judgment to be suspended until official dispatches arrived. The acknowledgment prompted caustic debates in the Commons and the Lords—"warm skirmishes," Walpole called them, "in both the Temples of Honour and Virtue, Lord Chatham himself heading the troops of the Opposition." Germain "received several wounds from Charles Fox," who hoped to see him brought to a second trial. Fox had already been ejected from a dinner party for proposing a toast to General

Washington. "Does the noble Lord know the extent of his criminality?" Barré challenged. Burke asked acidly whether "a whole army compelled to lay down their arms" and receive "laws"—surrender terms—from the enemy was something new in the kingdom's history, and Alexander Wedderburn, the solicitor general, had to be restrained from challenging him to a duel.

"Dreadful news indeed," wrote historian Edward Gibbon, who had been elected in 1774 as a supporter of North. He had no "particulars" yet from the papers, but foresaw "a general cry for peace." The Earl of Chatham, still William Pitt to most, had his opportunity in the Lords on December 5. Rumors arose that because of his immense prestige he would replace North as prime minister in a conciliation Cabinet, but realists knew he was too feeble to resume office. Even propped on a crutch he could barely stand to address the peers. That day, however, arguments from both sides, according to the *Annual Register,* "rekindled the flame of Lord Chatham's eloquence." Wrapping his folds of flannel more securely about him, he declared, "I know that the conquest of English America is an impossibility. You cannot, I venture to say it, you *cannot* conquer America." Its people were not "wild and lawless banditti, who have nothing to lose." The war against the unalienable rights of Americans was "unjust in its principles, impracticable in its means, and ruinous in its consequences." Employing "mercenary sons of rapine and plunder" from the Continent guaranteed incurable resentment. "If I were an American as I am an Englishman, while a foreign troop was landed in my country, I would never lay down my arms—never—never—never!"

Chatham's motion that copies of all orders and instructions to General Burgoyne related to the "northern expedition" be laid before the dwindling numbers in the House of Lords was rejected on a division by 40 to 19. A legislative investigation into a quagmire portended government embarrassment. In the Commons, meanwhile, Fox and Wilkes were equally acerbic to another hostile majority. Conquering America, Fox claimed, was "in the nature of things absolutely impossible" as the attempt sprung from "fundamental error." Attacking Germain personally, Fox charged, "For the two years that a certain noble lord has presided over American affairs, the most violent, scalping, tomahawk measures have been pursued: bleeding has been his only prescription. If a people deprived of their ancient rights are grown tumultuous—bleed them! . . . If their fever should rise into rebellion, bleed them, cries this state physician!" Thomas Pownall, a former royal governor now an MP, followed Fox and claimed that a reunion "with rebels" was now impossible: It was better to part company with America completely. The "mere principle of self-defence" could not be justified.

Finally, Lord George had his opportunity to reject targeting as a scapegoat. Attacking Fox, he declared, according to the third-person report of the debate, "The hon[orable] gentleman who spoke last but one had represented him as delighting in blood; he begged leave to assure him, he was entirely mistaken; he had always abhorred the effusion of blood could it have been possibly avoided." He was ready to compromise with America on many things, but peace could only come with the concession that the colonists remain subjects of the Crown. "This was my decided opinion before I came into office; I have been uniform [since] in language."

The next day, Colonel Barré called on Germain as "a man of honour" to explain the surrender to the Commons, and Lord George pleaded with the House not to be "over anxious in condemnation." The surrender had not been unconditional. Burgoyne's army was not to serve again in America, but it was to have safe passage to a port and return to England.* He was ready himself to have "the censure of the House fall upon him. He was ready to abide it; as every minister, who regarded the welfare of his country, ought at all times to have his conduct scrutinized."

After more objections were voiced, the prime minister had the last word: "As to the noble lord in the American Department, he trusted he had acted on the soundest principles of candour and deliberation. He could not possibly make any objection to the inquiry into that noble lord's conduct as he made no doubt but that he would acquit

---

*Hair-splitting reinterpretations and reservations on both sides, but largely by Congress, would delay and finally prevent the ranks from going home before the end of the war. On January 8, 1778, Congress would move that the embarkation of Burgoyne's troops to England "be suspended till a distinct and explicit ratification of the Convention of Saratoga shall be properly notified by the Court of Great Britain to the Congress." To do so would constitute a recognition of the legitimacy of Congress, as the king realized, and refused to do, and Congress intended to keep the troops hostage to the impossible.

himself before that House." Edward Gibbon wrote from the vantage of his seat in the Commons that although the prime minister could secure a majority on any ballot, "If it were not for shame there were not 20 men in the House but were ready to vote for peace," even "on the humblest conditions."

To end further infighting Parliament adjoined for the holidays on December 10. The stock market continued to fall; once more, North offered to resign. The king insisted to North that he "had too much personal affection for me . . . to allow such a thought to take hold in your mind." Besides, North was "loved and admired by the House of Commons, and . . . universally esteemed by the public." Impossibly, he proposed the greatly admired Chatham to replace him and wind down the war. The king would not hear of it. "Honestly, I would rather lose the Crown."

With fears that France would now exploit British distress, the discussions in Whitehall were about how to wear down American resolve by blockade and battery of the coastline where it was populated enough to make a difference. Even those remote from decision making were becoming exasperated by the uselessness of prolonging what more and more seemed an unwinnable war. Lady Sarah Bunbury wrote letters to friends conceding her "*incapability* in polliticks" and her realization that she should "talk of things more suited to me," but by December 1777 she confessed her opposition to "so vile a war. . . . I grow a greater rebel every day upon principle."

On December 15, the hawkish Earl of Denbigh wrote his friend Lord Loudoun, retired now to military sinecures, that, departing London for Christmas, he "left all the King's friends and well wishers . . . in very low spirits indeed, not only on account of the very extraordinary misfortune that has happened to General Burgoyne, but also what may happen in consequence. . . . The Cabinet seems very irresolute whether to raise new corps and to carry on the war by land (which in our present situation I think impossible) or to stand upon the defensive in the few places we have got in our hands, or prosecute it very vigorously by sea. There is not a foreign soldier more to be got for love or money. . . . We have hitherto kept our great majority in both houses of Parliament but what will happen when we'll next meet God only knows."

Doomsayers now had license. A mock ode in the *Evening Post*

(December 9) and in the *General Advertiser* (December 12), by Jeffery Dunstan, reversed the Burgoyne fiasco into a celebration of his victory, followed by the hanging of members of Congress, with Dr. Samuel Johnson presiding at the scaffold. A premature "Ode on the Success of his Majesty's Arms" was answered in the *Public Advertiser* on December 27, 1777, by "No Triumphs of our gracious King." A cartoon, "The State Tinkers," showed Sandwich and Germain, assisted by North, hammering obviously inadequate patches onto a huge two-handled pot while the king looks on complacently. The caption begins,

The National Kettle, which once was a good one,
For boiling of Mutton, of Beef, & of Pudding,
By the fault of the Cook, was quite out of repair,
When the Tinkers were sent for,—Behold them & Stare.

Whether or not George III was the cook (open lèse-majesté—insulting the king—was common in opposition broadsides), he was not about to let the compliant Lord North go, although North almost daily pleaded his inadequacy. The king responded by paying off North's personal debts, which had reached an enormous eighteen thousand pounds, writing, "You know me very ill, if you do not think that of all the letters I have ever wrote to you this one gives me the most pleasure, and I want no other return than your being convinced that I love you as well as a man of worth as I esteem you as a minister."

The *Evening Post* on December 4, 1777, had predicted in panic that Howe would now be trapped between the army of Washington in the south and that of Gates in the north, and "all will be over." Burgoyne even became something of a hero for having done, according to the *Morning Post,* "more than could naturally be expected of him in his unfortunate situation"—a conclusion that implicitly maligned Howe. No one yet took note of the opportunities possible at the end of the month, when many of Washington's soldiers outside occupied Philadelphia, poorly paid or even unpaid, badly clothed for winter, and inadequately fed and housed, would again reach the close of their yearlong enlistments and refuse to return.

All that Howe would write to the American Department (on De-

cember 13) as Parliament adjourned across the Atlantic was that Earl
Cornwallis was returning on the *Brilliant,* again on alleged "private
business," which offered an opportunity to explain various inconclusive skirmishes in the corner of Pennsylvania that they held. Most
had been to secure forage "for the winter supply." Washington's intention, Howe hazarded, was "to take their winter-quarters at
Carlisle, York and Lancaster, and probably they may have a corps at
Reading, and another at Burlington in Jersey." A rebel encampment
he did not mention, to the southeast of Reading, and much closer to
Philadelphia, was inhospitable Valley Forge, on the west bank of the
Schuylkill, where Washington intended to keep Philadelphia under
watch.

The war had miscarried badly for Britain, but it seemed not beyond retrieval. In some English and Scottish cities royalists signed petitions of support to the king. The Glasgow council offered even
more, unanimously resolving to give "aid and assistance to [the] government at this critical time in order to enable them to quell the . . .
rebellion." Three days later it voted to raise a local battalion and
began the subscription with £1,000. The Trades House in Glasgow
furnished an additional £500; following that lead the bakers and
weavers each contributed £200, and the barbers £100. "A general
gloom hangs upon the countenances of every one," Edward Oxnard
wrote in his journal. "The town of Manchester has agreed to raise
one thousand men & clothe them." A feeling of urgency generated
by Saratoga was spreading across the country.

Some saw the catastrophe differently. In "The Halcyon Days of
Old England," with a "ta-ra-ra-ra" chorus, and an opening about a
war that had begun about tea, and feathers, and tar, an anonymous
songster, publishing in the *Evening Post,* closed with,

Some folks are uneasy and make a great pother
For the loss of one army and half of another;
But sirs, next campaign by then thousands we'll slay 'em
If we can find soldiers—and money to pay 'em!
I've sung you a song, now I'll give you a prayer;
May peace soon succeed to this horrible war!
Again may we live with our brethren in concord,
And the authors of mischief all hang on a strong cord.

On Christmas Eve Lord Stormont, the British ambassador, paid a courtesy call upon the French foreign minister, the Comte de Vergennes, at Versailles. Stormont had heard through leaks, and his own agents, that expectations were high that America would soon be recognized by France as an independent nation qualified to enter into treaties. The flow of war matériel to the colonies from Cherbourg and Brest was already substantial. Never officially recognized, it was arranged on loans by ostensibly private companies, although the Americans had no funds. War seemed inevitable.

Vergennes offered nothing but polite chitchat until, as Stormont arose to leave, the count asked whether the ambassador had "anything new."

"Nothing from England, Sir," said Stormont, "but if one half of the news from Paris is true, it seems to me very doubtful whether I will have an opportunity of wishing Your Excellency a happy new year."

7

Except in Parliament
January 1778–June 1778

Tenant: Pray, Squire, when do you think the war will end?
Squire: At Doomsday, *perhaps* sooner; but this is certain, the nation is almost ruin'd, and we country gentlemen are the greatest sufferers.

—From *"A Dialogue between a Country Squire and his Tenant," the* London
Gazetteer, *1778.*

Sir Fretful Plagiary. "The NEWS-PAPERS! Sir, they are the most villain-
ous—licentious—abominable—infernal! Not that I ever read them!
No—I make it a rule never to look into a news-paper."

—*Richard Brinsley Sheridan,* The Critic *(London, 1781).*

"THE general is well, but much worn with fatigue and anxiety," Martha Washington wrote from Valley Forge as winter
enveloped the Continental encampment above Philadelphia. Her marital visit involved none of the hardships of her husband's eleven thousand troops, who had no fieldstone house with
fireplaces. At best they cobbled small log huts, and were grateful for
meager clothing, blankets, and rations. Most soldiers did not be-
grudge "Lady Washington" her luxuries, which were nothing like
Mount Vernon. Yet three thousand men were not fit for duty; many
more were not fit for fighting. Some walked away when their enlistments expired; others deserted.

In his general orders, which could be read in London coffeehouses
before the snows at Valley Forge had thawed, he had declared, "The
General ardently wishes it were now in his power, to conduct the
troops into the best winter quarters. But where are these to be
found?" He hoped at best for huts "that will be warm and dry," but
they were neither. He hoped for material support from the middle

colonies, but farmers wanted hard cash, and only the well-provisioned British, in commodious Philadelphia, had that.

The Continental Congress, in exile westward in the village of York with only a rump membership (seldom as many as twenty delegates), was weak and inept. Washington's soldiers were often fortunate to have firecake—an unleavened bread. Uniforms and shoes were in tatters, and they wore whatever clothing kept them warm. "I can assure these gentlemen," Washington wrote of the delegates, "that it is a much easier and less distressing thing to draw [up] remonstrances in a comfortable room by a good fireside than to occupy a cold bleak hill and sleep under frost and snow without clothes or blankets." Although Congress demonstrated "little feeling" for the plight of the soldiers, "I feel abundantly for them, and from my soul pity those miseries, which it is neither in my power to relieve or prevent."

Howe's comfortable and well-equipped army might have overwhelmed the Americans that winter—if the redcoats had any desire to do battle. Few skirmishes tested Washington's defenses. Except in Parliament, little serious fighting took place in early 1778. As a sardonic verse in the *Evening Post* (to be sung to the tune of "Ye Medley of Mortals") explained,

Give ear to my song, I'll not tell you a story,
This is the bright era of Old England's Glory!
And tho' some may think us in pitiful plight,
I'll swear they're mistaken, for *matters go right!*
Let us laugh at the cavils of weak, silly elves!
Our Statesmen are *wise* men! They say to themselves!
And tho' little mortals may hear it with wonder,
'Tis *consummate* WISDOM that causes each *blunder!*

Criticism in Parliament would be little more restrained. Washington's dwindling troops could do little more than to occasionally harass Howe's warm and well-fed occupiers of Philadelphia. Gates's snowed-in northern army, in its winter quarters on the upper Hudson, was no threat to comfortable New York, and even less to Newport. Yet, by confining the British largely to a strip of a hundred miles between New York and Philadelphia for more than two years, whatever strategy Whitehall might have intended for subduing the rebellion was stalled. Little appetite for more war existed elsewhere in what remained of British America. There was even less enthusiasm in Britain, now worried about an imminent French alliance with the colonies, and gambling that a sweetened offer of conciliation would ward off, and isolate, the French. The stake in the colonies reflected pride of empire; the long-contested sugar plantations in the Caribbean represented consumer desire—and revenue. As army chief, Lord Amherst advised the ministry that continuing a land war in America as part of a larger conflict "must be feeble in all parts and consequently unsuccessful." And a prolonged, enfeebling war would only be to the advantage of the French.

Politicians did not wait for Parliament to resume on January 20 to debate the alternatives. In the first weeks of 1778 Earl Cornwallis was again in London, arriving on the *Brilliant* on January 18 to defend the prosecution of the war. The day before both Houses met, Lord North was asked whether the army had comfortable quarters in Philadelphia, and he quipped, lamely, "So good that I wish I was to pass the next three months there." (Rather, he meant any place other than a less than civil House of Commons.) He had just heard from Germain that a party of Howe's redcoats had successfully crossed the Schuylkill to the village of Darby to seize enough stored forage to feed their horses through the winter. Despite Saratoga, all was not lost, but "the anxiety of his mind," North wrote to the king in the usual third person, hoping to be relieved, "had deprived Lord North of his memory and his understanding." He felt incompetent to continue as the country was dividing more sharply. Soon he would plead again, but in the more emotional first person, "Let me not go to the grave with the guilt of having been the ruin of my king and country."

Mocking North's political anguish, and the hopeless solutions that the outwardly amiable, unwarlike prime minister was expected to propose, Edmund Burke coldly compared the obese, gouty Lord North to Pericles in his last days, when "exhausted with misfortune, wasted with disease, and lingering with pain, [he] walked abroad, bedecked with amulets, charms, and the saws* of old women."

---

*sayings, maxims

Although regimental colonels employed recruiting officers who usually pocketed five pounds for every man accepting the king's shilling, volunteers remained few. Appeals were made to show the spirit of "Jack England," a precursor to "John Bull," who dated back as symbol to 1712 but had not yet become the personification of the English nation. Radical broadsides sold in the streets and aimed at likely recruits; one titled, "Six-Pence a Day" (when a loaf of bread cost fourpence and a pot of ale a penny), ridiculed army life. "An Exact Representation of Manchester Recruits," with a cartoon of weird, dehumanized volunteers, made soldiering a grim option. "The Master of the Arses, or the Westminster Volunteers" showed six motley recruits spurred on by redcoats, front and rear, one walking with crutch and stick, the other with gouty, swathed legs.

Parliament remained reluctant to pay more for a war going nowhere. The land tax had been raised to four shillings per pound in 1776, and a variety of petty new taxes was picking the pockets of the ministry's adherents in both city and country. One statute had been the Servants Act of 1777, declaring "a duty on all servants retained or employed in the several capacities therein mentioned," which included gardeners and coachmen, laborers and footmen. The annual assessment for each male servant (females were untaxed) was twenty-one shillings—a guinea. The fine on failure to pay was twenty pounds. An irate letter to the editor in *Town and Country Magazine* in January 1778 proposed, "as the war with America does not seem likely soon to end," a luxury tax on foreign workers of either sex at double the rate for domestic employees—"barbers, peruke-makers and hairdressers," for example—and "professed smugglers," "perfumers" who profit "500 per cent on every article," and a tax, also, on "running horses, which are the source of gambling, and various kinds of dissipation." Further, a tax on "bagnios"—brothels—and hotels. "These," the writer declared, "would not burden the poor and industrious, who are already incapable of bearing the load under which they groan."

To avoid increasing taxes to support more soldiery, a Tory scheme had been devised to raise regiments by local subscription, but its Cabinet spokesman, the American Secretary, was unavailable to make the initial presentation. His wife, Diana, was dying, the victim of a child's less severe measles, and when the end came on January 15, 1778, Lord George sequestered himself at the family estate, Knole.

She had been faithful and supportive, and he took her loss hard. Lord Suffolk immediately sent a sympathy note that also recognized Lord George as the Tory center of war planning and administration, however badly served by his military and civilian colleagues, and however vainly he attempted to micromanage affairs an ocean away. "Zeal for the public welfare," Suffolk wrote, "urges me to endeavour to rouse your attention even in the first agonies of grief. I shall confine myself at present to saying that we won't be idle during your absence; but we can't go far without your assistance."

On the day that Parliament sat, Suffolk wrote again. "Allow me to express my hopes," he urged Germain, "that calmer and maturer reflection will have convinced your lordship that it can neither be for the king's advantage or your own credit that you should retire at such a moment as the present. On the contrary, I wait with anxious expectation to hear that you mean shortly to come amongst us again, and avail yourself of the best relief from private affliction, public busyness. These are not only my sentiments and wishes but those of others who have great respect for your lordship."

Sensitive and acute, Suffolk reflected the Tory consensus. As much as Lord George was vilified in the opposition press, and by the peace advocates in Parliament, he seemed the best war partisan available—managerial and disciplined despite criticism of his sharp temper and shrinking options. He would be attacked for abetting Burgoyne's catastrophe and condoning the Howe brothers' inaction, yet when Parliament sat in his absence on the twentieth, Walpole wrote to William Mason that the House of Commons could do "little or nothing as they wait for Lord George to lead up the Blues." It was the usual nasty aspersion to Minden, where the British cavalry—"the Blues"—had delayed its advance until it was too late to matter. Three radical newspapers in "Captain Parolles★ at M[i]nden" would compare Germain's alleged cowardice nearly twenty years earlier, which he could never live down, to British failures in America, claiming that he could not manage military strategy from the distant safety of Whitehall, "Three Thousand Leagues beyond the Cannon's reach." A broadside cartoon showed Burgoyne, costumed as a stage mountebank and carrying copies of his plays, leading his troops into captivity, their wrists bound.

★Parolles is the worthless braggart in Shakespeare's *All's Well That Ends Well*.

The Secretary was again in the Commons on January 26, supported ironically in the opposition *Morning Post* on the twenty-first by a catalog of rebel generals ridiculed for their contemptible origins and prewar occupations—a boat builder, a bookseller, a servant, a milkman, a jockey, a clerk. The satire on British snobbery suggested that commanders of noble birth and little else could be beaten by officers reaching the top by merit in classless America. A progovernment broadside took a contrary view, depicting a member of Congress snug in a fur-lined coat and clutching a large pocketbook accompanied by two warmly uniformed officers who are cheering on tattered and freezing—and clearly unhappy—Continentals.

Germain's return appeared prompted by a message from James Hutton, a bookseller with connections among his Moravian brethren in America, and Germain's secret agent in Paris, just arrived in London on January 25. Lord George knew that Benjamin Franklin, with associates, was in France to negotiate a treaty of assistance. After Saratoga and the apparent standoff at Germantown, Franklin could bargain from unanticipated strength. North had instructed Hutton that he was prepared to offer the Americans, to separate them from the French, everything "except the word independence." On February 1, 1778, Franklin followed up their talks with a letter asking not only for independence but, assuredly tongue-in-cheek, much more. He sought "generosity" and "good will" on a grand scale: "For instance, perhaps you might, by your Treaty, retain all Canada, Nova Scotia and the Floridas. But if you would have a real friendly as well as an able Ally in America, and avoid all occasions of future Discord, which will otherwise be continually arising on your American Frontiers, you should throw in those Countries. And you may call it, if you please, an indemnification for the needless and cruel burning of their Towns, which Indemnification with otherwise be some time or other demanded."

With Whitehall and St. James's Palace showing renewed interest in accommodation with America, although not at a level which Franklin took seriously, the French had the added element of self-interest to prevent it. After a hurried seventy-three-hour trip from Paris, Hutton reported that one of the American delegates—obviously Franklin—had suggested that if the king acknowledged the independence of the colonies, a deal could be struck that would ward off "the treaty on the carpet." He had all of ten days to come back quickly with a proposition.

Without overt intervention by George III, *quickly* would not be operative in the vocabulary of his bureaucrats. But the government was working on alternatives to persuade the Americans to come to terms. The first—military force—was clearly in jeopardy. Whitehall had to parry skeptical questions in Parliament about funding new regiments through local subscription, evading budgetary limits, and raising alarm about other uses for them. Lord Camden called the unpopular scheme illegal, as, in the Commons, did John Dunning and others. The attorney general and the solicitor general defended the proposal, but the financial backers were ridiculed—with no names named—as military contractors, appointees in the pay of the government, and Jewish stockbrokers. On February 2, Charles Fox declared that with the looming threat of a "foreign war" (with France) and the military establishment in Great Britain six thousand men below its peacetime strength, "it would be madness to part with any more of the regular army" in a war in America that had become "impracticable." He moved "that no more of the Old Corps be sent out of the Kingdom," and the Duke of Richmond made a similar motion in the Lords. Both attempts would fail, but the army in America thereafter would receive little more than replacements.

The Commons also called for an investigation into how General Burgoyne's campaign had collapsed, and demanded the texts of messages sent to him by the American Secretary. An anonymously written ballad, "The Heads," to a "derry down" refrain, condemned the unwisdom of the "thick skulls" which had approved the expedition:

On Britannia's bosom sweet Liberty smiled,
The parent grew strong while she fostered the child,
[But] Neglecting her offspring, a fever she bred,
Which contracted her limbs and distracted her head.
Ye learned state doctors, your labours are vain,
Proceeding by bleeding to settle her brain;
Much less can your art the lost members restore,
Amputation must follow—perhaps something more . . .

Back at work at Whitehall, the American Secretary sent a saccharine message to General Howe that was much less than honest. Lord George had "the satisfaction to acquaint you that his Majesty has received the most uncommon testimonies of affection and support in the prosecution of the war, if the obstinacy of the colonies in rejecting the generous terms held out to them shall make it necessary to continue it, not only from Parliament but from the people in general."

What appeared to be a spontaneous groundswell was something quite different, as, reading between the lines, Howe must have understood. Obviously, Parliament could not be counted upon to pay more for the war. An embarrassment was the release of figures showing that in the two years ending on February 1, 1778, the government had spent £111,550 on rum for the forces in America, at five shillings threepence per gallon. "Were the spirits of our brave forefathers who won the battles of Crécy and Agincourt, or of Oliver [Cromwell]'s fighting saints," a critic objected, "kept up by such means?"

"Several noblemen and gentlemen of extensive influence and [also] some great cities have undertaken to raise new corps," the Secretary again explained, to mollify pocketbook concerns, "and in London, Bristol, and many other towns, considerable sums have been subscribed to be given in bounties to recruits for the old regiments." Since the campaigning season would be "far advanced" before Howe could receive and employ such forces, Germain urged him to detach "such a number of troops as can be spared consistent with the defensive plan you have proposed" for coastal raids in conjunction with the fleet. Howe was not being offered much, or asked to mount more than token harassments in the interim, and the emphasis remained "defensive." No strategy surfaced to end the rebellion in 1778.

"We are not only *patriots out of place,*" Sir George Savile, MP for a Yorkshire seat, told the Marquis of Rockingham gloomily, "but patriots *out of the opinion of the public.*" Concurring, Rockingham responded that they had yet to win over enough voices. "This Country is altogether as determined as the Ministers, to continue the Pursuit of measures which must end fatally." The only hope he saw was to wait "till the Publick are actually convinced of the calamitous State we are in." In the Commons, John Wilkes read one of Burgoyne's more extreme letters to the American Secretary about buying the loyalty of savage Indians. "Surely, Sir," he said, ostensibly to Lord North, "an enquiry into those horrors, & the failure of an expedition, which has not only disgraced our arms, but obscured the name of Englishmen, and fixed a foul stain on our national character, is still more worthy of our enquiry than even the waste of public treasure, altho' we are, I fear, if the war continues, too near the brink of a general bankruptcy. . . . The Ministers have at length confessed we cannot conquer America. To what purpose, then, are more torrents of blood to be shed?"

To ward off growing discontent Lord North promised that he would have a new conciliation plan ready for Parliament on February 17, a Tuesday following the traditional very long weekend. A strongly worded petition signed by fifty-four hundred inhabitants of the county of Norfolk, including the city of Norwich, was delivered for reading to the Commons, warning of government "misrepresentation of our situation. . . . An empire is lost. A great continent in arms is either to be conquered or abandoned." It asked the House to inquire into the "calamitous" situation, as "your constituents have been gravely deceived and deluded. . . . Without wise councils at home, we cannot have empire or reputation abroad."

The day before, Thomas Walpole, MP for King's Lynn, and his MP cousin Horace, had discovered through contacts across the Channel that an American treaty with France had already been signed. British agents in Paris knew how busy Dr. Franklin was, arranging to secure privateers to harass shipping and the coasts; buying and conveying arms through French financial subterfuges; and negotiating with seekers of military commissions from across the Continent, attempting to turn away the utterly spurious claimants while recruiting those with useful social, political, and monetary backing. Whitehall knew that war would come when France was ready, and treaty recognition of America implied that.

An hour before the House met, the Walpoles alerted Charles Fox. He rose immediately after North and asked whether conciliation remained meaningful, for he had learned that an American commercial treaty entered into as an independent nation, the United States of America, had just been concluded with France. If true, the government's propositions to grant virtual but not explicit independence would have no effect. George Grenville, when prime minister the sponsor of many of the prewar sanctions such as the Stamp Act, took the floor to acknowledge that he had seen an extract of a letter from Dr. Franklin himself, confirming the signed treaty. Of what use, then, were these flaccid conciliatory bills? He felt "the humiliating blush that must spread the cheek of my Sovereign when he should be called to give his assent to them."

Edmund Burke then charged that he had offered the plan belatedly proposed by North two years before, and was voted down. Now he called on the prime minister to answer to the facts of the French treaty. When Lord North stood silent, Sir George Savile argued that it would be an impeachable offense not to reply, and closed tauntingly with "An answer! An answer! An answer!"

Shaken, North confessed that he had heard such reports, but had no "official intelligence" on the matter. "Peace, at all times," he claimed, had been his "governing principle." French officials had denied collusion with the colonies, North asserted, while knowing much more. He would look into it.

Three days later, the melancholy news was confirmed, yet the conciliatory bills that now had no practical value were formally introduced anyway. One authorized the king to appoint a new group of peace commissioners to replace the Howes, with broad negotiating authority; however, the conditions offered would be subject to parliamentary approval. The other declared the intention of Parliament to recognize the de facto authority of Congress, and promised that rather than exercise the right to tax the colonies, they might devise a voluntary contributory system. Wryly, Fox complimented the prime minister on his "conversion."

From Edinburgh, once the news reached James Boswell on February 28, he wrote to Dr. Johnson, "What do you say to 'Taxation No Tyranny' now, after Lord North's declaration, or confession, or whatever else his conciliatory speech should be called?" He regretted that the king "does not see it to be better for him" to receive revenues "from his American subjects by the voice of their own assemblies, where his Royal Person is represented . . . ?"

In Hanley, pottery entrepreneur Josiah Wedgwood was incensed by the tone of North's reversal of tax policy for America. "After spending 30 millions & sacrificing 20 thousand lives, to tell the House the object was a trifle—a something, or nothing worth the trouble of collecting!" He had long been critical of the waste of "blood and treasure" in a "wicked and preposterous war," as he objected in his letters, and he had privately produced intaglio medals for his pro-American patrons showing the colonial "Don't tread on me" motto with coiled rattlesnake. To his business associate Thomas Bentley he wrote that he was not concerned that the nation might lose a war with the French "and blessed my stars and Lord North that *America was free."* He had neither need nor desire to leave England, but approved "of a refuge being provided for those who chuse to flee rather than submit to the iron hand of a tyranny. . . . We must have war, and perhaps continue to be beat. . . . If our drubbing keeps pace with our deserts, the Lord have mercy on us."

In the Lords, the Duke of Richmond again called for Germain to explain Burgoyne's abandonment, and in the Commons, Thomas Connolly, an Irish MP related by marriage to the Howes, asked Lord George to cite the reasons General Howe had given when he asked to be relieved. The American Secretary refused to divulge them. The opposition in the Commons asked for immediate repeal of the Tea Act as a show of good faith, and to its surprise the bill passed. (The Lords was another matter.) But when members sought to have Parliament, rather than the king, appoint the peace commissioners, the resolution failed. The futile patchwork alternatives succeeding repeal of the Stamp Act had come and gone even before Germain came to office, but the *Evening Post* and the *General Advertiser* focused on his ministry in a cruel parody of King Claudius's conscience-stricken soliloquy in *Hamlet* (the literate were expected, also, to be literary): "Oh! My offence is rank; it smells to Heav'n."

To promote the seriousness of the official turnabout, which included an offer to suspend hostilities until June 1779 (to accommodate parleying), the king proclaimed still another day of fasting and prayer for February 27, which the *Evening Post* and the *General Advertiser* were not alone in condemning as hypocrisy. (Horace Walpole called it unnecessary, as the seventeenth had already been, in Parliament, "a day of confession and humiliation.") When the proposed order of service was drawn up and published, one instruction to churches for a reversal in attitude led to wry interpretations: "Then shall all the People say *after the Minister,* 'Turn us, O Lord, and so shall we be turned!' "

A blunt satire on the annual solemnities condemned the failed commanders who had made begging for a blessing on the royal arms apparently necessary:

First General Gage commenc'd the war in vain;
Next General Howe continued the campaign;
Then General Burgoyne took the field; and last,
Our forlorn hope depends on *General Fast.*

Another in rather weak rhyme quoted a psalm of David about washing one's hands in "innocency" and went on in scorn,

With *cruel hearts* and *bloody hands,*
The *Ministry* were stain'd,
A *Fast* was publish'd thro' these lands,
That they might all be clean'd.
But oh! What blunders time affords!
Thro' want of *grace* and *sense,*
They washed them in—*a form of words* . . .

Fast Day was, Parson Woodforde recorded in Norfolk, "bitter cold with cutting winds," but he met "a large Congregation" for "Prayers only," prudently offering no sermon on the war, or the abstinence prescribed.★ A different variety of divine had already preached on the war at Oxford—Myles Cooper, exiled president of King's (later Columbia) College in New York, a devout loyalist who had narrowly escaped with his life. Cooper attacked the "violent and corrupt" rebels for "enslaving the colonies." They had failed to "fear God [and] honour the King," and to recognize that every man must be "contented with his station, and faithfully discharge his respective duties," for "when men's principles are wrong, their practices will seldom be right." Hawkishly, he blamed "divisions at home" in Britain for the disharmony in America.

★Even the Continental Congress, in unusual religiosity, had called for a day of fasting late in 1776, during a period of military disasters. "According to the custom of our pious ancestors in times of imminent dangers and difficulties," it declared, it was crucial "to implore of Almighty God the forgiveness of the many sins prevailing among all ranks, and to beg the countenance and assistance of his Providence in the prosecution of the present just and necessary war."

Throughout the kingdom the disillusionment about English arms became more vocal. "An Indignant Briton" published a long screed in the *Bristol Journal* on February 28 wondering how and why "the queen of the seas, the conqueror of France, and the scourge of Spain" was "FORCED by her own provinces to grant terms." It was, the outraged writer declared, "want of *unanimity* that ruined us: there were adders in our bosom, that gave us much more mortal wounds than the swords of our enemies." An anonymous pamphlet soon followed, identified as by "an Officer returned from that [American] service—a *Letter to the English Nation, on the Present War with America . . . from which the absolute Impossibility of Reducing the Colonies will sufficiently appear, and the Folly of continuing the contest demonstrated.*" Implicitly agreeing, the *Gazeteer* acknowledged that "the finest troops in the world could not win in America," and the *General Advertiser* summed up the cost in money and men, concluding that "at the end of every campaign we are worse off than we were at the beginning."

It was no laughing matter, but a wry pseudobulletin allegedly from Doctors' Commons★ reported, "We hear that a *divorce* of a very extraordinary nature, between *John Bull* and his wife *Americana,* is shortly to take place. . . . The cause of [the] quarrel originated one morning over their *Tea,* which would have been instantly made up, but for the *roguery* of Mr. Bull's servants, who had an interest in keeping them at variance. Now it has spread so wide, that a *reconciliation is thought impracticable. . . .* The consequence of this divorce will be that *John Bull* will have nothing to live on but the *little original farm* he had before marriage; whilst his wife will be in *sole* possession of the *great estate she brought him.*"

When in April the Court announced that Queen Charlotte was expecting her thirteenth child, the *General Advertiser* suggested that "for each revolted province," the queen had presented the kingdom with a burden on its treasury. When Charlotte was pregnant the year before, an American paper reported, ostensibly from the official *London Gazette,* and with a purportedly loyal twist at the close, "that the King and Queen were both with child; but upon strict inquiry into

★Doctors' Commons, below St. Paul's Churchyard, was demolished in 1867. Dickens refers to it in *David Copperfield*. It was occupied by the College of Advocates and Doctors of Law, in which legal business relating to wills, marriages, and divorce proceedings was transacted.

the matter, by a jury of matrons, of which his Grace, the Archbishop of Canterbury, was foreman, it was found to be true only with respect to her Majesty, and as to our most gracious sovereign, the detestable falsehood is discovered to have been invested by the more artful, and greedily swallowed by the weaker and more credulous abettors of the American rebellion, who fondly wished his most sacred person pregnant, and undoubtedly with twins, from the malicious hope of his expiring in childbed." Freedom of the press seemed to have few limits in troubled Britain.

The prospect of war with France had caused the ministry to proliferate further its tented training camps for militia across southern England, which Richard Brinsley Sheridan derided in his popular musical comedy *The Camp.* After fifty-seven performances at Drury Lane it reopened in Bristol. One character, the effeminate Sir Harry Bouquet, is scorned by women acquaintances for not yet having joined the militia. Merchants made quick fortunes supplying the camps. A notorious trader, Hutchinson Muir, secured the commissariat contract to supply rum at a 50 percent markup, then acquired a lucrative contract for bread. Regimental colonels, often local worthies, fed and clothed their own troops, profiteering on the side.

The cantonments at such locations as Maidstone, St. Edmundsbury, and Winchester soon became a spectator sport. Much as trenches in Flanders would be named for streets in hometowns early in the 1914–1918 war, tenting sites were laid out to recall the regions from which regiments had been drawn, and the curious came to visit. As Mr. Bluard declares in *The Camp,* "Ah! Monsieur Gauge, I am so very glad to find you, by Gar I was hunt[ing] you all over the Camp—I have been thro' Berkshire;—Cross Suffolk, and all over Yorkshire, and hear no word of you." Newspapers published columns of "Camp Intelligence," and one review of troops near Salisbury, according to diarist John Marsh, was "a glorious day for the Turnpike, as I believe the cavalcade of Coaches[,] Chaises[,] Waggons, Carts, Horses &c extended near 2 miles."

Even Samuel Johnson's curiosity was piqued by the camps, prompting his visit to the Lincolnshire militia at Warley Common in Essex, where his young literary crony Bennet Langton was stationed as a captain. Dr. Johnson accompanied a major on sentry rounds after dark, supped in a general's tent, and watched a shooting exercise.

"The men indeed do load their muskets and fire with wonderful celerity," he marveled. And after inspecting the "superiority of accommodation" for officers and the "inferiour ones" for the ranks, he thought approvingly that he had never "so distinct a view" of the class system. He dined, drank, and bedded with the gentlemen, and according to Langton was "very well pleased with his entertainment."

The Reverend Woodforde went from his village to Norwich to gawk at the soldiery, taking his servant, Will, with him, "& supped & slept at the King's Head." It was a grand occasion for the minister, who usually kept close to Weston Longeville. "In the Evening about 9 o'clock there was a great Riot upon the Castle-Hill between the Officers of the Western Battalion of the Norfolk Militia, and the common Soldiers & Mob owing to the Officers refusing to pay their men a Guinea apiece as they were to go Morrow towards the Place of their Encampment—several of them refusing to go without it & would not resume their Arms after Roll calling for which they were put into the Guard Room & the Mob insisting on having them out, which occasioned a great Riot. The Mob threw stones & some of the Soldiers running their Bayonets at the Mob wounded them. Some of each Side were hurt but not mortally wounded or any killed. It lasted until Midnight." Apparently Norfolk newspapers employed discreet self-censorship. The incident vanished into the shadows of Woodforde's diary.

Every debate in Parliament would reflect domestic agitation, but the reluctance to relinquish America in the face of military failures and the looming French threat persisted. The appeal to damaged pride remained powerful, even when, on March 11, the Earl of Thanet revealed that, through General Burgoyne, he had received a friendly letter from a former intimate once a British officer—General Horatio Gates, the victor at Saratoga. Born in England, the son of the Duke of Leeds's housekeeper, Gates wrote that he could not help "feeling for the misfortunes brought upon his native country, by the wickedness of that administration, who began, and had continued this most unjust, impolitic, cruel and unnatural war." The new United States, he insisted, was eager to be the friends but not the slaves of "the parent country," to which it was "more attached" than any other. "Therefore, spurn not the blessing which yet remains. Instantly withdraw your fleets and armies; cultivate the friendship and commerce of America. Thus and thus only can England be great and happy."

So hoarse with a cold when he proposed to read the letter to the House of Lords on March 16 that he could barely introduce it, Thanet asked for permission to have the clerk do the reading. The Law Lords★—perhaps the most conservative members in the Upper House—objected that it would be "exceedingly improper . . . to enter into any correspondence with a rebel officer or General, or to frame any resolution upon his information; and also that the letter might also contain matter which it would be highly unfitting for their Lordships to hear."

Arguments erupted, the dovish peers noting that Parliament had just appointed commissioners to deal with persons "of weight and importance" in the colonies, such as Gates, and that such sentiments were vital to learn. Thanet's motion was rejected, guaranteeing the Gates letter wide publicity.

In America, Gates had acquired a different kind of notoriety. His victory at Saratoga was in dramatic contrast to Washington's succession of withdrawals in losing Philadelphia. Recognizing that, Congress had attempted to weaken the authority they had given him the year before by creating a board of war under Gates. Humiliated by defeats and the halting support of Congress, Washington had already written to his delegate friend Richard Henry Lee, "I have been a Slave to the service: I have undergone more than most Men are aware of, to harmonize so many discordant parts." While he was attempting to revive confidence in his ragtag troops at Valley Forge by drilling them under the self-styled Baron von Steuben, a Prussian émigré officer recommended by Franklin, Gates turned up in York, discrediting the commander-in-chief to Congress and covertly seeking his job. The scheme went awry. His relationship with Washington deteriorated, and he was directed back to command of the Northern Department in New York. By the next winter he was relegated to the backwater of the Eastern Department in Boston.

When, on March 17, 1778, as expected, Dr. Franklin was received formally at Versailles as ambassador of the United States of America,

★Those members of the House of Lords qualified to take part in its judicial business.

and the French government claimed falsely to the Court of St. James that only a treaty of commerce was involved, both houses of Parliament were irate at the recognition and the implication of military aid. War appeared inevitable, and instructions were sent to the British ambassador, Lord Stormont, to leave Paris immediately.

Two days later, the painful and prolonged inquiry on Burgoyne was concluded in the Commons, with Lord George wearily responding to question after question. He had already told an MP crony that he would resign if the vote against the ministry made the secretaryship a "useless place." In an early division on the matter, won by the government 164 to 44, the Secretary voted, reasonably, for himself. Before the second of the three ballots, he defended his actions in the matter once more, reminding the House that he had urged (although not ordered) Howe to complete his campaign in time to assist Burgoyne. That Howe failed him was something which could not have been anticipated many months earlier and three thousand miles distant. Yet a ditty was making the rounds about Sir William, who had launched no spring operations, and appeared not to be pressed into action by Whitehall,

> Awake, arouse, Sir Billy!
> There's forage on the plain!
> Ah, leave your little filly,
> And open the campaign.

In the early hours of the morning Charles Fox, although prepared to move censure of Lord George, realized it was futile. Angrily ripping up his draft proposal, he left the chamber. Alexander Wedderburn, who had managed the ministry's case, moved for closing the "humiliating and degrading" inquiry, which succeeded, in the emptying chamber, by fewer than forty votes. Still, motions by the opposition intended to embarrass the ministry kept both houses agitated. On grounds of need to defend the British Isles from France, Richmond moved in the Lords "that all the ships of war and land forces be immediately withdrawn from the ports and territories of the thirteen revolted provinces and disposed of in such manner as should seem best calculated for the defence of the remaining parts of the empire, in the difficult situation in which we are unfortunately placed; humbly beseeching his Majesty to take into his particular consideration the condition of England and Ireland to repel a foreign invasion." The motion would fail.

To the ministry's embarrassment, Burgoyne himself, on formal parole from his prisoner-of-war status by act of Congress, arrived in England. The press paid him more court than did the Court. On the technicality that he was still a prisoner of war, for Congress was an illegal body, he was refused admission to the royal presence. He demanded a court-martial to clear his reputation. According to the law officers of the Crown, Burgoyne on parole was "incompetent to any civil function and incapable of bearing arms in this country." He was declared "dead to all civil, as well as military purposes."

A parliamentary inquiry on the parlous state of the Royal Navy also had been ongoing. The Admiralty's case was not helped by the theatrical raids of feisty John Paul Jones and thirty-one volunteers from the *Ranger* who landed at Whitehaven, attacked two forts ineffectively guarding the harbor, and attempted to set fire to vessels anchored offshore.★ The actual damages were pinpricks, but not since 1667 had an English seaport been attacked. Suddenly ordinary citizens within reach of the sea felt vulnerable. More would be heard of Paul Jones.

In France, Franklin, who had backed Paul Jones, wrote to the Congress that his "little Cruisers [had] insulted the Coasts of the Lords of the Ocean." The Royal Navy's impotence was derided in the press. The *General Advertiser* published an "epitaph" on the unseaworthy frigates laid up at Spithead: "Here, continue, ingloriously to rot," the verses began.

An anonymous songster in the wry ballad "Paul Jones" pilloried the incompetence that made the Yankee depredations possible, and especially the greed of military suppliers, and its economic price:

Through a mad-headed war which old England will rue,
At London, at Dublin, at Edinburgh, too,
The tradesman stands still, and the merchant bemoans

★When George Roberts, once a seaman on the *Ranger,* died at seventy-three in May 1829, his obituary noted his claim that the raid was "a desperate attempt to capture Lord George Germain." His inherited country estate, Drayton, however, was unapproachably eastward across England, remote from the Irish Sea.

The losses he meets with from such as Paul Jones.
Contractors about this bold rebel harangue,
And swear, if they catch him, the traitor they'll hang;
But amongst these devourers of ten per cent loans,
Are full[y] as great robbers as any Paul Jones.
Now happy for England would fortune but sweep
At once all her treacherous foes to the deep;
For the land under burdens most bitterly groans,
To get rid of some that are worse than Paul Jones.
To each jolly heart that is Britain's true friend,
In bumpers I'd freely this toast recommend:
"May Paul be converted, the Ministry purged,
Old England be free and her Enemies scourged."

England's enemies, the balladeer charged, were within. Corruption in the Admiralty was common knowledge, and the "epitaph" in the *Advertiser* identified at least one culprit. The First Lord—John Montagu, 4th Earl of Sandwich—was notorious for his jobbery, graft, and bribes which ate into the sums for keeping warships at the ready. Still His Majesty's Order in Council would continue the expensive reenlistment bounties for sailors at five pounds for every able-bodied seaman and half that payment for "ordinary seamen" who would sign on for another year.

Sandwich's earldom and his cabinet position notwithstanding, he was known widely and parodied in political cartoons as "Jemmy Twitcher," one of Captain Macheath's crooked cronies in John Gay's popular *Beggar's Opera*. Sandwich's mistress, Martha Ray, was notorious for selling naval commissions to enhance her wardrobe. When the blatant Tory cover-up of navy corruption stretched on, the Duke of Richmond, on April 7, moved to close the proceedings. He had failed, he conceded, "through the prevalence of that power he wished to correct, in several of the objects for which he had proposed the committee." Richmond closed with a condemnation of the conduct of the ministry. "The arts of wicked men," he railed, have "left nothing that can do honour" to His Majesty's government.

The Earl of Chatham, contrary to the advice of his physician, insisted on being at the debates. He had been staunchly, even eloquently, pro-American, but now feared the ruinous cost of sweeping withdrawal. Nearly seventy, wrapped in his familiar flannel and leaning on two crutches as well as supported by one of his sons, the younger William Pitt, and Chatham's son-in-law, Lord Mahon, he hobbled to his seat in mid-afternoon, in time for his protest. In a barely audible voice, but heard nevertheless through the sudden utter silence in the House, he began, "I am old and infirm, with one foot, more than one foot, in the grave. . . . I have made an effort, almost beyond my strength, to come here this day to express my indignation at an idea which has gone forth of yielding up America. My lords, I rejoice that the grave has not yet closed upon me, that I am still alive to lift up my voice against the dismemberment of this ancient and most noble monarchy." And he scorned the likelihood that by dividing its military energies "this great kingdom" would now "fall prostrate before the House of Bourbon."

Rejecting the inevitable, he continued, "Let us at least make an effort, and, if we must fall, let us fall like men. My lords, as ill as I am, yet as long as I can crawl down to this House, and have enough strength to raise myself on my crutches, or lift my hand, I will vote against giving up the dependency of America on the sovereignty of Great Britain." Richmond began a response, and Chatham rose feebly to reply, then clutched at his chest and fell backward. Parliament adjourned, and he was carried to an adjoining chamber, then to a house in Downing Street. He died on May 11, 1778. The City of London asked that he be buried in St. Paul's, but Parliament would not permit that distinction to the outspokenly pro-rebel constituency.

Two weeks later, on May 26, General Burgoyne appeared dramatically in the House of Commons to defend himself. The House was so crowded that strangers—visitors to the Commons gallery—had to be turned away. Sir John had arranged that Robert Vyner, MP for Lincoln, would introduce a motion for a committee of inquiry into his conduct. Burgoyne, an MP himself, seconded, in the process praising the American forces (whose official hostage he remained) and complaining about being forbidden the king's presence.

Germain contested the legality of Burgoyne's being examined, but the general argued that Congress (however unrecognized) had permitted his parole to enable him to clear his character. The word "permitted," Lord George rejoined, proved Burgoyne's conditional prisoner-of-war status, but taking the general's side, Charles Fox re-

minded the House that the American Secretary himself had a conflict of interest, having been the subject of a legal inquiry—a formal
court-martial. When the combative Temple Simon Luttrell rose to
contrast Burgoyne's military conduct with the questionable gal-
lantries of other generals in America, and also with that of an unnamed but quite obvious Cabinet official who had been cashiered
for disobedience, Lord George reached angrily for his dress sword.
Though he was an old man, he raged, he would not condone "a
wanton and unprovoked rebuke" from a foolish younger one—Luttrell was thirty-nine and a veteran of duels—who was an assassin of
the most wretched character.

Clamor engulfed the House, which appeared more warlike than
anything across the Atlantic since Saratoga. In a rare gesture, the
Speaker removed his hat as a signal for members to sit down. Luttrell
fled the floor, but the Speaker ordered the doors "stopped," and summoned Luttrell back to retract his words. Not a syllable, Luttrell insisted—it was all on the record and he would go to prison rather
than retract anything. Lord North conceded that the American Secretary had been excessive, but for good reason. John Buller, MP for
East Looe and the spokesman for the Admiralty in the Commons,
rose in favor of expelling the incendiary Luttrell, but Buller also condemned the impulsive Lord George. Passion spent, the American
Secretary apologized for his conduct, and improbably called Luttrell
his "noble friend," a characterization which the stubborn Luttrell rejected indignantly. Two hours later, the confrontation finally quieted,
the motion for a committee of inquiry for Burgoyne was rejected,
144 to 96.

Two days later, on May 28, David Hartley, MP for Kingston-
upon-Hull and a supporter of conciliation, moved to ask the king to
adjourn the Parliament "in the present dangerous crisis." Burgoyne,
still at his seat, joined in the debate. The motion failed. A crisis existed nevertheless, and on the thirtieth, as Lord North sat with friends
in the King's Theatre, Haymarket, for the first night of *Il re pastore,* an
opera by Tommaso Giordani, a booted messenger arrived at his box
with a panicky report that the French had landed. They had not, and
would not, but a squadron of sail out of Brest had been seen offshore.

The opposition press continued to support Burgoyne as cynically
as it excoriated Howe, contending that recovering the colonies was

an impossibility whatever the strategies employed or the commanders on the scene. And there was a new commander in America,
Howe's deputy, Henry Clinton. On March 8, Lord George had instructed Clinton that "his Majesty's firm purpose" was to prosecute
the war "with the utmost vigour," while "keeping possession of
Philadelphia." Clinton would learn that in May, months away in
communications, Germain was changing his mind. The city was not
worth keeping. The British did not control the adjacent counties in
Pennsylvania or New Jersey, struggled to feed troops or horses from
the land, and had to import nearly everything. Passage of provisions
across the Atlantic, evading Yankee privateers (who had captured 733
vessels by February 1778), involved real risk. Sailing up the partially
pacified Delaware Bay was little safer; and despite having made landfall in the upper Chesapeake the British had no means of extending
their reach from there into Maryland or Virginia—or westward
across Pennsylvania.

A scornful look at the futility of keeping Philadelphia appeared in
Westminster Magazine on March 1 as "A Picturesque View of the State
of the Nation." From the Delaware, a beached ship suggests the stagnation of commerce. Across the river an Indian saws off the horns of
a cow; a Dutchman milks the cow (an unlikely occurrence, given its
horns); a Frenchman and a Spaniard hold bowls for milk, and a
British lion, asleep, is being befouled by a dog.

Even before the French crisis led Germain to order the evacuation
of the city and removal to New York, Clinton, as Howe's successor,
ignoring earlier orders from Whitehall to stay, had no plans to remain
where occupation had become a burden. Yet Germain conceded to
the new conciliation commissioners appointed on April 12 and
about to voyage to America that he lamented the withdrawal, "as the
army under the command of General Washington is reported to be
sickly and ill provided, whilst His Majesty's forces are in the best condition."

In Philadelphia, Howe and his entourage had indeed had a good,
if ineffective, war. In Paris, Franklin jibed that Philadelphia had
"taken" Howe. Aside from some patrols along the porous frontier between the two sides, and a few minor skirmishes, the putting down
of the rebellion from Philadelphia largely involved empty, oft-printed
proclamations "to repair to the British standard" and receive remis-

sion of political sins. Even then it was obvious that the city's self-interested elite would return to the Stars and Stripes once the red-coats were gone.

In May, as the occupiers were reluctantly preparing to leave, having dined, drank, and danced away the occupation months, Admiral Lord Howe called Ambrose Serle aside after breakfast on the twelfth "and gave me a long & full account of the Disgust w[hi]ch [the] Govt. had conceived from his Brother's Conduct, and his own Intentions to resign his Command." Serle did not need chapter and verse. Even in London the press would refer smirkingly to General Howe's amorous dalliance with "the very Cleopatra to this Antony of ours" and its effect on his generalship. Clinton would write to the American Secretary of his concern that "nature" had not given Howe "an enterprizing and active spirit, capable of pushing the advantages he may have gained in battle" against Washington's "inferior army."

Tory mothers and daughters had made life pleasant for Howe's aristocratic entourage, and ladies of the evening, including a shipload of tarts imported from England, had no difficulty finding employment, even among the poorly paid but very bored ranks. One hell-raising cavalry cornet of twenty-five, Banastre Tarleton, who would rise quickly to lieutenant colonel as one of the most cruel, and effective, of commanders in the southern colonies, was discovered in bed with the Philadelphia mistress of his senior officer, and the challenge to a duel that followed was reported in the London press. (Tarleton would claim to have butchered more men and lain with more women than anyone else in the British army, and when Horace Walpole mentioned the boast later to Richard Brinsley Sheridan, the playwright of *The Camp* and *The School for Scandal* scoffed, "Lain with? He should have said ravished. Rapes are the relaxation of murderers."

To keep a semblance of order floggings and even hangings were a routine response to looting and violence, attributed as always to Hessians. A Scottish subaltern in the Guards, Lord Dunglass, wrote to his father, the Earl of Home, from Philadelphia, "This once happy Country exhibits a scene of desolation too horrible for language to express." While services for ordinary people were neglected and running down, balls and races and plays and gambling, and the lure of

Smith's City Tavern, the Bunch of Grapes Tavern, and the Cockpit in Moore's Alley, left the army hierarchy wondering how Philadelphia had received its reputation as the dour Quaker City.

Confirmation that the withdrawal already being organized had been approved in Whitehall reached Philadelphia on May 22, four days after a farewell event for the indolent Howe that would become legendary. The "Mischianza" was produced by his debonair and efficient aide Captain (soon to be Major) John André. His production was a lavish twelve-hour extravaganza at the Wharton mansion, which boasted a tree-lined park sloping down to the Delaware. The revels included a party staffed by twenty-four black slaves in oriental dress, a regatta with music from a band on a barge, tilts and tournaments, a procession through triumphal arches, fireworks, a midnight banquet for 430 guests, and a ball. At eleven an unplanned pyrotechnical display occurred. Slipping in from Valley Forge, where Washington had again reorganized his army, Captain Allen McLane and his scouts crept through the lines and set fire to a length of felled-tree barricades shielding the merrymaking. Answering muskets cracked, and the silken-clad ladies cringed. Howe's officers assured guests that it was part of the entertainment. The feast continued.

The next day (May 19), appalled that reports of the bizarre event would inevitably reach London, Ambrose Serle deplored, "It cost a great Sum of money. Our Enemies will dwell upon the Folly & Extravagance of it with Pleasure. Every man of Sense, among ourselves, tho' not unwilling to pay a due Respect [to Howe], was ashamed of this mode of doing it." The entire litany of the "Mischianza" would be published in the English press. The *London Chronicle* described the orgy as "nauseous." *Gentleman's Magazine* described it as "dancing at a funeral, or [at] the brink of a grave."

Before relinquishing his command, Howe received anxious Philadelphia worthies whose loyalty to the Crown was now leaving them in jeopardy. The general advised them frankly, "Make your Peace with the States, who would not treat you harshly." It was "probable," he thought, that "on Account of the French War," British troops would be withdrawn from rebel America. The loyalists anticipated confiscation of their properties and ropes round their necks, and some sought to accompany the departing British to New York, and even to England. "The contest," Serle thought, prematurely, "was at an end. No man can be expected to declare for us when he cannot be assured a Fortnight's Protection."

On the twenty-fourth Sir William turned over Philadelphia to General Clinton. On the twenty-eighth Lord Howe returned to oversee the embarkation by sea. Serle left on the *Porcupine* for Plymouth. Most troops were to march overland through New Jersey toward New York City, despite orders from Whitehall to sail. There were insufficient ships for redcoats and refugees. Clinton expected to be harassed by Washington but chose to take his chances. Early on June 18, the last five thousand troops, some of them Hessians, crossed to New Jersey from Gloucester Point, two miles below Philadelphia, after which the footbridge over the marshes was destroyed. A temporary bridge over the Schuylkill constructed from cut masts was burned, as was another over two narrow channels of the Delaware at Mud Island that had been fought over fiercely in October 1777.

General Clinton was to be a peace commissioner with the unwanted triumvirate sailing from England. "I am joined in a commission," he complained to the American Secretary, "the instructions to which are very unsimilar to those I receive as commander in chief. . . . Is it expected that America in her present situation will agree to terms when the army is avowedly retiring?" His orders were personally odious. "I cannot misunderstand them, nor dare I disobey them. I am directed to evacuate Philadelphia. My fate is hard; forced to make a retreat with such an army is mortifying."

The evacuation of Philadelphia taking place just as the inexperienced young Earl of Carlisle, the ambitious Sir William Eden, and Germain's erratic old adversary George Johnstone were arriving, left them with even less bargaining clout than previous commissioners. The likely intervention of the French had also energized the British to defend the sugar islands in the Caribbean, and some of the Philadelphia garrison was ordered to lush St. Lucia. The land war in America was expected to languish. Yet it would not.

8

The French Connection
June 1778–December
1778

"We must hope that the rebels not having reaped that advantage from their new allies which they were taught to expect, and our superiority at sea being again restored, may incline many people to return to their allegiance and to live happy under the protection of Great Britain."

—*Lord George Germain to the Commissioners for quieting disorders,*
November 4, 1778

*F*ROM Valley Forge, as Washington was preparing to reoccupy Philadelphia and pursue the evacuating British, news arrived of the French treaty. "This is great, 'tis glorious news," he wrote to his brother, John Augustine Washington, "and must put the Independence of America out of all matter of dispute." He also expected a friendlier and more representative Congress in Philadelphia than the "thin Assembly" that had met in York—in future "replete with the first characters in every State." Washington speculated that the British would soon have to decide whether to hold on to the North American continent or to the "Islands"—the commercially attractive West Indies also fancied, and settled, by their European rivals.

At home, the British were masking their new worries with artificial merriment. Although it should have been clear that the war could not be won, during the early summer at Vauxhall Gardens on the Thames bankside evenings were enlivened by patriotism as well as pleasure. "Rouse, Britain's warlike throng," a martial anthem inspired by France's intrusion into the American war, was sung at twilight, to loyal cheers, by the popular Joseph Vernon. In season he performed in operas at Drury Lane, and according to local gossip had a taste for lurid sexual escapades. Other appeals inspired by the French intervention soon followed, one a recruiting song, "To arms! To arms! Britannia calls!"—reminding young men that "Britain's enemies insult her coasts." In America, to mark the king's fortieth birthday on June 4, 1778, British prisoners of war on an island in the Delaware inaccessible to Sir Henry Clinton's departing forces in Philadelphia chorused, longingly, "O'er Britannia's happy land."

The day before, Clinton had written confidently to Whitehall, "I am prepared to expect every obstruction that can be thrown in my way but I am not apprehensive of any great delay. . . . I hope to arrive at New York in about ten days after I leave this [city]." The new peace commissioners, before embarking with Admiral Howe, had urged Clinton to delay the evacuation long enough, Sir William Eden explained in futility, to lay their proposals before Congress and elicit a response "before this weak story becomes public." Angry in particular at Germain, who had only hinted at the withdrawal before they sailed, Eden added hopefully, "In the course of that delay there might be some fortunate change of men or measures in England, or of both." The commissioners' transatlantic mission, Eden predicted, would be "a mixture of ridicule, nullity, and embarrassments." His plea arrived too late to matter.

A colorful cartoon broadside with dialogue, published by Matthew Darly in the Strand before the commissioners left, anticipated the nullity of their mission. Past and future peace commissioners were caricatured in a begging posture:

ADMIRAL HOWE: We have block'd up your ports, obstructed your trade, with the hope of starving ye, & contrary to the Laws of Nature compell'd your sons to war against their Brethren.

GENERAL HOWE: We have ravaged your Lands, burnt your towns, and caus'd your captive Heroes to perish, by Cold, pestilence & famine.

EARL OF CARLISLE: We have profaned your places of Divine worship, derided your virtue and piety, and scoff'd at that spirit which has brought us thus on our knees before ye.

SIR WILLIAM EDEN: We have Ravish'd, Scalp'd, and murder'd your People, even from Tender infancy to decrepit age, although supplicating for Money.

GOVERNOR GEORGE JOHNSTONE: For all which material services, we the Commissioners from the pious and best of Sovereigns, doubt not your cordial duty & affection towards us, or willingness to submit yourselves again to remain the same [colonials], whenever we have the powers to bestow it on ye.

What the commissioners wanted materially, despite the cartoon Johnstone's ambiguity, was an agreement that would reclaim the English trade in tobacco, indigo, and other products their domestic clientele craved from America, and for which prices had shot upward with scarcity.

As transports and frigates dropped down the Delaware, the last redcoats taking the overland route to New York City marched from Philadelphia on June 18, shadowed ineffectively by Continentals. Had the French fleet arrived in time, the evacuation up the coast into the Narrows at New York harbor might have ended in catastrophe, but the outgunned armada made port by July 5, 1778, while the approaching enemy squadron was only off the Virginia capes. Clinton's supply wagons, which stretched for fifteen miles, should have been even more vulnerable through New Jersey, but to protect the front and rear of the train, Clinton divided his troops into two corps. "The slow advance of the Enemy," Washington explained lamely to Henry Laurens, president of the Congress, on July 1, "had greatly the air of design, and led me, with others, to suspect that General Clinton desirous of a general Action was endeavouring to draw us down." To avoid being lured into a trap, Washington lost his opportunity to scatter the supply train.

Avoiding possible contact with General Gage's northern forces which Clinton assumed, erroneously, to be approaching the upper Jerseys from the Hudson for a junction with Washington, the British and Hessians proceeded east, then north, often in darkness, toward Sandy Hook, to be ferried across the harbor. The mistaken intelligence also helped Clinton to evade pursuit.

What Whitehall knew was months out of date. The ministry assumed that the evacuation of Philadelphia would be entirely, and safely, by sea. Howe had brought his army there that way. What obsessed Germain was not the risk of the operation, of which he knew nothing, but to have the new proposals for conciliation considered by Congress. Paradoxically, it was a body which the previous commis-

sioners had been instructed to ignore as illegal. The implied recognition of Congress was more than Parliament and the king were willing to formally accept; yet the ministry would have been delighted to
acknowledge, belatedly now, anything but an utter break.

Although the most nominal connection of the colonies with England might have salvaged sufficient pride upon which to end the war,
Congress spurned any linkage with the mother country. Still at York,
Henry Laurens as president of the Congress wrote to the commissioners on July 17, 1778,

> The acts of the British parliament, the commission from your Sover-
> eign, and your letter, suppose the people of these states to be subjects
> of the crown of Great Britain, and are founded on an idea of depend-
> ence, which is utterly inadmissible.
>
> I am further directed to inform your Excellencies, that Congress
> are inclined to peace, notwithstanding the unjust claims from which
> this war originated, and the savage nature in which it hath been con-
> ducted; they will therefore be contented to enter upon a considera-
> tion of a treaty of peace and commerce, not inconsistent with treaties
> already subsisting, when the King of Great Britain shall demonstrate a
> sincere disposition for that purpose. The only solid proof will be an
> explicit acknowledgement of the independence of these states, or the
> withdrawing his fleets and armies.

Only in early September did that rebuff—that independence
would not be hedged by any form of words—reach London. Autho-
rizing the commissioners to return home, Lord George conceded,
"The express resolution of the American Congress not to treat without the removal of his Majesty's troops or a preliminary acknowl-
edgement of the independence of the American colonies, together
with the public reception to which they have since given to a minister from the Court of France, have put an effectual stop to all pacific
advances on our part."

Returning to the unhappy task of suppressing the rebellion,
Whitehall also learned that the opposing armies had collided briefly
at Monmouth in New Jersey on June 28, 1778, as Clinton moved
cautiously north. Musketry had given way to weather, as scorching
summer heat in the upper nineties had overwhelmed both sides.

Near Monmouth Court House the enemies met in a confused battle that was close to a draw. Clinton's redcoats and greencoats with their long baggage train managed their escape; the Americans held their ground. Washington reported burying more than 200 enemy dead; others on both sides died later of heat exhaustion. Over 600 enemy deserters, 440 of them Hessians, straggled their way back to Philadelphia. Five hundred Americans were dead or missing, of which about 100 prostrated by heatstroke later rejoined their units. Although Clinton's troops were far from unscathed, Germain reported to him that His Majesty commended "the unexampled event of conducting an army encumbered with so long a train of baggage through a very difficult country without the loss of a single carriage."

That Clinton had got through—although not as easily as the king assumed—was blamed by Washington on the always difficult Major General Charles Lee. He had allegedly disobeyed instructions and ordered a retreat "without having met any opposition." Other American battalions on Lee's flanks were thrown into confusion. Angrily dismissing Lee, Washington turned his corps over to Nathanael Greene. Lee (whose double dealing as a prisoner of war remained unknown) would claim to a court-martial that suspended him for a year that he was only resting his tired troops after dark, but Washington's hair-trigger temper had finished Lee as a commander.

The occupation and evacuation of Philadelphia now seemed no solution for either side to ending the rebellion. A nearly seditious book to be published in London about the events, with a typically elongated title, closed with Howe's notorious Mischianza, damning its futility and its decadence. *Historical Anecdotes, Civil and Military: in a Series of Letters written from America, to different Persons in England, containing Observations on the general Management of the War, and on the Conduct of our principal Commanders in the revolted Colonies,* claimed acerbically that one could not account for the many "blunders" committed "on any other principle but strength of skull."

Although Pennsylvania and most of New Jersey were lost, as well as much of New York other than the city and environs, hawks in London could not change their thinking. They assumed another year's campaigning much like the last. A dispatch on July 30 claimed that the rebel government was in a bad way financially. (The colonies were never otherwise.) "America owes, at this moment, thirty millions [in pounds], and five millions have been voted for the service of the current year; so that the debts of America already amount to near as much as all the lands there would sell for." To make the rebel population further sick of war, the coast was to be ravaged; as more easy pickings, the southern states, assumed to harbor loyalists, were to be invaded; and France was to be distracted from assistance to the provinces by threatening her most economically advantageous Caribbean islands. As each province returned to the king's allegiance, loyal delegates would be named to a royalist rival Congress. Whitehall's strategy seemed unassailable only to itself.

By the time such instructions were dispatched, French admiral the Comte d'Estaing, who had sailed from Toulon on April 13 with eleven ships of the line provisioned, British spies reported, for nine months at sea, had appeared menacingly off Sandy Hook on July 11. Hardly back in New York City, Clinton's more than twenty thousand troops seemed bottled up. Yet it was an age of sail, dependent on winds and tides and depth. D'Estaing lingered off the harbor sandbar, reluctant to chance running his seventy-four-gun deep-draft frigates aground. Then, after wallowing indecisively for eleven days, he withdrew toward Rhode Island.

To spur naval preparations, King George had visited Vice Admiral John Byron's fleet at Portsmouth, which had been awaiting sightings to determine d'Estaing's direction. When the fleet of "Foul Weather Jack" materialized off New York on July 30, and the watchful Washington had still not attacked from across the harbor—no easy operation, and never intended—Clinton seemed safe. Slipping out the packet *Grantham,* he sent the news of the double reprieve—from the Americans and then the French—to England. Fearing invasion themselves, His Majesty's subjects at home were more concerned about the English Channel than remote American waters. Redcoat reinforcements would be token, and few.

Again in the formal third-person traditionally used toward royalty, North explained to the king that he was unequal to the war. The Cabinet needed someone "capable of leading, of discerning between opinions, of deciding quickly and confidently, and of connecting all the operations of government, that this nation might act uniformly, and with force. Lord North is not such a man." On July 2, 1779, the king, unaware yet of the favorable news from New York, wrote back,

"No man has a right to talk of leaving me at this hour." North remained.

As the conflict with the colonies was becoming an international war, the widowed American Secretary's domestic troubles took on an unanticipated note of horror. The *Public Ledger* on July 22, 1778, printed a report "respecting Lady George Germain having burst her coffin & of her being reburied. Steps were taken to hush up this catastrophe. The state of mind in which Lord George finds himself whenever that unhappy subject of Lady George's death is brought back to his mind makes Mr. de G[rey, the undersecretary*] anxious to prevent his Lordship from seeing it in any other paper." Thomas De Grey intervened with the opposition editor John Almon, publisher of the *Parliamentary Register,* to use his influence to keep the tasteless story of what seemed a botched embalming from appearing in other papers.

Among the Secretary's public problems was the lingering and embarrassing presence of Sir John Burgoyne, who still claimed a hearing despite the parliamentary recess. Congress had declined to honor, on petty obfuscations, General Gates's "Convention" with Burgoyne permitting his troops to return across the Atlantic if they were not to be employed further against America. With France in the war, however, they could be used lawfully against the new American ally— something the French would rightly regard as an unfriendly act. On June 5, after Burgoyne had been in England only a few weeks, Lord Barrington, the Secretary at War, a lesser figure than Germain and largely assigned administrative authority, wrote coolly to Sir John, attempting to get rid of him, "The King, judging your presence material to the troops detained prisoners under the Convention of Saratoga, and finding in a letter of yours to Sir William Howe, dated April 9, 1778 that 'you trust a short time at Bath will enable you to return to America,' his Majesty is pleased to order that you shall repair to Boston as soon as you have tried the Bath waters, in the manner you propose."

Burgoyne's parole had come from the enemy, not the king, but his legal status in England had been questioned, even his taking up his seat in the Commons to which he had been duly elected. Sir John

*Later Lord Walsingham.

chose to defy the order by claiming to Barrington that his doctor had ordered "repose, regimen of diet and repeated visits to Bath."The Secretary at War could only repeat lamely that it was the king's pleasure "that you return as soon as you can, without risk of material injury to your health." Burgoyne's doctor—if he really had one—had effectively vetoed a royal command and left the general free to vindicate his honor and harass the embattled ministry.

Bath was popular not only for its salubrious waters but for its gambling clubs. One could not be immersed indefinitely. And Charles Fox, formerly a political enemy but a patron of the card tables, wrote sympathetically to the embattled Burgoyne in gaming idiom, "At whist, as you very well know, it is often right in a desperate case to play upon a supposition of your partner's having a good hand, though there might be the strongest symptoms of the contrary; because if he has not, the game is lost. Just so, I think of the present state of affairs. It is the duty of those who mean to act upon public motives to suppose many things which they cannot believe."

While His Majesty snubbed Burgoyne General Howe returned to England to a polite royal reception, and on July 2, as the king was renewing his confidence in North, Howe was received at Kew Palace. Since Sir William had sailed from Philadelphia on May 24, he could report nothing of the evacuation from Philadelphia other than that it was being prepared as he weighed anchor. He would have his inconclusive but embarrassing hearing in Parliament, after which it seemed that his military career was over, but promotions never required success. Eventually he secured new commands and rose to full general.

Writing to Howe's successor with no hope of a new campaigning season in 1778, Lord George urged Clinton to keep "the coasts of the enemy constantly alarmed. . . . At least it would prevent their sending out that swarm of privateers, the success of which has enabled and encouraged the rebels to persist in their revolt."

More serious nautical challenges loomed: Neither Britain nor France had issued a formal declaration of war, but war existed, at least at sea. Finally, on July 10, 1778, a letter from Louis XVI to the duc de Penthievre that was released to the press referred to repeated insults "to my flag" by ships belonging to "the King of England," and called for appropriate responses. To his Privy Council on July 20, George III alleged "many injuries and acts of hostility"on the part of the

French. As Walpole would write to Horace Mann on August 4, "We are in the oddest situation that can be; at war in fact, but managed like a controversy in divinity."

France was slow to play an active role beyond offering money and munitions. The French fleet seemed to be exploring for targets of opportunity, but cautious about exploiting them. Britain had to hope that a policy of supporting the overthrow of a monarchy would continue to seem perverse to sovereigns. When Emperor Joseph II of Austria visited Paris incognito as "Count Falkenstein," and Louis XVI asked for his view of the American insurgents, the emperor answered that he had none: "It is my profession to be a royalist."

Reconciling that with French aspirations in Europe and beyond required a return to the ideas of the late duc de Choiseul, foreign minister before Charles Gravier de Vergennes. In 1770, Choiseul had written a confidential memorandum, "Means for France to employ to reduce England to the position it ought to occupy in the Balance of Europe." American independence was crucial, he predicted, to prevent England's further monopoly of transatlantic trade, to weaken its financial position, to tie up its manpower and seapower in attempting to put America down, and to make more precarious England's hold over its colonies, including the sugar islands in the West Indies. The "balance of Europe" in the French view required gambling upon America.

Although the perennial enemy, France, was just across the Channel, uneasy Ireland was less watched, and a fleet of desperately needed victuallers for Clinton's garrison, en route from Cork, was able to bypass the French, who were sailing on another failed expedition, this time to Newport. Under orders from Whitehall, Clinton was to send troops to defend Canada from the French, if needed, and troops to take—or defend—more of the "Saints" in the Caribbean, and, if necessary, abandon New York for Halifax. Germain's thinking did not seem a recipe for winning, and by fast packet Clinton complained to his cousin, the well-connected Duke of Newcastle, "You have but one army [in America]; 'tis a good one. It has never been affronted. You may want it. You ought to have kept it together, nursed it, cherished it. By the present arrangement I wish one half of it may not be under ground [in the disease-ridden West Indies] by Christmas and the rest reduced to an ignominious flight to avoid still greater disgrace." He hoped that Newcastle would employ such strong language on Lord George as Clinton by protocol could not exercise himself.

The Rhode Island affair in early August was no victory for either fleet, won only by the winds. Violent Atlantic gales damaged and dispersed ships on both sides, canceling the French advantage in heavy guns. To the chagrin of the Americans, the ineffective d'Estaing sailed to Boston for refitting, and went on to the Caribbean. A wry song marked the Yankee frustration, beginning,

> As Jonathan so much desired
> To shine in martial glory,
> D'Estaing with politesse retired
> To leave him all the glory.

The French connection was proving of little use to "Brother Jonathan" (the original of "Uncle Sam"), except for diverting critical English resources from putting down the rebellion. That it could go on indefinitely was the subject of a mock futuristic cartoon broadside issued by John Williams, a bookseller with premises "near the Mitre Tavern in Fleet Street." In "The Royal George's Cruise in the year 2777 with the Short-sighted Cookswain at the Helm . . . and the Devil at the Lead," the English ship of state is steered by George III as the vessel is about to be swamped by "the Breakers of America." Nothing has changed in a thousand years. "I cannot see twice the length of my nose," confesses the king in balloon dialogue. There is no need to worry, says one crewman to another. "My Lord has provided cork jackets for all of his Party as soon as this damned Ship is wrecked."

Restricted to New York, the peace commissioners hung on disconsolately, issued a futile appeal over the heads of Congress, then, in November, sailed for home, accompanied by Earl Cornwallis, who seemed almost a commuter across the Atlantic. Clinton sent a letter with him to Germain explaining how valuable Cornwallis's knowledge would be to the ministry. All that Whitehall would learn was that while the land war was going nowhere, the French had again failed at sea.

As d'Estaing's Rhode Island expedition, still unknown in London, was falling apart to English advantage, another confrontation with the French was materializing closer to home. The ministry had determined to maintain its presence in the upper colonies, at Newport and New York, to initiate another in the southern colonies, and to put its resources into the sugar islands in the Caribbean and the threatened Channel coast. French frigates had been reconnoitering the British home fleet, commanded by Admiral Lord Augustus Keppel. A pillar of the pro-American opposition in Parliament, he nonetheless prepared to do battle with the detested French. Anti-French feeling had compartmentalized the war.

"Every body talks of an invasion," a marine officer wrote late in June, "every body's mind is fixed on Keppel's fleet." Like all commanders, however, Lord Augustus thought he was inadequately reinforced for his mission. "I don't wonder at the alarm of the merchants, and wishing the fleet [were] at sea," he wrote rather acidly to the Earl of Sandwich on July 2 from a seaport town on the Isle of Wight. "[B]ut when they do that [complaining] they should hope also that it is in [adequate] force for the services required of it. The King's councils have determined twenty-four ships' force sufficient. I will sail when I am joined by that addition of ships." He got his ships.

On July 26, cruising the Atlantic approaches to the Channel, and skirting the Bay of Biscay sixty-six miles west of what the English called Ushant (the Isle d'Ouessant), Keppel and his second-in-command, Sir Hugh Palliser, encountered the French under the Comte d'Orvilliers. Each fleet had thirty ships of the line. Fierce cannon fire boomed, with heavy damage and casualties suffered by both sides, after which the fleets withdrew to lick their wounds.

Wars with the French seemed continuing and perpetual, and inevitably conducted mostly by sea. Soon after, with the striking French successes in flight by balloon, a cartoon would depict anticipations of aerial warfare in nautical terms. "The Battle of the Balloons" imagined two futuristic English balloons fighting two French craft, each with sails and signal flags, and open boats hanging from the air bags. Three men per boat—a navigator, musketeer, and cannoneer—do battle. According to the caption,

Behold an odd fight, two odd nations between,
Such odd fighting as this was never seen,
But such fights will be common . . .
In the year of one thousand eight hundred and odd.

When accounts of Ushant reached the newspapers, the confrontation at first was seen as a victory, and a hawkish printer in High Holborn published a broadside, "Monsieur sneaking Gallantly into Brest's
sculking Hole after receiving a preliminary Salutation of British Jack
Tar." A Frenchman with a frigate for headgear is being whipped into
his harbor by a sailor brandishing a cat-o'-nine-tails. Further details
arrived in London, and the "victory" seemed at best a draw. Sir Hugh
Palliser, on land a spokesman for the Lord Sandwich's Admiralty in
the Commons, seemed accused of much the same reluctance to join
battle (by failing to respond to a signal) as charged to Lord George
years before. "Mindenian finesse," Horace Walpole called it. Although
Keppel distanced himself from the affair, Palliser responded angrily
by charging his chief with failing to press home an initial advantage.
The *Chronicle* reported falsely that the admirals had fought a duel,
and the *Public Advertiser* claimed that one combatant had been
wounded. In the remarkably hot late summer the battle of words became openly political and heated. The prowar Palliser was close to
Sandwich, while Keppel, a sympathizer with the colonists, was
smeared—allegedly with the king's encouragement—as lacking in
desire to win against the new ally of the Americans.

Almost certainly encouraged by Sandwich, Palliser filed a charge
of misconduct and neglect of duty against Keppel on December 9,
1778. Formal notice to appear before a court-martial came the next
day. Both sides mobilized their adherents.

At midnight, as the tenth became the eleventh, George Rogers,
Keppel's secretary, arrived at the Grosvenor Square town house of the
Marquis of Rockingham, leader of the opposition in Lords, carrying
a letter describing the five articles of the charges. They talked until
two; then Rockingham dismissed Rogers and scratched out a brief
note to Edmund Burke that the matter would immediately come up
in Parliament. A messenger awakened Burke with the news. "What
diabolicall villainy," Rockingham wrote. "[D]o come up as early as
you can in the morning."

In the Commons that afternoon, Admiral Palliser—like Keppel,
also an MP—elucidated his charges. Tories were pleased with the discrediting of an opposition stalwart. Whigs realized what the divisive-
ness would do to the navy. Keppel responded to the House,
according to his son, Thomas, "like a man inspired."

The Duke of Richmond, Keppel's influential Whig friend, was lord lieutenant and colonel of the Sussex militia. Because the Channel coast was threatened, the role, usually little more than honorific, had vaulted Richmond into increased prominence. A critic of the war with America, he was yet another of the opposition whose loyalties were split by historic hostility to France. To the embarrassment of the government, Richmond had declared in the House of Lords on April 7 that the loss of ground forces in America "by death, desertion or otherwise" was already—and his figures were obviously not up to date—19,381, in addition to 5,336 prisoners of war. (The term "desertion" was an especially loaded one.) Lord Amherst, the army commander-in-chief, although another, but far more subdued, opponent of the American war, found himself, to his surprise, attacked by the duke for government unpreparedness to defend against France. (It was crucial for the pro-American leadership to remain publicly anti-French.) "Lord Amherst is asleep, or dares not act," Richmond had charged unreasonably in October, "& it looks as if the same Man who has lost 13 provinces intends by equal bad management to risk the Loss of 3 Kingdoms." Most peers in attendance understood that it was indirectly an attack on the American Secretary.

Currying favor with the ministry by again suggesting what it wanted to hear, New York governor William Tryon wrote in a self-serving message that Germain had received in mid-October, "Were I at this crisis to dare to give an opinion on public affairs, it would be that British forces on the continent . . . were never in so good a condition as at present to reconcile America to the dependency on Great Britain, the army being as it were united and in possession of the four islands, New York, Long Island, Staten Island and Rhode Island (the centre of the American coast), from whence it might make such vigorous and hostile depredations . . . as would oblige Americans to call aloud for the settlement offered by the King's commissioners."

Two weeks later, the frustrated negotiators themselves wrote to Lord George from New York (collectively Tryon's first three islands) that the authority of His Majesty's forces in America was so "greatly impaired" that it was hopeless to remain. Their orders home were en route. To justify their mission—as they were being paid quite handsomely—the commissioners issued a final public proclamation on October 3, 1778, offering to remove all the grievances which had stirred the rebellion and promising pardons for treasons committed if the colonies returned to the royal fold. However, if a colony "mortgages herself and her resources to our enemies"—clearly, France—". . . Britain may by every means in her power destroy or render useless a connexion contrived for her ruin." Few colonists were listening.

Privately, Eden wrote home that stubborn ignorance of America among the leadership in London doomed any efforts at reconciliation. To his brother in England he deplored "that our Rulers instead of making the [Grand] Tour of Europe did not finish their education round the Coast and Rivers of the Western Side of the Atlantic." He knew "little more of it than I saw in coming 150 miles up the Delaware," but he was full of regrets for wasted opportunities." Repeating much of what he had unburdened to Alexander Wedderburn, the attorney general, he wrote, with full realization that his words would go the rounds of Whitehall, "It is impossible to see what I can see of this Magnificent Country and not go nearly mad at the long Train of Misconducts and Mistakes by which we have lost it." Walpole predicted gloomily, although he supported American independence, "We shall be reduced to a miserable little island, and from a mighty empire sink into as insignificant a country as Denmark or Sardinia!"

Seeing a land war going stagnant on both sides, the English press reflected the wishful thinking that the populous and comfortable empire, although deprived temporarily of its American holdings, could outlast the impoverished and disunited states and force them to yield. To the imminently departing commissioners, Germain, who knew nothing of Eden's confessions already on a packet crossing the Atlantic, remained stubbornly buoyant. "We must hope," he wrote on November 4, "that the rebels not having reaped that advantage from their new allies which they were taught to expect, and our superiority at sea being again restored, may incline many people to return to their allegiance and to live happy under the protection of Great Britain."

From the standpoint of William Franklin, Ben's royalist son, despite the failures of the French, no American strategy was working for the English. Exchanged after more than two years of captivity in Connecticut, the former colonial governor of New Jersey wrote lengthily

and bitterly to Germain on November 10, 1778, from New York that
during his confinement in Litchfield prison he was even denied parole to visit his dying wife. Yet he remained optimistic about suppressing the rebellion. Through rose-tinted spectacles similar to those
worn by Lord George, Franklin predicted that royalism needed only
one grand and visible defeat of Washington to evoke "great clamour
for peace in spite of all the arts and endeavours of the Congress to
prevent it." He saw Washington's army (which he perceived as a
small, unstable entity, although most colonies seemed under widespread Continental control) as better disciplined and clothed than
ever before, but chronically weakened by short terms of enlistment.
And to Lord George's likely delight he concurred with Whitehall's
cost-conscious strategy: "Were the principal ports blocked up . . . and
[our] privateering encouraged, their trade would soon be destroyed,
without which they cannot carry on the war."

Another uninvited adviser to the American Secretary was Manhattan printer and publisher James Rivington, recently back from a
business trip to England and eager to curry further favor through
Germain's busy aide, playwright Richard Cumberland. Since General
Howe was now in disfavor, Rivington safely rubbished him for
"abandoning the Hudson and . . . sacrificing the northern army."
Then turning his attention obsequiously to Lord George, he described Cumberland's chief as "the most elegant nobleman in the
British realm." Although Rivington closed with more honesty than
he intended by modestly deprecating his letter as "tedious trumpery,"
in his postscript came the real reason for the length of his appeal. He
wanted clearance to import ten tons of "printing letter and printing
paper" promised to him in England for propagandizing Americans
through his newspaper. "His Majesty has honoured me with a commission under the royal sign manual to be his printer and the Lords
of the Treasury have given me an establishment for my salary, but
alas! It is to be paid out of the quitrents in this country so that there
is no fund for the purpose and my salary is purely nominal." There
were no quitrents—charges on estates—in chaotically administered
New York. Rivington hoped humbly that he may be "thought worthy of some further indulgences by my ever gracious and noble
benefactor Lord George Germain." Shrewdly playing both sides,
Rivington was also a spy for Washington.

Another royal governor, restricted to a small wedge of New York, had a further bargain suggestion for the Secretary. The irrepressible Governor Tryon suggested a device that had never been successful in wars past or present—"That a proclamation from the Crown or Parliament issue with a reward of one thousand pounds for every member of the General Congress and civil governors, [and] usurpers, that shall be delivered up to the King's troops." Lord George would ignore it.

Promising news, however, did emerge from America. General Clinton reported that in the near suspension of ground hostilities (both sides had their eyes on the French), he could send some troops to the West Indies, and others to once Spanish Florida, never part of the American colonial structure. He had tested the strategic situation by skirmishes into northern New Jersey to secure fodder and provisions, and "General Washington did not show the least disposition to assemble his army, and the militia kept at a distance."

Less happy news came from the members of the peace commission, who had returned late in November. Only one of the three, the dueling prone ex-governor George Johnstone, MP for Appleby, read anything favorable in events. Johnstone called on Edmund Burke in London just before the reconvening of Parliament on November 26. Hopefully, he told Burke, there was "very ill blood" and "divisions" among the Americans, despite the failure of the Howes to exploit opportunities. Johnstone planned to attack both brothers in the Commons, Burke wrote to his son Richard. "The whole talk of the Town is about him. . . . He is to animate the House to the Continuance of the War. He is also to attack the Ministry—and to promise success under more effective Generals, and more able Ministers. . . . It is certain, that he loudly condemns every thing done in the Military and Naval Lines both in America and Europe."

Until his seductive letter to Robert Morris, financier of the rebellion, was widely published to Johnstone's embarrassment, it was little known in England that he had been accused by American lawyer Joseph Reed of attempting to bribe his way into Congress's acceptance of the conciliation plan. After a devious opening declaring fulsomely that the men who conducted the affairs of America could never be influenced by improper motives, Johnstone got to his motive—that in "all such transactions, there is risque; and I think that

whoever ventures [accommodation] should be secured. . . . Honour
and emolument should naturally follow the fortune of those who
have steered the vessel in the storm, and brought her safely to port,
[and] that Washington and the President [of Congress] have a right to
every favour that grateful nations can bestow, if they could once
more unite our interests, and spare [us] the miseries and devastations
of war."

According to Reed, Johnstone suggested gifts of ten thousand
pounds, together with any offices in the colonies in the gift of His
Majesty. As proposed conduit of the offer, Reed replied scornfully
that he was "not worth purchasing; but such as he was, the King of
Great Britain was not rich enough to do it." In a declaration on August 11, Congress spurned the bribe and closed off any further deliberation as "incompatible with the honour of Congress." The door on
reconciliation by that route seemed closed.

Hoping to win over the opposition to his contention that only increased military pressure could bring the Americans to compromise,
Johnstone had first gone to Brighthelmstone, the country estate of
the Duke of Richmond, attempting to sway him before Parliament
reassembled in late November. "Next Thursday," Burke wrote, "we
are to open Business; but what that Business is to be; whether we are
to send more Troops to America or not; or what steps are to be taken
in any matter no one pretends to guess. As to the people, they are
pretty much as usual. All is wrapt up in [the] Clouds."

The day before Parliament resumed a satirical pamphlet appeared,
pretending to be a summary of what chieftains in the Lords and the
Commons would say about the rebellion, and catching their tone.
Deliberately not sparing the Court party in order to suggest a sort of
balance, "Anticipation" had been written by Richard Tickell, a friend
of Lord North's principal secretary. Much talked about, it had little
impact on events. The majority could work its will. Welbore Ellis,
MP, gibed, "It is well written, but I perceive the author takes me for
a dull fellow." At a shilling and sixpence was a more mordant production, "America Lost. A Poem of Condolence. Addressed to Britannia." And even more troublesome was a play with music, *Second
Thought is Best,* by John Hough, a lawyer at the Inner Temple, which
had to be performed at Drury Lane without its strongest song, which
had been blue-penciled by the Lord Chamberlain, who had the

power to license (or reject) productions and mandate excisions on grounds of blasphemy, sedition, or moral offense. Lost to perform-ance (but not to publication) was a ballad beginning,

> The nation is in ruin, Sir,
> The nation is in ruin, Sir;
> I rave! I swear! Aghast I stare;
> To see such mischief brewing, Sir.

The king's formal Address on November 26, 1778, reopening both Houses railed against the "violation of the faith of treaties" by France and its "clandestine supply of arms and other aids to my revolted subjects in North America." The provocative French had abetted the failure of conciliation. The opposition led in the Lords by Lord Rockingham used the opening to take exception to the departure proclamation of October 3 by the frustrated peace commissioners, which threatened desolation of America for its intransigence in "mortgaging herself, and her resources, to our enemies." It was "in-consistent with the humanity and generous courage," Rockingham claimed, "which, at all times, have distinguished the British nation." On December 4, the brothers Howe, both now back from the war and in their seats in the House, condemned the "cruelty" in the proclamation, which vowed to make the colonies useless as "an ac-cretion to France," and blamed military unsuccess on "the head of the American Department." Neither victory nor peace was possible, Sir William Howe declared, as long as the noble lord held office.

Germain seemed astonished by the charge, and rose to avow in all honesty that he was not in "sole management of the war," and indeed was only a humble servant of the Crown. Pressure on Lord North to replace him with someone less hard-line had increased through 1778, but the king saw his American Secretary as the only Minister whose tough views on the colonies paralleled his own. North had to keep him. Germain had to stay. The protest in the Commons died, 209 to 122. On December 7 a similar motion in the Lords, declaring "the displeasure of this House" about the commissioners' retaliatory manifesto, was rejected 71 to 37.

In the Commons, Burke cautiously at first declined to speak. When he did, on December 4, he altered his expected strategy to suggest that since the outcome of the war with America was irreversible, the British should swallow their pride and fight only the French. Others tried out similar ideas. A pamphlet by William Pulteney, MP for Shrewsbury, "Thoughts on the Present State of Affairs with America, and the Means of Conciliatio," suggested making peace proposals so attractive that Congress would break off its French connection and agree to a federal union with Britain. The *Public Ledger's* "How best to till, or sow the fertile field," in "The Georgi-con, or The First Georgic of Virgil, Imitated," also recommended uniting the kingdom and the colonies against France by giving some vague independence—but not freedom—to America, a subtle distinction unlikely to persuade a Congress that had rejected every mode of linkage.

It was the fashion for generals returned from America to blame London rather than their own deficiencies. On December 14, before the Commons recessed for Christmas, Sir John Burgoyne, technically still on leave from his status as prisoner of war, expressed indignation that excessive administration tied the hands of officers, and criticized recommendations that any further troops be sent to America, "when it is impossible to terminate the war while the present American Secretary had the direction of it."

Lord George again rose in self-defense. He had not lost Saratoga. "The very moment the House wished him to retire," he was reported to say, "he was ready to resign, and he would certainly do so if the army now in America should be ordered to abandon it."

A contrary note to Burgoyne was sounded in the *Gloucester Journal* on December 21, quoting a two-months'-old letter from New York. "You may rely on it," reported the obdurate loyalist, "that the rebellion is much weaker than it was this time twelve month; and nothing but a little wisdom in planning her schemes, on the part of Great Britain and vigour in their execution is wanting to crush it." Then followed a litany of American weaknesses. "The French alliance is greatly disliked by many of the violent rebels. . . . Taxation is now grievously felt. The credit of the Congress money is irretrievably sunk. . . . Men can scarcely be prevailed upon to take up arms, either by compulsion or for money. Washington has not 10,000 men, and these are divided into different parties. . . . What dependence there is to be placed in these [militias], and what [futile] resistance they make to regular [British] troops, repeated experience has shown." Much of what the writer claimed was true, yet to the exasperation of White-hall, the colonies hung on.

From his headquarters at Middlebrook, New Jersey, in a letter dated only "December," Washington wrote to fellow Virginian Benjamin Harrison, a delegate to Congress, ostensibly about his possession, as a veteran of the Seven Years' War, of a land grant in the "back Country" dating to 1763. That he could even think about his "5000 Acres of Land in my own right" suggested that he saw an end to the war, but if so he was unusually hopeful. "I can assign but two causes for the enemy[']s continuance among us," he judged, "and these balance so equally in my Mind, that I scarce know which of the two preponderates. The one is, that they are waiting for the ultimate determination of Parliament; the other, that of our distresses; by which I know the Commissioners went home not a little buoyed up; and sorry I am to add, not without cause." He saw, as he would always remind the Congress, the need for more unity as a nation than the selfish separateness of the states evidenced both at home and abroad. "I think our political system," he explained almost as might Dr. Franklin, "may, be compared to the mechanism of a Clock; and that our conduct should derive a lesson from it for it answers no good purpose to keep the smaller Wheels in order if the greater one which is the support and prime mover of the whole is neglected."

Britain also faced a crisis of confidence as the impending court-martial proceedings against Keppel opened increasing divisions, becoming more worrisome to many than the American war. Further, unknown at home, even yet to the American Secretary, as General Clinton's urgent plea of December 15 was still at sea, the army in New York, now greatly augmented by the Philadelphia evacuees, had more problems than anyone knew. Clinton prefaced his message by calling the "situation" an "embarrassment."

"Your lordship," the general began with some dramatic exaggeration, "will be startled when I inform you that this army has but a fortnight's flour left. I hear no accounts that can give me hopes that supplies are on the coasts and the north-west winds which blow violently and almost incessably at this season make the arrival of any fleet in this port very precarious indeed. Our meat [rations] with the assistance of cattle purchased here will last about forty days beyond Xmas, and a bread composed of pease, Indian corn and oatmeal, can be furnished for the same time. After that I do not know how we shall subsist. The military chest, my lord, is empty."

Since the turnaround for communications was three months or more, and the gathering and loading of provisions would add weeks at best to that, Clinton's appeal was beyond immediate fulfilment. His army would have to live off the land. The plea may also have been strategic—to anticipate withdrawals or casualties taken in foraging or punitive raids. It may also have been a covert appeal for more of everything denied to him since he acquired his command, and since France had distracted Whitehall. He could not even "quit this place," he contended. He didn't have the transport capacity. He wasn't complaining, he explained—only lamenting his situation. He wanted nothing militarily significant to be expected of him, "circumstanced as I am."

The public which purchased broadside cartoons at stationers or in the streets did not need access to Clinton's confidential message to sustain its anxieties. One in mezzotint showed the familiar face of Dr. Franklin looking up from the case of an opened pocket watch. His homespun look had made him famous in London before the war, and in Paris his avuncular likeness appeared everywhere objects were sold—on medallions and lids of snuffboxes, and in prints. The mezzotint from Fleet Street featured a moral lesson in clock metaphor alluding to his treaty with France that had upset British calculations:

> Had but our nation mov'd like this great man
> With widsom's wheel to regulate its plan,
> Not urg'd by rancor, nor disturb'd by rage,
> But guided by the prudence of this Sage;
> The spring of State had still been strong and tight,
> Its chain of Friendship, lasting, pure and bright,
> Our hand of time had pointed still at noon,
> And sable night had not approach'd so soon.

Equally critical, "An Extraordinary Gazette or the Disappointed Politicians" showed ministers in a coffee house doing what such establishments existed for—smoking, drinking, and reading the latest papers. On the wall behind them were a 1762 map of North America displaying broad British accessions at the expense of France and Spain—and a 1778 map of America. Only a fragment of America in the north remained British, and it was crawling with writhing serpents.

9

The War on Trial
January 1779–June 1779

"How stand the interests of the nation, and the characters of individuals, while our Commanders reserve their activity for attacks, justifications, and recriminations at home?"

—*Monthly Review, April 1781*

"War is like other gaming; when one is out of luck, it is wise to leave off."

—*Horace Walpole to George Selwyn, MP, October 4, 1779*

WHEN news from London arrived circuitously at Valley Forge, where Washington awaited Howe's evacuation from Philadelphia, that a new conciliation commission was being appointed, he had renewed hopes for peace. It was then May 1778, and the general, unusually elated, wrote to John Augustine Washington, "I am mistaken if we are not verging fast to one of the most important periods that America ever saw." His information—it would be mistaken—was that the royal commissioners would be Lord Amherst, who deplored the war; Lieutenant General James Murray, who had also battled the French in America, and was then governor of Minorca; and Lord Augustus Keppel, reputedly a sympathizer with the aspirations of the colonies. It was too good to be true.

In London, although the hawks were still in control, they needed a scapegoat. A pillar of the Whig establishment, Vice Admiral Lord Augustus Keppel through 1778 was a target for pro-war Tories who saw him as insufficiently belligerent—unwilling (like the unassailable Amherst) to cross the Atlantic and put down rebel Americans. In early 1779, Keppel's court-martial obsessed England. The admiral was the grandson of Arnold Joost van Keppel, who had accompanied

William of Orange from Holland in 1688 and was created Earl of Albemarle. Despite his impeccable family connections, after the indecisive encounter with the French off Ushant he became the target of the despised Earl of Sandwich, First Lord of the Admiralty.

Exchanges of charges from both sides about the conduct of the war continued to agitate the House of Commons. The business of the Commons was regularly disturbed by embarrassed generals and admirals who were using the chamber to regain honor lost on the battlefields and in the boudoirs of America. Three years of futility on land and sea had taken its toll of statesmanly nerves, and some members saw incapacity and negligence everywhere they turned, not excluding Whitehall and St. James's Palace. Opposition politicians demanded that Palliser, Keppel's deputy and a toady of Lord Sandwich, be dismissed for his conduct against the French. Palliser countered that Keppel should be court-martialed for mishandling the fleet at Ushant. The government then found itself under attack for mishandling the war.

To stifle public controversy, the Admiralty had filed charges against Keppel. A career was to be ruined, and if it were Keppel's he could be executed on the deck of his own flagship—the fate in 1757 of the maligned Admiral John Byng after his failure against the French off Minorca.

The extreme penalty was rare indeed for serving officers blue of blood and elevated in rank. Public hangings of lesser men and women were the most dramatic free entertainment available to ordinary folk, and a hangman made additional money by selling anything the victim owned or wore as souvenirs. On one ordinary day at the Old Bailey—the central criminal court in London—nine convicts were sentenced to death—for stealing silverplate, for highway robbery, for robbing a bank, for theft of a letter from the mails, for stealing a mare, and for murder. Two were condemned for counterfeiting, and another two for shoplifting. Four were women.

On the first day of 1779, as wintry winds raged down the Thames, much of the showplace Royal Hospital at Greenwich, a symbol of the Navy, was destroyed by fire. It seemed like an omen. "If storms have any meaning," Horace Walpole wrote to Lady Ossory from Strawberry Hill, where a skylight was demolished by a falling tree, "I believe they do not come to give hints to individuals, but to nations."

On January 7 the court-martial of Admiral Keppel opened at the Portsmouth naval base, where Byng had been shot after his conviction. Although the arraignment outwardly had nothing to do with America, other than that the French had allied with the colonists, the American war, and the largely Whig opposition to it (parties had not yet formalized), was implicitly on trial.

The press took sides, with the rebel colonies often as subtext. As scatology was the norm in political broadsides sold in the streets, one cartoon, "State of the Nation," showed Lords North, Sandwich, and Mansfield in consultation on adjoining privies, with North's toilet paper decorated with jews' harps* and labeled sixty thousand pounds, alleging his means of financing the war. Sandwich is tearing apart a British naval ensign for his own lavatory needs. "Ministerial Purgations, or State Gripings," in six panels, again showed a state council in which ministers perched on latrines—each a bench with a hole in the seat. Typically, North, Germain (his broken sword hanging on the wall behind him), and Sandwich were in each such attack, which here included their moans about the state of the nation, with the caption below,

Oh, who must Pity the case of Great Britain,
When its Ministers purge thus,—that must be beshitten.

Relatedly more directly to the Keppel trial was "Britannia and Her Daughter," another recurrent motif, in which a nubile Miss North America is chided for encouraging advances from France and Spain:

Britannia beheld her with tears in her eyes.
O' Daughter return to your duty she cries.
But she replies no I'm a Woman full grown,
And long for to keep a good House of my own.
If you'd used me kind when I was in your power,
I then had lived with you at this very hour.
But now on my Lovers so much do I doat,
That we're Arm'd and I'll help 'em to cut your old throat.

*a lyre-shaped musical device akin to a mouth-organ

Another more nautical but progovernment cartoon showed D'Orvilliers and Keppel, backsides opposite, bombarding each other with excrement. "What a Smack and what a Stink!" the caption read, "& yet neither prevails. For how can it be? When both they turn their tails." In a William Humphreys broadside titled "Who's at Fault? A View of Ushant," Keppel was shown as a head without a body, his legs attached to his shoulders. In the background are ships' masts seen through clouds. According to the caption, "The Anatomists will have it that it can have no Heart, having no Body—but the Naturalists think it has a Heart, [but] it must lay in its breeches." Another attack on Keppel, "Britannia's Assassination," was a broadside in which Keppel turns his back on Lady Britannia, hauls down his flag from its staff, and explains, lamely,

> He that Fights & runs away
> May live to fight another day.

Those who recognized that the American war lay behind the attempt to undermine the reputation of one of England's leading—but opposition—admirals were open in their skepticism about the charges. Yet there was no question that of the rival fleets the French were back on station in the Channel in two weeks. The British needed three weeks to refit the least damaged warships, while replacement vessels were far off in American waters, and unavailable. An anonymous engraving sold as a broadside showed American seaports being burned, with the king, blind to the carnage, happily oblivious in hunting garb. Beneath is a caption adapted from Joseph Addison's once popular, and politically charged, *Cato:*

> Oh Washington is there not some Chosen Curse,
> Some hidden Thunder, in the Stores of Heav'n,
> Rid with uncommon Wrath, to BLAST these MEN,
> Who owe their Greatness to their Country's Ruin.

"These Men" included the Earl of Sandwich and his stalking horse, Vice Admiral Hugh Palliser. Ironically, *Cato* was Washington's favorite play, and Martha Washington had arranged to have it performed by soldiers when she visited wintry Valley Forge.

The war seemed in limbo as Englishmen held their collective breath about the court-martial, wondering whether the proceedings would further divide the kingdom. However, to Germain it was an Admiralty matter. He was preoccupied with plans to resume the suppression of the colonies once the seasons changed. Joseph Galloway, a Quaker Tory and former speaker of the Pennsylvania Assembly, was in London to lobby for action, and forecast almost certain victory. Visiting North, whose military acumen was minimal, he explained that if Washington's army were "driven away," the loyalist resurgence in America would overwhelm the noisy rebel minority. North wrote to the king that Galloway, a Philadelphia lawyer who had run civil affairs for General Howe during the occupation, visualized Virginia as key to reunion, and believed that "a most happy success" would follow if a new campaign there proceeded "with vigor and ability."

Galloway had seen neither vigor nor ability in either Howe, and was pamphleteering in London for reconciliation based on a continuing connection with the mother country. He would testify on his proposals to a committee of the House of Commons, and eventually would be charged in absentia with high treason by Pennsylvania and his properties ordered sold.

The charges against Keppel ostensibly had nothing to do with the faltering American war. He was alleged guilty of "Misconduct and Neglect of Duty" off Ushant on the twenty-seventh and twenty-eighth of July 1779. The first indictment maintained that he left his deputy, Sir Hugh Palliser, unprepared to engage the enemy, abandoning him "singly and unsupported." The second charged that Lord Augustus "stood away from the enemy to a great Distance," while the third specified that he "did not do the utmost in his Power to take, sink, burn or destroy the French Fleet." A fourth paragraph charged "that he led the whole British Fleet away from them, that he gave them"—the French—"the Opportunity to retire unmolested," and that this inaction "was disgraceful to the English Flag." The final clause, largely repeating the fourth, was that "the Admiral did not pursue the flying Enemy . . . and the Honour of the British Navy was tarnished."

In Portsmouth, the president of the Court, Admiral Sir Thomas Pye, seated with four admirals and eight captains, declared the proceedings open. No one anticipated a trial that would last thirty-one days and keep many members away from their parliamentary duties. Among the spectators were the political elite on both sides of the American question, the Whig opposition including the Marquis of Rockingham and Edmund Burke.

Sixty-seven, and commander of the Portsmouth base, the slender, unobtrusive Pye had once been court-martialed himself for neglect of duty, in 1755. Although acquitted of all serious charges, he had been reprimanded for carelessness, which did not impede his promotion, or a knighthood in 1773. Walpole meanly derided him as "an old dotard," but Pye conducted the proceedings with scrupulous objectivity, very likely remembering his own experience in the dock.

Vice Admiral Marriot Arbuthnot, who had already served unmemorably in American waters, sat on the court. Also, Walpole wrote in his *Last Journals,* "Admiral Campbell, the intrepid Lockhart Ross, and Sir John Lindsay, though the nephew of Lord Mansfield, stood forth as the champions of Keppel in the most undisguised manner. Admiral Montagu . . . acted more as counsel for the prisoner than as one who was to hear and pronounce. . . . Palliser acted with no address. . . . Lord Sandwich's finesse seemed to have deserted him, too, . . . but he was busied in tampering with the witnesses and the log-books, and in all those little tricks that were the flowers of his genius."

Once the charges were read, a stipulation was agreed upon by prosecution and defense "that each Master on delivering his Logbook be sworn, that the Book he delivers is the Ship's Original Logbook . . . without any Alteration or Addition." Immediately afterward, Robert Arnold of the *Robust* objected to taking the oath, contending that his log had indeed been altered once it became "known that the Admiral was to be tried." Consternation arose. His testimony was postponed.

Captain Samuel Marshall of the *Arethusa,* was sworn and questioned:

"Did Admiral Keppel make the Signal for Battle . . . ?"

"Yes"

"Was there a general Signal for the Whole Fleet to chace at this time?"

"Not that Day; but I considered ourselves in chace of them from the first Time we saw them. . . ."

"From the Day you first saw the French Fleet to the time you lost sight of them—Do you from your own Observations or Knowledge know of any Act of the Commander-in-Chief, Admiral Keppel, behaving or conducting himself unbecoming a Flag Officer?"

"No, as God is my Judge."

Sir William Burnaby, captain of the *Milford,* was sworn:

"During the Day of the Action, to your Knowledge, did Admiral Keppel negligently perform the duty imposed upon him?"

As the witness hesitated, the jury asked to have the question repeated, and Burnaby carefully chose his words:

"It appears to me that it comes before this Court to judge from the Facts given in Evidence. Admiral Keppel is a very brave and gallant Officer, and it does not become me to presume to give my Opinion, which can be of little Weight."

Captain Robert Digby of the *Ramillies* was next to testify:

"Did Admiral Keppel neglect to do his utmost? Did you that Day see him run away from the French Fleet?"

"No."

"Was the Ship you commanded engaged?"

"Yes. . . . Our Maintopsail was cut to Pieces, our running and standing Rigging very much cut, so that we were not able to wear [our ensign] for some time; our Foremast wounded in several Places, particularly in one, it was cut Half through, and several of the other Masts and Yards were wounded, Mainyard and Mainmast particularly. . . ."

"Did you see Admiral Keppel with the British Fleet run away from the French Fleet on the Day of the Action, or the Day after?"

"No."

The press (and thus the literate public) was mesmerized by the proceedings, which were always seen as representing something beyond both men. As *Freeman's Journal* put it on January 14, 1779, although the opposing combatants were "brave Keppel, who long sustain'd the fight," and "base, degen'rate Palliser," beyond them were

Germain and Sandwich, who it contended should not be permitted to further guide the war.

As the trial proceeded morning after morning, additional commanders of vessels at Ushant were called and sworn, each with his log in evidence. When Captain Alexander Hood of the *Robust* arose, he felt forced by earlier testimony to explain that his log had originally been "written up carelessly. . . . I never considered a Ship's Log-book to be material Evidence. . . . The corrections in it respect the narrative part only. . . . The Winds, the Courses . . . stand unaltered. . . . When I found my Ship's Log-book likely to be produced in Court, . . . I judged it proper to revise and correct it for the Good of the Ship. . . . Sir, I stand here an attacked Man . . . , my Honour has been wounded. . . . There can be no Criminality in the Thing, unless the [altered] words convey Criminality."

His log, Hood added, would indicate that much of his vessel's upper decks and sails had been shot away—"The Ship made a great deal of Water."

> "Could you have obeyed the Signal for re-attacking, had it been made . . . ?"
> "No, not at that Time; it was impossible."
> "Do you think the Admiral of the British Fleet was flying from his Enemy?"
> "At that Time, to be sure, there was no Appearance of Flight."

Hood was recalled on January 15 to continue, and again asked about the seaworthiness of the *Robust* after the engagement. The ship was not, he recalled, "in a perfect condition to chace."

> "Did Admiral Keppel, by his Conduct on either of those Days tarnish the Honour of the British Flag?"
> "His Character is above my Praise. . . . The Court must decide upon that Question."

The interrogation continued on the visibility of various signals and flags, after which the Court adjourned, accepting Hood's excuses. After all, he was from a famous nautical family and his brother

Samuel, an admiral and future Baron Hood of Catherington, was governor of the naval academy at Portsmouth. The public, however, was less generous, and for a time the epithet "hooded" was in use to refer to false testimony.

On January 16, Captain John Carter Allen of the *Egmont* was called, summing up his recollections with "As I look upon it, the Admiral [Keppel] behaved with much Honour." "Honour" was a key word among gentlemen. Implied throughout the hearings, as meticulous as was the emphasis upon detail, was the questionable honor of Keppel's accuser, Vice Admiral Palliser, whose name remained unmentioned, if sometimes suggested.

On January 20, Captain John Bazely of the *Formidable,* Palliser's flagship, was called, and the hours ticked away with navigational details, as before. But as early winter twilight was darkening the candle-lit courtroom, the distraught Bazely dramatically waved off closure. "It gives me great pain to detain you beyond the usual Hour of Adjournment," he began. "But the three Leaves [of the log] containing the Narrative of the 26th, 27th and 28th of July, having been taken from the *Formidable's* Log-Book, and supplied by others, carry with it so extraordinary an Appearance that I trust the Court will not think me unreasonable in begging that the Master be immediately called in to explain it. I could look down what Signals I could recollect myself. . . . The Admiral"—he meant Palliser—"gave me a piece of Paper with some Remarks he had made; so between the two I made up a Log for that Day of what I though were Facts."

The contentious log was produced. Three original pages were missing—allegedly thrown away by the ship's master because someone "had spilt some ink on it." New leaves had been reconstructed and inserted. Asked to explain what had happened to the pages, Bazely confessed, "I do not know, so help me God—I hold a ship's Log sacred."

"Suspense, still," Walpole wrote to Horace Mann on January 29. "The court martial continues, and everything respectfully awaits its determination—even France and America seem to lie on their oars till the oracle at Portsmouth has pronounced. The response, however, is not likely to be ambiguous. There has been so much juggling to warp the judgment of the priests of Neptune, and the frauds have been so openly detected, . . . that Palliser and his accomplices, high and low, will probably rue the tempest they have brewed." Reporting the testimony while covertly taking sides, *Gentleman's Magazine* cautiously evaded the evidences of fraud, observing only that a logbook "gave rise to some very severe suspicions, of which Adm. Keppel did not fail to make the proper use."

The hearings continued into January 30, when Keppel arose in his own defense. The charges his accuser had brought forward, if true, he conceded, were "very heinous." But "the Circumstances of my Accuser's Silence for Months is strong Evidence of itself, that even in his Opinion, my Conduct was liable to no Reproach." Only the newspaper attack on November 4 had stirred his unnamed accuser into a counterattack, and the testimony had made it clear that the logbook alterations suggesting Keppel's misfeasance had been made as late as December 12 in Plymouth by order of Captain Hood. By no coincidence, it seemed, Hood's superior—and Keppel's accuser—had been in Plymouth on December 12.

The trial recessed, and inevitably a patriotic fast-day intruded, on February 10, for which the tireless Charles Wesley wrote an ostensibly loyal hymn, "Tremendous God, Thy work we see." However, in a sign of the times, the divine dimension in the anthem appeared rather ambiguous and even defeatist. Wesley included references both to "our guilty brethren" who continued the war against America, and to the partisan intervention of those who protested the war, whom "thee [God] and thy viceregent [the king] scorn." Apparently God and George III only scorned the rebels and their accomplices.

On the thirty-first day, February 11, 1779, the proceedings continued symbolically on the HMS *Britannia* and then concluded at the residence of the governor of Portsmouth Harbor. Admiral Pye sequestered the jury for deliberations into the evening.

The verdict was read on Wednesday, February 12: "that the Charge is malicious, and ill-founded; it having appeared that, the said Admiral, so far from having, by Misconduct and Neglect of Duty . . . , behaved as became a judicious, brave and experienced Officer. The Court do, therefore, unanimously and honourably acquit the said Admiral Augustus Keppel of the Several Articles in the Charge against him."

"Inexpressible Joy here," Edmund Burke wrote buoyantly that Thursday to Frances Pelham. Lord Rockingham hastened to London to move a vote of thanks in the Lords to Keppel for his "eminent services," while at the Marquis's Yorkshire estate, Wentworth-Woodhouse, locals celebrated by burning an effigy of Palliser. Lady Rockingham protested that it "was not proper at one[']s own House, because foolish people might think it was done by order." As early as the eighth, anticipating an acquittal, Rockingham had ordered the illumination of Wentworth-Woodhouse at the appropriate time, but he had not anticipated that the illuminations would include incinerating a symbolic Sir Hugh.

"Swiftly, ye Sprits of the sea and air"—a broadside by William Hayley—appeared in the streets, deploring "the dark stab of ministerial art," the false accusation against Lord Augustus, now exploded, that was the "pernicious child of a corrupted state." The disordered minds of Palliser and Sandwich had not conceived the plot, Hayley alleged, blaming instead the utterly innocent Secretary for America:

> . . . Germain plans the dire campaign,
> The curse of Minden's Field, or Saratoga's plain.

Two days after the verdict Keppel requested to return to duty and the authority to rehoist his flag over the HMS *Victory;* then he asked for a temporary leave of absence "to attend my private Affairs." Such matters would include his speaking his mind on American issues once more in the House of Commons.

When news of the acquittal reached London, a mob attacked the Admiralty building in Whitehall, lifting the gates from their hinges and chasing after Palliser, who had reached London after fleeing Portsmouth at five in the morning in a hired post chaise. Although mobs continued to wander about in search of targets, violence in the rubbish-strewn streets in Westminster subsided at dusk, once houses were illuminated and soldiers and special constables were called out. At three in the morning, however, Charles Fox, Lord Derby and his younger brother, Major Stanley, and several other men "of quality" who were still drinking at Almack's Club, decided to explore local streets to see what was going on. Torches in hand and tracking the murmuring of a mob, they discovered in the throng before Palliser's town house the young 4th Duke of Ancaster, twenty-one and very drunk. Some of the rabble had just smashed the admiral's windows and pushed inside, only to find that his furniture had been prudently removed. Seeing their disappointment, one of the young lords asked, "Why don't you break Lord George Germain's windows?"

The minister's residence was also in Pall Mall, but most of the malefactors, innocent of newspapers, had no idea who he was. After someone explained, they attacked the Secretary for America's lower windows, reachable from the street, then broke in and heaved some furniture out, leaving his daughters cowering in their beds. Alerted nearby, Lord North escaped through an opening in the roof of his house before the Guards arrived and prevented further mischief.

Awakened and alarmed when his own windows were smashed, Lord Sandwich picked up his courage and fled through the back garden with his longtime mistress, Martha Ray. They found refuge in the Horse Guards's headquarters in Whitehall.

Martha Ray's terrors were not over. James Hackman, a one-time army ensign who had just become an Anglican clergyman, had met Miss Ray, daughter of a Soho stay maker, at Sandwich's estate at Hinchingbrooke and conceived a passion for her that she did not reciprocate.* When Hackman's offer of marriage was spurned, he purchased a revolver and followed her to Covent Garden Theatre. On April 7, 1779, as she was leaving a performance of Isaac Bickerstaff's comic opera *Love in a Village,* Hackman shot her dead. She was thirty-four. Sandwich felt robbed of "all comfort in this world" but stubbornly returned to the Admiralty. Hackman, who had turned his gun on himself but botched the job, was soon executed.

Irreverence about the earl and the unfortunate Miss Ray abounded. An illustrated broadside published by Isaac Harris of Sweetings Alley, Cornhill, depicted "the Bull of the State" out of control, and while the American Secretary deplores, "This reminds me of Minden," and George III complains about the depredations to his "Treasury," the bull has flattened Lord Sandwich, who moans, "O! I'm as dead as Miss Ray." No press was more free than in Britain. In the colonies, especially the more righteous ones like Massachusetts, papers were shut down for disloyalty or impiety. It rarely happened in London.

---

*She had nine children with Sandwich, who had kept her cozily since she was eighteen.

A cartoon broadside "drawn by Capt. Bailly of the *Porcupine*" and engraved by Christian Vincent went on sale at Berwick Street in Soho to celebrate the Keppel trial's outcome. Above the caption, "Great is the Truth and it shall prevail," was the figure of Fame flying over ships in full sail. Round one of the six medallions framing it were the words,

With Marling Spike I Knot and Splice
With Log-Book Vampt Up Wondrous Nice
With H—d's★ Ovations and Advice
Keppel [would] die and Triumph Vice.

Another broadside depicted a hanged Earl of Sandwich—labeled, familiarly, "Twitcher"—on a ship's deck and Palliser dangling in chains, a logbook weighting down his legs, and the corpse of "Kitty" Ray beneath. Above the ship, supported by the devil with forked tail, Lord North sits placidly on a pile of clouds holding in one hand his monocle and in the other—as his formal title was First Lord of the Treasury—a book titled *The Art of Financing*. Although the gibbet has their bodies, North declares of Palliser and Sandwich, their hearts and souls were his.

On March 3, Fox moved in the Commons to condemn Sandwich for shortchanging Keppel with an inadequate fleet, losing the division 240 to 170. Then he moved an attack on government naval policy, losing 246 to 174. The outcome for each critical resolution was inevitable, but the debates were aspects of a series of hostile inquiries, some from the opposition and others initiated by generals and admirals tarnished by the American war who exploited their dual status as MPs.

Early in February Sir William Howe called for American documents related to him to be made public, and both North and Germain gave in and evaded any division in the Commons. Howe moved that Lord Cornwallis be summoned to testify, and spoke at length in the "enquiry." Burgoyne followed. Cornwallis and eighteen other officers were ordered, on May 18, to attend the House, and Major General Charles Grey, who was accused by the Americans of

---

★Captain Alexander Hood of the *Robust*, later an admiral, and created Viscount Bridport.

the Paoli bayoneting "massacre"* near Philadelphia, defended his chief by claiming that "there could be no expectation of ending the war by force of arms" with the inadequate numbers of troops "assigned to its prosecution." Major General James Robertson, summoned long before from New York, added that only "the loyal subjects . . . returning to the King's government" could free America "from the tyranny of the rebels." None of it was what the ministry wanted to hear, and further examinations were postponed indefinitely. Adding to what was already public scandal about corruption in the Admiralty, the hearings reeked of embarrassment about the conduct of the war.

The Earl of Bristol's motion in the Lords to dismiss Lord Sandwich for misuse of the navy would fail, 78 to 39, but by then, inevitably, Palliser had to be tried, for the Court had pronounced his charges as "malicious and ill-founded." He had already resigned his appointments to avoid dismissal, and applied for a court-martial to clear himself. Keppel was asked to prepare the charges and refused, realizing the outcome would be fixed, but proceedings in Portsmouth harbor aboard the man-of-war *Sandwich,* a carefully chosen venue, began anyway on the same day—April 12, 1779—as the Bailly broadside appeared.

Despite the catastrophe to Miss Ray, Lord Sandwich continued as before, and contrived as expected to pack the Palliser jury with loyalists and to order all ships to sea which appeared to be captained by officers hostile to the admiral. Other ships were called in to Portsmouth if it appeared that favorable testimony from their commanders might be needed. The atmosphere would remain heated long after the trials. At a by-election the next April at Windsor the vindictive king came out openly against Keppel, although his contrary teenage son, the Prince of Wales, spoke openly for Lord Augustus. "I shall in consequence," said the sovereign, "get my Tradesmen to appear" for Portlock Powney, Keppel's undistinguished Tory opponent.

---

*In the Philadelphia campaign, in the darkness of early morning on September 21, 1777, Grey's troops, learning that General Anthony Wayne's Continentals had bivouacked for the night near Paoli, sprang upon the sleeping soldiers with bayonets. According to John André, Grey had forbidden his men to load their muskets, and ordered them to use only their bayonets. About 150 Americans were killed and wounded, and 71 taken prisoner.

Defeated at Windsor, Keppel was offered an alternative seat in Surrey and was returned, despite Lord North's supplying four thousand pounds from the Treasury to the campaign of the admiral's opponent.

The heavy hands of both George III and the Earl of Sandwich lay on the Admiralty deliberations as Palliser was acquitted on May 5, 1779. Although he told the Court that he was "inflamed with resentment" at Keppel's refusal "to excuse or exculpate me," his conduct was declared by a divided panel as "in many ways highly exemplary and meritorious." Yet the Court also deplored that he had not obeyed Keppel's signals, and he was even found "reprehensible in not having acquainted the Admiral [Keppel] . . . of his [ship *Formidable's*] distress."

To demonstrate royal support, His Majesty invited Palliser to a levee at St. James's Palace on May 7, where the loyal press reported that he was greeted "graciously." Palliser requested reinstatement, but even Sandwich understood that the admiral's active career was over and his unpopularity assured. Sir Hugh had, nevertheless, earned a sinecure for his loyalty to his patron, and Sandwich, abandoning "all sensibility and honour," so Charles Fox of the opposition charged, would appoint Palliser ("that object of universal detestation") governor of rebuilt Greenwich Hospital.

The king's troubles were many, and increasing. As the Keppel affair had made clear, the contrary young Prince of Wales represented yet another rebellion. Restless heirs to the throne had often become opponents of Court policy, and in self-interest, potential future favorites encouraged the breach. George III and his grandfather, George II, had a cool relationship at best, and the wayward Prince of Wales's friendships with antiwar radicals exasperated his hawkish father. In the cycle of aggrieved royal parents the king would soon entreat the future George IV, seeking loyalty, "The numberless trials and constant torments I meet with in public life, must certainly affect any man, and more poignantly me," he explained, "as I have no other wish but to fulfill my various duties; the experience of now twenty years has convinced me that however long it may please the Almighty to extend my days, yet I have no reason to expect any diminution of my public anxiety; where am I therefore to turn for comfort, but into the bosom of my own family?"

The king appealed to his son to associate only with those of re-

spectable character, and by example to help "restore this country to
its former lustre." But the precocious prince, not yet eighteen but already a gambler and womanizer like his crony Charles Fox, even
shared briefly, with Fox, a taste in mistresses, both enjoying the
charms of the bosomy actress Mrs. Mary Robinson, whose talents
were more of the boudoir than the boards.

Some Englishwomen, if one believes what was appearing in print,
had ambitions of a different nature. A print, "A loud-crying Woman
& a Scold shall be sought out to drive away the Enemies," issued by
James Daveny, opposite the King's Head public house in the Strand,
depicted two formidable Cockney wenches, one with elbows raised
and the other with fists clenched, daring the surprised French to
cross the Channel. A column, possibly echoing Aristophanes and his
Lysistrata, suggested that if ladies led armies they could quickly bring
the "tedious" war to an end. Another, in the *Evening Post,* suggested
in what might have been a sexual as well as a nautical pun, "Women
wish to fight, too, and do not fear impressment." In the *Morning Post*
a long letter to the editor appeared, replete perhaps with sexual innuendo, and captioned "Female Corps." It began, "I am a young woman
of spirit & long to exercise the portion of abilities Heaven had allot-
ted me for some noble end." The writer was "hurt" when she reflected on the "no meaning figure our sex cut, at the present
alarming crisis," when war with France seemed to add to Britain's
burdens. "A considerable addition to our troops may be found necessary . . . to be raised to make up the deficiency occasioned by those
in America; and as every part of the kingdom is in a manner stript,
and recruits grow scarce, I cannot see why an army of *women,* well
trained and disciplined, should not prove as essentially useful as one
of *men*!"

She had read much about the Amazons, who seemed worthy of
imitation, even if some of their history, like "demolishing their
males," appeared fabulous. Although she was "but five feet three
inches and a half," she would gladly serve. She had been thinking
"that if every stout, well-made woman, *measuring six foot,* in London,
and different parts of the country, were collected together, formed
into regiments, and habited *en militaire,* they would make as noble,
and as formidable an appearance as the *Grenadiers,* or *Blues.*" The
ladies at Coxheath and other encampments—she may have meant

those selling their services—"may probably imagine they are already acting for the common good; whether they are or no, is not for me to say." But she felt that many women not handicapped by a "delicate frame" could volunteer. As it was, war had emptied both town and country of interesting men—"the army, and navy, are banished from us."

"I ardently wish," the lady closed, "that every game-minded* individual would interest themselves in this universal calamity, praying that we may be allowed liberty, and opportunity, to display those talents, which are capable of being cultivated for the noblest uses, and which were never intended to lie buried in obscurity, or remain in a state of inactivity." It was signed from Sunbury by "Thalestris." Knowledgeable readers would recognize the adopted name as that of the legendary queen of the Amazons.

The seas around the British Isles remained the cockpit of the war in 1779, as little was happening in America, although the war had not taken a holiday. Washington was without resources to exploit Clinton's withdrawal to New York City, and Congress remained weak and ridden by dissension. From his encampment in New Jersey Washington wrote to George Mason, a Virginia delegate, "Friends and foes seem now to combine to pull down the goodly fabric we have hitherto been raising at the expence of so much time, blood, and treasure." Britain, however, was distracted by the threat of the French fleet and the relative pinpricks of Paul Jones. Its lengthy coastline was highly vulnerable to attack, as only the Channel shore could reasonably be protected. It was an opportunity for the rash former privateer captain from America.

When the revolution broke out in 1775 John Paul Jones was only twenty-seven. He had been living quietly in Fredericksburg, Virginia, for a little more than a year after fleeing to the New World to escape a murder charge—claiming later to Benjamin Franklin that he had to kill a sailor in self-defense. As the Continental navy needed not only vessels but officers, he managed a commission as a first lieutenant, with more ambition than merely to seize as prizes lightly defended British merchant ships plowing to the West Indies. The privateers, however, no longer hugged the shoreline, and ranged outward into

*The writer was using "game" in the sense of "plucky, resolute, ready and willing."

the Atlantic. There the fictional loyalist refugee Jonathan Corncob, now purser on an armed brig in an early English novel about America, is taken captive by the Yankee privateer *Picaroon*. On a prison ship in Boston harbor he hears a British tar pray violently,

> O L—d, our father, which art in heaven, of thy infinite goodness and mercy, look down and d—n, c—se, bl-st, blow, burn, blind, sink, and utterly destroy the thirteen united states of America.

With little more than audacity Paul Jones saw the three thousand miles of the Atlantic as a bridge to bring the war to the enemy's shores. All the colonies could furnish him was a twenty-gun sloop out of Portsmouth, New Hampshire, the *Ranger.* Soon there were two Portsmouths in the eye of the war—the seat of the Keppel court-martial and the base from which the son of a Scottish gardener, with an apprenticeship on a ship out of Whitehaven in Cumberland but unable to win a commission in the Royal Navy, would wreak his revenge on the "wooden walls" with sails that were to protect England. He had been third mate on a slave ship, then captain of a small brig. Whitehaven lured him back, and he came ashore with his crew, burned a boat, and spiked the coastal batteries. As the local earl was away, Paul Jones made do with the worthy's silver platter and teapot and sailed to Carrickfergus, across the Irish Sea, where he took on the HMS *Drake.* Neighboring seaports were alerted.

All England was apprehensive about his next strike, which was imagined as part of a concerted plan. The governor of the Isle of Man called out the Manx militia. London newspapers reported the actually small success of the Whitehaven raid as due to the "defence-less" state of the coasts and the "inexcusable" laxness of the Admiralty. The response was helpful to the colonies, as it meant that more resources would be kept at home.

"We are all in a bustle here," a Whitehaven correspondent reported to the London *Morning Post,* in a letter printed on April 28. As a result of the "late insolent attack of the provincial privateer's men," locals were cleaning rusty old swords and making up powder cartridges. The report identified Jones as "John Paul," who had apprenticed on the *Friendship* in Whitehaven and was "well known by many people in this town." When he raided Selkirk in Scotland he panicked thousands along the exposed coasts, and the *Morning Chronicle* reported that the northern shores of England and Scotland were so fear-stricken "that a general intimidation discovers itself on every appearance of a sail." He was "not in arms as an American," he wrote to the Countess of Selkirk, whose estate he had raided, and whose family silver he was returning, but "in the present generous struggle for the rights of men." He asked her to use her "soft persuasive arts" upon her husband, the influential Earl of Selkirk, "to endeavour to stop this cruel and destructive war, in which Britain can never succeed." (He did not explain that he had intended to kidnap the earl to effect an exchange of prisoners, but Selkirk was fortuitously away.) A satire by the prolific John Freeth in the *London Evening Post* (October 12, 1779), to the familiar tune of "Stick a pin there," suggested Paul Jones's potential as irritant.

When he failed to reappear it was assumed that he was off to France for refitting, and indeed he did voyage to Brest to seek a larger man-of-war, obtaining a rather sluggish French vessel he renamed after Franklin's early nom de plume as "Poor Richard." The *Bonhomme Richard* prowled along the east coast of Scotland from the Firth of Forth to Leith, but when he attacked the formidable HMS *Serapis,* his smaller accompanying vessels deserted him. Off Flamborough Head in Yorkshire a mismatch began. Many in both crews were dead before the better gunned *Serapis* struck its colors, its captain unaware that Paul Jones's battered ship had been so severely damaged that it would soon sink. The Americans seized the *Serapis,* and the accompanying *Countess of Scarborough*.

Lord Rockingham, who was High Steward of Hull, put aside his pro-Americanism to offer a battery of shore cannon at his own expense. "In this southern part of the Kingdom," Burke wrote to him from Bristol about the offshore threat from the French, "I have not for several years found the people any thing like so well disposed to any Effort of Vigour for the Salvation of the Country. The loss of some of our possessions, and our fears for the rest begin to excite . . . feeling. The Blisters begin to rise, and there are signs of life in the body."

It was no longer only the Americans, of whom Paul Jones was nearly unique in his proximity, whom the British feared. The French reportedly were gathering strength in Normandy for a cross-

Channel landing, and General Clinton's garrisons across the Atlantic were, given the anxiety at home, largely ignored. Civil defense was taking precedence over unleashing the redcoats in America for yet another campaign somewhere. The American Secretary urged Clinton to stage coastal raids to keep Washington guessing. After all, John Paul Jones with a single ship had caused consternation along the British shores, and was even celebrated accordingly, as in the "Heroi-Comical" verses "Paul Jones: Or the Fife Coast Garland," in which the "Oyster Wives of Newhaven" appealed to Lord Sandwich to order warships north or be "pleas'd with our disgraces." For the moment, the rebellion, which had to be won on the land, was a trial by sea.

10

Moderately Feeding the War
June 1779–December 1779

"Much as it behoves us to profit of every means and occasion which present themselves of bringing the American war to an honourable conclusion; the powers Great Britain has to contend with in Europe are so potent as to require her utmost efforts to withstand them."

—*Lord George Germain to Sir Henry Clinton, August 28, 1779*

"BOTH Armies continued quiet in their Winter cantonments till about the middle of May," Washington wrote to the Marquis de Lafayette after the young general had returned home to France to seek further aid. Paul Jones had hoped that Lafayette might even lead a raiding force across the Channel to harass the English, but the only effective raids were organized by the English, via New York. General Clinton sent troops up the Hudson to King's Ferry, to take Stony Point, across the river from Peekskill, and Sir John Collier took a brigade under Major General Edward Mathew from New York to towns inland from Hampton Roads, Virginia. Exploiting complete surprise, they landed unopposed. Downplaying the embarrassment, Washington told Lafayette lightly that "after plundering and destroying the property (chiefly private) in those places and stealing a number of Negroes [they] returned to New York the moment they found the Country rising in Arms to oppose them."

In reality, Portsmouth, Norfolk, Gosport, and Suffolk were razed after valuable stores of ammunition and tobacco were seized; 137 small vessels were destroyed; patriot sailors had to burn a 28-gun warship still on the stocks to keep it from the enemy; and two un-loaded French merchant ships had to be scuttled with their cargo. Without having lost a man the expedition returned to New York. It was a costly intelligence failure, as was the Hudson highlands affair. Washington was not always the scrupulously honest paragon of the cherry tree legend propagated by Parson Mason Locke Weems.

When Lord North recommended in the Commons that in order to hoard resources to defend the home islands, the American war should be only "moderately fed," he did not yet know the success of moderate feeding. It could not win the war, but it kept the war from being lost. His listeners understood only that taxpayers would not be further burdened to pay for the expanding conflict, although some-how it had to be paid for. Edmund Burke gave North's guarantee a different gloss, rising to blast the prosperous entrepreneurs—many of them MPs—who he alleged had applauded most loudly. Predators rather than patriots, they were the "twenty fat contractors at his Lordship's back" who shouted in effect *"feed! feed! feed!"* in approval that their profits would continue. They were "ravens and birds of prey" less interested in the country's future than "to suck her inner-most vitals, to feast on her entrails." Burke's targets were the forty-six men who held major supply contracts to keep the American war going, eighteen of whom were MPs, seven more close relatives or "connections" of MPs, and eleven others business partners of mem-bers. The patronage network fed on the war.★

The American Secretary reminded North nevertheless that "exer-tions must be made, for no measure can be so fatal as a tame defen-sive war." The king also warned of the domino effect of losing America, for "then this island would be reduced to itself, and soon would be a poor island indeed." Yet financing the wider war with France, and soon Spain, was impossible if Sir Henry Clinton were to be unleashed to recover the colonies. Clinton had written to the American Secretary hopefully in January, as winter further weakened Washington's cantonments, "Signs of disunion among the rebels are apparent; great discontent is said to prevail in the army owing to the insufficiency of pay, and the supply of provisions and forage is very

---

★A bill moved by Sir Philip Jennings Clerke in February, and supported by Burke, to ex-clude contractors from Commons as a conflict of interest had failed.

limited." But discontent in England over the war was making it difficult to augment Clinton's garrison.

Realizing that his message might not arrive until June, on April 4,
1779, Clinton had proposed to the American Secretary his recommended operations for the summer months. Any reply from Lord
George, sent against the certainty of unfavorable winds, would reach
New York too late to matter. The best possibility, Clinton had suggested without much enthusiasm, was a landing in South Carolina, as
the southern colonies seemed to have the least affinity with the hard-
core rebels. "The small force which the *present* weakness of General
Washington's army would enable me to detach, might possibly get
possession of Charlestown (tho' it would certainly require a siege)."

A southern strategy required massive shipping, and Sir George
Collier, the latest fleet commander in New York, offered a glum assessment of his potential when he wrote to Germain on April 19,
"The weak enfeebled state of the ships both in point of numbers and
of men give me the most painful sensations. . . . I have great pleasure
in finding Sir Henry Clinton so much inclined to co-operate; but
my power is so little proportioned to my wishes that I am at a loss as
to what to undertake or how to supply the convoys, guards of ports,
and various other services which this extensive command necessarily
has occasions for." Because of the adverse weather in the North Atlantic, he also noted, "at least a fourth part" of his fleet was regularly
"blown off their stations."

Commanders in the colonies always claimed that they could
barely maintain forces for garrisoning what they occupied, but the
view from Whitehall as always was more optimistic. On May 5, Lord
George, whose informants furnished him with what they thought he
wanted to hear, wrote to Clinton of "the favourable appearances His
Majesty's affairs now put on in America," and referred to reinforcements being sent—in actuality, replacements. Germain saw Georgia
as about to fall off the rebel tree, and also claimed from his sources
that "Carolina no longer makes remittances for the Congress."

The secretary expected much from Clinton that Sir Henry, concerned to hold New York, could not perform without risk. Complaining (within the family) on May 21 to the Duke of Newcastle,
his chief partisan, of frustration, Clinton alleged to be "worn down
with grief and mortification," although he had four homes, a farm,

and a pretty mistress, Mrs. Mary Baddeley, in New York City and Long Island, and an annual salary and expense account of twelve thousand pounds—an income far in excess of the prime minister. He occupied himself with amateur theatricals and concerts usually arranged by Captain John André, manager of the notorious Mischianza. The general often played the violin. "I grow old, my dear Lord," Clinton maintained, nevertheless, to Newcastle, seeing his military future in jeopardy, "and though my constitution in appearance may not have suffered much, I feel it greatly impaired. Seven long years have I been absent from my motherless babes; 'tis time to attend to them.* To risk fortune, health, and even reputation upon events to which I cannot . . . give the least bias is hard indeed."

In that frame of mind the next day, ignoring protocol, Clinton began a long and angry letter before he received Germain's newest upbeat gloss. "How mortified I must be, my Lord," he wrote on May 22, "at finding movements recommended for my debilitated army which your Lordship never thought of suggesting to Sir William Howe when he was in his greatest force and without an[y] apprehension from a foreign enemy!"

Written emotionally with numerous slips of the pen, Clinton's outburst would be sent off in haste without a fair copy being made. He conceded that Germain did only recommend, rather than order, plans for further action, but that meant that Lord George reserved "the right of blaming me if I should adopt other measures and fail." Clinton realized that the approaching summer was his opportunity for some initiatives, but only on the basis of his own information. "I am on the spot," he reminded Germain. "The earliest and most exact intelligence . . . ought to reach me. It is my interest as well as my duty, more than any other person living, to inform myself minutely and justly of the particular views, connections, state and temper of every province—nay, of every set of men—within the limits of my command; and it is my business to mark every possible change in their situation. Why then, my Lord, without consulting me, will you adopt the ill-digested . . . suggestions of people who cannot be competent judges of the subject?"

*Clinton was only forty-one. His wife had died in 1772; he had been in America since May 1775.

The opposition-minded Earl of Shelburne in the Lords had charged Germain with putting too much irrelevant minutiae into his instructions to America, and Shelburne did not need access to state papers to discover it. Messages sent by packet in both directions across the Atlantic in multiple copies for safety were often intercepted by American privateers and then published in both colonial and British papers. However belated by many months, those releases made the war an open book. (Similarly, the Royal Navy seized American messages en route to France and Holland, and some deemed embarrassing to the rebel cause would turn up in print.)

"For God's sake, my Lord," Clinton concluded volcanically, "if you wish me to do anything, leave me to myself and let me adapt my effects to the hourly change of circumstances. If not, tie me down to a certain point and take the risk of my want of success."

Germain could have sacked Clinton for his frankness (or arrogance), but only at the risk of a further year's delay in the already sluggish war. Although separating fringe colonies from the rebel strongholds seemed possible and would look good at home, both men realized that the only way to win was to decisively defeat the evasive Washington on home ground. The dream ("to stir Mr. Washington") had long tempted Howe and Burgoyne, Cornwallis and Clinton. As Sir Henry had reminded Germain a week earlier in a message still weeks away from Whitehall, "To force Washington to an action upon terms tolerably equal has been the object of every campaign during this war."

In the country at Strawberry Hill, Horace Walpole, writing about the news from New York of May and early June, wrote on July 10 to General Conway's wife, Lady Aylesbury, "Are we not at the moment assured that Washington cannot possibly amass an army of above 8000 men? And yet Clinton with twenty thousand men, and with the [loyal] hearts, we are told, of three parts of the colonies, dares not show his teeth without the walls of New York! . . . We have bullied and threatened and bayed, and nothing would do."

Frustrated because Washington refused battle in order to keep an army in being, Clinton could only attempt patrols and skirmishes. Washington's battlefield tactics remained to avoid the battlefield until he was certain that he could prevail.

One result of the continuing strain with what he assumed was an overly cautious Clinton was that Germain, as a strong hint about the future, sent the always aggressive Earl Cornwallis, who had once more returned to England on leave, back to New York as Clinton's deputy, the general disembarking on July 21. The two seldom got on, but Sir Henry, eager to extricate himself from America, recognized the expertise of Cornwallis and soon sought permission to resign his command to the earl. Restless about inaction from New York, the king preferred General Carleton, who was already nearby in Canada. Since Minden, however, he was despised by Germain, who blocked the appointment by threatening to resign and by demanding a peerage ("some mark of his Majesty's favour") so that he could move pridefully to the Lords. He cited his health and "the fatigue of the attendance in the House of Commons added to the business of my office."

Backing down, the king offered to let Clinton stay, and it was only in November that he agreed to Cornwallis as successor in America if something happened to Sir Henry. (The "dormant commission" to Cornwallis was to ensure that a senior German general did not accidentally succeed to command.) Germain agreed "humbly to submit," but his appointment of Cornwallis on the king's consent, posted by packet in November, did not arrive in New York until the following spring and would never take effect. Ships often lingered in port for weeks or even months awaiting better weather, supplies slow to arrive, or additional cargo. With increasing impatience, Clinton hung on.

Debarking as deputy, Cornwallis arrived with the news that the French were deploying a fleet across the Atlantic, destination unknown. Yet another navy could make trouble. It was already known in London that Spain, on June 21, had formally declared war on the British, more in self-interest than to back France or the American colonies. The Spanish wanted to recover Gibraltar, and hoped to pry "the Rock" loose as the price for intervention. Germain would send his confidant, the playwright Richard Cumberland, to Madrid, warning him that as he consulted informally with Spanish officials he should keep in mind that their "grievances supposed and complained of relate solely to our conduct toward her, [employ] not a word of America. . . . You did wisely in avoiding all conversation upon the subject of America. There is an absolute necessity in preventing the interference of foreign powers in settling the terms to be granted by a sovereign to his rebellious subjects."

Before the French (or the ineffective Spanish) could have an impact, Clinton planned to detach troops for further assaults upon the weakly held southern colonies. The Virginia raid by Collier and Mathews showed that the Continentals could not be everywhere any more than could the king's men. Clinton did not think that Washington, with much of his army in New Jersey, could react in time by land, and had no way to do so by sea.

As promised by London, the aging and the unwanted Admiral Arbuthnot (Clinton dismissed him as senile) arrived at last on August 25, his ships carrying little more than half of the 6,600 men the American Department had promised. Nearly a thousand of the cooped-up troops—there were 3,800—were sick with fever. Arbuthnot downplayed it in a message to Germain as scurvy,★ but Clinton described it as "a malignant jail fever"—and more than 100 were already dead. The disembarking soldiers spread the illness further, sending "above 6,000 of my best troops," Clinton recalled bitterly in a memoir, "to the hospital." His operations in the South were put off.

Germain's impossible dream remained the defeat of Washington in a direct confrontation. Barring that he was open to any other workable alternatives that would have similar effect. His reports from spies and agents and informants were always buoyant. "The dissensions and jealousies among the members of the Congress," he wrote to Clinton on September 27, a message that would not reach the general before winter, "continue to increase and . . . the people's repugnance to serve in their army becomes every day greater. It will not, I am persuaded, escape your sagacity that the gaining over some of the most respectable members of that body or officers of influence and reputation among the troops would, next to the destruction of Washington's army, be the speediest means of subduing the rebellion and restoring the tranquility of America. Your commission authorizes you

★Scurvy was caused by a deficiency of vitamin C (from fruit and green vegetables) in the diet. Until lime juice was available onboard ships, British sailors—thereafter called "limeys"—died in considerable numbers. Also afflicted were the troops they transported on long voyages.

to available yourself of such opportunities and there can be no doubt that the expense will be cheerfully submitted to."

If Britain could not win the hearts and minds of Congress or the Continentals, Clinton was reminded that he might attempt to buy them. The fact that such efforts were made, and with very few exceptions—the most notorious to come the next year—failed, says much about the obstinacy of most Americans. Inhabitants lacking enthusiasm for independence were everywhere in rebel territory, but lacked any influence. They were numerous in lower New Jersey and in Philadelphia, where the British occupation had been a social and financial boon, and patriotism and prosperity seemed at odds. Little could be done by Congress to punish the royalists who reclaimed allegiance to America, and in any case they were useful and wanted back. London hoped for their private loyalty while learning little about what they were doing to reconcile the king's peace with their immediate comfort.

Reopening his glass and china shop on Fourth Street, the London-born Joseph Stansbury could move about for mercantile reasons while retaining a discreet connection with Clinton's people as an informer. He had been a member of the loyalist Sons of St. George, wrote poems and songs praising Howe and the occupation, and privately circulated verses in which he claimed to others lying low, "Britain's monarch shares your pains." He would be the go-between for the restless Major General Benedict Arnold with Clinton's adjutant general and spy chief John André.

By Washington's appointment Arnold was military governor of Philadelphia, evidencing a lavish and questionable lifestyle. Frustrated about promotion, he was furious with the Congress for denying it on the grounds that Connecticut already had its share of lieutenant generals—and Washington had apologized to him powerlessly for the blatantly political intrusion which exposed the selfishness of the disunited states.

Suspicious of Arnold's sources of income—which would lead to court-martial proceedings but only minor penalties—and of his high-living Society Hill connections in Philadelphia (he had married the beautiful Peggy Shippen, of a prominent loyalist family, on April 8, 1779), his political and military associates were reluctant to give him any new responsibilities. Wounded seriously in the failed Canadian adventure, the debt-plagued Arnold nursed a lame leg and used it to duck new military assignments while exploring ways to evade trial, make money, and rise in what he now felt from his new friends was the certainty of rebel defeat.

"About the month of June 1779," Stansbury recalled from exile to a postwar British commission investigating loyalist monetary claims, "General Arnold sent for me and, after some general conversation, [he revealed] his political sentiments respecting the war . . . , declaring his abhorrence of a separation." Stansbury's easy access to Arnold came via his furnishing—possibly at discount British secret service rates—of the newlywed Arnold's dining room, making possible, "under a solemn obligation of secrecy, his intention of opening his services to the . . . British forces in any way that would effectually restore the former government and destroy the then usurped authority of Congress, either by immediately joining the British army or cooperating on some concealed plan with Sir Henry Clinton."

As teasers, Arnold furnished nuggets of information for Clinton, some of it authentic, some of it guesswork. He disclosed—as he knew what limited resources the Continentals had available—that Congress had all but written off Charleston, South Carolina, should another attempt be made to take it. Negotiations with Arnold would be complicated and lengthy. If Clinton were to pay for treason, he wanted value for his money. A gimpy rebel general whose honor was suspect seemed no bargain.

Another informant, deposed New Jersey governor William Franklin, was long recognized as beyond Tory suspicion despite his past as one-time colleague of his famous father. Imprisoned and then exchanged, Ben's monarchist son was in New York organizing refugee sympathizers in New York and Long Island into the Board of Associated Loyalists. Coordinating information—and wishful thinking—from the like-minded, he also sent intelligence to London, but William—and Whitehall—as yet knew nothing of Arnold's sly eagerness to defect for a price.

The younger Franklin was also unaware of widespread British espionage in France. Stormont had a watch kept on the elder Franklin from the moment he set foot in France, admitting to Lord Weymouth, "I look upon him as a dangerous engine, and am very sorry that some English frigate did not meet with him by the way." It seemed that almost everyone in the ministry was busy manipulating an agent in hopes of co-opting the Americans. As early as December 1777, once the news of Saratoga had shocked London, Lord North, keeping his own agent secret from Germain (who had his personal agent), had sent Paul Wentworth, formerly a colonial representative for New Hampshire, then a London stockbroker, to Paris to feel out Ben Franklin on peace without overt independence. William Eden, undersecretary in the Southern Department, pulled the strings for North and paid Wentworth two hundred pounds a year, but the mission amounted to little.

Stormont's "engine" metaphor for Franklin, and the intense adulation offered to the unpretentious but lionized "American Prometheus" (one of his code names was *Prométhé*), suggested why he was invested by gullible English agents with uncanny powers. According to one naive report to Lord Stormont,

> We now entertain no doubt that the motive of Doctor Franklin's journey hither was entirely philosophical. . . .* Know then, that upon the principle of Archimedes, the Doctor with the assistance of French mechanics is preparing a great number of reflecting mirrors which will reflect so much heat from the sun as will destroy anything by fire at a very considerable distance.
>
> This apparatus is to be fixed at Calais on the French coast so as to command the English shore whereby they mean to burn and destroy the whole navy of Great Britain in our harbors.
>
> During the conflagration the Doctor proposes to have a chain** carried from Calais to Dover. He, standing at Calais, with a prodigious electrical machine of his own invention, will convey such a shock as will entirely overturn our whole island.

Often more shrewd than his ministers, King George took Franklin more seriously than they did, although he misunderstood the old sage's unfeigned affection for England, where he had resided for many years and from which he had tried to work out a rapproche-

---

*"Philosophical" was used then to also mean "scientific"—as in "natural philosophy."

**Chains with heavy links were then affixed across rivers and narrow entrances to harbors to deny access by shipping. One American barrier protected the Hudson below West Point.

ment that might have precluded rebellion. "The many instances of the inimical conduct of Franklin towards this country," the king charged to Lord North, "makes me aware that hatred to this Country is the constant object of his mind....Yet I think it so desirable to end the war with that Country, to be enabled with redoubled ardour to avenge the faithless and insolent conduct of France that I think it proper to keep open the channel of intercourse with the insidious man."

With Franklin as its resident eminence, the American commission in Passy, a village on the Seine between Paris and Versailles, included a secretary in Stormont's pay, Edward Bancroft, who exchanged useless information with Paul Wentworth. Bancroft, once of Westfield, Massachusetts, was in his mid-thirties, and had trained as a physician. He had become friendly with Franklin in his prewar years in England, and had volunteered to spy for him in London. A member of the Royal Society, he was a laboratory dabbler in Franklin's own tradition. The venerable Philadelphia printer was especially interested in Bancroft's toying with inks and dyes—and did not know that for four hundred pounds a year, soon increased to one thousand pounds, Bancroft was sending, in invisible ink, diplomatic confidences to London.

Bancroft would seal his papers in a bottle and place them in a bole in a tree in the gardens of the Tuileries, where every Tuesday evening they would be plucked and sent to another agent, the untalented Wentworth, who when in London was a recruiter for American-born potential traitors. Nearly every American agent employed by the Congress in France, from Paris to the seaports, had someone in British pay at his elbow. However, spying won few wars.

When the rebellion was suppressed, so Bancroft was promised to ensure his fidelity, he would be made a professor of divinity at King's College in New York, the future Columbia University. Despite being well situated to furnish intelligence, he supplied few diplomatic secrets that were not already known to the elegant ladies among Franklin's intimates, who purveyed the gossip from every salon. Little strategic use could be made in London of the messages in Bancroft's bottles, as the French were not to be wooed away from ties with America, but spies watching munitions transports take on cargo made possible the interdiction of some of them at sea.

Bancroft was also close to Franklin's early diplomatic partner, Silas Deane, who planned to profiteer with Bancroft in postwar trade and speculation in shares. As part of the bargain, Deane also sold French and American secrets to the British until his recall by Congress in May 1778. Bancroft's own spying would remain unknown for nearly seventy years after his death in 1820; however, King George knew that he was motivated far less by patriotism than his pocketbook, calling him a "stock-jobber unfriendly to England." Only Franklin's later desire to give the secretaryship to his young grandson, William Temple Franklin, nineteen in 1779, ended Bancroft's pose as American patriot. With his nefariously earned pounds he returned to London to work on textile dyes, publishing a book about them in 1794.

Others from Franklin's former circle in London, now covertly employed on missions for Whitehall, also came to Passy, professing displeasure with British policy in America. Involvement in experimental science would assure Franklin's attention. One visitor was William Alexander, a wealthy Scot with dilettante laboratory interests and money to spend. David Hartley, MP, who dabbled in chemistry and mechanics and openly favored conciliation, had long known Franklin, and was sent by Lord North to suggest a peace deal outside the French accord. Franklin explained to Hartley, who warned of the "fatal step" of a French alliance, "America has been *forc'd* and *driven* into the Arms of France. She was a dutiful and virtuous daughter. . . . In her future Prosperity, if she forgets and forgives, 'tis all that can be reasonably be expected of her." Hartley would invent a method of fireproofing, placing thin iron partitions between wooden planks in floors and ceilings to retard a fire's access to air. He and Franklin would see more of each other in Paris and Passy, but not to Lord North's advantage.

Despite Washington's intermittent despair about keeping his discontented and occasionally mutinous army together, the reluctance of some colonies to contribute even to their own defense, and even the refusal of many colonists to pay taxes—bribery would not buy America back, nor would persuasion. The Earl of Carlisle, considered a lightweight although named the chairman because of his peerage, recognized that reality while on his futile conciliation journey in 1778. Writing to his wife, he explained, "The common people hate us in their hearts, notwithstanding all that is said of their secret attachment to the mother country." Sir William Eden, who had been a commissioner, and was a deputy to Lord North, also recognized that reality and was feeling increasingly desperate. Being very well paid for a futile junket had not been entirely pleasant, although it had been an education. Writing to Clinton in a letter received in early summer, while the negotiations with Arnold were unreported and stretching out, Eden observed candidly, "Our spirits in general with regard to your prospects are not very high; therefore if by any fortunate or able stroke you can get us out of our scrape you will be worshiped by a very grateful country."

The individual seen as keeping the kingdom in its scrape, almost alone, was George Washington. England remained intensely curious about the extraordinary, almost godlike, Washington, who was far more a hero to the London press than anyone engaged in putting him down. Early disparagements had given way gradually to disgruntled admiration that he had withstood the mediocre best that could be marshaled against him. Although a German almanac in Pennsylvania very likely seen by some Hessians was already referring to him as *Des Landes Vater* (the Father of his Country), as late as August 17, 1778, "An Old Soldier" in *Lloyd's Evening Post* had written disparagingly, in what had become almost a cliché, that there was no likelihood of greatness in Washington. "There are insuperable impediments in his way. He is but of slow parts, and these are totally unassisted by any kind of education.... In the poor, pitiful unsoldierlike war in which he has hitherto been employed, it is romantic to suppose he must not fail, if ever it be his lot to be opposed by real military skill.... That he is alive to command an army, or that an army is left to him to command, might be sufficient to ensure him the reputation of a great General, if British Generals were any longer what British Generals used to be."

While Whitehall and the military hierarchy in America were still finding it galling to refer to him as "General," that title failed to ruffle London's voracious newspaper readership. One English account, published on September 23, 1779, purportedly from "an American gentleman, now in London, who is well acquainted with General Washington," exuberantly combined fiction and fact in creating a near paragon of higher humanity. He was "remarkably healthy" although "advanced in years"—he was actually forty-seven—and was "very fond of riding on a favourite white horse."* Reportedly only a single servant attended him: The English press did not know he was the devoted Mount Vernon slave Billy Lee.

Washington was "shy" and "very reserved"—which was true—and "loves retirement." (What that meant was uncertain, as he had not yet returned home during the long war.) He sought "separate judgements" from his officers, "without divulging his intentions," before making decisions. He had "no tincture of pride, and will often converse with a centinal with more freedom than he would with a general officer." Further, the general combined discipline with mildness:

> He punishes neglect of duty with great severity, but is very tender and indulgent to recruits until they learn the articles of war and their exercise perfectly; he has a great antipathy to spies, although he employs them himself, and has a regular aversion to all indians. He regularly attends divine service in his tent every morning and evening, and seems very fervent in his prayers. He is so tender-hearted that no soldier must be flogged nigh his tent. . . . He has made the art of war his particular study; his plans are in general good and well digested; he is particularly careful always of securing a retreat, but his chief qualifications are courage, steadiness, perseverance, and secrecy.

The general, one also learned, was quick to reward bravery, and humane to prisoners of war. And he was "very temperate in his diet," his only indulgence "a few glasses of punch after supper." Nothing was mentioned of women, but it had to be taken for granted that if womanizing was his weakness, it had not been discovered. From what Englishmen knew of the failings in America of their own leadership after public hearings in Parliament, columns in the daily press, and scurrilous tales told in penny broadsides, the enemy commander-in-chief was a majestic figure, a king lacking only a throne.

As the dream of reattachment with America would not die, an alternative approach was proposed to Lord Jeffrey Amherst by General James Robertson, who had served with Howe, and had returned late

---

*Thomas Nelson, who became governor of Virginia in 1781, had given Washington a fine horse, which he named Nelson. The horse survived the revolution. After the war, Washington returned Nelson to Nelson.

in 1778 to defend him in Parliament. Two-thirds of the colonists, Robertson contended in a memorandum, were loyal and "averse to the government they are now under," but felt that sooner or later the mother country would give up and abandon them to the rebels. Arnold was making that point himself, reflecting his own shifting allegiance. If his treachery failed, he wrote to New York via Stansbury, he wanted to be guaranteed that "the cause for which he suffers will hold itself bound to indemnify him for his losses and receive him with the honours his conduct deserves." Since there were not enough redcoats to subdue America, Robertson, like the more militant ex-governor Franklin, felt that more loyalists should be armed and put under civil governments with trading privileges with Britain restored. If a model experiment were to be tried, New York was the only possible venue.

Amherst consulted the king, and His Majesty apparently spoke to Germain, who settled on Robertson as the new governor of New York. But nothing went quickly in Whitehall bureaucracy, and good intentions seemed always overtaken by events. Robertson's royal commission was signed on May 11, 1779, with instructions from the American Secretary to create a civil government which would retain revenues raised and contribute some funds to the cost of imperial administration. But the general did not leave London until September 16, and found himself cooling his heels at Cork while a supply armada on which he was to sail was assembled. The fleet went instead to Georgia, and he landed at Savannah on February 16, 1780. A mail packet took him to New York, where arrived on March 21, 1780, a year after his appointment.

For a moment in the autumn of 1779—the hopeful signs of increasing rebel discord took until early winter to reach London—it seemed as if reattachment to the Crown might come about by default, and the king's subjects were relieved that such violent disruptions of civility could not happen in England. From its Quaker origins, Philadelphia seemed always a model of colonial decorum, but Pennsylvania Germans had settled the adjacent city to the northwest, Germantown, and fundamentalist Scotch-Irish Presbyterians had begun populating eastern Pennsylvania and nearby New Jersey as well as moving into the Appalachian backcountry. Both resented the opulent way of life of the Quaker and formerly

Quaker gentry, many of whom, like William Penn's own children and grandchildren, had become socially prominent Anglicans.

The politically radical Joseph Reed had become the autocratic president—the title of governor had not yet come about—of Pennsylvania in December 1778, and even Washington had congratulated him on triumphing over "those murderers of our cause," the wealthy merchants and speculators who had brought down the value of Continental currency. They were, Washington had written intemperately, "the pests of society and the greatest enemies we have to the happiness of America. I would to God that one of the most atrocious in each state was hung in gibbets upon a gallows five times as high as the one prepared [in biblical Persia] by Hamen. No punishment, in my opinion, is too great for the man who can build his greatness upon his country's ruin."

Such outrage, at far lower levels, simmered through 1779 until on October 4 two days of rioting erupted in usually placid Philadelphia. The former loyalists of the occupation were blamed for hard times, and Radicals plotted to seize royalist families and deport them by the boatload to New York. Handbills called for the expulsion from the city of those "disaffected persons" who called themselves Republicans and—by no coincidence in timing—were opposed to Reed's candidates in the assembly elections to be held a week later. Arming themselves, some Republicans—the local conservative faction—gathered at the three-story mansion of James Wilson, a signer of the Declaration of Independence but an opponent of the state constitution, which he considered too democratic. The building at 3rd and Walnut streets in Society Hill, with Benedict Arnold as one of the defenders, became known as "Fort Wilson."

In the streets were Pennsylvania German militiamen with two field artillery pieces, and Reed feared an explosion into urban anarchy. While he summoned the First City Troop, extremists seized suspected enemies from their homes and shot at anyone who appeared at Fort Wilson's windows. The front door was battered down by a large German, and others surged inside, but Reed had ordered the troopers to arrest all combatants, inside and out, and remove them to Walnut Street Prison.

At daylight the next morning, when other Germans learned that some of their number were dead and others in prison, they marched down Germantown Pike to free their comrades. Once met by the City Troop, which promised to release all prisoners, the militants turned back. In the renewed quiet, Reed went before the Pennsylvania Assembly to seek quick amnesty for all involved, explaining the violence and bloodshed as "one of the casual overflowings of liberty." James Wilson went into hiding across the Delaware in New Jersey.

Citing his position, Benedict Arnold asked the Board of War for guards, as "lawless ruffians" were still threatening his house. "This request I presume," he wrote, "will not be denied to a man who has so often fought and bled in defense of the liberties of his country." But Congress declared the matter a state affair, and refused to be involved. At nightfall the First City Troop again patrolled the rubble-filled streets, and quiet returned.

In London, Englishmen learned of the Pennsylvania disorders from their newspapers months later, and congratulated themselves that it could not happen there. London, the city that red-brick Philadelphia, on a much smaller scale, most resembled, seemed not to need a police force, and had none. Disunion seemed rampant in the colonies, and coexisted with a militant desire for independence. America seemed a barbarian country populated by the refuse of humanity. Until the war, Britain had transported criminals across the Atlantic to get rid of them.

The French squadron of forty-nine ships crossing the Atlantic, although primarily directed toward protecting the Caribbean sugar islands, and if possible plucking some belonging to Britain, anchored off Savannah in mid-September and landed five thousand troops to cooperate with a small Continental force seeking to secure Georgia. The inept and hesitant Admiral Charles d'Estaing, who had bungled the year before at New York harbor and the Chesapeake but was a favorite of Louis XVI, was thrown back with heavy losses, and was severely wounded himself. The redcoat success would soften the embarrassment of the surprise recapture of Stony Point on the Hudson in mid-July. General Anthony Wayne with 1,350 Continentals seized the fort—taken earlier in the year by Clinton—and 110 prisoners. The first press reports to reach England imaginatively estimated 800 prisoners, but even those numbers, Walpole wrote to Horace Mann, "seem trifles to me, who look on America as totally lost, and [I] do not take account of the modes by which we part with the ruins."

Although instructions from London on March 21, 1779—a collective Cabinet decision—were that Rhode Island was to be held against the French even if the rest of the lower colonies were to be abandoned, Admiral Arbuthnot felt that operations in the South could not begin with the limited forces at hand. He appealed for more ships and troops. The fancied threat of French invasion at home continued to squeeze resources and manpower, but cynics scoffed at the unreality of such fears. A comic broadside asked, "Can we Invasions dread, when Volunteers like these, propose to Fight the Gay Monsieurs?" (August 26, 1779). Subtitled "The Terror of France, or the Westminster Volunteers," it pictured chimney sweeps and other unsoldierly types being driven by a beadle with a raised stick, and suggested the level of local preparation. "The Master of the Asses—or the Westminster Volunteers A Mews—ing Themselves" offered another variant of the unsuccessful recruiting theme. Before the King's Mews at Charing Cross six motley volunteers in civilian dress but for cockaded hats are spurred on by redcoats front and rear, one of the soldiers with swathed, gouty legs, walking with a crutch and a stick. A James Gillray cartoon of September 5, 1779, "The Church Militant," satirized a different but equally useless level of belligerence. In the engraving, a group of clergy, some lean and ascetic, others stout and gross, led by bishops, sing with choristers, "O Lord Our God, Arise and Scatter Our Enemies." A solo—and fat—bishop, bottles arrayed behind him, sings,

Give us Good Beef in Store
And the Key to the [Wine] Cellar Door.

The British would evacuate Rhode Island and its perches in the Hudson highlands late in 1779. With the coming of the French altering priorities, ships and men were needed elsewhere. Unless New York City was at hazard, the Hudson at the moment seemed a poor investment because nothing, even seizing bits of rebel territory, seemed to tempt Washington into a confrontation. Fire raids and the plundering of the Connecticut ports, possible from New York and the sort of harassment Germain continually proposed, also did little but increase hatred for the British. Lord North's secretary, John Robinson, found him "in a state of mind such as it is melancholy even to reflect on," but the prime minister soon learned better news, which left him "in a good deal of vigour of mind and spirits" when word reached him of the American reversal at Savannah and the failed intervention of the French. Now the possibly loyal Carolinas appeared open for an assault.

Returning the southern colonies to the king's obedience meant dividing British forces into a defensive posture in the North, where they held little more than New York harbor, and loosely coordinated offensive operations in the coastal South, but from London it seemed perfect sense. Restoration of the king's obedience anywhere always tempted the remote ministries, often locked in fantasy.

Writing to Sir William Eden (and thus indirectly to George III) on November 11, 1779, Clinton crowed exaggeratedly about Savannah and its potential, "I think this is the greatest event that has happened the whole war. I need not say what will be our operations in consequence." When the news reached England, Tory papers published joyous odes, such as "Hark! from o'er the Western Main!" and the guns at the Tower of London were fired. Major General Augustine Prevost, the Swiss-born British commander who had moved up from East Florida to repel the French, boasted about Savannah to General Amherst in a message in the same mail packet bringing news of the new assault on Charleston. The seizure of a second southern port would be "a blow to the rebellious colonies [from] which they could not recover, and which might reduce them to reason much sooner than anything that can be effected to the northward."

The Continentals were reportedly reeling in the South and unable to cope with the fever-prone climate. Although the British controlled almost nothing in the interior, along the seaboard their civilized cantonments had hospitals, medicines, rum and other provisions from the Indies. "Despondency" and "sickness" among the Americans, Prevost predicted, "would soon reduce them to nothing."

The confident forecast was much to claim from an operation that had been modestly fed, but Whitehall also understood that ambitious plans were in progress to split off other southern colonies. Clinton's ambiguous assessment to Germain was that a further success in the region would be "of infinite consequence," but that he had "no assurances of any favorable temper in the province of South Carolina. . . . The force which the present weakness of General

Washington's army could enable me to detach, might possibly get possession of Charlestown. . . . But I doubt whether they could keep it." It could be only "a desultory advantage," exposing people "who might declare for us" to future abandonment and retribution.

For most soldiers assigned to the operation, Christmas was spent drearily in the crowded holds of ships being loaded for the southern campaign. Leaving General Knyphausen in charge of winter hibernation in the seemingly tranquil north, Clinton and Cornwallis, in 90 transports accompanied by 14 frigates, sailed from New York through harbor ice toward Charleston with 8,700 troops and 5,000 sailors and marines on Boxing Day, the day after Christmas 1779. They had every expectation of success. The New York command did not know that the revolution they hoped to suppress was opening a Pandora's box back at home.

11

The Time of the Tumults
January 1780–June 1780

"The Floods, O Lord, lift up their voice. . . ."
"Gallia exults and London burns!"

—*Charles Wesley,* Hymns Written in the Time of the Tumults, *1780*

As the new year opened, the Charleston expedition was early in what would become a thirty-eight-day voyage that had hardly proceeded beyond Sandy Hook when a winter storm began. Some ships foundered, and the Gulf Stream, soon encountered, slowed the convoy and threatened to sweep some transports into the mid-Atlantic. The armada had to bypass South Carolina and put in at British-held Savannah for repairs before setting out once more for Charleston. In England, Whitehall did not yet know of its whereabouts, but counted on it to end the rebellion in the South.

At home, revolution remained unthinkable. Since the government was deaf to internal discontent, it was also blind to signs that distant America could be exacerbating domestic restiveness. America meant empire, and national pride. Pacifism and dissent meant decline. As the king lectured Lord North on March 7, 1780, "I can never suppose this country so far lost to all ideas of self importance, as to be willing to grant America independence. If that could ever be universally adopted, I shall despair of this country being ever preserved from a state of inferiority and consequently falling into a very low class among the European states." North would again offer to resign. As usual, George III would not let him go. It had become a ritual.

The king's subjects looked back on what seemed, with or without America, to be fading glories. Taxes had risen; the slump in trade had cost jobs, as did the new steam-driven machinery in mills and the profit-driven enclosures of once common grazing lands. In Lancashire, thousands had demonstrated against Richard Arkwright's cotton-spinning machines at Chorley. Provincial associations and radical urban groups protested alleged corruption and demanded "economical reform." The opposition, led in the Commons by Fox and Burke and Wilkes, and by the Marquis of Rockingham in the Lords, was gaining strength. Critics saw the expanding and expensive war as squandering their birthright. Such alleged iniquities as the Game Laws, excise taxes, the standing army, endemic corruption, and the Riot Act seemed betrayals of ordinary people by government. As a result, English Nonconformists and working-class radicals, it has been said, "studied the faraway struggle of Americans like leaves in a tea cup."

The "General Fast," mandated for February 4, was intended as usual to bring to parishioners, however unaddicted to newspapers and however remote from London, a sense of "alarming crisis" (as one clergyman put it) on "a day of calamity" (as another divine claimed), and to renew "zeal for the government" (as still another urged). Again, religion was reinforcing politics. Within weeks, publishers issued texts of fourteen of the sermons in pamphlet form, with more to follow. The *Monthly Review* observed blandly that they evoked "the manly freedom and resolution of the honest Briton, so admirably blended with the moderation and piety of the good Christian."

Under a March 27 date a satiric newspaper column railed at the hypocrisies of North, Sandwich, and Germain, allegedly "amiable and constitutional Protectors" of the people but merely "loud in proclaiming that the Committees and Associations now forming by the several counties, to support their Petitions, are *dangerous assemblies* and *unlawful meetings.*" If gatherings exceeded twelve persons, they fell "expressly within the meaning of the Riot Act." Should such "riotous republicans" remain obstinate and refuse to disperse, "pursuant to the JUST-ASSES, who shall read the Act, a regiment of *Highlanders, Hanoverians,* or *Hessians,* may be ready to fire on them." Lawbreakers legally "*murdered,*" as well as any who might escape, would "forfeit their goods and chattels, lands and tenements to the Crown, [and] his Majesty's Ministers will not only *effectually* get rid of the Petitions and Petitioners, but by the forfeitures of their estates, raise a fund sufficient to carry on the *wise* war against America for twenty years to come."

A Society for Constitutional Information was organized by John Cartwright in April 1780 to document the existence in law of what seemed increasingly threatened freedoms. In the Commons, Edmund Burke employed the device of suggesting economies in government to attack the influence of the Crown. The king had large sums to influence policy through his titular medieval survivals and sinecures. For example, Burke ridiculed,

> Cross a brook, and you lose the King of England. . . . Go to the north, and you find him dwindled to a Duke of Lancaster; turn to the west of that north, and he pops up upon you in the humble character of Earl of Chester. Travel a few miles on, the Earl of Chester disappears, and the king surprises you again as Count Palatine of Lancaster. If you travel beyond Mount Edgecombe, you find him once more in his incognito, and he is Duke of Cornwall. So that, quite fatigued and satiated with this dull variety, you are infinitely refreshed when you return to the sphere of his proper splendor, and behold your amiable sovereign in his true, simple, undisguised, native character of Majesty.

Burke recommended selling the remaining Crown lands and eliminating such costly anachronisms as the Board of Green Cloth, the Great Wardrobe, the Jewel Office, the Treasurer of the Household, the Cofferer, and the Treasurer of the Chamber. If eliminated, he suggested sardonically, these and other sinecures that rewarded greedy politicians could help pay for subduing America. A bill which Burke proposed, mischievously, to abolish the Board of Trade and the American Department was defeated by only 7 votes, 208 to 201. It had no chance whatever in the Lords but demonstrated the growing disenchantment with the ministry.

Illustrated broadsides were much like later editorial cartoons, and public sentiment seemed also reflected in "The Heads of the Nation in a Right Situation," published by Matthew Darly in the Strand on May 1, 1780. The setting is Temple Bar, the barrier where the Strand became Fleet Street, and the City of London began.* Three severed heads on spikes—North, Germain, and Sandwich—are being pelted

*The gateway between Westminster and the City was removed in 1878.

with stones, dead dogs, and other rubbish by a crowd. A delighted woman says, "This is a sight I've long wish[ed] to see." A crone smoking a pipe heaves market objects from her basket. A codger waves his hat with delight; another flourishes his wig.

While Parliament once more debated the costs of the war, Clinton and Cornwallis were enduring the difficult passage southward to the Carolinas. Wintry Atlantic gales cost the convoy most of its artillery secured on decks. The pitching in heavy seas sickened the huddled troops aboard. Horses with legs broken by the plunging of bow and stern had to be destroyed and heaved overboard. The British public learned dramatically about the hazards of fighting a war at long distance when the *Anna,* dismasted during an overnight storm, wallowed out of sight of the fleet and drifted with its Hessians for seven weeks across the Atlantic to St. Ives in Cornwall.

It took a month or more for most ships to reach landfall in Savannah. Disembarking near Charleston began only on February 11, 1780—and that offshore on Tybee Island. Only on March 29 did the redcoat infantry reach a viable position fifteen miles upstream from the city. Assisted by supply ships from St. Kitts in the Caribbean, construction of a siege works began on April 1.

Enemy delays should have given General Benjamin Lincoln and his undermanned Continentals opportunity to slip away and fight inland, but he unwisely chose to dig in and defend the city. Charleston, after all, had survived an earlier invasion attempt.

In London, from which the war still appeared stagnated, John Dunning, opposition MP for Calne in Wiltshire,★ moved a resolution on April 6, declaring, "The influence of the Crown has increased, is increasing, and ought to be diminished," and further, that the House of Commons possessed the inherent authority "to examine into and correct abuses in the expenditure of the civil list revenues, as well as in every other branch of the public revenue wherever it shall appear expedient to the wisdom of this House to do so."

MPs waved papers, jeered, and cheered. Following the uproar, the first motion carried, 233 to 215, while the second passed without a division. Discredited by the result, North offered to resign. Again the king refused to see him out. The sovereign could en-

★Created 1st Baron Ashburton in 1782

courage or reprimand, but only his ministers with seats in Parliament could direct the war; no other prime minister seemed likely to take orders so dutifully.

Other than to validate a shift in mood, the motions in the Commons were meaningless, as the Lords would spurn them. "A little time will I am certain," the king wrote confidently on April 11, "open the eyes of several who have been led on farther than they intended." Indeed, when Dunning moved further, on April 24, that Parliament remain in session until economic grievances were redressed, he was defeated by fifty-one votes.

The "economical reform" bill introduced by Burke as an indirect criticism of the war was also defeated, but in the Lords the Duke of Richmond tried a different strategy to put pressure on the government, introducing a bill for universal male suffrage and mandating annual Parliaments. Predictably, it failed. With the opposition still on the offensive, the persistent General Henry Conway proposed, in the Commons on May 5, "A Bill for quieting the troubles now reigning in the British colonies in America, and for enabling commissioners, with full powers to treat, and conclude, upon terms of conciliation with the said colonies." The war, he argued, was "a fatal rebellion . . . preying upon our vitals," and that "the taxation of America" had been "impolitic and unjust," intended only "to rob three millions of British subjects of their liberty and property." The motion—and others before it and to follow—were voted down.

For royalists there could be too much democracy. A bill for civil relief for Catholics in England seconded by Dunning in 1778, and passed overwhelmingly in the Commons, intended to foster national unity and mitigate dissension in Ireland, became the unanticipated breaking point. The legislation was a modest beginning, ending liability to imprisonment for Roman Catholic priests and schoolmasters, in effect since 1700, and permitting Papists to purchase land. Riots directed against Catholic property in Glasgow and Edinburgh early in 1779 had delayed extending its provisions to Scotland, where Lord George Gordon, 3rd son of the late Duke of Gordon, was head of the militant Scottish Protestant Association. Gordon, who had long toasted American freedom with his friends, now had a new cause closer to home.

As Richmond's suffrage bill was being debated in the Lords on

Friday June 2, 1779, the lean, lank-haired Scottish Presbyterian, whose forbears had been Jacobite Roman Catholics, was marching on Parliament with a huge, clamoring mob. He carried a petition from the rigidly hostile Protestant Association to repeal, as a "betrayal of Protestantism," the relief granted Catholics the year before.

Recruitment of volunteer militias for America had drawn men from the Scottish Highlands and Ireland itself, raising anxiety among militant Protestants who did not want Papists, or recent rebels, under arms anywhere in the British Isles. Yet reinforcing Romish loyalty seemed useful at a time when Britain again faced its traditional Catholic adversary, France, and in April 1779 the Secretary for America had written to the lord-lieutenant of Ireland, the Earl of Buckinghamshire, that he knew of "no means of augmenting the army so Effectively as from Ireland."

MP for Ludgershall from a family seat, Gordon was twenty-nine. He had served in the navy in American waters, and had known sympathies with the colonists, but he had also showed signs of mental instability and was retired home as a lieutenant. Like his fellow MP Frederick Bull, a City alderman who was influential in the Protestant Association, Gordon was an outspoken critic of Lord North.

Eccentrics were not uncommon in either house of Parliament. Gordon had seemed more peculiar since his naval service. He shouted and wept rather than spoke, violated decorum in referring to members by name, and derided George III as a closet Papist. Offended when his parliamentary extravagances were ignored, he became even more extreme. Fanatical about the alleged evils of Catholicism, he had written a tract that he insisted upon presenting in person to the king. Since Gordon was the younger brother of a duke, the sovereign had reluctantly admitted him to an audience in January 1780. "The lunatic apostle," according to Horace Walpole, ". . . incontinently began reading his Irish pamphlet, and the King had the patience to hear him do so for above an hour, till it was so dark that the lecturer could not see. His Majesty then desired to be excused, and said he would finish the piece himself." Ignoring propriety, Gordon remarked, handing it to him, "Well! But you must give me your honour that you will read it out." Taken aback, the king was "forced to pledge his honour."

George III had not heard the last of Gordon. He advertised in

newspapers for signatures to a petition for repeal of legislation relieving "His Majesty's subjects professing the Romish religion, from certain penalties and disabilities." Then he chaired a meeting of the
Protestant Association in Coachmaker's Hall, near Cheapside, on May
29, 1780, to arrange delivery of the lengthy petition to Parliament.
Recognizing a market appealing to the association's prejudices,
Matthew Darly rushed out a print, "Father Peters leading his mangy
Whelp to be touched for the Evil." As the medieval tradition was that
rulers "by the grace of God" had healing powers, Darly punned on
the name of Lord Petre, regarded as head of the Catholic community
in England, as he was married to the niece of the Duke of Norfolk,
senior Roman Catholic peer. The caricature showed "Father Peters"
leading King George toward Rome. In the background, presumably
on the Thames, three derelict ships display brooms at their mastheads
to show they are for sale—probably an attack on Lord Sandwich and
his reputed corruption, and a comment on the wartime state of the
state.

Somehow, anti-Papist aspersions were also linked to the American
cause, suggesting that to be pro-Catholic was to be anti-American.
Anonymously written, "The American Times. A Satire. In which are
delineated the Characters of the Leaders of the American Rebellion," sold at two shillings. In it, purchasers could find attacks on
Franklin and Morris, Mifflin and Washington. Ostensibly the author
was "Camillo Querno, Poet-laureat to the Congress." The actual
Camillo Querno of Apulia, satirized in Alexander Pope's *The Dun-
ciad,* was a Vatican intimate of Leo X, who had attacked Martin
Luther as a heretic. The *Monthly Review* dismissed the pamphlet as "a
Jordan of invective."

In London newspapers and handbills, Gordon appealed for twenty
thousand militant Protestant supporters to accompany him and his
petition. They were to rally at noon on June 2, at St. George's Fields,
Southwark, across London Bridge, wearing blue cockades as emblems of the movement and carrying blue "No Popery" banners.
From there the faithful were to march in three separate paths in
order not to clog the bridges across the Thames.

Tens of thousands more irreconcilables massed than Gordon anticipated, many of them earnest and pious in their ways—as if, Edward
Gibbon wrote, former followers of Oliver Cromwell "had started out

of their graves." Their numbers were swollen further by gawkers, pickpockets, hawkers, and ruffians and even ladies of the evening joined, soliciting the afternoon trade. Not only were there crowds of Protestants by faith, but protestants of every sort—against the American war, against the French, against corruption, against taxes. By half past two the mob, four miles long and increasingly unruly in the mid-afternoon heat, was approaching the Palace of Westminster from several directions just as latecomers were seeking their seats.

MPs and peers already seated realized what was going on in the streets when new arrivals staggered in, and in the confusion demanded to be heard. "Some of the Lordships," according to a press account, appeared "with their hair about their shoulders; others smutted with dirt; most of them as pale as the ghost in Hamlet, and all of them standing up in their several places and speaking at the same instant. One Lord proposed to send for the Guards; another for the Justices or Civil Magistrates; many crying out 'Adjourn! Adjourn!' while the skies resounded with the huzzas, shoutings or hootings and hisses in Palace Yard."

Some mauled peers had clothes torn from them; others were bruised. Bishops, including the Archbishop of York, were missing parts of their habits. On his way from the Admiralty to the Lords, Earl Sandwich's carriage was stopped and smashed, and he fled to a nearby coffeehouse. Lord Mountford interrupted the Duke of Richmond's speech to report that Frederick Irby, Lord Boston, had been dragged from his carriage and trampled upon. He called on younger colleagues to draw their swords and come to His Lordship's aid. Others had their carriages stopped, the wheels wrenched off, and the glass panels beaten into shards. Noble lords straggled into Parliament whitened with the powder beaten out of their hair and wigs. John Verney, 14th Baron Willoughby de Broke, lost his periwig altogether. Fleeing the increasingly violent mob of alleged anti-Papists, the Bishop of Lincoln slipped into a private house, then escaped in woman's clothing. Meanwhile, presiding* anxiously from the woolsack as speaker pro tempore—"quivering like an aspen," Walpole wrote—was elderly Earl Mansfield, who had supported the Relief

---

*Edward, 1st Baron Thurlow, had been named lord chancellor in 1778 in part as reward for upholding the king's American policies; however, he was absent.

Act and was at a loss as to how to respond. En route to the Upper House his carriage had been attacked, its panels beaten in and its windows smashed, and he had barely escaped with his life. In the Lords he told the Duke of Gloucester, the king's chronically indebted brother, "This country is undone. A change of administration might be good, if any coalition be made."

Gordon had taken his case to the Commons, in the former St. Stephen's Chapel,★ where he was eligible to sit. Amid the uproar, which could be heard within as the great doors opened and closed, he arrived with a servant who balanced the immense petition on a porter's knot—a shoulder pad for carrying heavy burdens. Two officers of the House received it formally and placed it on the speaker's table for presentation. After opening prayers, never foreshortened for any reason, North called the petitioners illegal and refused to recognize a document presented less in parliamentary order than disorder. But desperately, as the tumult outside grew louder and more violent, he offered to take up repeal the following Tuesday, when the Commons next convened.

Threatening the prime minister that the impatient mob might tear him to pieces at any time, Gordon left the House to tease his adherents with inflammatory remarks. "They talk of considering the petition next Tuesday," he shouted, "but we must have it considered now!" Then he went to an outer gallery where some of his followers tried to press forward, although the inner doors, at the first reports of disturbances, had been closed and locked. From atop a staircase he declared, now more cautiously, as he was not entirely mad, "His Majesty is a gracious monarch, and when he hears that people ten miles around are collecting, there is no doubt that he will send his ministers private orders to repeal the bill." Turning to George Selwyn, who controlled the nominations for the two-seat Ludgershall constituency, Gordon asked, given the circumstances, whether he would be chosen again. Selwyn said no.

"Oh, yes," Gordon disagreed. "[I]f you recommend me, they would choose me [even] if I came from the coast of Africa."

"That's according to what part of the coast you come from," said Selwyn, invoking a monetary pun, and a reminder that the proper-

★Destroyed by fire in 1841 and replaced by the present Houses of Parliament

tied electorate usually supported the privileged. "They would, certainly, if you came from the Guinea Coast."

Many in the Commons were military gentlemen who, anticipating a demonstration, as it was advertised and crowds were already swarming toward Southwark, bore their swords to their seats. One angry MP, Colonel James Murray, brother of the Duke of Atholl, warned Gordon as throngs thundered at the locked doors, "My Lord George, I see many lives will be lost. By God, yours shall be one of them!" General Conway warned Gordon that the entrance to the House chamber was narrow—"and I shall protect the freedom of this place with my sword." Colonel Adam Gordon of the Cameronians identified himself as a "near relation"—he was a cousin—and shouted to Lord George, "If a man among this crowd, whose uproar strikes us deaf, crosses the threshold of the House of Commons, I swear to run my sword that moment—not into his, but into your body!" Captain John Baker-Holroyd warned Gordon that he ought to be sent to Bedlam; then he followed him up to the gallery to prevent his making further addresses to the mob from there. In both Houses it appeared nevertheless that the entrances would soon be forced.

The Lords were the first to adjourn, at about eight, and were allowed by the mob to leave, but they were warned that unless the Commons immediately repealed civil relief for Catholics, there would be "terrible mischief" at night.

Hurrying up, almost too late, at about 9:30, about five hours into the chaos, a rescue detachment of Horse Guards and Foot Guards began employing bayonets and the flats of their sabers to drive the throngs from the Parliament lobbies and the narrow streets around Palace Yard. In a space they had cleared an officer cantered up, accompanied by a magistrate and an official of the Commons, and the magistrate, dismounting, read the Riot Act as loudly as he could through the tumult. (Few others elsewhere in London would do so, but they would not have the Horse Guards around them.) When some in the mob stirred only to throw stones, soldiers began seizing some obvious leaders, taking them forcibly to Newgate Prison. Horses' hoofs were even more of an inducement to retreat. Protesters began dispersing nervously from Westminster eastward toward Blackfriars Bridge, demolishing the carriages of Sir George Savile and

Charles Turner, MP for York, en route. Exhausted, Gordon remained, as he lawfully could, dozing in a chair in the refreshment rooms of the Commons.

Darkness fell late in June, and the fanatics, the dispossessed, the rapscallions, and the rabble of London fanned out into the alleys and streets. With no goals but to vent its frustrations, the rabble, following self-appointed leaders, went roving for officials to harass, Catholics to abuse, and opportunities for plunder and profligacy. There was little to stop them. Without a police force London streets were patrolled only by the Watch, elderly and otherwise unemployed men hired by each parish and paid a pittance. Unarmed, each had only a lantern and a pole. They were useless in any emergency. The only other lights at night were feeble oil-and-cotton street lamps, which were often extinguished by local residents once the lamplighters left, as they furnished illumination for footpads and other thugs.

Buckingham House and St. James's Palace were bypassed by the mob and seemed immune to the disorders, but pandemonium engulfed central London, and the king wrote urgently to North, "This tumult must be gotten the better of, or it will encourage designing men to use it as precedent for assembling people on other occasions. If possible, we must get to the bottom of it, and examples must be made." Belatedly, North sent messages to magistrates and justices of the peace, who could bar assemblages of more than twelve if they did not disband after they were read the Riot Act. Until that formality, troops legally could not interfere. According to a letter from Horace Walpole to William Mason, the Cabinet Council, aware of impending trouble, had authorized North "to prepare the civil officers to keep the peace, and *he forgot it*"—failing to issue warnings until prompted. By then Gordon's supporters were swarming out of control.

In the City, where merchants and brokers looked forward hopefully to the collapse of North's war government, Lord Mayor Brackley Kennett, a prominent wine merchant and proprietor of the King's Head in Pall Mall, strained to keep the peace. Unwisely, he greeted, rather than warned, the hooligans gathering before the Mansion House, the imposing, pillar-fronted city hall of the financial district. The gesture emboldened demonstrators to further excesses. "There are great people at the bottom of these riots," Kennett claimed to a worried Irish Catholic silk merchant, deploring that he could not protect private residences.

Pillage and arson supplanted protest as the mobs swept eastward from Westminster. At nightfall that Friday the Roman Catholic chapels belonging to the Sardinian and Bavarian ministers, and legal under diplomatic practice, were ransacked and burned, although the Sardinian envoy, the Marchese di Cordon, at his Chapel of St. Anselm and St. Cecilia in Lincoln's Inn Fields, vainly offered the rabble money to rescue a large religious picture and a fine organ. The fire brigade (its engines owned by the fire insurance companies) arrived with water wagons and hoses to play on the adjacent buildings, but the belligerent crowd refused to let the firemen near the chapel and cut their hoses. As the Horse Guards attempted to save the ambassador's house from pillage, Thomas Walpole, Horace's cousin, seeing a lady in distress, took the terrified marchesa to his own residence nearby. Freiherr von Haslang, the Bavarian minister, at his house in Jermyn Street for which he had claimed diplomatic privilege and refused to pay the rent, tried to protect his adjacent chapel at 24 Golden Square, but the mob broke in and found sixteen sacks of untaxed tea and a quantity of smuggled lace under the altar. They were set afire. Haslang had prospered by selling smuggled goods as well as diplomatic protection from arrests.

As darkness came, many of the rabble remained. Breaking down railings, they camped in parks or slept in stables and other outbuildings. At his town house at 40 Berkeley Square, where Horace Walpole had servants add iron bars to his front door, a messenger arrived very early on Saturday morning, June 3, with a brief letter from General Conway, written "near 3":

> I have received a letter and communication of so extraordinary a kind and from so extraordinary a quarter this morning that I am very impatient to communicate it to you and talk with you upon it. I would have come to you this moment but that I have just made a long and hot walk from the Tower [of London] and am not sure of finding you at home. I shall dress now and then will either expect you here, or come to you before my dinner abroad as you like best.

Conway had received a message from an informant he would not identify that the king, concerned that the chaos would be more than the indolent North could deal with, was pressed by circumstances to replace him. Conway was invited to join a new government committed to strong action, but the king insisted that the price of coalition would be the retention in the ministry of Germain, Sandwich, and Mansfield, all of whom retained the royal confidence. Conway, His Majesty offered, could be commander-in-chief of the army; the Duke of Richmond would go to France as ambassador, to "treat of peace"; and Lord Camden and Mr. Burke could become well-paid commissioners for conciliation to America. Conway was invited to explore the possibilities with Lord George, meeting as if by accident, in the letter writer's house.

Walpole hurried to Conway's residence in Little Warwick Street, Charing Cross, and when asked his opinion, scoffed at the offer. The king's betrayal of North would solve nothing if North's accomplices remained. Not only would the devious scheme remove some of the king's strongest critics from England, no one whom Conway might ask to serve with him would do so if Germain remained as American Secretary.

"Dashing down the letter with warmth very unusual to him" (as Walpole recalled), Conway exclaimed, "And to think I would act a moment with Lord Sandwich!" Finding a pen, the general wrote a polite answer "declining the negotiation." Ineffectively as before, North would remain to cope as he could.

The weekend had begun almost calmly, as Sunday, June 4, everyone knew, was the king's birthday. Saturday dawned dead and silent as the mobs slept off exhaustion and the alcoholic booty from looted taverns. With his aides, His Majesty even visited the sentries at eerily tranquil St. James's Palace and Buckingham House and his accompanying servants brought them food and drink. Steeple bells pealed and flags were hoisted. Taking advantage of the temporary quiet, Edmund Burke had his books and pictures moved from Charles Street to safety, and sent his wife to the country. On Sunday into Monday morning he stayed with Charles Fox and Viscount Fitzwillliam at Rockingham's residence in Grosvenor Square, which soldiers, servants, tradesmen, and his political supporters had quickly garrisoned. "The rest," Burke wrote helplessly about his abandoned possessions in a rueful message delivered to a friend in Bristol by Burke's son, "is at the service of this Body of zealots."

By Sunday night the rioters were again as active as an overturned anthill, breaking into unguarded buildings to search for hammers, saws, pokers, axes, iron bars, barrel staves, and whatever else could be fashioned into clubs or crude tools. Catholic chapels were the alleged targets, but most mobs sought general mischief and the settling of personal scores. When Sir George Savile's house in Leicester Fields was threatened by the mob, he hurried to Grosvenor Square on horseback, borrowed Fox's carriage to save his papers, and escaped by the back door as the rioters were breaking in at the front. His furniture was thrown into the street and set afire. The Irish Relief legislation was known as "Savile's Act"—the Yorkshire MP had seen it to passage.

After camping in a nearby park overnight, some of the mob descended upon a Catholic area at Moorfields, just north of the City, torching houses and a chapel. One of the homes belonged to the merchant who had appealed unsuccessfully to Lord Mayor Kennett. Below Moorfields, Spitalfields and Wapping were set afire. Charles Dickens, who would describe the disorders in *Barnaby Rudge* (1841) from a mass of research he had collected, and interviews with survivors, wrote, "The contagion spread like a dread fever; an infectious madness, as yet not near its height, seized on new victims every hour, and society began to tremble at their ravings." To Dickens, the "honest zealots" had become outnumbered by "the very scum and refuse of London." In the atmosphere of panic, rumors spread that sympathetic soldiers were about to join the mobs, and even that thousands of wrathful miners from South Wales were marching on London. The outrages became disconnected from their supposed causes. In *Barnaby Rudge,* one rioter shouts, "No Popery, brother!" only to be answered, "No Property, brother!"

On Monday, June 5, a mob set fire to the debtors' prison, smashed its doors, and let the inmates, many gaunt and malnourished, escape. The horde straggled toward Bloomsbury Square and the mansion of Earl Mansfield, now seventy-five and dean of the judiciary, who was not only considered pro-Catholic but was further unpopular as the peer who had devised for North the prewar Prohibitory Acts. As Lord and Lady Mansfield struggled to escape out the back of their house, the mob forced the front.

Sir Nathaniel Wraxall, an official of the East India Company, was riding nearby, and his party sought shelter. In the shouting, onrushing throngs many brandished crude weapons improvised from the debris of looted buildings. "Quitting the coach, we crossed the square, and had scarcely got under the wall of Bedford House, when we heard the door of Lord Mansfield's house burst open with violence. In a few minutes, all the contents of the apartments being precipitated [by the intruders] from the windows, were piled up and wrapped in flames. A file of foot soldiers arriving, drew up near the blazing pile, but without either attempting to quench the fire or to impede the mob, who were indeed far too numerous to admit of being dispersed, or even intimidated, by a small detachment of infantry."

Finally, soldiers arrived with a frightened magistrate to read the Riot Act, but it was too late. Mansfield's law library, pictures, and manuscript collection were afire. Leveling their muskets, the incensed Foot Guards shot at men and women milling about for booty, and the crowd began to disperse. After the soldiers left, the mob returned to carry away the casualties in a rude procession led by a hooligan loudly ringing Mansfield's looted dinner bell.

That night, by the lights of flaming torches, a throng marched on Lord North's barricaded residence. A squad of Horse Guards, now deployed and ready, galloped toward the rioters, who retreated to seek easier targets. Three magistrates reputed to be harsh in sentencing were especially marked for mob vengeance. The houses of Sir John Fielding (presiding magistrate at Bow Street but lying ill at suburban Brompton), Justice Cox, and Justice Hyde were vandalized. Assembling some armed friends, and barricading all passages to his house in Pall Mall, Lord George Germain coolly awaited an attack but, his friend Wraxall wrote, "The rioters were too well informed of the precautions taken to venture making any attempt on him." Not so Lord Sandwich, whose house and effects were again vandalized after he escaped.

"Now Newgate!" someone shrieked. It was inevitable that the prison would be attacked, as some mob leaders had been taken there from Palace Yard. From the rooftop of the house of the prison governor, Richard Akerman, fronting Newgate, the keeper asked what they wanted. "You have got some friends of ours in your custody, Master."

"I have a good many people in my custody," Ackerman answered with false bravado before vanishing to take flight with his family. Vandals improvised ladders, tore away rafters, and set fire to the prison roof. Doors and locks yielded to flames, crowbars, and axes. Privileged prisoners who rented comfortable quarters within, sent out for quality meals, and lavishly entertained guests were outraged at being evicted. Wretched inmates from dismal cells and still in chains straggled into daylight—women as well as men. "Three of these," an onlooker reported, "were to be hanged on Friday. You have no conception of the frenzy of the multitude." One group of "about twelve women and eight men" was led to a blacksmith, who was forced to remove their fetters.

With little being done to suppress the worst mob chaos anyone alive could remember, the king urged North by courier, "Allowing Lord George Gordon, the avowed head of the tumult, to be at large, certainly encourages the continuation of it, to which must be added the great supineness of the civil magistrates. I fear, without more vigour, this will not subside." Although the army had been responding to urgent appeals, even protecting North's own town house, soldiers lawfully could not intervene where local magistrates, fearing their own safety, had refrained from invoking the Riot Act.

"Conflagration: A Satire," an anonymous pamphlet published early the next year, imagined (with much accuracy) "Boreas" (North) and "Germanicus" (Germain) calling for a meeting of the Privy Council while the mob riots. While conceding that he is to blame for the "revolted provinces" and the religious turmoil, "Boreas" presents his plan for suppressing the Protestant Association, confident that while he could not control the parliamentary opposition, he had enough votes from members long purchased to pass whatever bills were needed. General Amherst is blamed for failing to use the army to quell lawlessness, but Amherst declares that he is blocked by the failure of civil authority. "Germanicus" recommends levying additional taxes to furnish funds to compensate riot victims, and asks "Boreas" to call out the army.

Again on Tuesday, June 6, London shops were shuttered, windows boarded up, streets empty. Cautiously, people of every persuasion improvised blue cockades for their hats and hung Protestant Association "No Popery" banners on houses and shops and across narrow alleyways, or chalked the slogan boldly wherever they could. Yet popular anger (as well as the opportunity to loot) had gone beyond Romanism and was directed against anything which appeared to oppress the poor, from pawnshops to the tollhouses on the Thames bridges. Although the violence had become anarchic, Lord Stormont, secretary of state for the Northern Department since the death of Lord Suffolk, claimed to the king, "This is a deep laid Rev[o]lt. . . . The Ringleaders at least act with deliberate rage and upon a deliberate plan." There was almost certainly no such plan, beyond venting anger at the establishment.

Samuel Johnson wrote to James Boswell that Hester Thrale and her husband, Henry, a wealthy brewer, bought off the rabble when they surrounded their town house and adjacent bottling works in Southwark, just below London Bridge. It may have helped that Thrale had suffered several strokes and looked palpably very ill. Very likely Mrs. Thrale fended off the threat for him. Although they were "in great danger," Johnson recalled, "the mob was pacified, at their first invasion, with about £50 in drink and meat; and at their second, were driven away by the soldiers." Johnson's publisher, William Strahan, "got a garrison into his house, and maintained them a fortnight; he was so frightened he removed part of his goods."

"The riots in London were certainly horrible," Boswell replied innocently from Scotland, realizing that Johnson spent part of every week across the Thames with the hospitable Thrales, "but you give me no account of your own situation during the barbarous anarchy. A description of it by Dr. Johnson would be a great painting; you might write another 'London, a Poem.'"

Rumors spread that the mad in Bedlam would be freed by the mobs, and also the ten lions caged in the Tower of London. (They remained untouched.) The Bank of England was besieged; the Fleet, the Marshalsea, and the King's Bench prisons were broken into and set afire, and the inmates released into the streets. Bridewell escaped the flames when its doors were opened and the convicts allowed to stream out. Breweries and distilleries were alluring targets, as the Thrales learned. On Holborn Hill, near burned-out Newgate Prison, the Langdale gin distillery and its storehouses were set ablaze and the fetid gutters ran with alcohol. The rabble, even women and children, sopped up the slimy spirits in rags, shoes, caps, and buckets, drinking themselves insensible. Lurching for more drink too close to the burning buildings, some died in the flames.

The next morning, remembered as "Black Wednesday," Dr. Johnson, who lived nearby, "walked with Dr. [William] Scott to look at Newgate, and found it in ruins with the fire yet glowing. As I went by the Protestants were plundering the Sessions-house at the Old Bailey. There were not, I believe, a hundred; but they did their work at leisure, in full security, without sentinels, without trepidation, as men lawfully employed, in full day[light]."

In *Barnaby Rudge,* in the rare quiet of the Black Lion tavern, young Joe Willet, one sleeve empty, sits out the terror with friends. "It's been took off," says his father, the publican, with some confused pride. "Tell him where it was done."

"At the defence of the Savannah, father," Joe answers mechanically.

"At the defence of the Salwanners," the elder Willet repeats, looking round the table for loyal compliments.

"In America, where the war is," explains Joe.

"In America, where the war is," Mr. Willet repeats vaguely. "It was took off in defence of the Salwanners in America where the war is." In the circumstances, the successful repelling of the French and American siege of Savannah in October 1779 has no meaning. Round the table the real war is not a remote abstraction where Joe Willet was maimed. It is distressingly close in the London streets.

In urgent session now, the council of the City of London passed a resolution calling on Parliament for immediate repeal of Catholic Relief. Even in daylight, as Dr. Johnson saw from his home at 8 Bolt Court just off Fleet Street, "the glare of conflagration" filled the sky. "Our disgrace will be lasting," Edward Gibbon lamented, identifying "a dark and diabolical fanaticism which I had supposed was extinct." Better informed of the realities, the king concluded that although the monarchy was being respected by the mobs, in the absence of any effective government he had to assert control.

The day before, the king learned that Secretary at War Charles Jenkinson had advised Lord Stormont that most magistrates continued to fail their duty, fearing retribution if they invoked the Riot Act. In one instance, explained Jenkinson, "The Troops having been called out were left by the Magistrate exposed to the fury of the Populace . . . [and] insulted in a most extraordinary manner, and that in two other instances after the Troops had marched to the places appointed for them, several of the Magistrates refused to act. It is the duty of the Troops, my Lord, to act only under the Authority and by direction, of the Civil Magistrate."

Summoning the attorney general, Alexander Wedderburn, who had not fled into hiding, the king persuaded him that civil procedures including the Riot Act had been superseded by the violence and requested the attorney general to issue that finding to the remnants of the Privy Council. Meeting then with the council, which even the hostile but anxious Rockingham attended, the king asked Wedderburn formally, "Is that your declaration of the law as Attorney-General?" When Wedderburn agreed, the king declared, "Then so let it be done!"

Orders went to Lord Amherst at the Horse Guards to disperse the rioters everywhere and in any way he saw fit. Anticipating the summons, and already in action without it, Amherst had been hastily mustering men, and soon had nearly twenty thousand soldiers ready. Some were new militia to serve alongside the regulars, which later would cause unease among the opposition as setting precedents for domestic disturbances. Large fires remained burning where masses of troublemakers thronged Holborn Hill and Ludgate Hill, pouring in and out of the City. Troops raked the narrow streets with musket fire to scatter the mobs. Fleeing, some fell and were trampled where they lay.

That Wednesday morning, June 7, Lord George Gordon boldly turned up at the Porter's Lodge at Buckingham House and asked for an audience with His Majesty. Lord Stormont was then consulting with the king. "Not until he has given sufficient proof of his loyalty and allegiance," the king began in a response to Gordon, "by employing those means he says are in his power to quell the present disturbances and restore peace to this capital." In his agitation he could not finish writing the note. Stormont completed it.

When the council of the City of London received the proclamation of martial law, the formerly contrary lord mayor now seemed grateful. A cartoon published by Thomas Gatch of St. Giles showed a rowdy with a bludgeon, a "No Popery" ribbon in his hat but clearly with no religious intent, swinging at a burning building and bellowing, "Down with the Bank!" John Wilkes had already hastened to the Bank of England to assist in its defense, and even Gordon offered his services to Captain John Baker-Holroyd at its Threadneedle Street gates. They had met before—in the Commons. Baker-Holroyd refused him.

Eager to see what was going on, Walpole—so he wrote to Lady Ossory—decked himself with blue ribbons, for safety, "like a May-Day garland," and as it grew dark went to visit his cousin the Earl of Hertford in Grosvenor Street, finding him with his sons charging their muskets. That night, as fires about London still burned, soldiers continued to resort to their bayonets. Rioters trying to escape south over Blackfriars Bridge below the Bank of England were crushed in the bottleneck that the bridge approaches became. Others, feeling trapped, jumped over the sides, some to drown in the dark, rubbish-strewn Thames.

By daybreak on Thursday, June 8, 1780, all major buildings in Westminster and the City still intact were protected by the army. The Horse Guards patrolled Palace Yard and fifteen hundred regulars and five battalions of militia were encamped in Hyde Park at the ready. Artillerymen defended the Tower of London and iron chains closed many major streets. Sources of London's water were guarded, and drawbridges across the Thames raised. Charlotte Burney, who was staying with her friend Mrs. Thrale, wrote to her novelist sister, Fanny, soon after in the sudden tranquillity, "It sounds almost incredible, but they say that on Wednesday night last, when the mob was more powerful, more numerous, and outrageous than ever, there was, nevertheless, a number of exceedingly genteel people at Ranelagh [pleasure gardens, in Chelsea], though they knew not but their houses might be on fire at the time!" Among them were the Earl of Waldegrave with his daughter and niece. Without the distracted Conway, his wife, Lady Aylesbury, went to the Haymarket to see a revival of *Douglas,* the lauded drama by William Home, which had some ironic resonance as it was about a young Scottish officer fated for a tragic end.

Whitewash applied by work gangs covered the bloodstained and bullet-pocked walls of the Bank of England, and fresh earth concealed some of the carnage on Blackfriars Bridge. Some pathetic former inmates of the burned prisons, hungry, nearly naked, exhausted, and with nowhere to go, returned to what might once have been their cells and crawled to safety.

King George in his military uniform, 1771, by Johann Zoffan. *Royal Collections, courtesy of Her Majesty Queen Elizabeth II*

Charles Wilson Peale's portrait of Washington at the end of the war was reproduced in an engraving in *Harper's Weekly* on May 4, 1889, for the centenary of his inauguration as president. *Harper's Weekly*

Lord North by Nathaniel Dance. *Courtesy National Portrait Gallery*

Lord George Germain, portrait by George Romney. *Private collection*

The attack in this tavern scene is clearly one with no casualties—an attack on food and drink. The undated broadside cartoon is almost a recruiting poster in suggesting that war in America is a holiday from domestic tedium. Odds and bobs suggests a miscellany—here of food and drink. A syllabub is a hot milk drink laced with rum or other spirits. *Lewis-Walpole Library, Yale University.*

British troops plundering an American mansion, a later American magazine depiction imagining a home stately even by British standards. *John Grafton, editor, The American Revolution (Mineola, N.Y.: Dover, 1973); hereafter, Grafton.*

Angry old England trying to reclaim the colonists (untitled print, circa 1776, anonymous). *Private collection*

The Catch Singers, anonymous print, 1776. The two Howes, Lord George Germain (but identified as Sackville), and Lord North toast their gains—bags of gold on the table. The map behind them is reversed. *British Museum 1868-88-4546 (PS811908 1157)*

Unidentified print, 1774. A British view in 1774 of how authority was being challenged in Massachusetts. Before a "liberty tree" on which the Stamp Act placard is tacked upside down, a tarred-and-feathered Tory is being forced to drink taxed tea while in the harbor the Boston Tea Party goes on. A gibbet hangs from the liberty tree. *Grafton*

"Council of the Rulers & the Elders against the Tribe of ye Americans." North, left foreground, is buying support; the speaker draws attention to a map of America bursting into flames. *Westminster magazine, December 1774*

Edmund Burke, engraving from a portrait by Sir Joshua Reynolds. *Grafton*

The Parricide. A Sketch of Modern Patriotism (anonymous engraving for *Westminster* magazine, April 1777). Daughter America in Indian feathered headdress attacks Mother Britannia, who is held down by Yankee patriots. A British lion is being restrained by a New England clergyman. *British Museum 1876-3-16-441*

Benjamin Franklin being presented at the French Court in Versailles. Imagined by John Andrew in an illustration in *Ballou's Pictorial,* May 17, 1856. *Ballou's Pictorial*

Benjamin Franklin in 1778 in France (engraving from the portrait by Joseph Duplessis). *Grafton*

The surrender that brought the French into the war. Burgoyne (on the left) offering his sword to Gates at Saratoga in October 1777, in a romanticized French engraving of the scene. *Grafton*

General "Gentleman Johnny" John Burgoyne, from an engraving after Sir Joshua Reynolds. *Grafton*

The Yankee's Triumph or B———e beat (anonymous print, 1778). Horatio Gates receives Burgoyne's sword in surrender while his starving redcoats are fed by the Continentals. *Grafton*

THE YANKE'S TRIUMPH, or B——E BEAT

The Taking of Miss Mud I'land (anonymous print, circa December 1777). The Continental fortifications had blocked Howe's progress up the Delaware until October 22, 1777. *Michael Wynn Jones, editor, The Cartoon History of the American Revolution (New York, N.Y.: Putnam, 1975) (hereafter, Wynn Jones).*

Charles, Earl Cornwallis after the war in an engraving from a portrait by John Singleton Copley, an American expatriate artist in London. *Grafton*

(OPPOSITE PAGE, BOTTOM) *La visite du Camp Americain par les Comisaires Anglais* (anonymous French print, circa 1778). Although the title suggests a visit by English "commissioners" to an American camp, the print actually portrays visitors to an English camp training recruits for the American war. Thus the well-dressed ladies and gentlemen are camp tourists. *Grafton*

A Picturesque View of the State of the Nation for February 1778 (anonymous print). While Lord Howe's flagship languishes off Philadelphia and commanders sleep onshore, the British lion dozes as a Yankee dog urinates on him, while a British cow is being milked and violated at the same time. *Library of Congress*

"A view in America in 1778," a caricature by Darly, published in *Darly's Comic Prints of Characters, Caricatures and Macaroonies,* London, 1778. The well-clothed officers and member of Congress contrast with the cold and poorly attired soldiers and the wounded Negro in the foreground.

General Sir William Howe, by
J. Chapman. *Grafton*

Clinton's troops, with loyalist refugees, moving across
New Jersey after evacuating Philadelphia in June 1778 (a
later magazine engraving imagining the scene). *Grafton*

General Sir Henry Clinton in a contemporary
engraving from a portrait. *Grafton*

The Liberty of the Subject (engraving by James Gillray, 1779). While distraught women protest, an unhappy tailor (note the scissors and measuring tape poking from his pocket) is hauled away from his work by a naval press gang. The dome of St. Paul's is dimly seen in the background. *Lewis-Walpole Library, Yale University*

"The Distresses of the Nation. An Ode Performed in Honour of his Majesty's Birth-day" (anonymous illustrated broadside, June 4, 1779). The choir is conducted by Lord Sandwich; Lord North plays the violin. A crumpled paper under the kettledrums at Sandwich's feet reads "To the Blessed Memory of Miss Ray." *Library of Congress*

They reign'd a while but 'twas not long / Before from world to world they swung / As they had turn'd from side to side / And as the Villains lived they dy'd. (anonymous print, 1779)

The quotation from Samuel Butler's mock-heroic *Hudibras* (1663–1678) is employed to excoriate Palliser (Sir H.) and Sandwich ("Twitcher"). From Palliser's legs dangle the falsified logbook intended to incriminate Keppel. *Wynn Jones*

Monsieur sneaking gallantly into Brest's skulking-hole (anonymous print published by W. Richardson, 1779). Although the naval battle with the French that resulted in two British court-martials was essentially a draw, the cartoon gives the event a pro-Keppel spin. *Wynn Jones*

"A loud-crying Woman & a Scold shall be sought out to drive away the enemies" (anonymous print published by James Daveny, January 1780). The cartoonist imagines resolute English womanhood defending the coasts from invasion by America's allies, the French. *Wynn Jones*

The Bull Roasted: or the Political Cooks Serving Their Customers (anonymous engraving published by Isaac Harris, February 12, 1780). The "State Cooks"—the ministry—serving up pieces of the empire to America and her allies. On either side of the fireplace are Germain and Sandwich, with North doing the serving. *Wynn Jones*

John André's sketch of himself the night before he was hanged. *Grafton*

Benedict Arnold in Philadelphia in 1778. *Engraving from the portrait by Pierre Du Simitiere. Grafton*

Count de Rochambeau, French General of the Land Forces in America Reviewing the French Troops (print published by Thomas Colley, November 25, 1780). Rochambeau arrived at Newport, Rhode Island, to take over his command, which he is apparently doing, in the English view, with sublime arrogance. *Grafton*

Jack England Fighting the Four Confederates (print published by John Smith, January 1781). Jack England (left) fighting France, Holland, and Spain, with America (in Indian headdress) already on the ground to the right. Jack says, "Sink me but I cou'd beat them all if our Land Lubbers wou'd but Pull Together." *Wynn Jones*

The last battle. A British depiction of the defenses at Yorktown, September 1781. *Grafton*

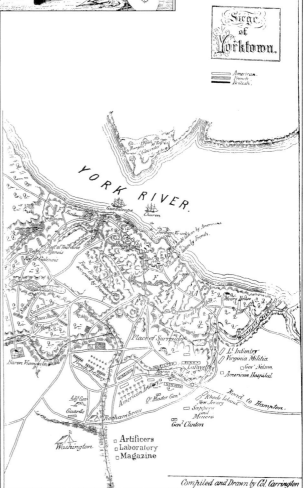

"Mrs. General Washington Bestowing Thirteen Stripes on Britannia," *Rambler magazine* (London), March 1783. RB 478018 *is reproduced by permission of the Huntington Library, San Marino, California*

Proclamation of Peace (anonymous print published by William Wells on October 21, 1783, to mark the signing of the peace treaty with America). As usual, the American is a Red Indian. The Englishman, second from right, is collaring the Dutchman to insist upon peace. *Lewis-Walpole Library, Yale University*

The undated and anonymous caricature suggests the American Secretary at the end of the long war—grim, drawn, and still defiant. *Lewis-Walpole Library, Yale University*

By Friday, June 9, most radical emblems and banners had disappeared from London. The dead were uncounted, but far exceeded the few hundred claimed by the government. Fifty-nine rioters and plunderers of the 192 tried were sentenced to death, although only twenty-nine were eventually executed.

On the afternoon of June 10, a Saturday, the king asked that Gordon be taken into custody. He had returned to his house in Welbeck Street, near Cavendish Square, and made no effort to flee. "If you are sure it's me you want," he said lightly to the Horse Guards who came to arrest him. "I am ready to accompany you." It was the only recorded instance of his modesty. "He always spoke on the people's side," Dickens thought, more kindly than most, "and tried against his muddled brains to expose the profligacy of both parties." He was interrogated for three hours by the Privy Council. Then, to evade curious London crowds, he was escorted over Westminster Bridge and back over Tower Bridge, to a cell in the Tower of London.

The ministers jointly wrote to the Duke of Gordon that it gave the government "the utmost pain" to commit his brother, Lord George, for "High Treason." In an address to both Houses on the nineteenth, His Majesty apologized for the unauthorized employment of eleven thousand troops in a domestic setting, but contended that necessity required it.

The proud world that was England had changed. Through the many newspapers across the counties most people learned of the disorders before they had ended. Steam engineer James Watt wrote to Glasgow professor and chemist John Black, "We have had terrible doings here but I hope it is now over. I never saw or knew so many people overawed by a most despicable mob." Yet the mob remained deferential to the monarchy, the historic symbol of England even to the unlettered and the destitute.

Weakened by events not of its own doing, the reform movement lost momentum as the shocked populace looked to authority for order. Elizabeth Montagu, a Tory colliery owner, concluded that Lord George Gordon had stifled discontent "and I hope in a great degree cured the epidemical democratick madness. The word petition now obtains nowhere, the word association cannot assemble a dozen people. We are coming to our right senses." Horace Walpole worried, on the other hand, in a letter to Lady Ossory, that he had no pity for the imprisoned Gordon: "If he is the source of our being ruled by an army, I shall abhor him still more."

The same day, June 16, 1880, news arrived from America that Charleston, with twelve thousand white inhabitants one of the most populous cities in the colonies, had been taken on May 12. The siege had ended without a final assault after Fort Moultrie had been surrendered to a storming party of sailors and marines, and howitzers had been brought up to fire into the city. Seven American generals were captured, and nearly six thousand other ranks, including sailors from twenty schooners and frigates in the harbor. But for the loss of New York City in 1776, the surrender of Charleston seemed the most profound defeat of the Continentals since the rebellion had begun, and on June 3, 1780, Clinton issued the usual proclamation pardoning anyone who now swore allegiance to George III. Many Carolinians who preferred, cautiously, merely to lay low while the king's obedience was in effect, were anguished. Clinton's deputy, Lord Rawdon, told him frankly that the order was "unfortunate" and that "nine out of ten of them" would go over to the rebels when they could. His implications, if Clinton understood them, were even more disturbing. However big the immediate victory, it meant nothing.

Departing for New York, and taking with him forty-five hundred men whom Cornwallis could have well employed in the South, Clinton wrote to Sir William Eden on June 8, 1880, "I leave Lord Cornwallis here with sufficient force to keep [Charleston] against the world." But if "a superior fleet shows itself, . . . I shall despair of ever seeing peace restored to this miserable country." Sir Henry meant the French threat, as the Continentals had only a makeshift navy. Although the British had superior manpower, they were unable, anywhere, to control the interior, and could move long distances only by sea.

More than 40,000 of His Majesty's troops were in the colonies, about 31,000 of them British and Hessians. New York also garrisoned about 2,000 Provincials in loyalist green, while Charleston and Savannah each had about 4,000 marginally reliable loyalist troops. Some adherents to the king were also in the Floridas. Lord George Germain had no plans to augment these forces, assuming from the upbeat estimates he received from American informants at second hand that domestic recruitment would only improve with further victories. After five years of rebellion Washington's army still depended largely on short enlistments, leaving him with troops who were little trained and seldom paid.

Sir William Eden, who had been the optimist on the returned conciliation commission but now knew better, was nonetheless the intermediary for transmitting sunny messages from loyalists he had met, writing from Downing Street to Germain about "private letters and rebel papers" he had received by packet from New York. Perhaps out of political ambition more than practical reality, Eden had documented "without a doubt that the credit of the rebel Congress is at its utmost stretch and actually breaking." The letters to him from New York were "fill'd with hopes of termination of the war." Now the news from Charleston seemed to validate Eden.

Although casualties were few, Charleston seemed a major success, the largest for either side since Saratoga. Like Burgoyne, Continental major general Benjamin Lincoln attempted to dictate his own terms, but got less than Sir John bargained for in 1777. A British band blared "God Save the King" at the surrender, and the Americans marched into custody with drums and trumpets sounding, and fifes playing "The Turk's March"—since they were not permitted an English tune.

Lincoln would be exchanged early the following year, in return for Major General William Phillips and Baron Friedrich von Riedesel of the Brunswickers. Both had been captured at Saratoga and were languishing in Virginia with the rest of the "Convention Army" which Congress remained unwilling to parole to Britain despite the agreement Gates had signed with Burgoyne.

Clinton now wanted to secure the rest of the Carolinas. It appeared that the southern colonies, now with little American military presence, were ripe for retrieval, but he worried about any premature moves into North Carolina. Although the capture of Charleston seemed to be "a great event," Walpole lamented to Lady Ossory, "it was not a good one, if it ensanguines us against peace." An optimistic ode in *Town & Country* predicted the return of the prodigal to "its parent's arms." To Edmund Burke, the royalist John Noble wrote on June 18 that he was "very fearful" that the public would see a connection between "the late Riotts, and the News from Charles Town, [for] party Malice will take the Advantage of every thing, that by false colouring May be made to answer its purpose." The rejoicings in Bristol, Noble wrote, were great, "but what made it unpleasant, was the unmanly Hints . . . against a part of their fellow Citizens. Nay a paper was circulated, desiring no Illumination on so Glorious and good News to prevent that tumult and Riott, which the *disloyal part of the City* would most probably take the Advantage of, to bring about."

The *Chronicle* reported that an American officer taken prisoner at Charleston—he was Brigadier General Charles Scott—told his captors "that Congress had with the utmost difficulty prevailed on the Americans to support the expense and inconvenience of the present campaign, and that the chief reason which induced them to enter upon it was a confident assertion that the cities of London and Westminster would be laid in ashes this summer." The invention was fanciful but it satisfied many that the frightening Gordon riots were somehow part of a transoceanic conspiracy to undermine the war.

Whitehall could not capitalize upon what appeared to be progress in putting down the rebellion by augmenting troops in America. The possibility of further civil unrest as well as continuing fear of French invasion made it prudent to keep much of the army, especially those in the new encampments in the south of England, where they were. In Yorkshire, a crowd gathered in the belief that Lord North had fled London during the riots and was hiding with the Earl of Dartmouth, the former American Secretary, in a local country house. A spokesman for the throng demanded an audience with the prime minister, who was not there. Such incidents suggested that the upheaval in London, although now put down, could materialize elsewhere.

Again uneasy about North's ministry, which had revealed how feeble it had become, the king felt out Rockingham about a coalition, but the opposition leader had a price—American independence, the jettisoning of Sandwich and Germain, and secretaryships for Fox and Richmond. The king would not pay it. "As soon as we have hobbled through the next session," he said, "there must be a general election." He thought confidently that relief over the suppression of the tumults and an infusion of Crown corruption would add to his majorities in the Commons. Parliament was dissolved on September 1, although it legally could have sat another year, and the king invested more than sixty thousand pounds in buying what elections he could. Although five years of the American war had divided the electorate even more than before, the loss of six seats was not enough to mandate change. Only losing America could accomplish that.

Later in the year, when the king reopened Parliament by proxy, his Address delivered by the Earl of Westmoreland, an unusual amendment to the formal vote of thanks was moved by the Whiggish Marquis of Carmarthen. He voiced cautious appreciation for "the moderation and virtue of not taking advantage of the opportunity afforded by the late riots, to unite the arms of an enraged populace with those of the military, and apply both to the overthrow of the constitution of this country, and the destruction of the liberties and rights of the people." Rather than an augury of the Bastille Day to come across the Channel, the end of the crisis had evidenced England's resilience.

The Cabinet had been informed by the Duke of Gordon that he would implore clemency for his brother, but his intervention became unnecessary. A lesser charge than treason might have resulted in a guilty verdict, yet a conviction on any grounds could have been explosive. Gordon himself seemed still unhinged by religious mania. From the box he threatened to read four chapters from the Old Testament Book of Zechariah, who described his eight visions of the end of the world. Gordon was excused from further testimony.

Burgeoning far beyond Gordon's intent as a demonstration against Popery, the "Gordon Riotts" had become a spontaneous insurrection against the established order. As, however, it could not be established that Lord George planned to overthrow the state, on February 5, 1781, he would be acquitted, after which he addressed the jury, confidently,

"You have done perfectly right in the verdict you have given. I am not the person I was charged to be. I declare to God, that I am as innocent as any of you, and never designed anything of treason against my king and country. Honourable gentlemen, it has been a wicked prosecution—"

"Have done my Lord," a juryman cried out; "it was a nice point."

"Gentlemen," Gordon concluded, "I beg your pardon; excuse my warmth. I heartily thank you, and God bless you."

At six the next morning he was released into the custody of his brothers. Prayers of thanksgiving were returned in many Protestant churches. The Reverend Charles Wesley loyally produced a series of thirteen hymns on the Gordon Riots, condemning "dark conspirators . . . who patient majesty blaspheme [and] doom Britannia to the fire," and somehow he also managed to blame American "felons," "savages," and "assassins," who were "Britain's most apostate sons."

Thanks to a supine and anxious Parliament, the repeal of Catholic Relief followed the flames, and it would be decades before the civil disabilities would again be removed. By the next year, Gordon's attraction to radical Presbyterianism over and his reason apparently restored, he wrote to the prime minister as if he would be listened to "that the independency of America" was in the "national, particular, and immediate interest" of Britain.

Causes proliferated for Gordon, in whom megalomania and idealism could not be separated. Campaigning against hanging and the transportation of prisoners to Australia, as well as other perceived injustices, including the financing of wars, he would be convicted again, this time for libel. To support his antiwar jeremiads he negotiated with both Quakers and Jews (however small their numbers), seeing each group as having crucial financial clout and hoping each would refuse to lend money further for carrying on wars. Moving to Birmingham, he converted to Judaism, grew a beard, and kept the Mosaic laws. But on January 28, 1788, extradited from Holland after fleeing charges of libeling Queen Marie Antoinette of France and libeling the "Judges and Administration of the Laws of England" in a pamphlet protesting the banishment of convicts to Botany Bay, he was sentenced to Newgate, now rebuilt after the excesses of 1780. He died there in 1793.

America, where Gordon had served briefly in the Royal Navy, and whose liberties he had toasted with William Hickey and his friends in 1776, had intruded into the riots quickly christened with Gordon's name. Beyond the bigotry, at least some of the societal discord convulsing the streets of London had been generated across the Atlantic.

12

A Dearth of Heroes
June 1780–December
1780

...And now I've closed my epic strain,
I tremble as I show it,
Lest the same warrior-drover Wayne
Should ever catch the poet.

—*John André,* The Cow-Chace, *1780*

*I*N late summer the news in London from America seemed unexpectedly promising after the frustrations of past campaigns.
The messages Lord George Germain received from the southern provinces were all positive. The Carolinas seemed to lure rebel
generals into mistakes, or worse. News from the north remained
mixed. In New Jersey, Washington was relinquishing towns he had no
men to hold, but Hessian general Wilhelm Knyphausen, a realist,
conceded that evidences of rebel discontent were overrated. The
British were not making it easier for themselves. As an unidentified
lady wrote about enemy raiding parties in the *New Jersey Gazette,*
"Who that has heard of the burning of Charlestown in New England,—of the wanton destruction of Norfolk and Falmouth,—of
their wasting★ the fine improvements in the environs of Philadelphia, . . . and the general havoc which at this moment marks their
footsteps in their route through a part of this state—but would wish
to avert from themselves, their kindred, their property, and their
country in general, so heavy misfortunes."

Loyalist informants, often rewarded, offered what they thought
their sponsors wanted to hear. "I found the disposition of the inhab-

★In the sense of despoiling or destroying.

itants by no means such as I expected," Knyphausen reported. "[O]n the contrary they were everywhere in arms, nor did I find that spirit of desertion amongst their troops which it was represented to me existed amongst them." Nonetheless, General Robertson boasted to the American Secretary in language welcome in London that rebel militia casualties were such that "in future they will not consider turning out as an amusement." Admittedly, campaigning on horseback was handicapped by a forage problem. Hay and oats in bulk were awkward and expensive—and slow—to ship across the Atlantic, or even from Georgia. In the New York area the British confiscated two-thirds of every harvest, permitting farmers the luxury of keeping the remaining one-third.

Since retaining the northeastern segment of New Jersey, on the western bank of the Hudson, was essential for the British for forage and to protect New York City, Anthony Wayne persuaded Washington to authorize an attempt on Block-House Point in Bergen County. Wayne denigrated the defenders, led by a regular, Captain Thomas Ward, as "refugees & a wretched banditti of Robbers horse thieves &c." Early on July 21, 1780, expecting to overwhelm the outnumbered loyalists with his two brigades, General Wayne had the fortified log house cannonaded by six-pound balls from "grasshoppers"—light artillery moved on horseback. Some of his men tried to storm the building and were driven off by fierce musket fire. Sheepishly, Wayne withdrew to Totowa with those of his sixty-four casualties sufficiently alive to carry back and a consolation prize of cattle that he had to abandon as he retreated. It was not his finest hour.

In early October, Lord George brought the news about Block-House Point to the king, who commended "the very extraordinary courage shewn by the Loyal Refugees—the brave SEVENTY." Any evidence of life in the loyalist cause encouraged hopes for further recruits. Clinton's adjutant-general, Major John André, obviously with too much time on his hands, derided Wayne in seventy-two stanzas of jogging verse, "Cow-Chace," after the Scots ballad, "Chevy Chace," in which the general, once a tanner, was ridiculed for having had his hide tanned. James Rivington offered to publish the three cantos in his New York *Royal Gazette*.

But for such episodes that changed little, the war in the North had stagnated, but the South seemed different after Charleston. Given the time lag in reporting across the Atlantic, the American Department did not learn of Cornwallis's follow-up victory at Camden in inner South Carolina until the autumn, when other events were already complicating efforts to exploit the gains. Clinton in New York learned the news on September 20 after a four-day sail of a schooner from Charleston, and immediately posted a mail packet to London. Since restoration to loyalty was crucial to retaining the colonies, Whitehall was especially heartened by the submission to the king's obedience of Henry Middleton, the second president of the Continental Congress and a major landowner in South Carolina. Also, Rawlins Lowndes, a former president (governor) of South Carolina, and hundreds of others reportedly acknowledged that the patriot cause was hopeless. Carolinians were unaware of Sir Henry's warning to the American Department: "To possess territory demands garrisons. The accession of friends, without★ we occupy the country they inhabit, is but the addition of unhappy exiles to the list of pensioned refugees."

On July 13 the Congress had named the politically popular Horatio Gates, hero of Saratoga, to command Continentals in the South and rally what remained of them after Charleston. Repeating his successes in New York, Gates realized, was impossible, as they were largely owed to the cunning of Benedict Arnold. Although Washington had recommended General Nathanael Greene as more qualified, he had been ignored. Greene, a Rhode Islander of thirty-eight and an efficient quartermaster general, was cautious and resourceful. General Charles Lee, who had been cashiered for incompetence in New Jersey and retired to Virginia, understood how erratic Gates, often immune to advice, was. Lee warned him, "Take care, lest your Northern laurels turn [in]to Southern willows." One did not have to be an arboriculturist to know that willows weep.

Sick, underfed, and sleepless, Gates's troops were unready. Some had already walked away from the war. He mustered only half the numbers he thought he had. Militiamen often drifted back to their farms, especially at harvest time—and only sometimes returned. On August 16, in the heat and haze near Camden, what troops Gates had, overwhelmed, would panic. Unhorsed and bleeding, Bavarian

★In present usage one would more likely write "unless."

volunteer Baron de Kalb* fought on foot until he fell, mortally wounded, while Gates and a wretched remnant fled sixty miles to Charlotte, North Carolina.

England learned about the humiliation of the Americans from Germain's *London Gazette Extraordinary,* dated October 9. It was the most embarrassing rebel collapse since Long Island and New York City in 1776, and Washington feared further erosion. Succeeding Gates, who would survive a court-martial for cowardice, Greene charitably called him "unfortunate but not blameable."

When Gates abandoned Charlotte it appeared that Cornwallis's southern strategy was on course. Soon, however, it would unravel, and there would be no heroes. At first there appeared to be one, the fearless Banastre Tarleton, a cocky redhead from a mercantile family in Liverpool who was a lieutenant colonel at twenty-six. Well known in socialite bedrooms of Anglophile Philadelphia in 1777–1778, he had become a ruthless leader of light cavalry, and near Camden had taken three field pieces and many more lives. On August 18, 1780, at Fishing Creek, Tarleton would add to his reputation when his horsemen would scatter and nearly wipe out the partisan force of the "Carolina Gamecock," Thomas Sumter.

Already known across the Atlantic was Tarleton's exploit of May 29 at the village of Waxhaws, South Carolina, where, brandishing sabers and bayonets, his troops had killed 113 Americans and captured 203 wounded, losing only 19. In the relentless barbarity, one dragoon officer conceded, "the virtue of humanity was totally forgot." Soon England was reading avidly about "Bloody Tarleton" and "Tarleton's Quarter," which meant no quarter. But Tarleton, a headstrong braggart who urged his men to be predatory and cruel, had made enemies even on his own side. When he was outfought, as he was often reckless, both rebels and redcoats exulted. Although he was admired by the Prince of Wales, it was difficult for the English press to turn him into a paladin. In the colonies his tactics created a pretext for reciprocal savagery.

By the time Whitehall knew of further successes in the South,

---

*Johann Kalb, sponsored by Lafayette and created a major general, was a bogus baron but an efficient military professional, whose luck ran out when the incompetent Gates was placed over him in the Carolinas.

there were other problems to confront. One worry closer to home was the imminent intervention of the Dutch. A steadfastly commercial and seafaring people, Hollanders, despite treaties with Britain, supplied the French West Indies, ran the blockades to trade with the Americans, and even refitted John Paul Jones. The British began stopping Dutch convoys, and early in September the press reported that Henry Laurens, a former president of the Congress and current American commissioner to the United Provinces of the Low Countries, was captured aboard one. Facing seizure, he threw his sack of confidential documents over the side, but they floated long enough to be retrieved with a pole and hook. The soggy papers when dried were taken to England and—as a trophy—bound for the king in rough calf, gilt, and leather, in eighteen folio volumes.*

Among Laurens's documents was a proposed Dutch-American treaty and loan. Britain demanded that the agreements be disavowed; in November, Germain even visited the Dutch envoy at his home, ostensibly for cards, where Horace Walpole found Lord George appearing "remarkably cool." When no satisfactory reply was forthcoming from Holland, war was declared on December 20.

The Dutch navy, as well as the larger French and Spanish fleets, were matters of serious concern to the Admiralty. Britain had to defend a large, exposed coastline not even impervious to lone entrepreneurs like John Paul Jones. The Continental navy, minus some ships captured or lost, numbered only 57 vessels by the end of the war, most of them remaining near the American coast, while the British fleet, the mightiest in the world, included 230 warships and hundreds of service vessels. But the colonies had also authorized 449 privateers bent on profit and plunder, stronger motives than abstract patriotism. Although Paul Jones had gone from free-spirited pirate to nimble naval captain, self-employed privateer skippers roamed the shipping lanes like buzzing bees while keeping clear of the cannon of ships of the line.

The juggernaut of the Royal Navy had more pressing business than one-on-one engagements with fast if flimsy antagonists, and was spread thin in frigates and in leadership. In 1779, Lord Augustus

---

*When Laurens was finally released from confinement as a prisoner of war, his papers, so enhanced, were returned to him.

Keppel, long at odds with the Admiralty, had relinquished command of the crucial Channel fleet, and Admiral Sir Charles Hardy was drawn from retirement to replace him. The public had confidence in few of Lord Sandwich's other flag officers. Luckily for Hardy, a combined but little integrated French and Spanish force off Plymouth, seeking an opportunity for landfall, was blown off course by eastern gales while Hardy was vainly trying to find the armada farther west, off the Scilly Islands. With sails less than sound afterward, the enemy ships limped to Brest. It was a victory of sorts.

The overly cautious Hardy had been no hero, but when he died the next spring, at Portsmouth on May 18, 1780, it was the occasion for dipping of flags in mourning at Spithead, and for gloomy reassessments of the war at sea. The past was always a better place, and one London newspaper, growing bitter if nostalgic, wrote, "The glory of the nation, under George II, seems to have vanished like a dream, and, on waking, we find only a reality of sadness, shame, and disappointment: all this we owe to the ignorance and obstinacy of Ministers."

On October 6, 1780, a letter signed by Germain and Stormont for the ministry authorized Earl Cornwallis, the absent Lord Constable of the Tower of London (one of his sinecures), or his deputy, to commit Henry Laurens to the Tower of London "on suspicion of High Treason." Since Britain recognized no American citizenship, the Carolinian remained a rebellious Englishman, subject to its penalties.

England's dearth of authentic heroes ended on November 13, 1780, three days after a grand jury had returned an indictment of high treason against Lord George Gordon. A fast packet from New York had arrived with shocking news about Major John André. On the very day that the *Royal Gazette* had published the final canto of his "Cow-Chace," September 23, 1780, copies of which were carried to London on the same vessel, André had been captured with concealed evidence of Benedict Arnold's treason, a long-simmering plot still to be unraveled. The last stanza of André's verses was,

And now I've closed my epic strain,
I tremble as I show It,
Lest the same warrior-drover Wayne
Should ever catch the poet.

The official *London Gazette* and other papers in London rushed to publish accounts of André's seizure, trial, and soon, execution, as well as of Arnold's concurrent joining "the King's standard," a coup overshadowed by the catastrophe. In acknowledging General Clinton's distraught dispatches about the affair, the Secretary for America responded, "His Majesty read with much concern the very affecting narrative of Major André's capture and the fatal consequence of that misfortune. . . . His Majesty has further extended his royal bounty to Major André's mother by the grant of a pension and has offered to confer the honour of knighthood on his brother in order to wipe away all stain from the family that the ignominy of the death he was so unjustly put to might be thought to have occasioned."

Since the André-Arnold conspiracy to capture West Point with defenses deliberately sabotaged by Arnold, its commander, was now abandoned, Germain hoped to Clinton "that you will be able to form another plan which, executed with your spirit and ability, will hasten the dissolution of the rebellion which is evidently declining fast." However, Clinton's spirit was gone and the injunction was thoughtlessly cold. The general was still mourning André.

On September 1 Robertson had written to Germain with a touch of fiction that the authoritarian French disliked "levellers" and did not get on with their American allies, and that Washington's increasingly miserable militiamen "will finally prove an addition to ours. They desert by the dozens tho' they swim miles to get at us, and they relate that hundreds hide in the woods or sculk in the marshes, waiting for a possibility to escape." Encouraged, Lord George saw in the successes in the South, the arrival at New York of a fleet commanded by Admiral Sir George Rodney, and the defection of General Arnold, auguries of victory in America. The multiple "disappointment[s]" of the rebels, he wrote, "cannot fail to lessen the confidence of the people in the assurances of Congress and the minister of their boasted ally [Chevalier de La Luzerne of France] and show them the vanity of their hopes of establishing independence through their means; and should Mr. Washington suffer any disgrace at such a time the most important consequences to the king's affairs might be expected from it."

Rodney was a problem. A potential hero to many, he had a taste for high life he could not afford, and had gone thirty thousand pounds in debt to finance his election to the Commons in 1768. Sandwich had refused him the sinecure as governor of Greenwich Hospital, which would have helped pay for his extravagances. To evade his creditors he had gone to Paris in 1774, but returned when war with France seemed imminent, and had been in command of the *Eagle* off Ushant. In his early sixties, he was past his prime, but he had a reputation for audacity, a trait in short supply in the Admiralty. He would have problems with the choleric Admiral Arbuthnot.

To Horace Walpole, the report that the "much commended" Major André had valiantly "begged to be shot" rather than hanged when Washington's offer to exchange him for General Arnold ("the author of the mischief") was rejected made him more of a hero. The British badly needed one. The less than admirable leadership in America had not furnished a gallant role model. "That atrocious villain," as Walpole described Arnold, was hardly eligible, having sold himself. A fighting general with an excess of flamboyance, he had earned another step in rank, but Washington could not extract it from the politicized and often petty Congress. He had to commiserate to Arnold that it was "not for want of merit in you," explaining, "The members from each state seemed to insist upon having a proportion of general officers, adequate to the number of men they furnish, and that as Connecticut had already two major generals, it was their full share. I confess this is a strange mode of reasoning."

Marrying a Philadelphia loyalist daughter, and enjoying when military governor of Philadelphia the elegant life of the wealthy Anglophile set that survived into the postoccupation almost unscathed, he was ready for self-rewards when patriotism palled. Learning in France of Arnold's treachery, Benjamin Franklin would observe, "Judas sold only one man, Arnold three millions [of Americans]. Judas got for his one Man 30 pieces of silver, Arnold got not a halfpenny a head. A miserable bargain!" General Robertson in New York, however, wrote exultantly to Lord Amherst (and ignoring André's certain end—it was still September 26 and the trial and judgment were three days away), "Arnold, the boldest and most enterprising of the rebel Generals, lives with me and sits by me while I write."

Despite Robertson, there would never be much enthusiasm for Arnold in Britain. A later Rowlandson drawing, engraved by William

Hinton of Sweetings Alley in Cornhill, "The Loss of Eden—and Eden Lost," recalled the bribery of Arnold when the always ambitious William Eden was "bought off by a [postwar] place." In the engraving, Eden and Arnold, the general shown in his new regimentals, embrace. From Eden's coat pocket three documents protrude—his lucrative but futile conciliation commission appointment, another labeled "Commercial Negotiator to France," and a third, "£6,000 per annum." Written across the design, scornfully, is "Every Man has his Price." Arnold had quickly become a byword for profitable treachery.

The *London Chronicle* would report (in early December 1880) that Arnold had written to Washington after escaping on the aptly named *Vulture* in Tappan Bay, threatening that if André were executed there would be retaliation "on such unhappy persons of your army as may fall within my power," and he warned of a "torrent of blood." Under the Articles of War, Washington could have ordered André hanged without a trial, as he had been seized in disguise with damning papers on his person.

The delicacy of the André case was such—the prisoner was an exquisite young gentleman—that Washington did not want to make the decision on his own. He named fourteen generals, including Lafayette and von Steuben, to preside over a one-day trial convened in an old Dutch church in what was then called Orangetown, New Jersey, on September 29. (Wayne, the victim of André's verses, was excused but would be an observer at the poet's hanging.) André owned up to the obvious and called his quitting his regimentals a "great mortification." He claimed that the hidden papers had been pressed on him by Arnold, and that he was "betrayed into the vile condition of an enemy in disguise within your posts." No witnesses were called.

In a unanimous opinion Washington's board recommended that André "ought to be considered a spy from the enemy and that, agreeable to the law and usage of nations, . . . he ought to suffer death." Under British usage, no deserter was ever exchanged. Arnold would not be relinquished to save André.

From New York, Arnold pressed to have a British command, and to further justify the expense of his betrayal he sent letter after letter to Germain offering strategic advice and information on American weaknesses. Since money had bought him it was natural that he would suggest money strategies. In a letter of October 28, 1780, he wrote to London that "a reward of fifteen or twenty guineas should be given to every private soldier or non-commissioned officer in the rebel army who would come over and join the King's army, one-half to be paid in hand and the other half at the end of the war. Such an offer I am convinced would thin their ranks." He even proposed offering Washington a peerage to defect as it "might not prove unacceptable." While the bribing of the austere Washington seemed impossibly absurd to the American Department, Germain did raise the bounty to deserters from three guineas to ten, seven payable only at the conclusion of hostilities.

Inconsolable (in Robertson's description), Clinton wrote rather pathetically to his sisters in England that he had "assured" Washington that if André, "whom I regard as an innocent, should suffer," the British would take the lives of forty imprisoned rebel South Carolinians. "To those who do not feel the private losses we have met with, the defection of such a man as Arnold will appear important." But the conspiracy to suborn Arnold in no way seemed compensation.

Many wondered then and since whether the Clinton-André relationship had something in it of father and son,★ or something overtly or passively sexual. André even wrote erotic verses for Howe about the passionate entwinement of limbs in a "Storm of delight." Although addressed to a "Sally," the lines could be suggestive of other pleasures, fancied or real.

★In a somewhat parallel situation, George Washington was forty-five and Marie Joseph Paul Yves Roch Gilbert du Motier, the Marquis de Lafayette, was twenty, with six years of very minor French army experience, when they met in 1777, Congress (eager for influential French connections) having granted him the rank of major general when he offered to serve as a volunteer at his own expense. In France he had been only a captain. At Brandywine, when he was wounded in the leg by a musket ball, Washington told aides who helped him off the field, "Treat him as though he were my own son." In early 1778 he was given his own division and served with distinction through Yorktown.

    The childless Washington treated him with paternal tenderness—with a masculine affection that could then in the continental fashion include embraces and kisses——over the rest of his years. "I do not know a nobler, finer soul," he said later, "and I love him as my own son." Lafayette was orphaned when he was two years old, his father killed in the Battle of Ninden; only in Washington did he find a surrogate father.

The heroic element in the unwarriorlike André seems almost entirely related to how he died rather than how he lived. Aside from Quebec in December 1775 (where he was taken prisoner, and later exchanged), and his involvement in the night attack on Anthony Wayne's rear guard at Paoli in the Philadelphia campaign in September 1777, André saw little action. Clinton reached deep into in his officer corps, and caused tongues to wag, when he made a junior captain of nine years' service known more for his elegance and charm than his fire-and-sword qualities his adjutant general, and then tried every means, going directly to the top, to achieve a promotion for him. Yet Sir Henry was forced to settle for provincial major—invalid in Britain—when even Lord Amherst questioned the request, and wondered why it was made, having some knowledge of the young man before he sailed to America. "He once injured me," Clinton would recall bitterly of Amherst.

Son of a merchant from Geneva but born in London, André was fluent in German, French, and Dutch; he composed music and poetry (including flirtatious verses to young women for whom he felt no passion), and wrote satires, as well as new prefaces to older plays; he sketched and painted, and created stage sets and masks and disguises; he danced, acted, and played the flute; he designed party dresses for Philadelphia debutantes; he loved fancy and colorful uniforms, even to wearing pink bows on his Meschianza attire at the farewell gala for Sir William Howe. But his closest known relationship in America, very likely only avuncular, was with a boy from Lancaster, John Cope, with whom he spent many hours early in the war teaching him to draw.

During the Philadelphia occupation he was adored by aristocratic young loyalist ladies, but his gracefully mannered responses were just that. The only woman to whom he had ever proposed marriage—it was before the war—was the wan, consumptive Honora Sneyd, a Derbyshire heiress unlikely to make serious physical demands upon him—and her father broke off the engagement. Yet Anna Seward would make much of the thwarted romance in her *Monody on Major André,* published in Dr. Johnson's hometown, Litchfield, the next year. Upon his capture, she imagined sentimentally, André concealed a miniature of his beloved in his mouth.

The hero in André emerged in the dignity of his conduct once he was condemned. He even drew an affecting self-portrait from his cell. The usually aloof Washington felt an avuncular interest in the handsome and unflinching major. To Henry Laurens's son, John, comparing André to Arnold, "so lost to all sense of honor and shame," Washington valued what he saw as gentlemanly integrity. Breaking his usual decorum, he sent meals to André from his own table, and the general's hand reportedly trembled when he signed the death warrant. At the scaffold on October 2, 1780, André grimly bound his eyes with his own handkerchief; and when he was told that he would be allowed to speak before the trap—a wagon on which he stood—was sprung, he lifted his blindfold and said, "I pray you to bear witness that I meet my fate like a brave man." Unimpressed, a Continental soldier at the scene said he watched, a few moments later, André "flouncing on a rope."

In "The British Hero in Captivity," published as a pamphlet, the anonymous author praised the nobility and humanity of Lord Cornwallis, the courage of Arnold for vainly offering his own life for André, and the major as the epitome of the patriot. "Faithless America" is castigated for its "revengeful hate," and the shade of the hanged André materializes to call "vengeance down" on the rebels for their "dire barbarity and guilt."

André fulfilled the national need for a hero after nearly six years of blunderers and mediocrities. No Englishman involved in the war would so capture the popular imagination. General Robertson's daughter, Anne Loudoun, wrote to him, "Major André's fate has been the universal topic of conversation. His Mother, and Sisters, bear the shock with astonishing fortitude." Shortly, in the Poets' Corner in Westminster Abbey, paradoxically an appropriate place, a marble cenotaph would be erected by order of George III, "Sacred to the memory of Major John André, [who,] employed in an important but hazardous enterprise, fell a sacrifice to his zeal for his King and Country."

Disillusioned after the death of André and now privately defeatist, and still awaiting the acceptance of his resignation, Clinton sent an aide across the Atlantic to Germain to demand the recall of Admiral Arbuthnot as the price of remaining in New York. Unmoved, Lord Sandwich wrote sardonically to Germain, "As there may be some difficulty of finding a person exactly to our mind to relieve Admiral

Arbuthnot in the command of the fleet in America, and as I think it almost a certainty that Sir Henry Clinton [will] quit on his not being appointed sole [Conciliation] Commissioner, could it not be contrived that, in case of his quitting, . . . Arbuthnot might remain where he is?" The wry proposal suggested how diminished America had become in Whitehall's priorities.

Rivalries and animosities had multiplied as the war dragged on. Arbuthnot was not nearly as doddering and obtuse as his antagonists made him out to be. Although when writing to Germain in December he conceded that "the complicated labour of this command is too much for me at my advanced age, 68, near 55 years in actual service," he was shrewd enough to point out that if Washington moved his augmented forces southward, he might "thereby render Lord Cornwallis's situation very precarious, without remedy." Earl Cornwallis was riding high, however, and Lord George would not take Arbuthnot seriously. The admiral went on to deplore that "the disappointment that accompanied the death of that honourable youth, Major André" may have postponed useful punitive expeditions, which could now be led by General Arnold, who knew the country. What Arbuthnot did not realize was that the renegade general would be sent south on a raiding mission, and that Clinton, not trusting Arnold, had given Thomas Dundas and John Simcoe, both lieutenant colonels, sealed commissions to accompany Arnold and relieve him should some "impropriety" in his actions appear not to be in the best interests of the king.

To Germain, Arbuthnot also deplored the "abuse of power" of Admiral Rodney, who had "strip[p]ed the storehouses of all the necessaries for both ships and men" when taking crucial naval stores to the West Indies, and had "debilitated me." However, Clinton had discovered in September, when provision fleets from England were delayed, that Arbuthnot was accountable for similar improprieties. He had redirected three army victualler vessels from New York, where supplies were running low, to Halifax, where there was now a surplus, and had delayed for six weeks sending a convoy to Nova Scotia to return some of that excess to needy New York. Misunderstandings and mistakes in communication continued to dog the war effort.

Feeling guiltless of impeding the war in the North by taking it to the French in the Caribbean, Admiral Rodney, from St. Lucia on

December 22, would send Germain a passionate memorandum deploring "the procrastination with which the American war seemed to me to have been and still was conducted." And he attacked dozens of unnamed time-servers and self-servers he assumed were identifiable in Whitehall. It was one of the strongest messages the American Secretary would ever receive:

> I can with truth and honour aver [that] no personal resentment, pique, or hatred, to any man whatever, either in the army or navy, biasses my thoughts. Nothing but the natural affection an Englishman bears or ought to bear to his King and country irritates my mind when I behold her treasures squandered, her arms inactive, and her honour lost, and by the very men entrusted with the most important and honourable confidence of their Sovereign and his Ministers, paying not the least regard to the sufferings of their country, but retard[ing] the completion and extinction of the rebellion to make the fortunes of a long train of leeches, who suck the blood of the State, and whose interest prompts them to promote the continuance of the war, such as quartermasters and their deputies, *ad infinitum,* barrack masters and their deputies, *ad infinitum,* commissaries and their deputies, *ad infinitum,* all of which make princely fortunes, and laugh in their sleeves at the Generals who permit it, and by every means in their power continue to discountenance every active measure.

Germain would confess unhappily to his deputy, William Knox, "How miserably we have been served in this war." But the king, who prized loyalty above all else, was deaf to such reproaches, insisting, "The giving up the game would be total ruin; a small state may certainly subsist, but a great one mouldering cannot get into an inferior station, but must be annihilated." To His Majesty, the reunion of the empire was a necessity beyond negotiation.

Another prominent American, after Henry Laurens, was soon in a British prison. On November 20 Benjamin West received a letter from young John Trumbull hand-delivered from the Brown Bear tavern opposite the police station on Bow Street. Undeniably a son of the revolutionary governor of Connecticut, Trumbull had been arrested before he could get very far in studying painting under West, which was his bona fides for being in London. Although warned that he was under no compulsion to respond to charges of treason before his trial, he answered with Yankee feistiness,

> You appear to have been much more habituated to the society of highwaymen and pickpockets, than to that of gentlemen. I will put an end to all this insolent folly by telling you frankly who I am. I am an American. My name is Trumbull. I am the son of him whom you call the rebel governor of Connecticut. I have served in the rebel American army. I have had the honour of being an aide-du-camp to him whom you call the rebel General Washington★. . . . Lord George Germain knows under what circumstances I came to London, and what has been my conduct here. I am entirely in your power; and, after the hint which I have given you, treat me as you please, always remembering that as I may be treated, so will your friends in America be treated by mine.

Trumbull claimed protection under the general amnesty offered by the conciliation commission in 1778, and had been working in London under West. Following his outburst he was taken to Clerkenwell Prison, where he spent the first night in the same bed with a highwayman, and the next day was delivered a writ of suspicion of high treason. London newspapers carried stories of his arrest, reporting a letter found in his possession from William Temple Franklin in Passy, grandson and secretary of the archenemy of England, Dr. Franklin. Trumbull was suspected of covertly working for Franklin. More likely the arrest was in retaliation for the execution of Major André.

West rushed to Buckingham House, requesting an audience with the king. A familiar figure at Court, he was admitted, and explained that the arrest of one of his students for treason, of which he was blameless, might reflect on West's own character and diminish his relationship to His Majesty. West pledged himself for Trumbull's future conduct.

"West," said the king, who knew little about the case, "I have known you long and have conversed with you frequently. I can recollect no occasion on which you have ever attempted to mislead or

★Trumbull was with Washington in December 1776 when he crossed the Delaware.

misinform me, and for that reason you have acquired my entire confidence. I fully believe all you have now said, and assure you that my confidence in you is not at all diminished by this unpleasant occurrence. I am sorry for the young man, but he is in the hands of the law, and must abide the result—I cannot interpose. Do you know whether his parents are living?"

"I think I have heard him say," West replied cautiously, "that he has very lately received news of the death of his mother. I believe his father is living."

"I pity him from my soul!" said the king, who was the fount of pardons. "But West, go to Mr. Trumbull immediately, and pledge to him my royal promise that, in the worst possible event of the law, his life shall be safe."

Going on to Whitehall, West applied to see Lord George Germain, and his secretary and favorite Benjamin Thompson. A New Englander, as West knew, Thompson had been a spy for Germain and General Howe. When he had found it dangerous to remain in the colonies he had sailed for England, where Germain gave him a sinecure as absentee secretary of the province of Georgia and a second salary to work in the American office. By 1780 the opportunistic Thompson had succeeded Thomas De Grey as undersecretary for America.

Officially assured that Trumbull would be released once the stir about his arrest had quieted, West went with the news to Bridewell, where he found him ensconced in a room in the keeper's house—a furnished parlor with folding bed—for which he was to overpay one guinea a week. Although Trumbull had been sentenced to Clerkenwell, the magistrate, Sir Sampson Wright, had apologized for the poor conditions there resulting from the Gordon riots. Trumbull then sent a message immediately to Germain about the "detestable companionship," and Lord George replied affably that Trumbull could choose any prison in England in which to be confined.

West and another American student, Gilbert Stuart, brought Trumbull paints, and he spent seven months as "Bridewell Jack"— Stuart's flippant term for what was a very mild incarceration— preparing work for the Royal Academy's next exhibition. Advocates from the pro-American opposition visited, including Fox and Burke, who promised to bring the case before Parliament, but it took until

June 1781 before a writ of discharge freed Trumbull. He sailed for Amsterdam, then home to Connecticut.

The general election called by North in October in the hope of rallying support around the encouraging news from America was a Tory disappointment. Royalist printers and the purchased press had tried to smear the opposition cause. In an engraving, "The Virtuous and Inspir'd State of Whiggism in Bristol," a candidate is seated in a chaise drawn by two men; behind them is the Devil. Satanically inspired, the candidate declares, "I come to establish America's Independence. Listen to the Voice of my People." In his hand is a striped flag inscribed "The Voice of Rebellion is a supreme Law which passeth all Understanding."

The few of the king's subjects qualified to vote remained uneasy about the wartime rise in the national debt. Only £127 million in 1775, it had doubled to more than £250 million, which foreshadowed higher taxes and higher prices. In a Commons of 552 members, many unopposed for reelection, the absolute majority of guaranteed supporters of the Crown was reduced to twenty-six. However skimpy the mandate, the Ministry had one. Yet it did not seem that way in the Commons when acceptance of His Majesty's Address to the new Parliament was moved on November 6. King George had referred to the signal successes of the king's arms in the Carolinas, which he predicted would have important consequences in bringing the war to a happy conclusion. An amendment was moved and seconded that the traditional complimentary language be replaced by the lines, "In this arduous conjuncture we are determined to unite our efforts for the defence of our country; and we beg leave to assure your Majesty that we will decline no difficulty or hazard in preserving the essential interests of this kingdom."

Spirited debate arose as to whether the substitution implied supporting or abandoning the American war, and the amendment failed, 212 to 130. A similar motion in the Lords lost, again with many abstentions, 68 to 23. There was much more unanimity on closing proceedings for a long Christmas hiatus. Christmas was celebrated more festively than piously. Yule logs blazed and much food and drink consumed. Christmas mince pies and plum pudding were ingested after the roast turkey, and wine and punch quaffed all through the day. In America, the holiday was largely ignored in the North but for the

Dutch tradition in New York; in the South, Christmas would have been more merry in the English manner but for the dislocations of war.

As Christmas approached in the Carolinas, Cornwallis's most efficient commander other than the unpredictable Banastre Tarleton was Lord Francis Rawdon, already noticed in the London press. (Later, after India, he would be created Marquess of Hastings.) In his early twenties as a lieutenant colonel in the New York garrison, he had been André's predecessor as adjutant general to Clinton. Taking a dislike to the ambitious boy wonder, Sir Henry had transferred Rawdon to a combat role. At Portsmouth, Virginia, his troops combined with those of Major General Alexander Leslie, who had sailed from New York with twenty-five hundred men to undertake raids with the fleet. Cornwallis had appealed to Germain over Clinton's head for a more aggressive posture. Raids, north and south, were Sir Henry's substitute for a campaign.

Above Rawdon, with a raiding party in the Chesapeake, was Benedict Arnold, now a British brigadier general. In Virginia he reportedly took a rebel captain prisoner, and while interrogating him, asked what he thought the Americans would do if the situation were reversed and they caught him—Arnold. "Why, Sir," said the captain, "if I must answer your question, you must excuse my telling you the plain truth. If my countrymen should catch you I believe they would first cut off that lame leg, which was wounded in the cause of freedom and virtue, and bury it with the honours of war, and afterwards hang the remainder of your body."

Despite the prospect of more strength in the South to split the Continentals, Cornwallis felt increasingly uneasy. The arena was too vast. Daniel Morgan, who had led a company on Benedict Arnold's ill-fated march to Quebec late in 1775, and at forty-four was a major general known as the "Old Wagoner," threatened redcoat incursions inland with a small force of Maryland and Delaware Continentals. Cornwallis guessed that there were far more of the enemy lying in wait, as guerrilla groups kept arising in the hinterlands he thought he had pacified. A London paper with Whig leanings would observe, "The facility with which the Americans recruit their scattered forces, is truly alarming, and affords the strongest proof of the firmness and sincerity with which they are attached to their new rulers, and their new form of government. The superior skill and appointment of the English soldiers may gain them some occasional conquests, but the American forces recruit more strong and collected from every defeat. Facts will speak for themselves."

Whenever the rebel cause flagged, patriots seemed to emerge from nowhere, some in the middle South commanded by tough Colonel William Washington, a cousin of the commander-in-chief who had fought at Cowpens, while the supportive southern loyalists continued to seem a mirage. Observing the phenomenon some months earlier—it was an ongoing predicament, now worsening—Horace Walpole wrote to Henry Seymour Conway, an old soldier, about "believing the magnificent lies that every trifling advantage gives birth to. If a quarter of the Americans had joined the royalists, that have been said to join, all the colonies would not hold them. But, at least, they have been like the trick of kings and queens at cards; where one of two goes back every turn to fetch another."* The irreversible situation seemed recapitulated in a wry song:

Parliaments squabble and gabble,
Ministers wonder and stare;
Armies march backwards and forwards,
Americans stand as they were.

In a cold rain on uncelebrated Christmas Day, 1780, Morgan's partisans reached the Pacolett River below Cowpens, deep in the South Carolina interior, after a fifty-eight-mile slog. After a forty-mile ride, Colonel Washington's mounted militia, hovering nearby, surprised a British detachment and gave them "Tarleton's quarter," taking no prisoners. How disquieting the southern Christmas was for restoration of the king's peace would not be known in England until the winter was nearly past.

From the perspective of London, portents for America seemed bleak at each year's end. It took no feat of intelligence for the British

---

*Walpole's metaphor appears to refer to such two-player games as piquet, known in England as cent, where one discards and draws replacement cards from stock. Other French variants were *brusquembille, briscan, mariage,* and *la bataille* (war), some of which may have been known by then across the Channel.

to learn of General Washington's annual forebodings, as on October 18, 1780, he had sent a circular letter to all state governments informing them of "the present state of the troops of your line, by which you will perceive how few Men you will have after the 1st of Jany. next. . . . The greatest part of the misfortunes and perplexities we have hitherto experienced, are chiefly to be attributed to the system of temporary enlistments." He also warned of devalued Continental currency, and his inability to resupply troops. Each new year, as he faced reconstituting an army, nothing saved his command, he conceded, "but the supineness or folly of the enemy." He could not count upon that indefinitely.

To Franklin at the end of December, concerned about the continuing disappointments from the French, especially at sea, Washington wrote from New Jersey, "Latterly we have been obliged to become Spectators of a succession of detachments from the Army at New York, [sailing] in aid of Lord Cornwallis; while our Naval weakness, and the political dissolution of a large part of our Army, puts it out of our power to counteract them at the Southward, or take advantage of them here." He hoped for an end to "the folly of temporary expedients," but the calendar seemed a more formidable enemy than Clinton or Cornwallis.

13

Marching About the Country January 1781–July 1781

"I assure you that I am quite tired of marching about the country in quest of adventures. If we mean an offensive war in America, we must abandon New York and bring our whole force into Virginia; we then have a stake to fight for, and a successful battle may give us America."

—*Earl Cornwallis to General William Phillips, April 10, 1781*

*I*N England nearly a century after the rebellion in America, a shy Oxford mathematics don writing under a pseudonym pub-lished a dream fantasy that included a line of dialogue that Earl Cornwallis, as a military tactician, would have ruefully understood. "Here, you see," the Red Queen explains to the uncomprehending Alice in *Through the Looking-Glass,* "it takes all the running you can do to keep in the same place. If you want to get somewhere else, you must run at least twice as fast as that!" London assumed until the always belated news reached across the Atlantic that it was the rebels who were on the run.

In mid-February, encouraging intelligence reached Whitehall that General Washington's chronic troubles retaining his Continentals after each New Year's Day had reoccurred. Lord George saw to it that the report appeared in the official *London Gazette,* on February 17, 1781. The American Secretary had learned of it from Clinton, while Robertson wrote to Lord Amherst that the first intimations "that the Pensilvania line discontented with Congress would quit the rebel service" had come as early as the previous July. A contagion of militia mutinies in 1780 and early 1781 suggested that the American cause was faltering. Troops were refusing further service, Clinton reported

to London, "without either pay, clothing or provisions. A riot en-
sued." Rebel zeal had its limits.

The first soldiers to storm off were from General Anthony
Wayne's brigade, in winter quarters at Morristown, New Jersey. After
an accumulation of grievances over many months had not been addressed by Congress, which had been granted by the states little
power of the purse, leaders of the protest, from the brigade's Board of
Sergeants, contended that many soldiers had enlisted "for three years
or during the war," and since "whichever comes first" was implied,
their contracts had terminated. One reluctant regiment was forced to
join the protest at bayonet point.

Since troop strength was relatively small—Washington's army in
New York and New Jersey was only 6,583 officers and men—the
1,500 who left camp with their field equipment, guns, and ammunition to take their complaints to the Congress in Philadelphia were a
potentially crippling loss. Patriotism was not a factor. Soldiers left unpaid often had families subsisting in hardship. Reaching Princeton, a
village of seventy houses, the militants established themselves at the
college in the ruins of Nassau Hall to wait for a response from
Philadelphia. A congressional committee led by Joseph Reed, also the
Pennsylvania governor (but called president), escorted by twenty
horsemen of the City Troop, met them on January 6, 1781, to negotiate. The sergeants insisted on parleying only with General Wayne.

Washington was too far away to join him, and in any case he had
to keep the mutiny from spreading through the army. Learning of
the rebel disobedience even before Washington, Clinton had sent
agents to meet secretly with the mutinous sergeants. As Walpole
would write sardonically to Horace Mann when he heard of it, "We
consoled ourselves with the revolt of a large body of Washington's
troops—but when Sir H. Clinton invited them to his standard, they
impolitely bound his messengers hand and foot and sent them to the
Congress. We are apt to sing *Io Paean* too soon; and only show how
much we want good news, by accepting everything as such."★

Clinton had offered pardon, pay, and the privilege of declining

★The Greeks in Aristophanes's time invoked Apollo or Artemis with a hymn, the "Io
Paean": a joyful cheer. In his satirical *Lysistrata* the Chorus of Athenians sings, "*Io Paean! Io
Paean!* Dance, leap, in honor of a victory won!"

British military service. Realizing the potential treason, the sergeants wanted to send the British agents back with a taunting message, but Reed objected to any communication. When rumors surfaced about a possible enemy move from Staten Island into New Jersey, involving four thousand men with boats being readied by General Robertson, bargaining with the mutineers accelerated. Wayne promised amnesty and discharges for three-year enlistees who claimed their release; Reed offered arrears of pay and clothing as soon as possible. He had to raise the money in "hard cash"—coinage validated by one's teeth, not worthless paper currency. On the tenth, compromises were arrived at and the mutineers agreed to turn in their weapons. (On the same day, Clinton's emissaries were arraigned and convicted for spying, and hanged the next morning.)

It took until January 29 for Wayne to arrange the discharge of 1,315 men at their request, some of whom subsequently reenlisted.

At Pompton and Suffern in northern New Jersey five hundred of the New Jersey militia struck, demanding the benefits won by the Pennsylvanians. His patience exhausted, Washington insisted on unconditional submission. A key offender from each of three regiments was identified and tried, and two shot by a firing party of twelve chosen harshly from other mutineers. As guns were being reloaded, the third soldier was reprieved. Smaller mutinies of Connecticut and Massachusetts men had occurred in 1780, and more incidents would follow as Congress failed to meet its financial obligations. In each case the news heartened Englishmen at home.

Little else reaching the London press seemed hopeful. The acknowledged plight of desperate Continentals was not turning them to what the ministry insisted on labeling, to its continuing detriment, the king's obedience. Walpole wrote to the Reverend William Mason, with no information but the newspapers, that "Lord Cornwallis . . . has found the [Carolina] country as hostile as it was proclaimed to be friendly." The Prince of Wales learned of the state of affairs in America when Lieutenant Colonel Gerard Lake, his best friend, only recently appointed his First Equerry, was ordered to America and left for Portsmouth on January 19. "Our parting," Prince George wrote to his brother Frederick, just sent off to Hanover for military training, "as you may suppose, was a very severe trial to us both." Just before Lake embarked he penned a warning to the prince that many people would try to gain his "favor" by encouraging him to do "things that they would be perhaps the first to condemn." He was to refrain from writing "any more letters to a certain sort of ladies," and to avoid politics, "becoming the dupe of those who have no other design than to make use of you for their own advantage." That meant entrapment by the pro-American opposition.

Soon Lake would be writing frankly to the prince from Yorktown, Virginia, where he assumed command of "the Light Company, which is still remarkably fine, notwithstanding the great loss of men they have sustain'd." Colonel Robert Conway, who was being dispatched to England by Clinton to report on the increasingly desperate situation in Cornwallis's sector, would "in all probability deliver this letter to you." Lake claimed to be "exceedingly happy" under Earl Cornwallis. "I most sincerely wish his exertions may be crown'd with the success they so justly deserve, tho' I fear . . . this war will never be finish'd in the way we have all so much reason it should, as I have no doubt that every American is so entirely averse to a reconciliation with the mother country, so exasperated against us, at the same time so fertile in resources, that it is not possible this country can ever be conquer'd."

"What gloomy prospects strike th' apparent heir," candid verses "On the Heir Apparent" in the *London Courant* began. Published on January 24, 1781, just after Gerard Lake departed, the lines forecast the lamentable future the Prince of Wales faced—losing an empire before his succession. It was almost as if the writer had read Lake's letters. Given the victories at Charleston and Camden, the bleak mood in London early in the year recognized a reality openly at variance with what the ministry promoted as a promising turn in the war. The *Morning Post* and *Morning Herald* were blaming Clinton in New York for supporting Cornwallis insufficiently. Joseph Galloway, now totally relocated to England because he could not return to Philadelphia, was still sending on to Germain empty fantasies from his New York friends that if only the indecisive military furnished the many thousands of covertly loyalist Americans with the opportunity, they would return to their allegiance.

As late as February 17, 1781, Germain's *London Gazette* was reporting American news of early December, which seemed replete with ill omens. "We expected to hear that all Washington's army was catched in a drag-net," Walpole wrote to William Mason, "and that Lord Cornwallis had subdued and pacified all Virginia and Carolina." Instead, readers were informed "that his Lordship and his handful of men had been sick, but thank you are a little better, and that Colonel Ferguson was beaten, and Colonel Tarleton had a puny advantage, all of which we knew two months ago." Patrick Ferguson, the inventor of the breech-loading rifle, which the hidebound army would scorn for a further century, had been killed at King's Mountain in North Carolina on October 9, 1780.

Although Walpole was more interested in the immediate budgetary crisis, and the reverse at King's Mountain had not been mentioned in the *Gazette,* he had other sources of information. The Commons, he also noted, had put off a second reading of Edmund Burke's bill to pare the sinecure-swollen civil list, which had been defeated six months earlier, "because Wednesday is the Fast day, and Thursday Vestris's benefit.★ God has his day, a French dancer his, and then the national senate will be at leisure to think whether it will save three-halfpence-farthing out of eighteen millions that are to be raised in hopes of protracting the war, till we want at least eighteen millions more." It was government strategy to put off asking for more money for the war until the need was so great as to be beyond debate.

Securing the king's obedience remained a financial and logistical nightmare for Lord George. Rum, for example, was not only supplied for morale reasons. As a water purifier, it was used at the rate of one quart for every six canteens. Transported from the Caribbean, shipments had to evade American privateers. Many did not. As Lieutenant Colonel Lake understood before he had set a foot on colonial soil, the fertility of the land was of little benefit to the British, often not even for forage. But for the expanse of Long Island, with its hundreds of small farms, His Majesty's forces did not control the countryside. Most provisions had to be obtained abroad. With the war not remotely over, the army had already imported and consumed 3 million gallons of rum, 11 million pounds of salt beef, 40 million pounds of salt pork, and was only able to secure, in America, 3 million

★Auguste Vestris, a spectacular Florentine-born dancer, had been a star of the French stage. Benefit performances for theatrical personalities were common sources of income for them.

pounds of fresh meat. Flour, rice, oatmeal, vinegar, butter, and other provisions had to cross the stormy Atlantic, as did replacement clothing, boots, and military equipment, and as early as Burgoyne's failed campaign, boots for his men vanished en route. Fewer than half the tens of thousands of horses survived the voyages, and many thousands of wagons shipped proved too heavy for the poor to nonexistent American roads. Radiating optimism about the outcome was not easy for bureaucrats in Whitehall or senior officers reporting from America.

January 19, 1781, when Gerard Lake had departed for Virginia, had not been an auspicious date. The Russian ambassador, Ivan Smolin, called that day on Lord Stormont, who now handled foreign affairs as secretary of the Northern Department, and presented him with an angry message from Empress Catherine II. An Armed Neutrality League formed by nations profiting from the American war had been proclaimed by the empress early in 1780. Since Britain claimed the belligerent right to seize enemy goods, Russia, Sweden, and Denmark had joined to protect their freedom of navigation, and asked Britain, France, and Spain to accept the principle of unrestricted neutral trade. The Dutch, hostile to England although William V was a cousin of George III, and helpful to the rebel colonies, planned to join. If they did, and were attacked, it would commit Russia (on paper, at least) to support Holland with armed force.

It had been a Dutch trader from which Henry Laurens had been seized. Holland, Franklin noted wryly, was "no longer a Nation, but a great shop, and I begin to think it has no other Principles or Sentiments but those of a Shopkeeper." When the Dutch signed on, London (in December 1780) had declared war, furnishing the provocation to seize rich Caribbean islands colonized by Holland. But how would Russia respond? France and Spain had accepted the principle of free navigation by neutrals, but Britain had ignored it, and Catherine charged that the treaty without Britain was an "Armed Nullity." At a meeting of the Cabinet, Lord Sandwich warned the others that if Russia entered the war, "We shall never again figure as a leading power in Europe but [will] think ourselves happy if we can drag on for some years a contemptible existence as a commercial state."

To soften the empress's hostility, the government offered the Mediterranean island of Minorca just east of Spain if Russia would use its influence to mediate peace. Catherine had no interest in property so remote from St. Petersburg, but the tensions with Russia eased.

Fast days to pray for a divine onslaught on America had become routine, and the opposition *London Courant* published, contrarily, a tirade against supine bishops who not only promoted the endless war from their churches but voted to support the military from the seats in the House of Lords. Addressing politicized clerics, the *Courant* charged,

Although you have not actually wielded the sword of war, and plunged it into the bottoms of your fellow creatures; although you have not personally appeared on the field, nor tinged your white sleeves with reeking blood; yet you have voted for those measures which have strewed the plains of America with many thousand human bodies; you have been accessory to the departure of thousands of souls into the awful presence of God.

How inconsistent has your conduct been with the religion which you profess, and the characters you ought to sustain? Instead of being the promoters, you ought to have stood forth as the mediators between America and England; instead of tacitly or publickly bowing at the nod of the Minister, because he is the Minister of the State, or crouching to the will of the King, because he was born a Prince, you ought to have been urgent for peace and the prevention of bloodshed; and, instead of waving the banners of war, you should have presented the sheathed sword. . . . Repent, my Lords, while you have the power of repentance. . . . Abstract from your minds all thoughts of encreasing grandeur, of the favour of Kings, & the accumulation of wealth, and act so that you may be translated from a world of vanity, to that place where you may indeed be Priests unspotted and unblemished.

It was signed "One of the PEOPLE."

After Charleston and Camden, the London press had been busy praising the overreaching Cornwallis, often called now a Caesar or Hannibal, at Clinton's expense. The *Chronicle* observed that "the intelligent and intrepid" Cornwallis had marched his army 120 miles through South Carolina in less than four days, while Clinton several years earlier in New York had managed only eighteen miles in sixteen days. Even the opposition *Public Advertiser* quoted Shakespeare's *Othello* in praise of Cornwallis, that

> The man commands
> Like a Full soldier.

The *Courant,* nevertheless, warned on April 5, 1781, that the earl was leading his army into an inextricable position in Virginia reminiscent of Burgoyne's entrapment in upper New York. Late in April Cornwallis argued to Germain—a communications turnaround of months made any response of his useless—that experience had proved that there was little allegiance to the Crown in the Carolinas despite "the strongest and most public assurances." Charleston, he assured the American Secretary, was safe, but otherwise he risked "embarrassing circumstances" if he returned southward. In London, unaware of how little control Whitehall now had over events about which the press could only guess, the *Gazeteer* on May 21 bluntly asserted that the retaking of America was in imminent collapse, yet that Cornwallis was more victim than perpetrator. The "blunders, folly and madness" were those of the ministry in London.

What seemed in Whitehall to be the flagging rebellion in America was, at the moment, proving otherwise on the ground, but the time lag left the ministry still awash in optimism. A colored engraving issued from Cheapside late in January, "Jack England and the Four Confederates," had the confident caption, "To Arms, you Brave Britons, to Arms. The Road to Renown Lyes before you." The four enemy confederates were "Yankee Doodle," "Monsieur Louis Baboon," "Don Diego," and "Mynheer Frog," with the American complaining that he could "beat them all" if his allies "would but pull together," but the other three confessed their incompetence, the Frenchman admitting, "I have almost forgot how to fight."

"The Balance of Power," issued by a printer in Cornhill, also satirized America's European allies. On one side of a pair of scales a heroic, Roman-clad Britannia, declares, "No one injures me with impunity." A verse below the cartoon of foppish, greedy France, Spain, and Holland, on the other balance, reads hopefully,

America, dup'd by a treacherous twain,
Now finds she's a tool both to France and to Spain,
Yet all three united can't weigh down the scale:
So the Dutchman jumps in with the hope to prevail.
Yet Britain will boldly their efforts withstand,
And bravely defy them by Sea and by Land. . . .
[Then the Americans] will with Britain unite
And each to the other be Mutual Delight.

Fewer and fewer Englishmen retained that optimism about the likelihood of reunion. A protest gathering representing the county of York resolved unanimously, "That it is the opinion of this meeting that the prosecution of an offensive war in America is most evidently a measure which by employing our great and enormous[ly] expensive military operations against the inhabitants of that country, prevents this [kingdom] from exerting its united, vigorous and firm efforts against the powers of France and Spain, and has no other effect on America than to continue, and thereby to increase the enmity which has so long and so fatally subsisted between the arms of both." Not only could the fratricidal war be "productive to no good whatever, but, by preventing conciliation, threatens the . . . final ruin of the British Empire." It was a middle path espoused by more and more Englishmen—that one could be a pacifist and a patriot by reducing the war to the traditional European rivals.

In the cities, especially London, many readers continued to learn the dismaying news in the coffeehouses, where they repaired to read the papers. A cartoon, "The Coffee-House Patriots," depicted the decidedly unwarlike clientele settling the nation's newest dilemmas, including the Dutch and the French, both considerable sea powers. Yet "Jack England" was more than their match when at its best. The Dutch possessed largely a merchant fleet; the capricious French navy, even when used effectively, could not reach the American interior. Washington's apparently dwindling army in the North was remote from Virginia and the Carolinas, where the French could assist, if present, through broad rivers and bays. Still, on January 13, 1781,

with new confidence that he could hold onto his troops (the mutinies had been in the North), General Greene sent a message to
Daniel Morgan, the "Old Wagoner," that Tarleton "is said to be on his
way to pay you a visit. I doubt not that he will have a decent reception and proper dismission."

Hannah's Cowpens was rolling land near Camden where cattle
were wintered. On the seventeenth what promised to be another
rout led by Tarleton turned into a trap. Morgan exhorted his men to
aim for the epaulets of enemy officers. William Washington's
mounted militia also came forward. In an hour the British lost 100
killed and 229 wounded; another 600 were taken prisoner. Wounded
himself, Tarleton escaped with 40 horsemen.

Despite the small numbers it was the most severe British defeat
since Saratoga. The *Chronicle,* improving the reality for coffeehouse
hawks when the news arrived in London on March 29, claimed, "By
all accounts Col. Tarleton was never more distinguished for spirit and
gallantry than on this occasion." Cornwallis acquitted Tarleton of any
blame. But he was very likely the inspiration for a massacre of Tories
on February 25, several weeks later, when troops led by "Light Horse
Harry" Lee and Andrew Pickens, after fighting Tarleton and covering
Greene, encountered a column of 400 loyalists recruited locally
under Colonel John Pyce. Ninety were killed; then six prisoners
were hacked to death in a reprise of "Tarleton's quarter." Greene
punned coldly if ungrammatically, "It has had a very happy affect on
those disaffected persons, of which there are too many in this country."

News of redcoat reinforcements from New York disembarking on
the Chesapeake coast of Virginia emboldened Cornwallis to strike
north again. On March 15, at Guilford Court House, below Hillsborough in North Carolina, his outnumbered but skillfully led army
pushed back Greene's troops with heavy casualties on both sides.
Again the numbers were relatively small, but large losses in a lean
force were critical. Greene committed 4,449 rank and file; 1,670
were Continentals, the others militia. Cornwallis had only 1,900
men, but they were seasoned professionals who kept their nerve in
trying terrain, and irreplaceable. Although figures differ, he probably
lost 532 officers and men. Tarleton was badly wounded. Greene's
troops lost 12 officers and 312 men, and the field.

Cornwallis could not afford the price of the Pyrrhic victory. He confessed to Major General William Philips, a prisoner at Saratoga but active again after his exchange (for Benjamin Lincoln), "My situation here is very distressing. . . . To form a junction with you [on the Chesapeake] is exceedingly hazardous." Because of increasing sickness among his men he wanted to escape the Carolina summer and move northward again, despite "the almost universal spirit of revolt which prevails." Interest in the king's obedience was proving increasingly rare.

News of Cornwallis's apparent victory first reached England in May, along with his incautious proclamation claiming the defeat of Greene and urging loyalists to the king's peace, but in early June came the reality. The countryside was inhospitable and difficult to supply. Cornwallis's army after Guilford Court House was even without bread for two days. Into April, troops had to backtrack for forage and food, enduring a miserable eighteen days' march to the Atlantic coast at Wilmington, North Carolina.

Unaware, because of the time lag, of Cornwallis's increasingly dismal prospects, Germain wrote, "I make no doubt your Lordship will, by this time, have had the honour to recover the province of North Carolina to his Majesty; and I am even sanguine enough to hope, from your Lordship's distinguished abilities and zeal for the King's service, that recovery of part of Virginia will crown your success before the season becomes too intemperate for land operations."

In the Commons on June 12, Fox laid bare the reality that the earl's brilliant success resembled a decisive defeat. He had "relinquished all the advantages he had gained with so much difficulty." Accepting that assessment, Walpole wrote to William Mason on June 14, 1781, "What can I tell you? That Lord Cornwallis has conquered his troops out of shoes and provisions, and himself out of troops."

Cornwallis had criticized his chief's alleged dawdling, often over Clinton's head to Germain and Amherst. Now Clinton attempted what seemed like small revenge—Cornwallis needed help anyway—by ordering General Robertson to command in the Chesapeake, suddenly perceived as the crucial theater of war. It appeared to Clinton that Cornwallis was trying to force the conflict into Virginia and the Chesapeake rather than return all the way—arduously, perhaps, by sea—to Charleston. Preparing to leave on the frigate *Amphitrite* with reinforcements drawn from New York, Robertson wrote on May 8 to Amherst with his usual blend of unrealism and platitudes, responding to a message of January 4, only just arrived. The Chesapeake, he explained, is "a great object to the french and to the rebels," the reason that Arnold had been sent there earlier, and General Phillips with 2,500 men after him. Now, Robertson added, 1,600 more troops were being landed—"these prevented La Fayette from coming down, and drove him ashore [prematurely] at Annapolis—where he remains entrenched."

Robertson expected more rebel soldiers to be ordered to Virginia to confront Cornwallis: "We hear that Wayne has marched from Philadelphia* southward with 1,200 men, that the Congress scheme of forming an army for the war fails, that even by taking men for a few months, their levys do not fill—and that Congress is now bankrupt, the people at Philadelphia refusing to take paper at 250 for one [authentic dollar]—dogs have been drove about the streets tarred and covered with it."

On May 20, having been relieved as governor of what there was of New York, Robertson sailed toward a discomforting new reality. Despite his claims that the rebel cause was falling apart, he confessed to Amherst as he concluded his message that he did not "see any solid national object" to be secured where he was heading. "Lord Cornwallis recommends operations in Chesapeake—and says if they cannot be carryed on, New York should be given up." (Germain had written to Cornwallis in a message not yet received, "I cannot help expressing my wishes that the Chesapeake may become the seat of war, even, if necessary, at the expense of abandoning New York.") To Amherst, Robertson pontificated, "We contract Ideas of the superior importance of places where we have lived or acted—this may have led my Lord to think the possession of Virginia and the provinces to the southward all that is desirable and attainable. Perhaps it is from the same prejudice that I have learned to think the giving up of this place would lose us every friend and every thing in America."

Robertson's orders, and earlier ones to an army under General Phillips, were attempts by Clinton to keep Cornwallis on the move while the New York garrison continued to hibernate. Cornwallis had

*Actually from York, Pennsylvania, which the British also called York Town

written disconsolately, almost cynically, to Phillips, an old friend in whom he could confide, from Wilmington on April 10 that he and Clinton appeared at cross purposes: "If we mean an offensive war in America, we must abandon New York and bring our whole force into Virginia; we then have a stake to fight for, and a successful battle may give us America. If our plan is defensive, mixed with desultory expeditions, let us quit the Carolinas (which cannot be held defensively while Virginia can be so easily armed against us) and stick to our salt pork at New York, sending now and then a detachment to steal tobacco, etc."

Arguing on April 25 to Germain in London that returning southward was useless as insufficient loyalists existed there to hold the hinterland, Cornwallis explained his Chesapeake strategy as a means of cutting the colonies in two rather than "to remain here for transports to carry us off," which would be "ruinous and disgraceful for Britain." The contradictions between Cornwallis's activism hedged by hopelessness and Clinton's wagering that war weariness on both sides would lead to conciliation, betrayed a desperation little understood in London. There the victories in the Carolinas and the apparent futility of the French fleet portended an imminent turnaround in the war. Yet the British held little more than Savannah, Charleston, and Wilmington in the South, as pockets in the interior disappeared under pressure from partisan forces as well as from units of Greene's army. Cornwallis had explained confidently to Germain in a message long moot when received that Greene had "left the back part of Virginia open" to a junction with Phillips. But the British could not control the "back part" of any colony.

With Robertson on board, the *Amphitrite* sailed no farther than Sandy Hook, anchoring to await the next fast mail packet from England. Yet before it came a message from Clinton arrived that Cornwallis had moved into Virginia and that Robertson, now redundant there, should return to New York. Again a combat command had eluded him.

Washington may have been disappointed—both sides had informers almost everywhere. He had written to Lafayette about General Robertson, "You may have something to apprehend from his age and experience but not much from his Activity."

On March 6, 1781 (in London time, given west-to-east communications, it was nearly May), Washington had traveled to Newport, Rhode Island, to discuss joint strategy with General Rochambeau, whose French forces had filled the British vacuum there. More vindictively than with any war-ending strategy in mind, Washington wanted support for a move against Benedict Arnold in Virginia. He hoped to capture the traitor and send him to the gibbet. It would turn out that Washington's instincts to take the war southward would validate his incautious emotions, but that was not yet evident. Lafayette had been sent ahead with a brigade, and felt in a precarious position as Cornwallis, with a stronger force, moved in his direction, but Cornwallis was unconcerned. He wanted to disperse or capture the patriot politicians in Charlottesville, where the House of Burgesses met, whose ideas had fueled the war, and disrupt the government of the state. Governor Thomas Jefferson, nearby at Monticello, fled with his young family.

Although affairs in Virginia looked more promising than they were, Clinton, still unrelieved in New York despite his pleas, worried about where the French would go from Newport. "I owe it to my country & I must in justice to my own fame declare to your Lordship," he confessed to the American Secretary, "that I become every day more sensible of the utter impossibility of prosecuting the war in this country without reinforcements." He recognized that it was now "visionary" to see any significant number of loyalists joining their cause, as it was hazardous to espouse royalist leanings when the empire had shown it could not protect them.

Although the message would not reach Whitehall for many weeks, ministers in London were reaching the same conclusion—that America could neither be recovered nor held without many more men than England could supply. Years before, after Lexington and Concord, Empress Catherine II had refused to supply mercenaries, but Whitehall, where wishful thinking often reigned, again hoped for a reconsideration. Richard Oswald, who had made a fortune as a military contractor for the army in America, proposed, through Henry Dundas, Viscount Melville, a nineteen-page "Plan for an Alliance with Russia, in order to carry on the American War." His suggestion was that 5,000 to 6,000 Russians could garrison New York to relieve the British and Hessian troops there to fight elsewhere.

Why the Russians might do it baffled logic. When they had claimed armed neutrality, they had in effect recognized the Americans as belligerents rather than rebels. To maintain amicable relations with St. Petersburg, the Royal Navy had been under orders for months not to interfere with Russian shipping. To further curry favor, English courts sentenced several newspaper publishers for slandering the Russian ambassador, although the offenses were hardly as harsh as the libels which appeared almost daily against George III.

In March, with seemingly incurable optimism, the press reported that Russia had offered mediation, that all parties had accepted, and that the peripatetic diplomat Sir Joseph Yorke, whose "newspaper greatness" Walpole scorned, was about to depart "on the wings of winds to Vienna to conclude the peace." Shares rose 6 percent in two days, then deflated as nothing happened and Yorke remained home.

Help of any sort from Austria, a bastion of Catholicism, was even more unlikely than from Russia. On February 22, 1781, the *Morning Chronicle* had dismissed an earlier conjecture in the rival *Morning Herald* that Austria, which had no pro-American sympathies, would come to the aid of Britain by attacking the despised Dutch. When, some months later, Sir Joseph, former envoy to the Hague, was rumored to be seeking a separate peace with Holland, hopes rose again, but they had no substance other than to register public weariness with the war. The displeasure of commerce-seeking European neutrals with Britain, allegedly the chief cause of market instability, was on the rise. "What inference can we draw," a London newspaper asked, "but that the INDEPENDENCE OF AMERICA, secretly acknowledged by every other Court in Europe, must soon be that of St. James's?"

From his headquarters in Morristown, New Jersey, Washington, always prone to private despondency, registered even more defeatism than the London press or the ministry in Whitehall. Late winter snowfalls had mired the general's small army where it was, and Washington wrote to Lafayette, who had returned to France briefly to lobby for further support, "The oldest people now living do not remember so hard a winter." In May, with the snows melted, he confided to his journal, "Instead of having the prospect of a glorious offensive campaign before us, we have a bewildered and gloomy defensive one, unless we receive a powerful aid of ships, land troops and money from our generous ally." But in France, from which Lafayette had already embarked with the news Washington was waiting for, the venerable Franklin now radiated optimism, claiming that he could furnish Mr. Gibbon with materials for writing *The History of the Decline and Fall of the British Empire.*

Despite the claims of Cornwallis that a bold stroke into Virginia would bisect the colonies and end the war, Clinton remained unpersuaded. Whether it was from caution or inertia, he wanted to hold onto New York as a base of operations in the North while giving grudging support to his deputy on the Chesapeake. Three expeditions by sea, each hazardous because of the French potential in the Atlantic, had bolstered Cornwallis. Benedict Arnold (who had received £6,315 for "loss of property" after his betrayal) had taken his loyalist American Legion to Virginia, wintering in Portsmouth, then moving out as a raiding party. General Alexander Leslie then led 2,500 English and Hessian infantry by ship up the James River as far as Richmond, torching what they could. General Phillips had followed in March with 2,300 reinforcements, and Lafayette, returned to America and taking 1,300 Continentals southward, could not head him off when a French fleet, arriving too late, was driven off.

Operating independently despite Clinton's reluctant help and Whitehall's distant helplessness, Cornwallis dismissed anticipated objections from his supposed superior in command. "It is very disagreeable to me to decide upon measures so very important and of such consequence to the general conduct of the war," he explained, "without an opportunity of procuring your Excellency's directions or approbation, but the delay and difficulty of conveying letters, and the impossibility of waiting for answers render it indisputably necessary."

Cornwallis had more objectives than troops to achieve them. One was to draw Greene's battalions away from the Carolinas, but he refused the bait. Greene even set off with two regiments toward Camden, where Colonel Rawdon, with a smaller force, beat him off at Hobkirk Hill on April 25. Colonel John Cruger, then besieged at the interior outpost of Ninety-Six,★ also held off Greene. Yet the British forces in the interior, exhausted in the heat and with no likelihood of reinforcements, withdrew toward Charleston and Savannah. Although they had won the field in most engagements in the South, they could not keep it.

★Ninety-Six was a stockaded outpost in the interior of South Carolina below Lake Greenwood, so named because it was believed, erroneously, that it was 96 miles from the frontier post of Fort Prince George. It retains its unusual name.

Late in May Washington and his aides again conferred with the Comte de Rochambeau and his deputy, the Chevalier de Chastellux, this time in Connecticut. Comte de Grasse, Washington learned, would sail north from the Caribbean during the summer to link up with the French moving south from Newport, where Admiral de Barras and his fleet were protected by Rochambeau's five thousand troops. Franklin knew that the French were disappointed with the weakness of the American military effort and the disunity of the colonial government in the three years since they had been pouring funds and supplies into the war in hopes of damaging Britain. Yet France had been distracted into the West Indies, had come up short in the Channel, and had botched its naval encounters off the American coast. The Bourbon monarchy had already advanced so much to the American cause that the Comte de Vergennes, the French foreign minister, would warn Franklin's delegation that the investment was already more than Congress "had a right to expect from the friendship of their ally." There were no assurances of further aid. The war had to be won, and soon.★

Underhandedly, Chevalier de La Luzerne, the French envoy, had already begun exploring compromise with Britain on independence for the colonies, bribing General John Sullivan to persuade his colleagues in the Continental Congress. Humbling the enemy had become too expensive for the treasury of Louis XVI, and on June 15, 1781, in secret session, the Congress agreed to abide by French policies on peace and to hold the commissioners in Passy to what were effectively French interests. Delegate Thomas Rodney of Delaware, who voted nay, wrote in anger to his elder brother Caesar, a signer of the Declaration of Independence, "I think it must convince the French Court that we are reduced to a weak and abject state." Both Franklin and Adams, who disagreed about many things, would ignore the resolution.

Messages from Washington and Rochambeau coordinating plans for an offensive, intended by Versailles to be the last, were dispatched by couriers. One from Chastellux to Luzerne, then in Philadelphia,

★Aid to America would virtually bankrupt the French treasury, a drain on the budget that would lead, in 1789, to the summoning of the Estates General to cope with the debt, and indirectly to the French Revolution that would cost Louis XVI his head.

criticized Rochambeau's passivity in Rhode Island and noted the need for prompt action. Within ten days, copies of the documents were in Clinton's hands. Ensign John Moody had seized a mail pouch, and its messenger, near Sussex Court House in New Jersey. One letter dealt with spies in New York City; another warned Lund Washington, the general's cousin and caretaker at Mount Vernon, that the British already in Virginia might raid the estate; still another was from Martha Washington (then with her husband) to her house-keeper; yet another was from Washington to his dentist about secur-ing a tool to tighten his false teeth.

To Lafayette, Washington wrote that he and Rochambeau had de-cided to join forces in an attack on New York City. With its defenses depleted by diversions of forces to Virginia, it seemed an opportune time. New York seemed to have priority over Virginia. Clearly the enemy letters were authentic and not shrewd disinformation. How-ever apprehensive about how to respond, Clinton, unexpectedly forewarned, wrote to Germain on June 9 that their position in New York would become precarious.

The sense among those in London who could read the strategic tea leaves was that the entire British position was indeed in jeopardy, although perusing the belated papers in the coffeehouses might have suggested otherwise. Cornwallis and company seemingly had been gathering in southern harbors and terrorizing the rebel interior. Soon the loyalists could reemerge and claim their birthright. "As to the American war, Sir," Dr. Johnson had lectured Boswell in April, "the sense of the nation is *with* the Ministry. The majority of those who can only *hear* is against it." The literate bourgeois *knew*; the illit-erate mob learned only from rumor. "Opposition," he dogmatized, "is always the loudest; a majority of the rabble will always be for the Opposition."

Disloyalty to his hero was unthinkable—aloud. Only in his diary did Boswell differ: "My opinion was that those who could *understand* were against the American war, as almost every man is now."

That Boswell was more attuned to the realities became obvious when young William Pitt took the floor of the Commons on June 12, 1781. Second son of the late Lord Chatham, and only twenty-two, he had been one of the few new legislators arising—in his case, indirectly—from the general election of September 1780. Defeated when he first stood for Cambridge University, he was given a safe Whig seat, for Appleby, in January 1781. Since being elected he had spoken only twice. Just before Parliament was to adjourn for the summer, Charles James Fox determined to give the tottering North government a further shove, and offered a motion for an inquiry "into the management of the war in America."

With the excuse that he wanted to correct something said about his father, Pitt amended the misrepresentation and then referred to those in the debate before him who had spoken of "a wicked or accursed war." It was worse than that, he said. "I am persuaded, and I will affirm, that it is a most accursed, wicked, barbarous, cruel, unnatural, unjust and most diabolical war." Explaining, he went on, emotionally, "The expense of it has been enormous, far beyond any former experience, and yet what has the British nation received in return? Nothing but a series of ineffective victories or severe defeats—victories . . . over our brethren whom we would trample down, or defeats which fill the land with mourning." He lamented shrewdly "the loss of so much British blood . . . on whatever side Victory might be declared."

Fox's motion was defeated, in a depleted House, by twenty-eight votes, but before the division Henry Dundas, lord advocate and a staunch defender of the North ministry, complimented Pitt on "so happy an union of first-rate abilities, high integrity, bold and honest independence of conduct, and the most persuasive eloquence." Dundas was being more than gracious to an obvious rising star; he was recognizing the imminence of change.

Reports arrived in New York that de Barras had sent a frigate from Newport to the West Indies with American pilots to guide de Grasse's Caribbean-based fleet. But to where? And where were Rochambeau's troops in Rhode Island to march, as they were seen moving, and by land rather than by sea? That also suggested a closer destination than Virginia.

In London, the first days of July were laden with omens. On May 2, Lord George Germain had sent another of his rude letters to Clinton, deploring his dithering, and on July 2, having received it, Clinton, uncowed, wrote to General Charles Rainsford that "in his heart" the Secretary for America "approves of all I have done. But, *entre nous,* he knows I do not [approve] of all he has done." Since Cornwallis had no desire to move into Maryland or Pennsylvania, and endanger, both from north and south, the forces he commanded, he was willing to return a token force to Clinton and retire to the lower reaches of the Chesapeake. On July 4, 1781, he began moving from Williamsburg across the James River to Portsmouth. On the edge of the peninsula separating the James from the York River to the north was Yorktown.

Weighing whether to sit out a defense of New York City or to overtake the French advancing from Rhode Island, Clinton had been unwilling to coordinate any plans with Admiral Arbuthnot, who on July 4 sailed for England. "For some time back," Rear Admiral Thomas Graves reported to Lord Sandwich in London, "no operations had been concerted between the disagreeing Commanders in Chief; but the moment it was known the Vice Admiral was going home, the General proposed an expedition and opened himself up on future plans." With no new troops from Europe Clinton was prepared to delay his attack on Rhode Island until the levies from Cornwallis arrived, and to hold New York at all costs.

What Clinton did not know, despite usually good intelligence, was that the New York adventure was likely not to happen. By late June, Washington, camped near Peekskill on the Hudson awaiting a junction with Rochambeau's army from Rhode Island, had begun to feel out Clinton's defenses. His detachments encountered strong foraging parties at Fort Lee, on the west side of the Hudson, and warships in the river. Enemy outposts at the Harlem River proved formidable. It appeared that siege operations would be necessary and almost impossible across water barriers—and there was no likelihood of a French fleet. Washington and Rochambeau would have to reconsider their options.

The next day, July 5, from Staten Island, General Robertson wrote to Lord Amherst in London that rebel plans had changed since the intercepted messages from Washington and Rochambeau had been reviewed. "Washington's [strategy] was to proceed with the whole of the french sea and land force [from Rhode Island] to the relief of Virginia, [but] the naval force of the french being reckoned inferior to ours and the [summer] season destructive to troops who act in Virginia, this was laid aside—and it was fixed that this place[, New York,] should be attacked." He cited evidence that "the french have been moving and the rebels have been collecting. . . . The enemy are retired out of sight." Major General de Chastellux, he claimed from captured letters, wondered why the allies did not, "when Clinton's arms are so helplessly spread, by taking New York stab him to the heart. They look to the West Indies for aid in Soldiers and Ships, we know their calls have been frequent and that they have promises from de Grasse, these probably cannot arrive nor a force that can give apprehensions for this place be collected before the middle of August."

Also, Sir Henry explained to Whitehall that he was trying to extricate some of his troops from Cornwallis before the French sent another fleet toward America—from the evidence, perhaps, to New York. Inexplicably, Admiral Rodney, claiming sudden illness, consulted only himself and, leaving Sir Samuel Hood in charge, sailed home from the West Indies with several ships of the line, although Germain had urged him earlier, "In a matter of so great moment, no precaution should be omitted or possible contingency guarded against."

Despite Clinton's obsession with New York, on June 27 Lord George, clearly persuaded by Cornwallis, had rebuked Sir Henry for not paying enough attention to the Chesapeake, and conveyed an order from King George to concentrate on Virginia as soon as the season permitted. The Atlantic gales blew from west to east. Clinton would not receive the royal command for many more weeks.

14

"The World turn'd Upside Down" July 1781–December 1781

If ponies rode men and if grass ate the cows,
And cats should be chased into holes by the mouse . . . ,
If summer were spring and t'other way round,
Then all the world would be upside down.
—"The World turn'd Upside Down," played by a band from Cornwallis's
redcoats as they lay down their arms at Yorktown, October 19, 1781

JOINING forces on the Hudson with Washington's Continentals late in July 1781 were the Comte de Rochambeau's troops from Newport. From the highlands above New York City and across the harbor they could look over Clinton's occupation army and keep the British command guessing. The metamorphosis from garrison stagnation to potential action was electric. Little more than a month earlier, Washington had despaired, but now the French were making good on their promises, almost certainly for the last time. In the South, Cornwallis's forces were converging along the Chesapeake coast of Virginia. Even farther south, Lieutenant Colonel Nesbit Balfour, left in command at Charleston, had sent a message in duplicate on July 2 to update the American Secretary about troop dispositions, one copy to go to Plymouth by the packet *Prince William Henry*. He was seeking reinforcements for Cornwallis that he knew he would not get.

Acknowledging the "great fatigue" of troops pursuing General Nathanael Greene in the stifling southern summer, Balfour reported the "uncommon precipitancy with which the enemy retreated" and conceded the difficulties of having to "match the advance on the march." The British could not "effect any thing decisive"—which was exactly what Greene intended. Balfour assumed "that the object of Greene's march"—a redeployment rather than a retreat—"pointed towards Virginia, which I am rather inclined to believe, from the intelligence [received], to which however I do not give the fullest credit, . . . of his being ordered there to join the force now under Generals La Fayette and Wayne."

The last dispatches to New York from Cornwallis had come from Petersburg, Virginia, on May 25. A juncture had been made with brigades under the command of Major General Phillips until his sudden death little more than a week earlier from fever. "His Lordship was at that time," Lord Rawdon reported to London, "proceeding in the pursuit of La Fayette, who daily expected to be reinforced by a corps under Gen. Wayne, detached by Gen. Washington to his support." Rawdon did not yet know that Washington himself was coming to their support—nor did Washington—or that Lieutenant General the Comte de Grasse★ was commanding a squadron from France also en route to the Chesapeake, where the York River emptied into the Bay. Even Washington had no word yet from de Grasse.

The packet with Balfour's duplicate message was intercepted by a Yankee privateer and rushed on to Washington. Whitehall's newest intelligence came from a disembarking admiral grateful to be back. According to a press report in London on August 7, 1781, "Admiral Arbuthnot arrived the day before yesterday at Spithead, from North America, on board the *Roebuck:* he presented himself yesterday evening to the Admiralty, with dispatches"—they were months late—"from Sir Henry Clinton, leaving the great affair of the reduction of America to Lord Cornwallis."

Clinton did not want to leave the reduction of America to Cornwallis, his potential successor and rival for respect in England. Largely on the basis of intercepted enemy letters, especially one from Lafayette, Clinton on June 19 had asked Cornwallis to return some of his troops to New York, as the southern colonies, especially in the summer heat, were unlikely to remain an active front. "If, in the approaching inclement season, your Lordship should not think it prudent to undertake operations with the troops you have, I cannot but

★Lieutenant General François-Joseph-Paul, Comte de Grasse commanded a naval force in the French manner, without an admiral's title.

wish . . . you would send me as soon as possible what you can spare from a respectable defensive."

Clinton himself envisioned only a respectable defensive, to prolong the war into a campaign some other commander would take on the next year. He wanted three thousand men returned, and for the troops remaining in Virginia he was shipping two thousand tons of provisions. Frigidly reminding Cornwallis of his deputy status, Clinton also instructed him not to communicate with Lord George Germain in London directly, but only through New York. By July 20, the Queen's Rangers had embarked to rejoin Clinton, but few more men would leave.

At about the same time as the frustrated Arbuthnot had sailed home, a dispatch from New York dated July 12 went separately to London, to appear in the press on August 30. "Jonathan," it reported with some optimism—America was still "Brother Jonathan"—"is collecting all his forces, raising Heaven and Earth to besiege us, in conjunction with about four thousand French troops;* on this occasion the . . . Yankees seem to be very forward, and turn out in great numbers, in hopes of getting possession of this place. Hence we expect some warm work in about a month, as the lads are investing us on all sides; however, should they have formed the resolution of attacking us, as they threaten, from the strength of our lines, and the ardour of our garrison, which, I dare say, . . . consists of twenty thousand fighting men at least, [I] am in hopes they will pay dear for their presumption, and may, in its consequences, put an end to the rebellion."

Shortly—it was on August 16—opposition newspapers would report sardonically that the progovernment "prints," utilizing "a wonderful deal of ingenuity, have gathered good news enough from the late dispatches sent home by Sir Henry Clinton, to serve the Ministry . . . for the remainder of the Summer. The French fleet have but few seamen on board, and those for the most part sick and useless— the junction has been happily effected between Lord Cornwallis and General Arnold—the people in the Carolinas, and up the Delaware, hate and detest the Congress—Lord Cornwallis upon the point of pursuing the enemy with an army of 8000 men—Lord Rawdon

*The Comte de Rochambeau actually had about fifty-five hundred troops.

driving the rebels before him with another powerful detachment—the rebels out of Breath running away from the British troops, without cloaths, without provisions, bare-footed, and half-starved—and Sir Henry Clinton strong enough at New York to demolish General Washington whenever he pleases. The Lord have mercy upon the Americans!"

A British brigadier general since December 1780, Arnold had indeed been in Virginia in response to Cornwallis's request to Clinton for a diversionary gesture, and had assumed interim command of Phillips's troops as well when the general died unexpectedly on May 13. Phillips had been seeking out Lafayette's army, sent to the Chesapeake by Washington in pursuit of the renegade Arnold. The patriot price on his head was only a spur to Arnold, obsessed with paying off scores, and he had ravaged installations along the James River as far inland as Charlottesville. Arnold had led his forces, he reported to his own satisfaction, to Clinton, with "ardour and firmness," but his renegade status had earned him the enmity of senior officers, as had his candor in messages to Germain on how to win the war despite the lethargic command in New York.

When ordered back to New York in June, Arnold proposed another punishing raid, this time to relieve French naval pressure from Rhode Island. In August, with Clinton's blessing, he sailed with 1,732 men in British crimson and loyalist green to sack seaports in his native Connecticut. Early on September 4, just after Rochambeau's army had marched to sprightly band tunes through Philadelphia, Arnold's torching parties, to a rising level of patriot hatred, ruthlessly plundered and burned New London. To General Robertson, reporting candidly to Earl Amherst, it was "a dear bought place." Losses were heavy on both sides. On Arnold's return, Clinton mingled praise of the entirely useless venture with the observation that he could afford few such victories.

Recognizing the politics of place, French orders to the Comte Rochambeau had been to put his troops and supporting vessels under Washington. Rochambeau had more than five thousand men seasoned in European skirmishes, and eight ships under Admiral de Barras. They had been awaiting impatiently for something to do beyond garrisoning a seaport in Rhode Island. Washington wanted to take New York and deprive the enemy of its supply base from England. Rochambeau had helpfully moved in that direction, but from July 21 to 24, when he and Washington looked over Clinton's lines, they realized that the risk was beyond their numbers. Even before Clinton received 2,000 long-expected Hessian replacements—very likely, he realized, the last—on August 11, he had 11,000 British and German troops as well as 3,000 loyalist militia, and a formidable water barrier as a natural defense everywhere but at Westchester County to the north.

Washington's curiously uncoded letter to Lafayette revealed that he preferred to attack New York, "reduced" then in soldiery, to mounting a "Southern Operation, [as] we had not command of the water," and there were reports "that the enemy were about to quit New York altogether." Information seemed magically procurable on both sides. Not only did the British seize a copy of Washington's message; the Continentals somehow knew of Germain's priorities to value Virginia over the retention of New York.

Then on August 14 came de Grasse's message to Rochambeau that he would be arriving at the Chesapeake, en route to New York, by early September, after which he would have to sail to the Caribbean to assist the Spaniards. Raising anchor at Brest while being watched closely by British spies who had not learned where de Grasse was going, he carried three thousand marines aboard twenty-five warships. Assuming the contested sugar islands as the French goal, Germain assured Clinton in a misguided message that would arrive too late to matter that de Grasse had no plans for North America, and that in any case, the choleric Admiral Rodney (who had returned) would give the French their comeuppance from Jamaica.

In London, one of the ministry's embarrassments remained Sir John Burgoyne, who seemed to haunt Whitehall. On April 3, the Congress had directed Washington to recall him and other senior officers absent from America on parole. Burgoyne appealed to his political friends for protection, and on August 15, 1781, Edmund Burke wrote to Ben Franklin in Paris, contending that it was "very disagreeable to see the most opposite Interests conspiring in the persecution of a man formed by the unparalleled Candour and moderation of Mind to unite the most discordant parties in his favour."

Franklin replied that Congress had no "wish to persecute General Burgoyne," but seemed disposed to exchange him for Henry Laurens, a former president of the body, who was jailed in the Tower of London. "I have just received," Franklin closed, "an authentic Copy of the Resolve containing that Offer, and authorising me to make it. . . . If you can find any means of negociating this Business, I am sure the restoring another worthy Man to his Family and Friends will be an Addition to your Pleasure." Laurens would be released, after further delays, in time to assist Franklin in settling the peace.

While Clinton still anticipated an attack on New York, and wrote accordingly to Germain, the combined allied forces began moving farther south, leaving some troops to mislead the British. Given time constraints, it was clear that de Grasse could not be useful north of the Chesapeake. Rochambeau and Washington entered Philadelphia from Princeton early in the afternoon of Thursday, August 30, where Robert Morris, the harried superintendent of finance, proceeded to borrow hard currency from Rochambeau's war chest to furnish a month's pay for Washington's approaching troops. They went on to the posh City Tavern for dinner and thirteen toasts, punctuated by salutes from vessels along the Delaware. In the evening the city was candlelit, and as Washington walked through the cobblestone streets to the acclaim of Philadelphians, the shabby loyalist past seemed very remote.

Continentals in blue began marching jauntily through the city on September 2, en route to Head of Elk in Maryland, where the Chesapeake began, to await de Grasse. One patriot cheering on the Americans asked a sergeant in the advance guard what troops they were. "Cornwallis's physic," he said, using the term then for cathartic, or cure. "Then the British did not swallow you all," the citizen joked. "No," the sergeant agreed, "We have sufficient left to give them all a good dose." The next day the French legions followed, dazzling Philadelphians lining the streets by their splendid crimson-and-pink, blue-and-yellow, green-and-yellow, and red, blue, and yellow uniforms, each identifying their aristocratic commanders.

By the time the French ships from the Caribbean arrived at the Elk on September 6 to ferry troops down the Chesapeake to Williamsburg, Clinton, now alerted by informants and by his own picket ships along the coast, realized that the main event would be in Virginia, where Cornwallis would be vastly outnumbered. Clinton's aide, Captain George Damer, later 2nd Earl of Dorchester, wrote in bleak honesty to the American Secretary from Staten Island, before a mail packet sailed,

> What I feel most severely is, that from [our] past conduct I cannot judge favourably or confidently of future exertions. Is it to be believed that Rochambeau and Washington should form their junction on the White Plains in the beginning of July, should remain between that place and our lines at Kingsbridge six weeks, should cross the North [Hudson] River, the Jerseys, and the Delaware, without receiving during that period any check, interruption, or even disturbance from our army? . . .
>
> The truth is that, so far from any offensive attempt on our side, the movements of our troops confined to York [Manhattan], Staten, and Long Islands, strongly marked an apprehension of New York and its dependencies being attacked or besieged. . . . And humiliating as it may be and is to confess, yet it is most true that the apparent force which made us tremble within our lines and behind our [defensive] works did not exceed our own numbers.

His own side was "happy that this army was gone, yet ignorant where it was going," Damer confessed to London, although they had learned from spies that de Barras's fleet had simultaneously sailed from Newport and destroyed facilities there the British might have reoccupied. "But neither did this, more than any other circumstance or information, tend to discover Mr. Washington's true design." Only de Grasse's arrival and "immediate possession of the Chesapeak[e] . . . put an end to our infatuations and prove his"—Washington's—"sole object to be assembling his whole force for the purpose of destroying the Virginian Army."

Washington had only exploited circumstances, but to Damer, and, presumably, Clinton, the lengthy reconnoitering of the outskirts of New York seemed a brilliant feint, leaving them in a strategic quandary. To Lord Amherst, General Robertson explained from his sources that Washington had encamped, on "the White plains, . . . an army of about 4300 French and Seven thousand Mostly raw rebels.... The better to proclaim his intention he hauld from Boston to White plains thirteen-inch Mortars and heavy Cannon fit only for a Siege." When some of the allied army crossed the Hudson at Peekskill and moved to Paramus in New Jersey, Robertson went on, they were observed "preparing Waggons for a move, Staaten Island the declared Object." Clinton reinforced Staten Island.

Since a traditional method of gathering intelligence was to send patrols forward to seize prisoners to interrogate, most Continentals were not told where they were going, or when. "If we do not deceive our own men," Washington contended, "we will never deceive the enemy." A French officer complained, "We do not know the object of our march, and are in perfect ignorance whether we are going against New York, or whether we are going to Virginia to attack Cornwallis."

Essential to any British response was the fleet of Admiral Thomas Graves, who had been ordered by Lord Sandwich to keep a lookout for a convoy of supplies from France. Unwisely, Graves employed his entire squadron in the mission, costing him timely coastal intelligence, and missing the deployment of the French from Newport. Six days after Graves's departure the packet *Swallow* reached New York with news from Admiral Rodney in the Caribbean, and Clinton sent the sloop onward to report to Graves, but it was captured by a rebel privateer. Only three weeks later did Graves receive a duplicate with the news, and turn about.

The mouth of the Chesapeake could not be seen from Yorktown, which angled slightly inward toward the York River. Off Cape Henry, from the frigate *Charon,* a British naval lieutenant on August 31 discovered the incoming French fleet, dominated by de Grasse's 104-gun flagship *Ville de Paris.* Cornwallis rushed a coded message to Clinton by a packet which slipped out in the darkness: "There are between thirty and forty sail within the capes, mostly ships of war and some of them very large." In reality, de Grasse had 27 ships, with 3,200 troops aboard, to be landed before he ferried south the brigades encamped at Head of Elk. Cornwallis, rather than Clinton, was under siege.

"Nothing gave me greater pleasure," de Grasse would later write

from Cape Henry to the Chevalier de La Luzerne, in Philadelphia,
"than the approach of the armies under General Washington and the
Count de Rochambeau. In order to hasten their arrival [at York-
town] I had fetched out seven vessels that drew the least water to
transport them from the mouth of Elk down Chesapeake Bay." But
as the ships were about to sail to the rendezvous point a fleet under
Admirals Hood and Graves appeared in the Atlantic approaches.
Hood had sailed from the Caribbean on August 10 with fourteen
ships and an infantry regiment aboard. Arriving at the Chesapeake
before de Grasse, he saw no sign of the French, and proceeded north
to scout Delaware Bay. Again there was no visible French presence.
He sailed on to New York, arriving on August 28. Once Hood
learned that de Barras had left Newport for the Chesapeake, he
joined the only five ships that Graves had fit for service after his futile
Atlantic reconnaissance, and with Graves in command, the combined
fleet of nineteen returned southward on August 31.

Arriving on the fifth, the British took on the much larger French
force off Cape Henry in the open sea. "I have fought them," de
Grasse reported to Luzerne, "and their van has been roughly handled. I returned to the Bay on the 10th." In reality the damage to
both sides was heavy. "In the meantime," de Grasse continued,
"Count de Barras had arrived [from Newport], and sent up the
transports he had with him to bring down the troops, which induced
me not to send up the seven vessels . . . ; and I had only to add to
those sent by Count de Barras. . . . I fell in with two of the enemy's
frigates . . . sent by the English admiral to cut away the buoys of our
anchors—They have paid dear for them." Graves's fleet straggled
back to New York for repairs. Cornwallis would never receive the reinforcements.

The earl had written to Clinton—the messages went on from
New York to London—that "the works at Gloucester," across the
channel from Yorktown, were prepared against "sudden attack," but
that Yorktown itself would need at least six more weeks to be "in a
tolerable state of defense." As the heat was intense, he employed, for
constructing earthworks, local black slaves who had been promised
their freedom. He had left about seventy-five hundred troops, not all
fit for duty. Although he might have attempted, with heavy losses

likely, to break out to the south, he had been assured by Clinton—an outcome still possible—that a powerful fleet was being prepared for his rescue, and Germain had promised, months earlier, that Rodney would ward off the French—which had not happened.

As early as September 5 gloomy speculation appeared in the *Kentish Gazette* that if a French fleet bottled up the Chesapeake, thwarting reinforcements from New York or England, Cornwallis, whatever his generalship, would be at the mercy of his existing means. On September 14, however, the *London Courant,* assuming that Washington's thrusts toward New York City remained real, predicted that the decisive battle for America was looming there. On September 6, via a packet sent riskily down the seaboard and taking cover in inlets, Clinton again promised relief for Yorktown. Cornwallis replied on the sixteenth by the same sloop, "If I had no hopes of relief, I would rather risk an action, than defend my half-finished works, but as you say [Admiral] Digby is hourly expected, and promises every exertion to assist me, I do not think myself justified in putting the fate of the war on so desperate an attempt."

Change was in the air on both sides of the Atlantic. To fill the vacancy in the Commons created by the death on August 30 of George Hayley, the council of the City of London, still the center of radicalism in England, ruffled the hawks by asking Lord George Gordon to run. He had lost his seat in the snap election after the riots he had caused the year before. In the *Public Advertiser* for September 17, 1781, Gordon demurred, "I make no doubt but I might carry the election against all opponents but for fear of provoking public disturbances I must beg leave to decline the honour proposed to me at this time."

Early in October, in another augury of change, rumors rife in Westminster were that the American Secretary would be dismissed with the consolation of a peerage—if someone could be found to accept his unpromising ministry. By late October most of the English press had conceded that the Chesapeake was becoming a French lake and that Cornwallis seemed fatally overmatched. It was not reasonable for Englishmen, the *Courant* conceded on October 24, "to expect from the bravest of men, what is beyond the power of mortal endowments." Three days later the *Morning Herald,* which followed

Lord Sandwich's line, speculated whether "the brave Cornwallis should be Burgoyn'd," and suggested that if it happened, "the Minden Hero"—Germain—would again be to blame. Obviously the Secretary for America was the manager of the war, and at fault at the distance of three thousand miles for disasters about which he could only speculate. "O Germain! Sprung from War's great Kings," a sardonic attack in the *London Courant* began. A parody of the *First Ode* of Horace, it again suggested how classically educated newspaper-buying Londoners were.

A few hopeful notes were still heard. Clinton, who had failed to impede the southward march of Washington and Rochambeau, might still find a way to force a rescue. But on November 16 the *Courant* deplored that a "crimson coloured curtain" would soon fall on the "dreadful tragedy we have been acting in America," and the *Public Advertiser* acknowledged on November 23, "We are already too exhausted to prolong the contest much longer." The drama in America had already played out as London papers published their mortifying forecasts.

Postponing action, a dismayed war council convened by Clinton in New York on September 14 agreed to await the arrival from England of Admiral Robert Digby, replacing Graves, with three additional warships, before organizing a rescue mission by sea. Doing little materially to prepare, Clinton busied himself for days with detailed memoranda on strategic alternatives, essentially building a paper case to protect his posterior in the event of a parliamentary inquiry. On September 24 (in a message begun on the twenty-third), General Robertson had written to Lord Amherst that his last message from Cornwallis "conveys strongly a want of instant aid, [and] at a Council of War consisting of three Admirals, a Commodore, Sir Henry Clinton, Genl Knuphausen, myself, Lt. Genl Lesslie and Majr Genl Patterson it was represented that only a force that would make our Army in Virginia beat the Rebel Army could prevent the loss of the force with Ld Cornwallis."

The troop strength decided upon for the operation was six thousand, conveyed by at least twenty-two men-of-war that would have to "force their Way thro the French Fleet and land our Army at York." As a "measure of necessity" the plan was adopted, relieving Clinton of the entire burden of decision. But at that moment in writing his dispatch,

Robertson "got news that Admiral Digby was in sight....An Express sails instantly to tell Lord Cornwallis that the fleet will absolutely Sail in whatever Condition it may be got into on the fifth."

With Digby on the *Prince George* was a stocky midshipman of sixteen, Prince William Henry, the king's third son and future William IV. When the frigate had arrived off Sandy Hook, contrary winds and a running tide kept it below the sandbar. Clinton sent a shallow-draft cutter to fetch the prince who, already nautically knowledgeable, wrote graphically and without hope to his father on September 28, in a letter to arrive two months later, "The Fleet are lying some at New York and others at Staten Island in a most wretched condition. They expect to be ready about the 7 or 8 of next month. However, I believe they will not be ready [as] soon as that time, for many ships are lying without masts and there is a great scarcity of lower masts, and in short, of all stores here."

The loyal press made much of the prince, describing "joy ineffable and universal" in New York and suggesting omens in his arrival of favorable reversal of fortune. But when the news came into rebel hands, papers in the colonies imagined a wry dialogue (with some spellings now peculiar) in which His Royal Highness learns unwelcome realities from "Sir Harry" Clinton:

Sir Harry. Your Royal Highness has been deceived [in London]. The delays and blunders of the Ministry, and the mistaken severities of the military, have created a large majority in all the colonies in favour of the Congress.

Prince. But I must see Lord Cornwallis!

Sir Harry. This I fear will be impossible. His Lordship is now besieged at York[town] by an army of 15,000 men, & the only avenue to him through the Chesepeak is blocked up by a French fleet of 36 sail of the line.

Prince. The devil! But can nothing be done to relieve his Lordship[?]

Sir Harry. Every thing has been done that valor and zeal for his Majesty's service could do—Admiral Graves had well nigh sacrificed his little fleet in supporting the power and fame of Britain on the ocean in a conflict with the French fleet off the capes of Virginia; he has returned defeated, and shattered in such a manner that I fear half his ships will be rendered unfit for service.

Prince. And must they have Cornwallis, the idol of my father's heart, the boast of England, the American hero, fall?

Sir Harry. I see nothing to prevent it.

Prince. And pray Sir Harry, where is the rest of my father's territory in America?

Sir Harry. His Majesty's territory at present, in the thirteen revolted provinces, is confined only to the garrisons of New York, Charlestown and Savannah.

Prince. O heavens! What do I hear? Why, Sir Harry, you have petrified me. Damn the loyalists, all this comes from listening to their tales. They teazed my father into this cursed war. . . . O! My poor mother, how I pity her! My father will break her heart with [his] pouting when he hears these accounts from America. Poor Lord North and Lord George Germain will be torn to pieces by the populous. America lost! The brightest jewel in my father's crown is fallen! Alas! What will become of my brother George[?] The kingdom's hardly now worth inheriting.

Although it seemed doubtful that a mail packet could again evade the French, the unreassuring message from Clinton reached Cornwallis on the twenty-ninth, promising the impossible—a deliverance sailing on October 5. Since, inexplicably, the British had never outfitted a naval dockyard at New York harbor in five years of occupation, repairs to Graves's ships took until October 12. From Yorktown that morning, Cornwallis wrote to Clinton, "Last night the enemy made their second parallel [siege trench] at the distance of 300 yards. We continue to lose men very fast."

Washington's heavy artillery had arrived on the sixth. Once the guns were emplaced, bombardment began on the ninth, with the general symbolically touching off the first round from a French cannon. By darkness on the fourteenth the vulnerable British ordnance had been silenced. "Experience has shown," Cornwallis wrote coolly—but from the protection of a cave—the next day, "that our fresh earthen works do not resist their powerful artillery. . . . The safety of the place is therefore so precarious that I cannot recommend that the fleet and army should run great risk in endeavouring to save us."

The same day, October 15, 1781, Clinton wrote to his patron in

England, the Duke of Newcastle, "I informed the Minister [for America] that if the enemy should hold a naval superiority for only a few weeks we should in our insular and detached state, run the greatest risks [in covering our operations]." Yet if Cornwallis's army were defeated, the king would "have little hope of seeing a British dominion re-established in America, as our country cannot replace that army. If I succeed in a junction with Lord Cornwallis, and there is a possibility of attacking Washington afterwards, I shall certainly attempt it." Later, *Gentleman's Magazine,* criticizing the divided command (although distances made that inevitable), would quote *Richard III:*

> What do they in the North
> When they should serve their sovereign in the West?

With the rescue fleet still in harbor on October 17, but filling up with all the troops the warships could hold—transports were too slow—General Robertson wrote again to Lord Amherst, knowing that his messages would be passed on to the American Secretary. "I dread their coming too late," he agonized. ". . . I have taken pains in all Councils of War to represent the decisive influence this event would have on His Majesty's affairs—that not only America, but the importance of Britain hung on it—that every thing was to be risqued" Delay, he had warned, "would operate as fatally as defeat."

The refitted fleet, 25 warships with 7,149 troops aboard, finally sailed from its rendezvous at Sandy Hook on October 19. The preparations had been enormous. In addition to cannonballs and artillery, over half a million cartridges, flints, matches, and other ordnance and stores, according to a careful inventory, were loaded. The last dispatch from Cornwallis, Clinton wrote to London before he embarked, had been dated October 11. The enemy was "advancing fast."

"As we are now under sail with a fair wind," Clinton explained to Germain from his flagship, which required a cutter alongside to take his message to a seagoing packet, "I still flatter myself that notwithstanding the rapidity of the enemy's progress and our having been delayed by the necessary repairs of our fleet so far beyond the expected time, it may yet be in the power of our joint exertions to relieve his Lordship."

On the very day that the fleet began moving from New York to Sandy Hook, October 17, Cornwallis sent emissaries under a flag of truce to propose an armistice. It was the fourth anniversary of the surrender at Saratoga. "The newspapers on the Court side," Horace Walpole wrote later, "had been crammed with paragraphs for a fortnight, saying that Lord Cornwallis had declared that he would never pile up his arms like Burgoyne; that is, he would rather die sword in hand. He had probably made no such declaration." (American papers had alleged it.) A broadside in London would display "The American Rattle Snake"—Benjamin Franklin had pictured a disjointed snake in an "unite or die" emblem—with the caption,

Two British Armies have I thus Burgoyn'd,
And room for more I've got behind.

The next day, October 18, 1781, Washington agreed to the terms of capitulation except for the article Cornwallis wanted—"that no person may be punished for having joined the British troops." Washington was unwilling to protect loyalists in Yorktown, in or out of uniform, who would be turned over to civil authorities.

In practice, none were punished, but the abandonment would astonish the English, and Germain would write acidly, "The effect of such a proceeding requires no comment."

"At retreat beating last night," Major St. George Tucker of the Virginia militia wrote in his Yorktown journal, "the British play'd the Tune of 'Welcome Brother Debtor'—to their conquerors[,] the tune was by no means disagreeable." The song by George Bickman dated back to 1738 and the title suggested a sneer. Ebenezer Denny, an ensign in the Pennsylvania Continentals, recorded, very likely from another location that night, only "the sound of a single drum; but when the firing ceased, I thought I never heard a drum equal to it—the most delightful music to us all."

Since music to be played at the formal surrender ceremonies was established by ground rules forbidding the derisory playing of an enemy tune, the Yorktown garrison was directed to march past beating "a British or German March." Yet any tune could be played in march tempo, and each of the ten surrendering regiments had what remained of a band. Military stores seized included eighty-one drums, twenty-eight bugles, and five French horns; and bandsmen kept their own fifes. Aedanus Burke, a South Carolina assemblyman in the Continentals, wrote to Arthur Middleton, a congressman captured at Charleston and exchanged, that on the afternoon of the nineteenth the surrendering troops, their flags furled, trod between parallel columns of Frenchmen and Americans "in a slow pace, and to the sound of music, not military marches, but of certain airs, which had in them so peculiar a strain of melancholy, and which together with the[ir] appearance before me excited sentiments far different from those I expected to enjoy."

The Germans passed through smartly, perhaps realizing that as hired troops they were only going home to practice their profession elsewhere. Redcoats, many weeping, some drunk, bore the burden of defeat. Some would heave their muskets onto the rising piles of weapons in hopes of damaging them. All filed out slowly to relinquish their arms while British bands played, perhaps to lighten the humiliation, the originally spirited "The World turn'd upside down." No one sang.

Ballads with that title and "upside down" lyrics had existed since Cromwellian days—and the world had certainly turned topsy-turvy for the British. A 1766 version published in *Gentleman's Magazine* and sung to a "derry down" tune, perhaps too jolly to be thought of then as melancholy, nevertheless had lyrics also relevant—even prophetic—for the occasion:

Goody Bull and her daughter together fell out,
Both squabbled and wrangled and made a great rout.
But the cause of their quarrel remains to be told,
Then lend both your ears and a tale I'll unfold.

"Having passed through our whole Army," Tucker wrote, the enemy "grounded their Arms & march'd back again thro' the Army a second Time into the Town—The sight was too pleasing to an American to admit of Description."

There are accounts of "The World turn'd Upside Down"—whatever the music—also being played when the British, under then lieutenant colonel (eventually lieutenant general) Alexander Leslie, evacuated Marblehead Neck, at Boston harbor, in March 1776. The ruefully appropriate air was reportedly also struck up by Burgoyne's unhappy bandsmen when they surrendered their arms near Fish Creek Bridge at Saratoga in October 1777. Given the ballad's subtitle (in one version), "The World turn'd Upside Down, or the Old Woman Taught Wisdom," it remained even more apt for a reprise at Yorktown.

Cornwallis had sulkily claimed indisposition and sent Brigadier General Charles O'Hara, escorted by Colonel Mathieu Dumas, to proffer a symbolic sword, ungraciously, not to Washington, but to Rochambeau. Much myth surrounds the intended indignity, and illustrations of the scene years later have varying depictions, all likely wrong. According to Dumas, Rochambeau motioned O'Hara toward Washington, who refused to accept the sword "from such a worthy hand." (O'Hara had been seriously wounded at Guilford Courthouse in March.) Under terms of the capitulation, all officers were entitled to keep their swords, and it is known that O'Hara dined with Washington that night.*

Off the Virginia Capes on October 24, five days later, the Clinton expedition encountered, and picked up, three men at sea in a small boat who brought the first news of the surrender. Still, the warships continued cautiously toward the Chesapeake to establish the certainty before turning round for New York. On one of the frigates in sight of the French fleet, Prince William Henry wrote to the king, "Unfortunately they were positioned to such advantage that we could not attack them without much loss, particularly after having heard of Lord Cornwallis's surrender." He told his father that Captain Dundas, under a flag of truce, had been invited with aides, who included an unidentified young midshipman (was it the prince?), aboard the huge French flagship *Ville de Paris*—in some ways it was still a gentlemanly war—and received by the Count de Grasse, "a very tall old man, a very good officer and a man of the greatest honour."

Clinton lamented afterward that if his ships had been able to sail earlier the catastrophe might have been prevented. Yet his fleet and his forces, even joined with those of Cornwallis had that been possi-

---

*Exchanged on February 9, 1782, he was given command of troops sent from New York to Jamaica and made major general. His last command, as a full general, was as governor of Gibraltar.

ble, would have been at very great disadvantage, and had he lost that gamble, undermanned New York might have fallen. Lacking New York City as a bargaining chip in the final negotiations for American independence might have cost the British possession of Canada.

Still at sea on the *Bedford* on October 29, Captain Damer wrote to Germain, with the "particulars" still not known but for what was learned from local informants and the visit to the *Ville de Paris,*

> The French fleet remain in the Chesapeak[e] between 30 and 40 miles up the bay. They have taken no notice of us, neither will they. M. de Grasse has done his business completely and is satisfied. Surely there was never an instance of an army, so commanded, falling a sacrifice to the negligence, irresolution, or absolute infatuation* of others. I will not venture to trouble your Lordship any further. Indeed, I feel such a mixture of grief and indignation I hardly know how to express myself as I should.

Damer would not shift the blame to Cornwallis and his troops, who had "done everything in the power of men to do." He did not need to name names. In effect echoing him, the *Public Advertiser* would publish a couplet,

> How strange, how perverse, is Britannia's Fate;
> In all their business, they are too late.

Unofficial reports of the disaster reached New York on October 24 through American sources in New Jersey. On October 31 the British frigate *Nymph* brought the news as Clinton had learned it off the Capes. Cornwallis was permitted to send his own sloop, the *Bonetta,* to New York with dispatches for Clinton, as long as the vessel returned to Yorktown. Only on November 23 did the first reports of the surrender reach England, across the Channel from France, where Louis XVI had already decreed, "All the inhabitants of Paris will illuminate on November 27 the fronts of their houses to celebrate with due respect the great victory gained in America, both by

---

*Damer, who had also employed "infatuation" earlier to Germain, was using the word in the contemporary sense of extravagant folly.

land and sea, over the English, by the armies of the King combined with those commanded by General Washington."

On November 25, a Sunday, at about noon, official intelligence from Yorktown reached Lord George Germain's house in Pall Mall. A packet had docked at Falmouth the day before. With the minister for America was Thomas de Grey, his undersecretary, who had just succeeded his deceased father as Viscount Walsingham. Lord George immediately sent a messenger with the news to the king, who was weekending in the country at Kew. With the opening of Parliament imminent, the king would have to reconsider the text of his Speech from the Throne.

According to the journals of Nathaniel Wraxall, from Pall Mall the two men then summoned a hackney coach and drove to Lord Stormont's residence in Portland Place. Taking him into the carriage, they clattered off to consult Lord Mansfield, then proceeded to Downing Street to present the dreaded dispatch to Lord North. He took the news, Lord George recalled, "as he would have taken a ball in his breast. For he opened his arms, exclaiming wildly, as he paced up and down the apartment during a few minutes, 'O God! It is all over!'"

There was nothing more for Germain to do than to return to Pall Mall, where he expected his three daughters, Walsingham and Wraxall, and several other guests for Sunday dinner. While they were at the table a reply from the king arrived. The American Secretary tore open the royal seal and read an obdurate message in His Majesty's own hand:

> I have received with sentiments of the deepest concern the communication which Lord George Germain has made me of the unfortunate result of the operations in Virginia. I particularly lament it . . . the consequences connected with it, and the difficulties which it may produce in carrying on the public business. But I trust that neither Lord George Germain nor any member of the Cabinet will suppose that it makes the smallest alteration in those principles of my conduct which have directed me in past time, and which will continue to animate me under every event in the prosecution of the present contest.

Putting down the royal reply, Lord George ordered dinner resumed, although he seemed too preoccupied for ordinary chitchat.

Returning to the letter when the ladies left the room, he invented, for the others, an explanation, as he had not read it aloud. The eighty-year-old Comte de Maurepas, he explained, was reportedly dying.

"It would grieve me to finish my career, however far advanced in years," said Wraxall, "were I First Minister of France, before I had witnessed the termination of this great contest between England and America."

"He has survived to witness that event," Germain confessed.

"My meaning," said Wraxall, "is that if I were the Count de Maurepas, I should wish to live long enough to behold the final issue of the war in Virginia."

"He has survived to witness it completely," Germain owned up, withdrawing another paper from his pocket; "not without visible emotion," Wraxall recalled. "The army has surrendered, and you may peruse the particulars of the capitulation in that paper."

After Wraxall read it to the others, Germain himself read aloud the message he had received from the king, commenting that it did "honour" to His Majesty's "fortitude, firmness, and consistency of character." Then he added, "The king writes just as he always does, except that I observe that he has omitted to mark the hour and minute of his writing with his usual precision."

Although it was a Sunday, George III was not yet done with public business as he saw it. He also wrote to Lord North, intractably,

Many men choose rather to despond to difficulties than to see how to get out of them. I have already directed Lord George Germain to put on paper the mode that seems most feasible for conducting the war, that every member of the Cabinet may have his propositions to weigh by themselves, when I shall expect to hear their sentiments separately, that we may adopt a plan and abide by it. . . . With the assistance of Parliament I do not doubt, if measures are well connected, a good end may yet be made of the war. If we despond, certain ruin ensues.

The next day, the painful news was in the London papers, with predictions of the fall of the government. "I cannot put on the face of the day," Walpole, refusing to act disconsolate, wrote to Sir Horace Mann. "Whatever puts an end to the American war will save the lives of thousands—millions of money too. If glory compensates such sac-rifices, I never heard that disgraces and disappointments were pallia-tives; but I will not descant, nor is it right to vaunt of having been in the right when one's country's shame is the solution of one's prophecy."

To many Englishmen the war was, in effect, over, but the king in-tended to deny reality when opening Parliament the day after with his formal Speech from the Throne. It was no problem for a stubborn man. He called for redoubled vigor in prosecuting what little was left of the war. He could not answer to the trust placed in him as sover-eign unless he preserved the strength and security of the empire. Losses in America—Yorktown went unmentioned—required even more support from Parliament and the people to undo.

Charles Fox reinterpreted the Address in the Commons. What the king had really said beneath the platitudes, Fox explained, was, "Our losses in America have been most calamitous. The blood of my sub-jects has flowed in copious streams. . . . The treasures of Great Britain have been wantonly lavished, while the load of taxes imposed on an overburdened country is becoming intolerable. Yet I continue to tax you to the last shilling." While George III carefully omitted Corn-wallis and capitulation, Fox specified them and declared that "hopes of victory" were forever gone, and that the continuance of war would lead only to ruin. "I prohibit you from thinking of peace," Fox wickedly paraphrased. "My rage for conquest is unquenched and my revenge unsated." Only "the total subjugation of my revolted Ameri-can subjects" would satisfy him.

In the few weeks of national dismay remaining before the in-evitable Christmas recess on December 20 there were renewed calls for the resignation of the Cabinet. By narrower and narrower majorities, Parliament supported North, who privately attempted again to resign. The *Salisbury and Winchester Journal* on December 3 declared that the army had not been defeated in the field but was undermined in Whitehall by the bungling American Secretary. The *Morning Herald* on December 4 castigated Clinton for his gall in asking the "gallant" Cornwallis to send troops back from Vir-ginia to protect New York, with its army of nearly twenty thou-sand, from Washington's seven thousand who had already slipped away. On the same day the Liveried Companies of London presented a "Remonstrance" to the king that sounded in invective much like Fox. "Your armies," it charged, "are captured; the wonted superiority of your navies is annihilated; your dominions are lost." Aside from "the brave Cornwallis," lionized in defeat, newspaper after newspaper excoriated the failed commanders who had served the nation "so ill."

In parliamentary debate Henry Dundas, Lord Advocate for Scotland, noted wryly "the special hand of Providence. The Colonel [John] Laurens who had drawn up the articles of capitulation, and in whose custody Lord Cornwallis was at that time a prisoner in America, was the son of Mr. [Henry] Laurens, late president of Congress, who had been committed a close prisoner to the Tower of London, of which Lord Cornwallis was himself the governor; and thus had become a prisoner to the son of his own prisoner."★

From Fleet Street copies of an illustrated broadside, "State Cooks, or the Downfall of the Fish Kettle," went on sale on December 10. Beneath a chef's hat was "Boreas"—literally, "North." Wearing aprons, the cooks, George III and Lord North, stand in a kitchen looking sadly at a large frying pan that has fallen to the floor from a hook over the fire. The fish, named after American colonies (and some irrelevant ones like the Floridas and Quebec, and with Delaware missing), have tumbled out. "O Boreas," laments the king, "the Loss of these Fish will ruin us for ever."

North consoles, "My Honoured Liege, never Fret. Minden & I will cook 'em yet." A map on the wall behind them labeled "Plan of North America" conspicuously displays Yorktown. In a pocket of North's apron is a paper titled "Plan of Taxes, 1782."

Even earlier, as catastrophe was expected but not yet exposed, a mock sales announcement had appeared, offering at auction by "James Twitcher and Co.," for "Boreas, Minden & Co., Estate and Stock-Brokers," all British rights to America, "consisting among many other articles, of the Thirteen Provinces," along with "reversions" of Quebec, the territories of the Hudson's Bay Company, the Floridas, as well as "a body of reduced, dispirited troops" and "overgrown Commissaries." Also tendered was "the remaining Stock in Trade of the Royal Navy of

---

★The younger Laurens would be killed in a useless skirmish with a foraging party in South Carolina late in 1782. He was twenty-eight.

Great Britain, consisting of a small number of old hulks, built with Stettin-timber. . . . They will be sold with all their furniture on board of old women in command, old men, and a young Prince. . . . Also the Garrisons of Gibraltar and Minorca, with all the empty store houses and magazines. Those are now upon sale, and will be knocked down without any loss of time." It was a devastating indictment.

Also from Fleet Street on December 10 came a Rowlandson engraving, "The State Watchman Discover'd by the Genius of Britain, studying Plans for the Reduction of America." Sprawled asleep on a sofa is George III. Deploring the sight, Britannia asks, "Am I thus Protected?" The market for such broadsides was reflecting opinion in the streets before it was mirrored in Parliament.

On December 12, in the Commons, Sir James Lowther, once a supporter of North, moved "That the war carried on in the colonies and plantations of North America, had been ineffectual to the purposes for which it had been undertaken, and . . . that it was the opinion of this House, that all further attempts to reduce the Americans to obedience by force, would be ineffectual and injurious to the true interests of this country, by weakening her powers to resist her ancient and confederated enemies." The motion was condemned by Lord North, Lord George Germain, and Welbore Ellis, MP for Weymouth and treasurer of the navy. Germain charged that it was a motion to end the American war altogether, and that if it succeeded, he would retire forthwith. It was defeated by only forty-one votes, a crumbling majority. Despite arguments to stay in session while the "alarming situation" continued, Parliament adjourned on December 20, to reconvene on January 21, 1782.

Although Lord George realized that America was lost, he returned to his desk at Whitehall and set to work on the king's mandate for a new strategy to follow "our late misfortunes in Virginia." He proposed retaining the seaports still in British hands, exploiting them to harass the American coastline. The Canadian border would be employed for the same purpose inland. He also wanted to mount operations to retake Rhode Island and repossess "the lower counties of the Delaware" below Philadelphia, "as they are from the situation easily defended, have in them plenty of provisions for the subsistence of an army, and the inhabitants in general wish to return to their allegiance."* On the other hand, he advised the king, if he abandoned sovereignty of the colonies and trusted in the negotiating faith of the Americans, who "would venture to treat with you?" As the colonies "appear to be under the control of their General, who becomes every day more independant of the Congress as he more closely connects himself with France; how long such a Government can exist is impossible to say.... Their natural aversion to the French nation, may incline them to return to their connection with this country, if we remain in a situation to receive and protect them." It was a desperate hope.

From New York on Christmas Eve 1781, Clinton wrote self-pityingly to the Duke of Newcastle, "I am fairly worn out, my good Lord. For God's sake let me return to my little family while I have something of life left. Your Grace can have no idea of the cares of this command under the circumstances [in which] I have held it, till you see what remains of what was perhaps as good a constitution as ever man had. The winter is coming; I am froze at the fire." He had very mixed feelings about going home. He would now be independently wealthy but a target of scorn, especially now that Cornwallis, on prisoner-of-war parole, had preceded him home. "No officer was ever so popular under misfortune," a friend would report of the defeated Cornwallis.

On December 26, 1781, the *London Courant* published a rhyming satire with a jogging "derry down" chorus, "It fell on a time, when plumb-pudding and peace," utilizing Christmas images to explode years of "Yank-Hunting" by North, Sandwich, Clinton, Mansfield, Germain, Amherst, Gates, Burgoyne, Cornwallis, and other largely futile managers of the American war. A host of jingling satires had already appeared with derry down choruses, with the victim of Yorktown the latest target, in:

> When southward, Cornwallis first entered the land
> [as] Commander in Chief, with the sword in his hand,
> He swagger'd and boasted, and threaten'd the fates
> [that] In spite of their teeth he would ravage the States.
> > Derry down, &c....

---

*Very likely Germain meant what is now referred to as the "Delmarva" peninsula, between Delaware Bay and the Chesapeake, including counties of Virginia and Maryland, and the entire three counties of the small state of Delaware. It was thinly populated and much of it considered Tory in sympathy.

The next day the *St. James's Chronicle* published "Angels of Light transmit from Heaven," an "Ode intended for Christmas-Day." It was a prayer, in all belated earnestness, for the suppression of the American rebellion and the triumph "o'er confederate Foes" like France and Spain. "The World turn'd upside down" would have been more appropriate.

15

The Failure of Fire and Sword January 1782–January 1784

"The conquest of America by fire and sword is not to be accomplished, let your numbers be what they may."

—*Earl Cornwallis on returning to England as a paroled prisoner of war*

"The difficulty with us is making peace. Every fool can pick a quarrel but I do not remember any Minister wise enough to end a war without forfeiting his own credit with the bulk of the people."

—*Lord George Germain to General Sir John Irwin before Lord George became Secretary for America.*

LATE in 1782 Benjamin West was again with King George when a functionary arrived with the traditional red box containing a draft of the Address from the Throne; prepared by his ministers, it conceded American independence. He would have been more content, the king told West, had the colonies remained within the empire, but he no longer wished them any ill. He hoped that they would be happy in their new state and would not change it for the worse.

Accompanied by his American student John Singleton Copley, West was in the gallery of the House of Lords on December 2, 1782, when His Majesty, in a manner more halting than his usually forceful style, read his lines. Afterward the painters parted, Copley to work on a portrait of Elkanah Watson, an American merchant then in London. Symbolically in the background was a ship. In the studio Watson

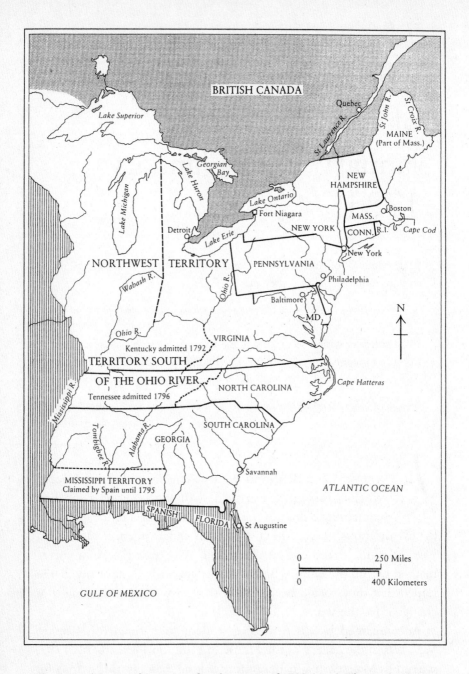

The United States of America after the peace of 1783 (map). The territories to the west were largely unmapped but claimed as far as known river channels.

From The Search for Liberty. From Origins to Independence, *by Esmond Wright (Oxford: Blackwell Publishers, 1995). By permission of Blackwell Publishers* watched Copley as "with a bold hand and a master's touch, he attached to the ship the stars and stripes. This was, I imagine, the first American flag ever hoisted in Old England."

Earlier in 1782, the ministry, unwilling yet to negotiate and encouraged by the king, endorsed Germain's memorandum for limited war. New York still garrisoned more than twelve thousand troops, and General Leslie had nearly five thousand in Charleston. Savannah and Wilmington also were in British control, as well as a few untenable interior posts, and a handful on the Canadian frontier. Potential further strength existed in the Caribbean, where the fleet was powerful, and in Quebec and Nova Scotia.

De facto peace remained distant. Privateers still stalked the coastline and the Chesapeake. Useless skirmishes on the edges of British enclaves still cost lives on both sides. In Virginia and Maryland hundreds of prisoners of war from Yorktown, indifferently guarded by patriot militia en route to holding camps in Pennsylvania, slipped away to lose themselves in the poorly mapped interior, plundering to survive. Except for a few settlements, largely along river routes, the colonial interior was an anarchic wilderness under no one's control, and prey to marauders who had sometimes flaunted a Stars-and-Stripes or Union Jack earlier to justify their banditry. Indians struggling to hold on to diminishing tribal lands, and menaced by squatters and migrants, travelers and traders, protected their hunting grounds with tomahawks and in turn were slaughtered by muskets. Frontiers demarcated in Paris or debated in London would not even be worth pieces of paper to rough backwoods illiterates with their long fowling pieces or to deserters from both sides still armed with their wartime firearms or whatever weapons they could steal.

On January 2, 1782, before Parliament could reconvene and establish a climate for winding down the war, Germain sent a dispatch by packet to Clinton, still awaiting relief, to maintain all positions on the Atlantic seaboard. Officially, the British were not about to quit the war. Clinton was instructed, further, to employ his troops, with naval support, to harass rebel ports and coastal towns, obstruct trade, and give encouragement to remaining loyalists. Lord George warned, however, "No more regiments or corps can be sent from this country. . . . It is not the King's intention that any operations should be carried on within land with the view to reducing any of the revolted

provinces or countries to His Majesty's obedience by force." Sardonically, Horace Walpole quipped to Lady Ossory that Britain, like
Roger de Widdrington in the old ballad "Chevy Chace," whose "legs
were smitten off" in a battle between the neighboring Percy and
Douglas families, "will continue fighting upon her stumps."

How useless further war would be was portrayed in a cartoon,
"The American Rattle Snake," issued by William Humphrey in the
Strand. Years before, in 1754, Benjamin Franklin had printed a cartoon of a disjointed snake representing the disunited colonies in an
"Unite or Die" manifesto, and thereafter a coiled rattlesnake became
an emblem of the union. In the Humphrey cartoon an enormous
coiled snake unleashes a forked fang from which a challenge
emerges:

> Two British Armies I have thus Burgoyn'd,
> And room for more I've got behind.

When Parliament reassembled after Yorktown on January 21,
1782, the antiwar opposition determined to bring down North,
Sandwich, and Germain. Almost the last act of the faltering ministry
was Germain's message to Clinton on February 6 that the appeal
made in his behalf by the Duke of Newcastle had been looked upon
favorably by the king. Clinton could return "at the first convenient
opportunity."

The letter did not reach New York until April 27, 1782. His temporary replacement would be General Robertson, whom Clinton
detested. Attempting to stop the tit-for-tat of raids and retaliation
that wasted lives, Robertson appealed to Washington. The bitterness
of defeat was agonizing redcoats in the limbo of barracks existence,
and waiting for formal peace that seemed never to come exacerbated
the hostility of the Continentals. Violence at "the hands of incensed
Men," Robertson wrote, was leading only to "universal Horror and
Barbarity." Little of that postwar war, which would go on for many
months, was known to the English press.

Robertson's tenure was brief. His formal successor would be the
hero of Quebec, Sir Guy Carleton, already en route, who was anath-
ema to Germain. The king wanted Carleton. Since North reminded
His Majesty that there was "little confidence" between the American

Secretary and Sir Guy, he suggested that the king "may find it convenient" to place the seals of the office in other hands. Reluctantly, the king agreed that "on the whole it is best to gratify the wishes of Lord G. Germain and let him retire." However, Lord George would not relinquish his seals without a seat in the Lords.

The day after Parliament reassembled, January 22, Lieutenant General Cornwallis disembarked in England, accompanied by Brigadier General Arnold, "that man of wretched fame," as Walpole described him. Cornwallis was reported as conceding that "the conquest of America by fire and sword" was hopeless, yet on his return to Exeter local admirers treated him like a conquering hero and carried him on their shoulders. That exercise in self-consolation failed to impress the pseudonymous "Fabricus," who, writing in the *Chronicle* and the *Morning Chronicle* (both papers in which Lord Sandwich had investments), charged that Cornwallis had brought his catastrophe upon himself by sequestering his army "inactive and idle in an unprepared and unfortified post, while a formidable force sufficient to overwhelm it was collecting."

Arnold wisely had little to say and found England less than friendly. *Gentleman's Magazine* quoted an unidentified peer as deploring "the placing at the King's elbow a man perhaps the most obnoxious to the feelings of the Americans of any in the King's dominions at the moment the House was addressing his Majesty to put an end to the American war." George III would never receive him.*

On the day before the annual abstinence mandated for a victory now vanished, February 8, 1782, the indefatigable Charles Wesley published *Hymns for the National Fast,* fifteen anthems, largely on the theme that God had punished Britain. Traitorous factions, the kingdom's internal enemies, had accomplished "their Country's fall." The fourteenth hymn prayed for an end to "this dire intestine"—domestic—"war," and the reconciliation of "all the British race." Several months earlier Wesley had collected and published his *Hymns for the Nation,* seventeen anthems including "For Concord," its title almost certainly an unintentional pun on where the war began, attacking Americans for blindly serving "the treacherous ends/ Of tyranny and

---

*The second most notorious loyalist in America, Ben Franklin's son, William, would slip out of New York City on August 13, 1782, in a British convoy sailing to England.

Rome," and "A Prayer for the Congress," damning the "Satanic" Americans for the spilling of "rivers . . . of guiltless blood."

Following the fast on the "present troubles," the king on February 9 granted Lord George Germain the titles of Baron Bolebroke in the county of Sussex and Viscount Sackville of Drayton in the county of Northampton. But vindictively recalling Minden, the Marquess of Carmarthen moved in the Lords that it would besmirch the honor of the House if a person under the censure of a court-martial were to be raised to the peerage. The motion was decisively rejected. Although most peers were grateful to have the American Secretary out of Whitehall, the press reminded ordinary people that establishment honors were seldom what they seemed:

> The Robe Patrician now shall cover all!
> Disgrace no more degrade, or fear appal; . . .
> Such is the magic of this crimson vest,
> When clasped with royal hands across the breast;
> It mounts the coward to the hero's place,
> Wipes from the recreant brow each foul disgrace.

On Tuesday, February 12, the newly created Lord Sackville took the oath in the House of Lords, and his seat on the Viscounts Bench. His war was over.

Welbore Ellis assumed Lord Sackville's office in Whitehall. Sandwich stubbornly hung on, as did North. Motions of censure in the Commons brought by Fox and Conway were defeated, by diminishing numbers, six times. "A nation must be sunk to a wretched state indeed," Fox charged, "which can place a blind confidence in men whose administration has lost America."

On February 25, the Morning Chronicle used three of its four pages to publish the debates in the Commons on the motion by General Conway to end offensive war in America. It failed by a single vote, 193 to 194. In the early hours of February 28, after another division on the peace proposal that took well after midnight to tally, North again submitted his resignation to King George, who predictably refused it. Yet the king could not hold out much longer, for Conway's resolution had now passed by nineteen votes, and the opposition General Advertiser used rare enlarged type to herald

"PEACE WITH AMERICA!" According to William Parker, its publisher, the tally "set England upon its legs again." The same day, from his home in Charles Street, a weary but exhilarated Edmund Burke wrote to Benjamin Franklin in Passy, underlining his words, "I congratulate you, as the friend of America, I trust, as not the enemy of England, I am sure, as the friend of mankind, on the resolution of the house of commons, carried by a majority of nineteen at two o'clock this morning, in a very full house. It was the declaration of two hundred and thirty-four; I think it was the opinion of the whole. I trust that it will lead to a speedy peace between the two branches of the English nation." Then he postscripted, "General Burgoyne presents his best compliments to you."

Three weeks later, after another peace motion passed by an even wider margin and the prime minister was further attacked for war loans "extremely disadvantageous to the public" but lucrative to his favorites in Parliament, North conceded to the House that his ministry was over.

To ward off change, George III had even threatened abdication and removal to Hanover, where he was also king, and early in March the royal yacht was openly readied. (He even asked Benjamin West to accompany him.) The king drafted a message to Parliament in the traditional third-person, claiming that the change of sentiment in the Commons "has totally incapacitated him from either conducting the war with effect, or from obtaining any peace but on conditions which will prove destructive to the commerce as well as to the essential rights of the British nation." Yet since he would have abandoned the throne to the foolish and unreliable Prince of Wales, the king on second thought put the draft away.

Although it took some time before the ill-kept secret of his threat became public knowledge, it did, and Thomas Rowlandson engraved a satire for sale by William Humphrey in the Strand: "The Times—Or a View of the Old House in Little Britain with Nobody Going to Hannover." The Old House, representing Britain, is an old-fashioned Elizabethan inn with projecting upper story and attic. To its left is King George, apparently asleep, being driven to Hanover in a coach with a crown on its roof. The implication was clear: The king's gesture was undramatically empty.

Insistently now, Lord North brought his own letter of resignation to St. James's Palace, where the king ungraciously refused to commend him for his thankless services, saying, "Remember, my Lord, that it is you who desert me, not I you."

In occupied New York, young Prince William Henry was being watched by rebel spies, who saw him as a potential bargaining counter in the peace negotiations about to begin, and Colonel Matthias Ogden of the 1st New Jersey Regiment suggested to Washington, now returned to his headquarters in Morristown, that the young midshipman be seized as a hostage. On March 28, 1782, Washington surprisingly approved, but on April 2 he warned Ogden that sentries at Clinton's residence, where the prince was staying, had been doubled "from apprehension of an attempt to surprise" Prince William Henry. General Clinton obviously had his spies, too. The plan was abandoned. The prince remained in New York with his tutor, the Reverend Henry Majendie, and embarked for home on November 27 on the frigate *Barfleur*.

The England that William Henry would rediscover had finally rid itself of Lord North, although political cartoonists were not yet done with him, perhaps because some satires were in production as he faded from office. One, in indignation over increased taxes on necessities to pay for the war, "Lord No__ in the Suds," depicted him in a washtub that froths with lather. Angry women surround him, and one applies a large scrubbing brush, saying, "Salt to the Scoundrel!" Beneath, the text declares,

> For the taxing of Salt, Tobacco and Soap,
> Some say that Lord North is deserving a Rope.
> His Lordship you see, he is now in a Tub
> While the old woman lathers & gives him a scrub.

But Lord North was gone. The ailing Marquis of Rockingham, abhorred by the king as leader of the detested Whigs, replaced North as First Lord of the Treasury (as the prime minister was still titled), accepting office on an understanding that the king had rejected earlier that there would be "no veto to the independence of America." The king also paid the price of consenting to restrictions on his purse, which eliminated much of his opportunities to buy influence over Parliament. In effect, thanks to the American war, popular government, even before electoral reform, had prevailed over the sovereign.

Other opposition figures took places in what was in effect a postwar ministry. Augustus Keppel became First Lord of the Admiralty. Having refused the royal offer in 1780 when it seemed a bribe, General Conway now became commander-in-chief of the army. The Duke of Richmond was named Master of the Ordnance. Burke and Barré became the well-salaried paymasters of the army and navy. The outspoken 3rd Earl of Effingham, who had signed seventeen protests in the House of Lords against coercion of America and been forced out of the military for his opinions, was reinstated and promoted from captain to lieutenant colonel. He was also made Lord Treasurer of the Royal Household—clearly a bone in the king's throat. Charles James Fox and the Earl of Shelburne (whom the king preferred as prime minister) became the two secretaries of state. The secretaryship for America was abolished.

To Sir Guy Carleton on April 4, in a letter that would arrive well after his taking command in New York, Shelburne advised, having assumed responsibility for America, "The first object of your attention must be to provide for withdrawing the garrison, artillery, provisions, stores of all kinds, every species of public property, from New York and its dependencies to Halifax. The same steps are to be taken with respect to the garrisons of Charleston and Savannah." Clearly the three occupations were to end with a peace agreement, although a treaty seemed complicated by American obligations to Versailles and the Hague, and by a Dutch defeat in remote Ceylon followed by Admiral Rodney's victory over de Grasse in the Caribbean. (On May 29, the *Caledonian Mercury* quipped about "the Coup de Grasse.") The admiral had been captured, embarrassingly for France, in the "Battle of the Saints" off Guadeloupe on April 12. With no information yet that Germain had been unseated, Rodney wrote to Lord George from the *Formidable* on April 15, "Permit me most sincerely to congratulate you on the most important victory I believe ever gained against our perfidious enemies, the French." At Stoneland Lodge, the new viscount was uninformed except by the newspapers.

Britain's worldwide position strengthened, and America's relationship with Holland and France was put under strain, just as emissaries from London, Richard Oswald (sent by Shelburne) and Thomas

Grenville (sent briefly by Fox) went to Paris to begin talks with Benjamin Franklin, to be joined later by John Adams from the United Provinces of Holland, Henry Laurens, released from the Tower of London, and John Jay, an ambitious young lawyer recently arrived from New York. On May 30, Parker's *General Advertiser* called for "Peace with America, and war with the rest of the Globe."

Settling America's future in concert with her allies was implicit, a broadside observed, to making "peace-porridge" with too many cooks, and talks began quietly to deal with the former colonies alone. Although the new nation had abjured a separate peace without France, Britain saw dividing the allies as good negotiating strategy. Franklin also saw good reason to parley independently, and would strain logic to justify his actions later to Versailles. The English press promoted the idea, and one broadside sold in the Strand, "Reconciliation between Britain and Her Daughter America," showed mother (wearing a St. George's cross) and daughter (in a feathered Indian headdress) embracing while France and Spain try to pull them apart. Another, also emanating from Printer's Row in the Strand, part of a series on notorious enemies becoming reconciled, blamed "Twitcher's Arts" (even after Sandwich's exit) for continuing hostility, and predicted useful dialogue between Britannia and a more pragmatic America:

"Come, come, shake hands and let's be friends."
"With all my heart, I've gained my ends."

A setback to negotiations occurred when the ailing Marquis of Rockingham died in early summer. Lord Shelburne, his successor, possessed more of the royal confidence as he was less dovish. Still, Shelburne, the future Marquess of Lansdowne, conceded that the Americans were "in full and actual possession" of the thirteen colonies. Once a semantic compromise was reached in describing the former colonies, official negotiations could begin. To salvage some pride over his lost policy of coercion George III had wanted to deal with "the thirteen united provinces," while the American commissioners insisted on "the United States." Both sides would agree on "the Thirteen United States."

From private life, Germain, now Viscount Sackville, perused the papers and wrote to his old friend General Irwin with sardonic pleasure about the new ministry's difficulties, "We swarm with abusive pamphlets, and Lord Shelburne is the object of their invectives." He remained certain that he had been a loyal servant of the king, and that the lethargy of Lord North had been instrumental in the loss of America. "What a dressing[-down] Mr. Pitt gave Lord North," he commented to his former aide William Knox in mid-1783, after a debate in the chamber from which he had been elevated. It had to be more than courtesy for young Pitt, when forming his first Ministry in December 1783, to write to Viscount Sackville to seek "the honour of a support . . . so important as your Lordship's." He would rarely be visible at his seat in the House of Lords, and the former American Secretary's appearance there in 1785 was even cause for notice in the press. Minden still obsessed him, as his political adversaries had never let him forget it, and his hard line toward America may have had as much to do with exorcising the ghosts of Minden as carrying out the commands of his king. On his deathbed—he died in his seventieth year, on August 26, 1785—he insisted to Richard Cumberland, his closest intimate, that he had never committed any act of cowardice at Minden, and that the court-martial had been an injustice.

Recognizing his own unpopularity as prime minister, Lord Shelburne privately employed his access to Secret Service funds not for intelligence but for covert public relations, bribing editors and publishers to applaud his policies. It helped, also, that British sea power was recovering its dominance, and that Spain's claim to repossess Gibraltar had been wrecked by its failure to break the tough British garrison's defenses. (As a sop, Spain would be promised Minorca, once offered to Russia.)

Although the turnabout would assist the British negotiating position, the public seemed not to care. America was lost anyway. In London the *Packet* observed that American affairs "are now scarcely attended to by the people of this country." Fox and Shelburne, predictably, disagreed about what to relinquish. Fox, in charge of foreign affairs, wanted to grant full independence as a starting point. Shelburne, who included the colonies in his portfolio, wanted agreements first completed with the European allies, to weaken America's bargaining position. A major concern in London was that continuing hostility to America in the treaty language would link the former colonies even more closely to the detested Bourbon regime. But with the defeats of the French at sea, Franklin felt able to negotiate without interference from Versailles. "The military Operations of the Campaign," Washington had advised Franklin, "are drawing to a Close, without any very important events, on the this side [of] the Water."

Little formal progress could be made on a preliminary treaty until Franklin was joined by the additional commissioners appointed by Congress, and William Whitehead, the prolific but aged poet laureate, published an "Ode for the King's Birth-Day, June 4, 1782," lamenting, "Still does reluctant Peace refuse."

Richard Oswald, a prewar friend of Franklin's, advised Shelburne to be accommodating, although not to the extreme of relinquishing "every part of Canada," as Franklin proposed, perhaps an extreme demand intended only to secure other claims in exchange. "We ought to deal with them," Oswald recommended, ". . . as supposed conciliated Friends. . . . I really believe the Doctor sincerely wishes for a speedy settlement, and that after the loss [to us] of Dependence, we may lose no more; but on the contrary, a cordial Reconciliation may take place over all that Country." (In his journal he wrote, "The more these States extend themselves in Population and Cultivation, the better it will be for England.") The king wrote to Shelburne sourly as negotiations proceeded that the "dismemberment of America from this Empire" might have a positive aspect, as "knavery seems to be so much the striking feature of its inhabitants that it may not be in the end an evil that they become aliens to this Kingdom."

Oswald had more difficulty with the ambitious young lawyer on the enlarged American commission, John Jay, and the acerbic John Adams. "The pride and vanity of that nation is a disease, it is a delirium," Oswald wrote. "[I]t has been flattered and inflamed so long by themselves and others that it perverts everything." Although parleying meant give and take, and Oswald had to consult painstakingly on every issue with London, Adams saw only the old enemy. "You seem to think," said the lean, argumentative Jay to Oswald, "that France ought to consider the Independence of our states as sufficient indemnification for all her expenses in the War." But French loans and grants to America were not Britain's obligation, and France and its

European allies were in a weaker negotiating position after Yorktown and the Saints than before.

On September 4, 1782, Parson Woodforde noted in his diary, "Nancy [Custance] read a long letter from her brother William dated the 28th June from Staten Island in North America brought by Mr. Custance's Servant from Norwich this Evening. . . . He is very well & has escaped many Dangers in America. He sent inclosed in his Letter some Continental Money Paper valued there at 10 Shillings and which he desired to be given to me." Staten Island in New York Bay was one of the few places in which redcoats remained. The British had abandoned Wilmington, North Carolina, toward the end of 1781. Savannah was evacuated on July 11, 1782, and reoccupied by General Anthony Wayne's troops. Charleston, under patient siege by Nathanael Greene's forces, creating a local shortage of food and forage, was on Washington's orders never assaulted directly, but its depleted garrison embarked for home on December 18, 1782.★ All that remained other than frontier posts on the Canadian border was New York and its harbor, the bargaining chip to be relinquished on the signing of the final treaty.

Whether the departures represented leaving indefensible locations or evidencing good faith, the differences between the sides were fading through the facts of distance and time. The ownership of the vast lands between the Appalachians and the Mississippi was contended for by all the parties in the war, but the Americans were already there. France and Spain had suffered military reverses elsewhere, and having overextended themselves were in even more financial difficulty than was Britain. A song in an illustrated broadside, "Peace Soup," summed up the negotiations:

France. "By gar, John English, you have well Crumb'd my dish."
Spain. "My peace soup is made very good by Stewing down Minorca & the Floridas."
England. "My loss is your gain, for my soup is very thin."
America. "I rest contented with a dish of Independent Soup."
Holland. "I will not taste it yet as it is not relish'd to my mind."
Waiter. "Taste it, Mynheer, 'tis better than you deserve."

★When the Saratoga Convention prisoners of war were finally permitted to sail for home, about fifteen hundred of them chose, rather, to stay in America.

In Paris on November 30, 1782, Anglo-American differences were settled by a secretly arranged preliminary treaty, the scene that Benjamin West, in London, hoped to portray on canvas. The evening before the signing Franklin informed the surprised Comte de Vergennes and told him that the British were also furnishing a safe-conduct ship to convey the text across the Atlantic. Vergennes stiffly protested the unilateral accord, which had proceeded contrary to the instructions of Congress, but the venerable Franklin, since Voltaire's death in 1778 the most admired personality in France, rationalized everything with his legendary tact. He courteously regretted the lack of "bienséance"—propriety—and promised, "No peace is to take place between us and England until you have concluded yours."

Craftily, Franklin added, removing the sting from the deviousness while suggesting yet another, "The English, I just now learn, flatter themselves they have already divided us; I hope this little misunderstanding will therefore be kept a secret, and that they will find themselves totally mistaken."

Richard Oswald's secretary, Caleb Whitefoord, celebrating with the Americans and their somewhat reluctant hosts at Passy that Saturday, got in the last word after a Frenchman perhaps inspired by champagne predicted that "the Thirteen United States would form the greatest empire in the world."

"Yes, sir," said Whitefoord, "and they will all speak English, every one of 'em."

The new nation received the boundaries it realistically wanted and complete recognition of its independence. It promised to honor its debts to departed as well as resident loyalists—an obligation defaulted upon later by the individual states. (A cartoon depicted four hanged Tories dangling from a tree, while one being tomahawked below cries, "Is this the return for our loyalty?") The Americans also received fishing rights in Newfoundland waters—an obligation largely defaulted upon by Britain. Although the French grumbled on about American ingratitude in settling a separate peace, France and Spain accepted allocations of territory to the south and, weary of war and the drain on their treasuries, acknowledged grudging satisfaction.

Britain signed separate articles of peace with France and Spain, on January 20, 1783. Arrangements with the Dutch would follow. No one in England wanted to take the dubious credit for the treaties with the Europeans and with America. But for denying Gibraltar, the concessions were surprisingly broad, and Vergennes remarked to his secretary, Gérard de Rayvenal, "The English buy peace rather than make it."

In a policy dispute with Shelburne as the talks proceeded, Fox lost out and left office. That pleased the king, as Fox was seen as a malign influence on the difficult Prince of Wales. But in February 1783 the unpredictable Whig effected a coalition with his old enemy Lord North to drive out Shelburne, and it took until April 2 before a respected peer could be induced to replace him. The American treaty still slumbered unsigned.

Faced again with the humiliation of accepting an unsympathetic government, George III once more contemplated abdication. In a letter he drafted that was never sent he confided to the Prince of Wales that to carry on the king would have to give up "every political principle on which I have acted" and permit in power "a ministry from among men who know I cannot trust them and therefore will not accept office without making me a kind of slave." It was "a cruel dilemma, and leaves me but one step to take without the destruction of my principles and honour; the resigning my crown, my dear son to you, quitting this my native country for ever and returning to the dominion of my forefathers." Reconsidering the gesture, he put the paper aside.

The Duke of Portland, who had been outspoken against the war from its beginnings, was prime minister when, on September 3, 1783, the Treaty of Paris was formally approved. This time for Britain the signer was not the ailing Richard Oswald, but Franklin's inventive London friend David Hartley, MP, who then returned to work on his fireplates retardant and to write a pamphlet about its efficacy. Horace Walpole wryly saw an American dimension in William Herschel's discovery of the planet Uranus, which he had first named, as a compliment, *Novum Sidus Georginium*. Writing to the Earl of Buchan on September 23, he teased, "Is there a bounded side to infinitude? . . . Mr. Herschel will content me if he can discover thirteen provinces there, well inhabited by men and women, and protected by the law of nations; that law which was enacted by Europe for its own emolument, . . . bestows the property of the whole realm to the first person to espy them, and can annex them to the crown of Great Britain, in lieu of those it has lost beyond the Atlantic."

Copies of the treaty were sent to America for ratification—a voyage westward that would take two months, and would find no quorum of the bickering Congress in session to approve it until early the next year. Sir Guy Carleton's redcoats and mercenaries evacuated New York anyway, and the last eight hundred troops in Washington's dwindling army that had not walked away from the war marched in. By then still another ministry was in place in Whitehall, and the king, hoping to be "no mere tool" to a faction in power, was trying to reconcile himself to the administration of the promising and brilliant young William Pitt. Untarnished, at least until defeat was imminent, by the politics of the failed war, he could not be faulted for losing America.

In January 1784 the treaty with the United States was approved by the Congress in Annapolis, Maryland, where the month before General Washington had submitted his formal resignation as commander-in-chief. Returning home on Christmas Eve to Mount Vernon and private life, he disappointed many Americans who, whatever their misgivings about George III, had lived their lives under a monarchy and would have preferred to see the godlike Washington ensure the unstable new nation's soundness as their king.

More than eight thousand Continentals had been killed or were missing in action in more than eight years of rebellion, and at least as many had died of disease or the hardships of weather—a comparatively large number given the small population of the colonies. Further thousands, mostly immured in convict hulks in New York harbor, had died as prisoners. Including hirelings, the British had lost far more men to death, disease, and desertion, and the war had also cost an estimated £115,654,914—an enormous sum in present-day purchasing power. Yet whatever the price, it was never enough in troops, stores, and ships in the vastness of America and its waters, or in the commitment of British leadership at home and abroad to a war that was very likely, in the circumstances, unwinnable.

"America is lost!" King George wrote in a thoughtful undated draft memorandum reconciling himself to the dreaded facts, and to his decision to eschew abdication. "Must we fall beneath the blow? Or have we resources to repair the mischief? What are those resources? And should they be sought in distant Regions held by precarious Tenure, or shall we seek them at home in the exertions of a new policy?" The "Colonial Scheme" had guided the direction of the kingdom for more than a century, he observed, but there were alternative avenues to maintain power and prosperity. "A people spread over an immense tract of fertile land, industrious because free, and rich because industrious, presently [will] become a market for the Manufactures and Commerce of the Mother Country." Now he realized that "the late conflict" had been "mischievous to Britain, because it created an expence of blood and treasure worth more at this instant, if it could be at our command, than all we ever received from America." The king saw the same as true of colonies remaining to Britain. "The more important they are already, the less are they fit instruments" to preserve "British power and consequence." Like America, he implied, they would also become disadvantageously detached from the mother country, and

> to add therefore to their value by exertions of policy which shall have the effect of directing any stream of capital, industry, or population into those channels, would be to add to a disproportion already an evil. The more we are convinced of the vast importance of these territories, the more we must feel the insecurity of our power; our view therefore ought not to be to increase but [only] to preserve them.

The document was a remarkable prophecy based on the American experience. Yet future governments would pour vast resources into conquering and absorbing the successor jewel in the Crown—India—and millions of square miles of Africa, eventually to relinquish them all at a cost to the home islands and their destiny still a matter of continuing controversy. Was an empire to be lost worth the burden?

Josiah Tucker, an economist and Anglican divine who had been Dean of Gloucester since 1758, had published "Four Letters" addressed to Lord Shelburne when he was prime minister and the preliminary articles of peace were signed. His ideas may have influenced the king. "*America,* I have proved beyond the Possibility of a Confutation," Tucker wrote assuredly, "ever was a Millstone hanging about the Neck of this Country, to weigh it down: And as we ourselves had not the Wisdom to cut the Rope, and let the Burthen fall off, the Americans have kindly done it for us." Tucker used such locutions as "Blood and Treasure," as would the king, and declared, "Trade depends upon Interest alone, and on no other Connection or Obligation. . . . Mutual Interest was the only Tie between America and Great Britain at all Times and Seasons, and this Principle will hold good, I will be bold to say, till the end of Time; whether they are dependent on, or independent of us. As to the Planting of Colonies for the sake of monopolizing, or exclusive Trade, it is the arrantest Cheat and Self-Deception, which poor short-sighted Mortals even put upon themselves;—at least in a *national* View."

From Cork in Ireland early in January 1784, where they landed after leaving New York City in the last evacuations, loyalist militants James De Lancey and Robert Watts, once thuggish Westchester County "Cowboys," penned a violent postscript to a letter they had surreptitiously acquired and opened, from a gentleman in Cahir, near Clonmell. It was intended for a recipient in Portsmouth, New Hampshire, and dated November 24, 1783, the very day on which the British were to begin departing from New York. Their properties confiscated for treason, De Lancey and Watts had embarked for England ahead of warrants for their arrest.

"I congratulate you, and every other spirited affector of liberty and independence," the Irishman had begun, buoyantly, "on your late happy and ever glorious revolution, whereby you have emancipated a flourishing, though infant empire, from the iron hand of tyranny and oppression."

"SIR," the emigrés added acidly before resealing the envelope, "A loyalist has perused this letter, and cannot help telling you, he thinks the writer must be a dam'd ignorant scoundrel; for America is, from the date of her independence, dam'd, and will live in broils and strife to the day of judgment." After their signatures they added, "*Loyalists.*"

Reactions were far different among the English in England, as appeared from a cartoon in *Rambler's Magazine,* "The Blessings of Peace," on December 1, 1783, a week after the Irish gentleman's letter to America had been violated. A crowded London street scene depicted a typical untranquil morning. In the center stands a man who appears to have been driven from his house by a harridan, very likely his wife, who threatens him with a long-handled ladle. On one of his shoulders perches a chattering parrot; on the other is a vocal magpie. A child at the woman's side is crying. A collector of rubbish is ringing a large handbell and shouting, "Dust hoa!" A mechanic noisily sharpens a two-handled saw on a whetstone. A fish hawker with a basket of his wares under one arm and another atop his head calls, "Come, buy my flounders!" A young woman turns the handle of a hurdy-gurdy held under her arm. Two large dogs in the foreground are barking at each other.

Everything—almost everything—was back as it was. At long last, the dubious blessings of peace with lost America had come to England.

Participants

JOHN ADAMS (1735–1826). Massachusetts lawyer and patriot. With Benjamin Franklin he edited Jefferson's draft of the Declaration of Independence. Joined Franklin in France as a peace commissioner. Washington's vice president and second American president.

SAMUEL ADAMS (1722–1803). Massachusetts patriot; radical who rose to prominence with the Stamp Act controversy and the opposition to the Intolerable Acts. A promoter of the Boston Tea Party, and of the Committees of Correspondence that led to the first Continental Congress. Despite a talent for making enemies he was elected governor of Massachusetts in 1793 and served until 1797.

ETHAN ALLEN (1738–1789). Settled in 1770 in New Hampshire Grants (present-day Vermont). Led Green Mountain Boys at Ticonderoga; captured in November 1775 before Montreal, taken to England, and exchanged in 1778. Campaigned for a separate Vermont.

JEFFREY AMHERST (1717–1797). British general who led the seizure of French Canada from 1758 to 1760, becoming governor-general of British North America. As Lord Amherst and army chief in England in 1780 he put down the Gordon Riots. Created field marshal in 1796.

JOHN ANDRÉ (1750–1780). London-born son of Swiss merchant. Captured by Americans near Montreal and exchanged a year later. Served in Philadelphia campaigns under Howe; became Clinton's deputy adjutant general as major in 1779. Seized near West Point in Arnold affair; tried and executed as spy at Tappan, New York, in September 1780.

MARRIOTT ARBUTHNOT (1711–1794). A career sailor from boyhood, he was appointed commander-in-chief of the American Station in 1779, where he was at odds with Clinton, although together they won at Charleston. He was succeeded by Thomas

Graves in July 1881. At eighty-two and in failing health, he became a full admiral.

BENEDICT ARNOLD (1741–1801). A Connecticut merchant and militia officer, he became a Continental brigadier general and distinguished himself before Quebec and at Saratoga. While commandant at West Point he sold his services to the British, fleeing to England as the war was ending badly for his career gamble. His name has since become a metaphor for treachery.

EDWARD BANCROFT (1745–1821). Born in Massachusetts, he became a physician and stock speculator in London, then secretary to Franklin's American commission in France while collecting emoluments from Britain as a government spy.

JACQUES-MELCHIOR SAINT-LAURENT, COMTE DE BARRAS (1719–1792). (Some biographies give his first name as Louis.) Commander of the French squadron at Newport, he outranked de Grasse off the Chesapeake capes but cooperated to ensure the victory at Yorktown. Retired in 1783 as lieutenant general of the Navy

ISAAC BARRÉ (1726–1802). MP, 1761–1790; colonel in Seven Years' (French and Indian) War, and afterward a friend of American aspirations; remembered in the name of the Pennsylvania city Wilkes-Barré.

JAMES BOSWELL (1740–1795). Scottish man of letters; cordial friend and biographer of Samuel Johnson. Contributions to *London Magazine* and other journals include pro-American sentiments.

JOHN BURGOYNE (1722–1792). Tory MP, 1768–1792; playwright (*Maid of the Oaks*); knighted after capture of Valencia in Seven Years' War; led redcoats to Saratoga, where he surrendered in October 1777; turned Whig, he was commander-in-chief in Ireland, 1782–83.

EDMUND BURKE (1729–1797). MP, 1765–1794; private secretary to Rockingham; sympathetic to aspirations of the colonies; renowned as orator and political philosopher whose influential speeches on American issues were widely distributed as pamphlets.

CHARLES PRATT, EARL OF CAMDEN (1714–1794). Lord Chancellor, 1766–1770; opposed Stamp Act and other coercive measures; towns named for him in New Jersey and South Carolina.

GUY CARLETON (1724–1808). Successfully defended Quebec 1775–1776, then became its governor. Knighthood, 1778. Political opponent of Germain. Military governor of New York; supervised its evacuation in 1783. Afterward, Lord Dorchester.

WILLIAM HENRY, DUKE OF CLARENCE (1765–1857). Future William IV; son of George III; succeeded his brother, George IV. Began long naval career in Admiral Robert Digby's flagship, on which he arrived in New York in 1781, just prior to Yorktown.

HENRY SEYMOUR CONWAY (1721–1795). Brother of Marquis of Hertford; cousin of Horace Walpole. MP, 1741–1784; in Rockingham camp from 1865. Career officer (lieutenant general, 1865); briefly secretary of state for the Southern Department in first post-Yorktown government. Retired as field marshal.

JOHN SINGLETON COPLEY (1737–1815). Boston-born painter; studied in London under Benjamin West. His historical paintings include *The Death of [Lord] Chatham* and, for the City of London, *The Siege of Gibraltar.* Elected to the Royal Academy, 1779.

CHARLES, 2ND EARL CORNWALLIS (1738–1805). As a major general commanded British troops in the southern colonies, defeating Gates at Camden but surrendering to Washington at Yorktown. Distinguished turnabout as governor general and commander in India, 1786–1793; created 1st Marquis Cornwallis.

WILLIAM LEGGE, 2ND EARL OF DARTMOUTH (1731–1801). Stepbrother of Lord North, he was Secretary for America, 1772–1775, ineffective in the ministry, as he was unable to reconcile his sympathies with the colonists and his insistence on parliamentary supremacy. Dartmouth College in New Hampshire bears his name.

SILAS DEANE (1737–1789). Connecticut delegate to Continental Congress, 1774–1776; first agent to France to procure aid. Superseded in authority in France by Franklin, he was nevertheless involved for his own profit with British spies Edward Bancroft and Paul Wentworth.

JOHN DICKINSON (1732–1808). Delaware lawyer, then Pennsylvania assemblyman, he was a delegate to the first Continental Congress and drafted the Articles of Confederation. president of Delaware, 1781–1782 and president of Pennsylvania executive council 1782–1785.

ROBERT DIGBY (1732–1814). Rear admiral sent to replace Thomas Graves on the American Station in 1781, finding that Graves was about to sail for the Chesapeake to relieve Cornwallis. He postponed taking up his command until the fleet returned in failure to New York.

HENRY DUNDAS (1742–1811). MP for Edinburghshire, 1774–1782; lord advocate, 1775–1783.

JOHN DUNNING (1731-1783). Solicitor general, 1768–1770, he was one of Shelburne's followers in the Commons and a persistent and vocal member of the opposition.

WILLIAM EDEN (1744–1814). MP from 1774; commissioner of trade and plantations, 1776; diplomatic adviser to Lord North and manager of his secret service on the Continent; member of peace commission in 1778. Created Baron Auckland in 1793.

THOMAS HOWARD, 3RD EARL OF EFFINGHAM (1747–1791). He resigned his army commission in April 1776, creating a furor when it was published in the press in September. In the opposition in Parliament throughout the war, he joined the postwar Whig government.

WELBORE ELLIS (1713–1802). MP, 1774–1790 and a supporter of coercion; treasurer of the navy, 1777–1782; American Secretary, succeeding Germain, February–March 1782.

CHARLES HECTOR THÉODAT, COMTE D'ESTAING (1729–1794). As a vice admiral he was ordered to America in 1778 to assist the rebellion, missing all his opportunities into 1779, when he failed at Savannah. Always afflicted by poor timing, in 1789 he became commandant of the National Guard. After the French Revolution he was executed as a royalist.

CHARLES JAMES FOX (1749–1806). Third son of the first Lord Holland. MP at nineteen, in and out of early North cabinets, then quarrelsome Whig opponent of the war and notable parliamentary orator. Cabinet offices in 1782 and after, then political rival to the young Pitt.

BENJAMIN FRANKLIN (1706–1790). Philadelphia printer, author, inventor, and civic leader; colonial postmaster general. Prewar agent to British government for Massachusetts and Pennsylvania. Envoy and peace commissioner in France; leading statesman in

Constitutional Convention, 1787–1788. President of Pennsylvania supreme executive council, 1785–1788.

WILLIAM FRANKLIN (1731–1813). Only son of Benjamin Franklin and (probably) his common-law wife, Deborah Read. Studied law in London; achieved various colonial posts via paternal influence; royal governor of New Jersey from 1763; prisoner of Continentals, 1776–1778; directed Associated Loyalists in New York; in pensioned English exile from August 1782.

WILLIAM TEMPLE FRANKLIN (1760–1823). Illegitimate son of William Franklin; secretary to his grandfather during peace negotiations in France; edited first collection of Benjamin Franklin's writings (six volumes) in 1818.

THOMAS GAGE (1719–1787). Royal governor of Massachusetts from April 1774 and briefly commander-in-chief of military forces in North America.

HORATIO GATES (1728–1806). Served in British army before emigrating in 1772 to the colonies and becoming a Virginia landowner. Commanding general at Saratoga, he owed his success largely to Arnold. Later, in the South, he was ineffective, taking flight at Camden. Moving to New York after the war, he served in the legislature for one term, 1800–1801.

KING GEORGE III (1738–1820). Eldest son of Frederick, Prince of Wales, and the first Hanoverian sovereign born and educated in England, he succeeded his grandfather, George II, in 1760 when Frederick predeceased him. In his later years he would suffer from episodes of mental derangement now attributed to porphyria. In 1810 his eldest son became Prince Regent.

GEORGE, PRINCE OF WALES (1762–1830). George IV on his father's death, he was erratic, debt-ridden, and dissolute as Prince of Wales, affecting Whig sentiments and adopting opposition friends, in open rebellion against his strict father.

LORD GEORGE SACKVILLE GERMAIN (1716–1785). Youngest son of first duke of Dorset, professional soldier wounded at Fontenoy (1745), court-martialed while a lieutenant general for not charging at Minden (1759), and dismissed from service. American Secretary 1775–1782; retired to become Viscount Sackville.

JAMES GILLRAY (1757–1815). London caricaturist and engraver of humorous scenes and political satire from 1779 to 1811; unafraid to lampoon George III and his followers.

GEORGE GORDON (1751–1793). A courtesy lord as third son of the Duke of Gordon, he served in the navy in America, 1766–1769; was retired in 1777 for mental instability; an MP 1774–1780, he instigated the anti-Catholic riots in June 1780 but was acquitted of treason. Convicted of libel in 1788, he died in prison.

SAMUEL GRAVES (1713–1787). Vice admiral and commander-in-chief of the American Station, 1774–1776; he was a cousin of Thomas Graves. His task was to carry out the restrictions of the Boston Port Bill, but with inadequate resources he largely failed and was relieved. Admiral in 1778 but with no duties.

THOMAS GRAVES (1725–1802). Commander-in-chief, North American Station, replacing Admiral Arbuthnot, in 1780. Relief of Cornwallis via his fleet from New York failed in October 1781. Vice admiral in 1787; admiral in 1794; created 1st Baron Graves.

FRANÇOIS JOSEPH PAUL, COMTE DE GRASSE (1722–1788). A sailor from age eleven, and a commander at Ushant in 1778, he became a rear admiral in 1781 with orders to assist Rochambeau in American waters. His success off Yorktown was marred by defeat by Rodney in the West Indies, where he was taken prisoner. After release his career was finished.

NATHANAEL GREENE (1742–1786). Massachusetts-born Continental general whose abilities led to his appointment as quartermaster general in early 1778. Desiring a field command, and fed up with Congress's bickering, he resigned briefly n 1780 and was victorious in the Carolinas in 1781. Perhaps Washington's best general, he was less effective in peace and went bankrupt in 1784.

JOHN HANCOCK (1737–1793). Massachusetts merchant and politician; president of the Continental Congress when the Declaration of Independence was approved, and its first signer.

DAVID HARTLEY (1730–1813). MP, 1774–1784; friend of Franklin and advocate for conciliation with America; sent to France in April 1783, replacing Oswald, to draft the definitive peace treaty.

PATRICK HENRY (1736–1799). A leading and eloquent Virginia radical, he became the first revolutionary governor of Virginia in June 1776.

ALEXANDER HOOD (1727–1814). Younger brother of Samuel Hood, he was a career naval officer who commanded the *Robust* off Ushant. He later fought against the French in the Mediterranean and the West Indies. He was created Viscount Bridport on retirement in 1801.

SAMUEL HOOD (1724–1816) Commanded in North America, the West Indies, and the Mediterranean, including the attempt to relieve Cornwallis in 1781. Created Viscount Hood of Catherington in 1796. He and his brother had naval cousins also named Alexander and Samuel.

RICHARD HOWE (1726–1799). Sailor elder brother of William Howe; son of 2nd Viscount Howe, became 1st Earl Howe. Distinguished service as admiral in relieving Gibraltar in 1782, but less effective earlier against the French navy in American waters.

WILLIAM HOWE (1729–1814). MP, 1758–1780; replaced Thomas Gage as commander in America late in 1775; took New York and briefly occupied Philadelphia. Knighted but known for his lethargy; replaced in 1778 by Sir Henry Clinton.

JOHN JAY (1745–1829), New York lawyer; delegate to Continental Congress, 1774–1779; chief justice of New York, 1776–1779; president of the Congress, 1778–79; minister to Spain 1779–1782; peace negotiator, 1781–1782; secretary for foreign affairs, 1784–1789; chief justice of the Supreme Court, 1789–1794; governor of New York, 1795–1801.

THOMAS JEFFERSON (1743–1826). Virginia lawyer, landowner, and politician; delegate to Continental Congresses; drafted Declaration of Independence. Governor of Virginia 1779–1781; American minister to France, 1785–1789; first secretary of state in 1789; vice president in 1797; third president of the United States, 1801–1809.

SAMUEL JOHNSON (1709–1784) Lexicographer and man of letters, he produced the first major dictionary of the English language in 1755. He edited Shakespeare, a multivolume lives of English poets, wrote poems, plays, and fiction, edited magazines, and was famed as a controversialist; his biography was written by his devoted follower James Boswell.

GEORGE JOHNSTONE (1730–1787). MP 1774–1780; governor of West Florida; a director of East India Company.

JOHN PAUL JONES (1747–1792). Born John Paul in Scotland; fled to Virginia in 1773 while a merchant ship captain after killing a mutineer. Officer in Continental navy in December 1775; as captain raided Scottish and English coastal towns; captured British frigate *Serapis* in 1779. Postwar mercenary service in Russian navy as rear admiral, 1788–1789; died in Paris.

AUGUSTUS KEPPEL (1725–1786). Second son of the Earl of Albemarle; possessing a courtesy title, he was MP, 1761–1780, vice admiral from 1770, and commander of Channel fleet in 1778, although opposed to the American war and an ally of Rockingham.

WILHELM, BARON VON KNYPHAUSEN (1716–1800). General and commander of Hessian forces in New York; despite his talents always a second-in-command to British generals by Whitehall policy.

MARIE JOSEPH DU MOTIER, MARQUIS DE LAFAYETTE (1757–1834). A wealthy and aristocratic junior officer in the French army, he sought service in America, and to curry French support he was commissioned a major general, serving with distinction through Yorktown. He then took his zeal for political reform back to France.

ANNE-CÉSAR DE LA LUZERNE (1731–1791). Second French envoy to the United Colonies, he arrived in 1779 and wielded great influence via lobbying Congress. He died while minister to Great Britain. A county in northeastern Pennsylvania is named for him.

HENRY LAURENS (1724–1792). South Carolina landowner, delegate to Continental Congress 1777–1780, and its president, November 1777–1778. Seized en route to Holland as American minister; imprisoned in the Tower. After his exchange for Cornwallis he was a signer of the preliminary treaty of peace in France in 1782.

JOHN LAURENS (1754–1782). Son of Henry Laurens; aide to Washington; wounded at Germantown and Monmouth; taken prisoner at Charleston and exchanged; fought at Yorktown as lieutenant colonel. Killed in skirmish in South Carolina after most hostilities had ended.

CHARLES LEE (1731–1782). A Virginia landowner who had served in the British army and the Polish army, he became a Continental general of dubious effectiveness and was eventually relieved by an exasperated Washington.

BENJAMIN LINCOLN (1733–1810). A Massachusetts militia commander, he became a major general of the Continentals in February 1777. Besieged at Charleston, he surrendered his army but was exchanged in time to be at Yorktown. Secretary of War from late 1781 into 1784.

TEMPLE SIMON LUTTRELL (1738–1803). MP, 1775–1780, with a reputation for cantankerousness.

WILLIAM MURRAY, 1ST EARL OF MANSFIELD (1705–1793). Lord chief justice of the King's Bench, 1756–1788. A power in the government, his decisions, however impartial, made him highly unpopular.

HUGH MERCER (1725–1777). Scots emigrant who fought in the Pennsylvania Regiment in the Seven Years' War, later (1776) a colonel in the 3rd Virginia Regiment, he became a Continental brigadier general. He died of wounds suffered at Princeton early in 1777.

RICHARD MONTGOMERY (1738–1775). A British officer in the Seven Years' War, he returned to America in 1773, became a brigadier general of Continentals in June 1775, and was killed in the failed attack on Quebec.

DANIEL MORGAN (1736–1802). Civilian teamster in the Seven Years' War, he became a Virginia militia captain in 1775, and was captured at Quebec, then exchanged. A Continental colonel at Saratoga, he was a brigadier general when his troops defeated the redcoats at Cowpens, South Carolina, in January 1781. Served in Congress 1797–1799 as a Federalist.

ROBERT MORRIS (1734–1806). Lancashire-born financier of the revolution from Philadelphia, where he became wealthy as a broker. Signer of the Declaration of Independence. Overextended in his financial dealings, in old age he was imprisoned for debt.

JAMES MURRAY (1719–1794) Governor of Quebec and Minorca, later governor of Hull, he became a full general in 1783. Known as "Old Minorca."

JAMES MURRAY (?–1794) Sometimes confused with his namesake (there were many James Murrays), he was an army colonel of the

72nd Foot and an MP; governor of Fort William and later a major general.

FREDERICK, 8TH LORD NORTH (1732–1792). MP at twenty-two, afterward chancellor of the exchequer, and (in 1770) prime minister. Presided over the loss of America, resigning in 1782. Served again briefly (1783) in a coalition with Charles Fox. Succeeded to his father's title as 2nd Earl of Guilford.

RICHARD OSWALD (1705–84). A Scots merchant, slave trader, and army contractor with commercial connections in America, he helped negotiate the 1782 preliminary peace treaty with the colonies.

THOMAS PAINE (1737–1809). English-born revolutionary agitator, he published the pamphlet "Common Sense" in Philadelphia in January 1776. Famous but unrewardingly so as a missionary of revolution, he relocated to Europe in 1787 and in France published *The Rights of Man* in 1791–1792 and *The Age of Reason* in 1794–1796. Returning to America, he died in poverty.

HUGH PALLISER (1723–1796). Comptroller of the Navy, 1770–1775; MP, 1774–1784; knighted as admiral and ally of Sandwich. Survived court-martial in 1779 to achieve a sinecure as director of the naval hospital at Greenwich.

PETER PARKER (1721–1811). Naval officer in American waters, 1775–1777; knighted belatedly (1782) for bravery at Charleston, where he lost his breeches; commander in Jamaica, 1779–1781; succeeded Lord Howe as admiral of the fleet.

HUGH PERCY (1742–1817). As eldest son of Duke of Northumberland he was styled Earl Percy. Served in America as a brigadier general.

WILLIAM PHILLIPS (1731–1781). Royal Engineers officer posted to America as a major general. Surrendered with Burgoyne at Saratoga and later exchanged. Died of a fever at Petersburg, Virginia, during the final Chesapeake campaign.

WILLIAM PITT (THE ELDER), EARL OF CHATHAM (1708–1788). An MP from 1735, he became, in 1756, effectively if not nominally prime minister, seeing Britain through the Seven Years' War. Spoke against harsh policies toward the colonies; left office in 1768 due to ill health.

WILLIAM PITT (1759–1806). Second son of Chatham, was known as Pitt the younger. A brilliant parliamentarian with antiwar sentiments on election to Commons in January 1781, he took office as prime minister in December 1783, the youngest ever, and held power for most of the next twenty years.

RICHARD PRESCOTT (1725–1788). Colonel, 7th Foot with rank in America of brigadier general from November 1775. Captured, exchanged, and recaptured again in July 1777 to exchange for Charles Lee. His reputation for arrogance was satirized in the British press

RICHARD PRICE (1723–1791). Welsh Dissenting minister, D. D. Glasgow; an early Unitarian. Pro-colonies moral and political philosopher gaining fame with his *Observations on Civil Liberty and the War with America* (1776).

JOSEPH PRIESTLEY (1733–1804). Controversial Yorkshire Presbyterian minister and self-taught chemist (*History of Electricity,* 1767); friend of Franklin; relocated to Pennsylvania in 1794.

ISRAEL PUTNAM (1718–1790). A militia officer in Connecticut, he became a major general in the Continental army in 1775.

FRANCIS RAWDON (1754–1826). Dublin-born career soldier; led (under Cornwallis) with distinction in the American South. Later governor-general of British India; purchased Singapore island, 1819; created 1st Marquess of Hastings.

JOSEPH REED (1741–1785). A Philadelphia lawyer, he was secretary to Washington, 1775–1776, adjutant general of the Continentals as colonel, 1776–1777. Declined bribe from a British peace commissioner. President of Pennsylvania supreme executive council, 1778–1781.

PAUL REVERE (1735–1818). Boston metalsmith and engraver; member of the Sons of Liberty. Courier for the Massachusetts Committee of Safety. Manufactured gunpowder for the colonies; opened foundry in 1788 and first sheet-copper mill in America in 1802.

CHARLES LENNOX, DUKE OF RICHMOND (1735–1806). Secretary of state for the Southern Department, 1766; antigovernment ally of Rockingham in the Lords.

FRIEDRICH ADOLPHUS, BARON RIEDESEL (1738–1800). Hessian general serving the Duke of Brunswick, he commanded the first Brunswickers in America under the agreement of 1775 with Lord North.

JAMES RIVINGTON (1724–1802). London-born New York bookseller, printer, and newspaper proprietor. Returning to New York with the British after his businesses were sacked by patriots, as king's printer he published the loyalist *Royal Gazette*. His attempt to keep his establishment going after the reoccupation of New York was ultimately unsuccessful.

JEAN BAPTISTE DE VIMEUR, COMTE DE ROCHAMBEAU (1725–1807). Commander of the French army in America from 1780 as a lieutenant general, he was successful at Yorktown in effective joint operations with Washington. Returning to France early in 1783, he received royal favor and governorships, and eventually became a marshal of France.

CHARLES WENTWORTH, MARQUIS OF ROCKINGHAM (1730–1782). As prime minister in 1765–1766, led repeal of Stamp Act. Leading opponent of North and his American policies; succeeded North in March 1782 but died four months later.

GEORGE RODNEY (1719–1792). An MP and career naval officer, he went into debt to finance reelection in 1768, escaping his creditors in 1775 by fleeing to France. Returning in 1778 he was promoted to full admiral. With audacity he relieved the Spanish siege of Gibraltar and defeated the French in the West Indies. Voted a large pension, he became Baron Rodney in 1782.

THOMAS ROWLANDSON (1756–1827). London caricaturist and engraver famed for lively domestic and tavern scenes and political satires.

AMBROSE SERLE (1742–1812). Undersecretary to Lord Dartmouth, then private secretary to Admiral Lord Howe in America, 1776–1778. Became a commissioner for the care and exchange of prisoners of war, serving into the Napoleonic years.

WILLIAM PETTY FITZMAURICE, 2ND EARL OF SHELBURNE (1737–1805). In Chatham's (Pitt's) second administration but declined to serve under North. Became a secretary of state under Rockingham, and brought the younger Pitt into the cabinet. Later Marquis of Lansdowne.

MOLYNEUX SHULDHAM (1717–1798). Governor of Newfoundland, 1772–1775; admiral in American waters in early years of the rebellion; MP, 1774–1784.

DAVID MURRAY, VISCOUNT STORMONT (1727–1796). Ambassador to France, 1772–1778, he became secretary of state for the Northern Department, 1779–1782, succeeding Lord Suffolk.

HENRY HOWARD, EARL OF SUFFOLK (1739–1779). Secretary of state for the Northern Department, 1771–1779; ally of Germain.

JOHN SULLIVAN (1740–1795). New Hampshire–born militia major in 1774, he became a brigadier general via membership in the Continental Congress. Served in Canada, at Boston siege; at Valley Forge; at Newport. Vain and ineffective, he resigned in 1779 and returned to Congress. Always politically astute, he was governor of New Hampshire, 1786–1789, then a federal judge.

THOMAS SUMTER (1734–1832). The "Carolina Gamecock," he was a militia leader, 1780–1781, more effective in plundering than in guerrilla war. Although long harried by debts, he served postwar in the South Carolina Senate, U.S. House of Representatives, and Senate, (1801–1810).

BANASTRE TARLETON (1754–1833). Rising via daring and ruthlessness from Dragoon Guards cornet to cavalry lieutenant colonel, he terrorized Continentals in the Carolinas. Paroled after Yorktown, he was MP for Liverpool, 1790–1806, and later a general and baronet.

BENJAMIN THOMPSON (1753–1814). Massachusetts loyalist; sailed to England in the evacuation from Boston; employed in Whitehall by Germain. Colonel in America, 1882–1883. Self-taught chemist (heat and explosives); knighted in 1784. While in Bavarian government service 1784–1795 he became Count Rumford.

HESTER LYNCH THRALE (1741–1821). Married Henry Thrale, a Southwark brewer. Close friend of Dr. Johnson from 1765; wrote memoirs of him and an autobiography. When widowed she married (1784) expatriate Italian musician Gabriel Piozzi.

JOHN TRUMBULL (1756–1843). Son of Connecticut governor Jonathan Trumbull, he left the army as a lieutenant colonel to study painting in London under Benjamin West. Arrested and imprisoned, he was finally released to return to America. He would become a major historical painter.

CHARLES GRAVIER, COMTE DE VERGENNES (1717–1787). French ambassador, then foreign minister; instrumental in the alliance with the colonies in 1778 and in the peace treaty of 1783.

HORACE WALPOLE (1717–1797). Youngest son of Sir Robert Walpole, Whig statesman, he was MP for King's Lynn and a prolific and gossipy letter writer, memoirist, and writer of gothic romances. His ornate pseudo-castle near Twickenham, Strawberry Hill, was the site of his private press hobby. Toward the close of his life he inherited from a brother the title of 4th Earl of Oxford.

JOSEPH WARREN (1741–1775). Boston physician and patriot firebrand who sent Paul Revere and William Dawes to warn of the redcoat advance on Lexington and Concord. Killed at Bunker (Breed's) Hill.

GEORGE WASHINGTON (1732–1799). A major under General Edward Braddock in the Seven Years' War, he became commander of the Virginia militia, then a delegate to the first Continental Congress, which in 1775 appointed him commander-in-chief of the Continental army. After the peace of 1783 he retired from military life but was recalled to chair the Constitutional Convention, 1785–1786. Elected the first American president, he served from 1789 to 1787.

LUND WASHINGTON (1737–1796). A distant cousin of George, he managed the Mount Vernon plantation during the war.

MARTHA WASHINGTON (1731–1802). Married wealthy planter Daniel Parke Custis in 1749; as widow with two children married George Washington in 1759. Spent winters with him and his army at Cambridge, Morristown, Valley Forge, and Newburgh. First "First Lady."

WILLIAM AUGUSTINE WASHINGTON (1757–1810). Described by George Washington as of Westmoreland County, Pennsylvania, he was the son of Washington's half-brother Augustine; commanded cavalry at Cowpens.

ANTHONY WAYNE (1745–1794). A Pennsylvania militia officer, he became a Continental brigadier general, serving in Canada, at Ticonderoga, Valley Forge, Brandywine, and Germantown, took Stony Point, and served in parallel with Lafayette in Virginia.

ALEXANDER WEDDERBURN (1733–1805). Scottish MP, solicitor general, attorney general, finally lord chancellor. Created 1st Earl Loughborough in 1801.

JOSIAH WEDGWOOD (1730–1795). English potter notable in the industry for dining and display products soon known as Wedgewood ware. Member of the Birmingham-based group of amateur experimenters (and mostly sympathizers with America) known as "Lunar Men."

BENJAMIN WEST (1738–1820). On settling in London after art studies in Italy, the former Philadelphian became official historical painter to George III and president, after Joshua Reynolds, of the Royal Academy. Spurned traditional classical garb for contemporary portraiture. Best known for *The Death of [General] Wolfe.*

CALEB WHITEFOORD (1734–1810). Writer and wit; London neighbor and acquaintance of Franklin; appointed by Shelburne to be peace commission secretary to Oswald.

JOHN WILKES (1727–1797). Feisty politician, son of wealthy London distiller. MP from 1757; expelled in 1764 for libel of the king; went into exile. Reelected, reexpelled, and imprisoned (1769–1770), increasing his popularity among the opposition. Elected lord mayor of London, 1774; reelected as MP, 1774–1790. Wilkes-Barré named for him and Isaac Barré.

JAMES WOODFORDE (1740–1803). The Reverend Woodford was a country parson who kept a diary from 1758 into 1803. From 1776 to 1802 he served a parish in a village near Norwich.

NATHANIEL WRAXALL (1751–1831). Served in the East India Company and on minor diplomatic missions; a writer of histories, notably *Historical Memoirs of My Own Time, 1772–1784* (1815). A follower of North, he went over to the younger Pitt. A baronet in 1813.

Source Notes

GENERAL

Many of the sources referred to under headings below for the first two chapters are further utilized throughout the book. These include the correspondences of Lord North, Lord George Germain, King George III, and Horace Walpole. For the first three, see below. Washington's letters are primarily from *George Washington. Writings,* edited by John Rhodehamel (New York, 1997). Perhaps no better picture of the domestic scene from 1775 to 1783 exists than the relevant volumes of *Horace Walpole's Correspondence,* edited by Wilmarth S. Lewis, et al., 48 volumes incl. indexes (New Haven, Conn.: 1939–1984), in particular Sir Horace's exchanges with Sir Henry Seymour Conway and his wife, Lady Aylesbury, and with Sir Horace Mann, William Mason, and Lady Ossory. Walpole, however, was opposed to the war, and his letters must be read from that perspective. A crucial volume also has been *Rebellion in America. A Contemporary British Viewpoint, 1765–1783,* edited by David H. Murdoch (Oxford and Santa Barbara, 1979), which reprints the texts of the *Annual Register.* Yet again, since its publisher, John Almon, was in the opposition, it must be kept in mind that his commentaries and choice of extracts may reflect his opinions. The *Register* includes parliamentary debates, the *Court Circular,* and brief contemporary accounts of military and naval engagements. (Inaccessible to it were the inner workings of government, which emerge from other documents.) For further parliamentary detail, see W. Cobbett and J. Wright, editors, *The Parliamentary History of England* (London, 1806–1820). Also referred to throughout as the major source of information on political cartoons and caricatures outside the contemporary magazines themselves is Mary Dorothy George's *Catalogue of Political and Personal Satires Preserved in the Department of Prints and Drawings, the British Museum, V, 1771–1783* (London: 1935).

Many sources are embedded in the text, especially contemporary newspaper and magazine references, and the texts accompanying illustrated broadsides. The press was sufficiently free to enable the reproduction verbatim of parliamentary debates and legislation, even the transcripts of sessions of the "enemy" Continental Congress, and speeches as well as the proclamations of "rebel" leaders, military and civilian. Although most of my references from English newspapers, magazines and broadsides are from the originals, also useful have been Solomon Lutnick's *The American Revolution and the English Press, 1775–1783* (Columbia, Mo.: 1967), and Martin Kallich's *British Poetry and the American Revolution. A Bibliographical Survey* of *Books and Pamphlets, Journals and Magazines, Newspapers and Prints, 1755–1800* (Troy, New York: 1988). The press was open and usually accurate about provisioning overseas troops, and Germain's correspondence furnishes further details, but also valuable has been R. Arthur Bowler's *Logistics and the Failure of the British Army in America* (Princeton, 1975), utilized throughout. Also employed throughout for domestic data has been Stephen Conway's *The British Isles and the War of American Independence* (Oxford, 2000).

PREFACE

The unfinished Benjamin West canvas, *The Peace Commissioners, 1782,* is in the Winterthur Museum, Wilmington, Delaware. Information about the painting is drawn from the canvas itself, and from Robert C. Alberts, *Benjamin West. A Biography* (Boston, 1978). The twenty-cent U.S. postage stamp issued in 1983 for the two hundredth anniversary of the definitive treaty misidentifies the scene as *Treaty of Paris, 1783,* adding, *US Bicentennial;* and in a travesty of West the stamp eliminates three of the Americans, leaving only Adams and Franklin, and adds two unidentified figures, presumably the English negotiators, while otherwise filling in the empty side of the canvas with a pillar-fronted building in the background and massive draperies, which are also added to the left behind Adams.

I   "COUSIN AMERICA": JANUARY 1775–DECEMBER 1775

"Cousin America" appears in a letter from Horace Walpole to the Countess of Ossory, August 3, 1775. The Walpole letters to a variety of correspondents, edited by W. S. Lewis et al. (see above), are referred to throughout. Walpole also kept diaries, also quoted from throughout, published posthumously as *Journal of the Reign of George III from 1771 to 1783* (London, 1859, repr, New Haven, 2000), also titled *The Last Journals of Horace Walpole* (London, 1890), and *Reminiscences* (London, 1819). The "My Master!" lines are from *The Last Journals* under an April 1774 date. Walpole's letter to Lady Ossory, November 9, 1775, reports Lord George Germain's assumption of Cabinet office the following day. The remark by Captain Heinrichs about a "Presbyterian Rebellion" appears in "The Letter-Book of Captain Johnann Heinrichs," *Pennsylvania Magazine of History and Biography,* 22 (1898). The Reverend Woodforde's *Diary of a Country Parson* (Oxford, 1985) was edited by David Hughes.

General Gage's letters are in *Correspondence of General Thomas Gage,* edited by M. Carter (New Haven, 1931–1933). Ambrose Serle's diary, also quoted from through 1778 when he returned to England, is *The American Journal of Ambrose Serle, Secretary to Lord Howe, 1776–1778,* edited by Edward H. Tatum, Jr. (San Marino, Calif.: 1940). Edmund Burke's letters (with very significant notes) are in *The Correspondence of Edmund Burke, III & IV* (Chicago, 1963), edited by J. A. Woods.

James Simpson's letter to Lord George Germain as American Secretary appears in the 1776 volume of Germain's official correspondence, published in annual volumes quoted throughout as *Documents of the American Revolution, 1770–1783 (Colonial Office Series),* edited by K. G. Davies (Shannon, 1972–1981). *The Private Papers of John, Earl of Sandwich* (London, 1932–1938) are edited by G. R. Barnes and J. H. Owen. George III's letters to Lord North appear in W. Bodham Dunne, editor, *The Correspondence of King George the Third with Lord North 1768 to 1783* (New York, 1971, repr. of the 1867 ed.). Further details about Lord North are from Peter Whiteley's *Lord North. The Prime Minister Who Lost America* (London, 1996.) The king's fuller correspondence is in Sir John Fortescue, editor, *The Correspondence of King George III* (London, 1927–1928). Lieutenant John Fielding's letters are in *The Lost War. Letters from British Officers during the American Revolution* (New York, 1975), edited by Marion Balderston and David Syrett. The Howes and their correspondence are best found (other than their exchanges with Lord George Germain, see above) in Ira D. Gruber, *The Howe Brothers and the American Revolution* (Chapel Hill, N.C., 1974). The most thorough modern biography of the First Lord of the Admiralty is N. A. M. Rodger, *The Insatiable Earl: A Life of John Montagu, Fourth Earl of Sandwich* (London, 1993). Sir George Rodney's congratulatory letter and preappointment letter to Germain are reproduced in the Stopford-Sackville manuscripts. For a full reference, see Chapter 2. Boswell is quoted from Peter Martin, *A Life of James Boswell* (New Haven, 2000) and from his published journals.

2   THE SECRETARY FOR AMERICA: 1775–1776

The epigraph is from George Grenville, Lord Lansdowne (1667–1735), as quoted by Horace Walpole in *Royal and Noble Authors of England, Scotland and Ireland* (Strawberry Hill, 1754). For Germain's early life and pre-

Revolution career, the best published resource is the Royal Manuscripts Commission's *Report on the Manuscripts of Mrs. Stopford-Sackville of Drayton House, Northamptonshire, I* (Hereford, 1904) and *II* (Hereford, 1910), which quotes substantially from both sides of his correspondence. The only full biography of the secretary is Alan Valentine's *Lord George Germain* (Oxford, 1962). A partial biography is Gerald Saxon Brown's *The American Secretary. The Colonial Policy of Lord George Germain, 1775–1778* (Ann Arbor, 1963). Both have been utilized for this chapter, and both rely heavily upon the Clinton Papers in the Clements Library, University of Michigan. The Minden court-martial is fully transcribed in *The Proceedings of a general court martial held at the Horse-Guards . . . upon the trial of Lord George Sackville* (Dublin, 1760). Franklin's letter to Priestley is quoted by Esmond Wright in *Franklin of Philadelphia* (Cambridge, Mass., 1986). Franklin's enforced appearance before the Privy Council is described vividly by Catherine Drinker Bowen in *The Most Dangerous Man in America. Scenes from the Life of Bejamin Franklin* (Boston, 1974), which includes the reaction by Benjamin Rush.

3   "A MOST UNACCOUNTABLE MADNESS":
    JANUARY 1776–JUNE 1776

Both Burke's letters and the *Last Journals of Horace Walpole* (on Germain) refer to heavy snow curtailing parliamentary business in early January. For Effingham, see Murdoch, editor, *Rebellion in America* (transcripts from Parliament in the *Annual Register*). For William Hickey and his friends, see *Memoirs of a Georgian Rake,* edited by Roger Hudson (London, 1995). The description of a cavalry's burden in America is from a London paper of March 30, 1776, as quoted in the *New Hampshire Gazette,* June 22, 1776. Edmund Burke is quoted from his *Letters* (see above). Parliamentary affairs are from *Rebellion in America* (see above). Lieutenant von Feilitzsch's diary as translated is *Journal of Several Campaigns in America* (1777–1780), from a Sotheby catalog. Of the many studies of Britons as foreign mercenaries one might note David Worthington's *Scots in Habsburg Service, 1618–1648* (Leiden, 2004).

As before (and following), Germain's correspondence is largely from *Documents of the American Revolution* (above). However, the description of his letter of April 7, 1776, about "unconditional submission" is from Peter Force, *American Archives, 4th Series* (Washington, DC, 1844). The petition of exemption from pressing by Thames watermen is from *Gentleman's Magazine,* November 1776. Self-mutilation to evade overseas service is described in the London press. The Bunker's Hill caricature is by London printer Mathew Darly. The affairs of the Howe brothers are detailed by Ira Gruber (above). The embittered bias in Peter Oliver's history of the war is referred to the *Dictionary of American Biography* account of him. Howe's unnamed officer was quoted in a letter dated March 25, 1776, and printed in the *Evening Post.* The *St. James's Chronicle* letter writer signed himself pseudonymously "Judaeus Apella." Another unnamed officer quoted from Nantasket about forage and provisions problems dated his letter variously from March 3 through March 17. It was first published in "a London paper" and reprinted in the *Freeman's Journal* on October 24, 1776. Germain's correspondence is from transcripts in *Documents of the American Revolution,* volume 12 (1776). Each subsequent volume also collects transcripts on an annual basis. Addresses to the king were regularly printed in full in the *St. James's Chronicle* and often also in the *Annual Register.* The *"Saint Yankey's day"* satire was quoted from a London press account dated April 18, 1776, in the *New Hampshire Gazette* on September 28, 1776.

4   A MOST PRECARIOUS INDEPENDENCE: JULY 1776–DECEMBER 1776

The broadside cartoon satirizing insufferable American patriots is dated October 21, 1776 (Lewis-Walpole Library, Farmington, CT). The pulling down of William Wilton's statue of George III in Bowling Green is recalled in a painting by William Walcutt (1854) and a steel engraving by John C. McRae (1859). Its shipment to Litchfield, Connecticut to be melted down into "some 42,000" cartridges is noted in Kenneth Silverman, *A Cultural History of the American Revolution* (New York, 1776). The fate of the surrounding fence is described by David W. Dunlap in "Greening Ye Olde Manhattan," *New York Times,* July 9, 2004, B-33. The shutting up of what is now Old St. Anne's Episcopal Church is told by Carol Child in "300-Year Journey," the Wilmington, Delaware *News Journal,* July 15, 2004, p. RC9-10.

The refusal of Washington's aides to deal with the Howes is from Serle's *Journal,* the *London Gazette* of August 10, 1776, and Gruber's *The Howe Brothers.* Captain Bowater's "taking nothing with them but their fears" is from his letter of September 26, 1776, in *The Lost War.* Germain's correspondence is from *Documents of the American Revolution.* The engraving "The Catch Singers" is number 5342 in the British Museum's Department of Prints and Drawings (hereafter, BM). The depredations of the naval press-gangs are described in H. Humpherus, *History of the Company of Watermen* (London, 1844), who quotes from Lady Mary Coke's journals. The Marquess of Hertford also wrote to Horace Walpole, October 31, 1776, about the press-gangs. Burgoyne's Christmas Day bet with Fox as recorded in the Brooks Club wagers book is quoted by Don Cook in *The Long Fuse* (New York, 1995).

Washington's "the game is pretty near up" is quoted from John C. Fitzpatrick, editor, *The Writings of George Washington* (Washington, D.C., 1937), VI. His own description (to John Hancock) of the Battle of Trenton is in a letter of December 27, 1776, also in Fitzpatrick. Another account, from the diary of Thomas Rodney, is in John Rhodehamel, editor, *The American Revolution. Writings from the War of Independence* (New York, 2001). David Hackett Fischer in *Washington's Crossing* (New York, 2004) notes that the boats used were high-walled ore-barges. Captain John Blunt's assistance in the Delaware crossing is described in Charles W. Brewster's *Rambles about Portsmouth* (1873), from a later facsimile edition (Portsmouth, N.H., 1971). John Fitzgerald's diary, December 25, 1776, quoted in *Songs of Independence,* notes his expectation of Christmas partying by the Hessians, "who make a good deal of Christmas." That Colonel Rall was warned by General James Grant, who had secured intelligence of Washington's intended attack, is substantiated from his private papers in Ballindalloch Castle, Scotland, reported by Carl Hartman in an Associated Press story on July 3, 2003, released nationwide. The Library of Congress copied Grant's papers onto fifty rolls of microfilm in 1999.

5   THE BEST-LAID SCHEMES: JANUARY 1777–JULY 1777

Most sources are identified in the text; others refer by subject to listings above. The Reverend Woodforde's patronizing of a tea smuggler is from his *The Diary of a Country Parson*. Sir Henry Clinton's own history of his American commands, *The American Rebellion. A Narrative of His Campaigns, 1775–1782,* edited by William B. Willcox (New York, 1949), is self-serving yet detailed in exploiting his own voluminous papers. Willcox's major expansion of his introduction is *Portrait of a General. Sir Henry Clinton in the War of Independence* (New York, 1964). The two works are drawn upon here and in later chapters. For Cornwallis's correspondence, here and elsewhere, other than to Germain and Clinton (although both appear in these volumes as well), see Charles Ross, editor, *Correspondence of Charles, First Marquis Cornwallis,* I (London, 1859); and Franklin and Mary Wickwire, *Cornwallis and the War of Independence* (London. 1971).

That parallel orders from Germain to Burgoyne and Howe missed a mail packet because of the American Secretary's weekend plans are oft repeated but clearly erroneous, as the narrative explains. However, the biographies of

Burgoyne, beginning with Albany de Fonblanque (London, 1876), perpetuate the myth that London—not General Howe—abandoned Sir John to his fate. While recent studies of the Howes (see Gruber, above, and T. S. Anderson's *The Command of the Howe Brothers During the American Revolution* [New York, 1936]) put the blame where it should be, the earliest biography of Lord Howe by Sir John Barrow, *The Life of Richard Earl Howe, K.G.* (London, 1838), fails to mention Philadelphia or even the Delaware River and Bay.

The complaint about rations irreverently using the Lord's Prayer is quoted by Bower in *Logistics and the Failure of the British Army in America* (see above).

6 SARATOGA TRUMPS PHILADELPHIA:
JULY 1777–DECEMBER 1777

Walpole's letters to the Countess of Upper Ossory are edited by W. S. Lewis with A. Dayle Wallace and Edwine M. Martz (New Haven, Conn.: 1965). His letters to Horace Mann, utilized throughout, are in *Horace Walpole's Correspondence with Sir Horace Mann,* edited by W. S. Lewis. Warren H. Smith, George L. Lam, and Edwuine M. Martz (New Haven, Conn.: 1967). Saratoga is much written about, and Burgoyne's intercepted letters to Germain were often published in the press as if an open book. They appear complete in *Documents of the American Revolution* for 1777. Aside from the Burgoyne biographies, the New York campaign is covered in Max M. Mintz's *The Generals of Saratoga* (New Haven, Conn.: 1990), where the rejoinder to Gates is repeated ("I am not glad to see you.").

Troup's lament to John Jay, July 22, 1777, is in *John Jay, The Making of a Revolutionary,* edited by Richard B. Morris (New York, N.Y.: 1975). Prescott's breeches embarrassment is recalled in Walpole's *Last Journals,* and the verse about the episode is quoted in *The Spirit of Seventy-Six,* edited by Henry Steele Commager and Richard B. Morris (New York, N.Y.: 1975). Captain Dansey's letter about the Delaware colors, and information about its return to Delaware in 1927, was furnished by Major General William Duncan of the Delaware National Guard. *The Takeing of Miss Mud Island* was printed by William Humphrey in the Strand on December 2, 1777, to illustrate Howe's dispatch of October 25, 1777.

Edward Oxnard's diary was published in the *New-England Historical and Genealogical Register, XXVI* (January 1872). Edward Gibbon is quoted from *The Letters of Edward Gibbon,* edited by J. E. Norton (London, 1956). The Mrs. Loring verses appear in many places, and are taken here from Philip Young, *Revolutionary Ladies* (New York, N.Y.: 1977). The cartoon "The State

Tinkers" was reproduced with caption in the *William and Mary Quarterly*, IX (July 1952).

7 EXCEPT IN PARLIAMENT: JANUARY 1778–JUNE 1778

The American Secretary's correspondence is found in the 1778 volume of *Documents of the American Revolution*. Clinton's correspondence with Germain and others is in Willcox. The *Annual Register* and the London press record parliamentary matters. Germain's personal distresses are recorded not only in Valentine but in the London press as cited. *The Closet* print was published by Isaac Williams, 39 Fleet Street, and is BM 5470. Franklin's relations with English politicians and agents are in Esmond Wright, *Franklin of Philadelphia*. Josiah Wedgwood's opposition to the war is described in Jenny Uglow's *The Lunar Men* (London, 2002). For Parson Woodforde see notes to Chapter 1. Walpole quotes the "General Fast" verses in *Last Journals*. For the Howes, see Germain, Gruber, Willcox, and press accounts cited. *Gentleman's Magazine* for August 1778, among the many publications reporting the Mischianza in appalling detail, referred to "the lap of Mrs. L———g" and to the affair as "dancing at a funeral." For the state of the Royal Navy and the swarms of rebel privateers see press accounts and Nathan Miller, *Sea of Glory. The Continental Navy Fights for Independence, 1775–1783* (New York, N.Y.: 1974). *Town and Country* for July 1778 reported the Luttrell-Germain imbroglio in the Commons in great detail. The spoof double pregnancy report, which would have been seditious if published in England as alleged, is from the *New Hampshire Gazette,* March 22, 1777, but facetiously credited to Lord George Germain's official *London Gazette* for the previous October 10.

8 THE FRENCH CONNECTION: JULY 1778–DECEMBER 1778

Germain's instructions to the peace commissioners and their responses through November are in *Documents of the American Revolution* and supplemented by other correspondence in the Stopford-Sackville MSS.

The cartoon satire, in color, on the commissioners as beggars, with captioned dialogue, was published by Mattthew Darly in the Strand (BM Prints and Drawings no. 5473). North's continued attempts to resign are in John Fortescue, editor, *The Correspondence of King George III* (London, 1927–1928). The verses on Franklin "by an Englishman, 1778" in the case of a watch are printed well after the fact in the *New Hampshire Gazette,* March 18, 1785. The print captioned "The Royal George's Cruise in the year 2777" was printed by J. Williams, Bookseller, "near the Mitre Tavern in

Fleet Street" (Lewis-Walpole Library). For the Ushant engagement with the French, see citations in Chapter 9, following. The cartoon of disappointed politicians in a coffeehouse, with maps of America behind them, is BM 5485.

9 THE WAR ON TRIAL: JANUARY 1779–JUNE 1779

The epigraph to this chapter from the *Monthly Review* is extracted from a review of *Remarks on Commodore Johnstone's Account of his Engagement with a French Squadron under the Command of Mons. de Suffrein, on Apollo, 1781* (London, 1781). The full transcript of the Keppel proceedings is *Minutes of the Proceedings at a Court-Martial, assembled for the trial of the Honourable Admiral Augustus Keppel on a Charge exhibited against him by Vice-Admiral Sir Hugh Palliser, Baronet as taken by George Jackson, Esq., Judge-Advocate of His Majesty's Fleet.* It was published at sixpence by W. Strahan and T. Cadell in the Strand, in 1779.

Illustrated and captioned broadsides, with BM Prints and Drawings codes, include *The Political Raree-Show* (BM 5548), from *Westminster Magazine,* June 1779; a hanged Lord Sandwich (5537); *Admiral Keppel's Tryal* by Captain Bailly (BM 5536); *The Birth-Day Ode,* with the corpse of Miss Ray at Sandwich's feet (BM 5540); *Who's at Fault?* Keppel as a bodyless head (BM 5570); *"What a Smoak and What a Stink!* D'Orvilliers and Keppel (BM 5626); *Ministerial Purgations, or State Gripings* (BM 5632); and *Britannia's Assassination* "He that fights and runs away . . ." is BM 5981. The futuristic navy-in-the-air cartoon, *The Battle of the Balloons* (BM 6709), was "printed and sold by Carrington Bowles, No. 69 in St. Paul's Church Yard" in 1784. The adaptation from Addison's *Cato* is from the caption to an anonymous engraving, *Mr. Trade & Family, or The State of the Nation* (BM 5574).

Charles James Fox's attack on Sandwich for giving the Greenwich sinecure to the disgraced Palliser was quoted in the *Annual Register* and printed in full in Fox's *Speeches, I* (London, 1815). Of the vast literature on Paul Jones, the most reliable life is Evan Thomas's *John Paul Jones, Sailor, Hero, Father of the American Navy* (New York, 2003). The British tar's blast at American privateers and the arrogant new nation is in the anonymous and probably autobiographical novel *Jonathan Corncob* (London, 1785).

10 MODERATELY FEEDING THE WAR: JUNE 1779–DECEMBER 1779

Germain's military correspondence is in the 1779 volume of *Documents of the American Revolution.* Ian Crowe's *Edmund Burke. His Life and Legacy* (New York, 1997) details Burke's reasons for attacking government "contractors." "The Council" cartoon issued by Humphrey Fox at 227 Strand on February 9, 1780, showed North, Sandwich, and Mansfield on adjoining privies (BM 5633). For General Clinton, Willcox, as well as Germain's correspondence, remain the major sources. Germain's correspondence with Richard Cumberland is in the Stopford-Sackville transcripts. For Joseph Stansbury's relations with Benedict Arnold and the brief Philadelphia urban anarchy, see Willard Sterne Randall's *Benedict Arnold. Patriot and Traitor* (New York, 1990). For Franklin and Stormont and other British dealings, see Esmond Wright, *Franklin of Philadelphia.*

The "Old Soldier" writing on Washington published his letter in *Lloyd's Evening Post,* August 17, 1778. The *"Des Landes Vater"* reference to GW is quoted in Esmond Wright's *The Search for Liberty* (Oxford, 1995). The September 23, 1779, word portrait of Washington by "an American gentleman now in London" was reprinted from an unidentified English newspaper in the March 4, 1880, issue of the *New Hampshire Gazette.*

General James Robertson's letters to Germain from New York are in *The Twilight of British Rule in Revolutionary America. The New York Letter-Book of General James Robertson,* 1780–1783, edited by Milton M. Klein and Ronald W. Howard (Cooperstown, N.Y., 1983). Robertson's letters henceforth are from this edition, although some are also in *Documents of the American Revolution.* The "Church Militant" cartoon by Gillray is BM 5553. The anonymous "Westminster Volunteers" cartoon is BM 5552; "The Master of the Asses," also anonymous, is BM 5551, and satirizes the militia being raised by local peers.

11 THE TIME OF THE TUMULTS: JANUARY 1780–JUNE 1780

For Burke's biography and letters, see above. Titles and descriptions of fourteen published General Fast sermons are found in mid-1780 issues of the *Monthly Review.* The many-sided (and often indirect) impact of the American war on British life and government is detailed by Stephen Conway in *The British Isles and the War of American Independence* (Oxford, 2000); John Derry in *English Politics and the American Revolution* (London, 1976); and Jenny Uglow in *The Lunar Men* (London, 2002). The "Just Asses" satire of March 27, 1780, on the Riot Act was reprinted from an unidentified London paper in the *New Hampshire Gazette* of July 29, 1780. The "tea-cup" image is from Joyce Appleby's review, "Self-styled men of destiny," *TLS,* March 24, 2003. Darly's "Heads of the Nation" cartoon is BM 5661. The pamphlet "The American

Times" was published at two shillings by Richardson of Fleet Street. The *Monthly Review's* condemnation appeared in its June 1780 issue.

The most comprehensive account of tumultuous June 1780 is J. Paul de Castro, *The Gordon Riots* (London, 1926). Also useful is a study by George Rudé, "The Gordon Riots: A Study of the Rioters and their Victims," *Transactions of the Royal Historical Society,* 5th series (1956). Dickens's *Barnaby Rudge* (London, 1841), while fiction, is vivid and largely valid but for some invented characters. Dickens did his homework. Also utilized here are Nathaniel Wraxall's *Historical Memoirs of My Own Time, 1772–1784* (London, 1815) and James Boswell's life of Samuel Johnson, with its reminiscences of the events that Boswell missed. The iron bars that Horace Walpole added prudently to his front door can still be seen, as Wilmarth S. Lewis had the door rehung at his home and library in Farmington, Connecticut.

The identification of Count Woronzow ("Rantzau") is made in the notes to a Walpole letter to William Mason. "Conflagration: A Satire" was published in London by Richardson in January 1781 as a pamphlet of twenty-nine pages.

The king's failed proposal to put General Conway into a coalition government is described in Walpole's *Last Journals* and validated by his correspondence with Conway of June 3, 1780. The letters by James Watt and Elizabeth Montagu are quoted from *The Lunar Men* (above). Germain's correspondence here and in Chapter 12 is in *Documents of the American Revolution* for 1780, and in the Stopford-Sackville MSS.

12 A DEARTH OF HEROES: JUNE 1780–DECEMBER 1780

The anonymous lady's sentiments about the British appeared in the *New Jersey Gazette* on July 12, 1780, and are reprinted in John Rhodehamel, editor, *The American Revolution. Writings from the War of Independence* (New York, 2001). "The Cow Chace, a poem in three cantos," by John André, is quoted from the 1866 reprint (Albany, N.Y.: J. Munsell). For Clinton, see Germain's correspondence and Willcox (above). General Phillips's role in the Chesapeake campaign is described by Robert P. Davis in *Where a Man Can Go. Major General William Phillips, British Royal Artillery, 1731–1781* (Westport, Conn.: 1999). The "Eden Lost" color engraving is BM 6815. The "Whiggism in Bristol" engraving is BM 5832. The most full account of Benedict Arnold's treachery and the involvement of André is in W. S. Randall (see above). *The London Gazette Extraordinary* continued to publish Germain's announcements from Whitehall about events in America, including the West Point fiasco, laundered into a patriotic tragedy and an Arnoldian triumph, and the arrivals and departures of significant officers and their aides. In his letters, Walpole not only got the rank of André wrong, assuming that an adjutant general was indeed a general, but in his *Last Journals* he referred to "Major-General St. André, the son of St. André, the surgeon." The London press in November 1783 published at great length the entire inscription on the monument to André erected in Westminster Abbey, with a detailed description of the monument designed by Robert Adam and executed in marble by P. M. Van Gelder. *The British Hero in Captivity,* a twenty-three-page pamphlet and one of the earliest of what would be a plethora of sentimental accounts, was dedicated "To His Royal Highness The Prince of Wales" and published in 1782.

Trumbull's arrest and subsequent imprisonment is described in far more detail than here in Alberts, *Benjamin West* (above, Preface).

13 MARCHING ABOUT THE COUNTRY: JANUARY 1781–JULY 1781

Charles Dodgson as "Lewis Carroll" published *Through the Looking-Glass,* a sequel to *Alice's Adventures in Wonderland,* in 1872. For the letters of Washington, Germain, and Clinton about the mutinies, see works above. For Phillips, see *Where a Man Can Go,* above, Chapter 12. For the confrontation of the Russian ambassador with Lord Stormont, see Michael Pearson, *Those Damned Rebels* (New York, 1972). The letters of the Prince of Wales and his equerry Colonel Gerard Lake are in A. Aspinall, editor, *The Correspondence of George, Prince of Wales, 1770–1812, I* (London, 1963). The mutiny of the Pennsylvania line is detailed in Carl Van Doren, *Mutiny in January* (New York, N.Y.: 1943). For British logistics and provisioning, see Bowler (in "General"), above. For Franklin, see Esmond Wright, above. "Jack England Fighting the Four Confederates" was released on January 20, 1781, by the printer John Smith (BM 5828); "The Balance of Power" was released on January 17 by R. Wilkinson, printer (BM 5827). Gillray's "The Dutchman in the Dumps" is dated April 19, 1781 (BM 5837). For the Vestris benefit, see *Italian Opera in London, I* (Oxford, 1995), edited by R. D. Hume, C. Prince, and J. Milhous. Cornwallis's costly campaigns (and Arnold's role) are described in detail, with maps, in William Seymour's *The Price of Folly. British Blunders in the War of American Independence* (London, 1995). For Robertson, Germain, and Clinton, see above. The quotation from *Othello* praising Cornwallis is from the *Public Advertiser,* August 22, 1781, and obviously referring to events months past.

14 "THE WORLD TURN'D UPSIDE DOWN":
  JULY 1781–DECEMBER 1781

For the culmination of the Virginia campaign I have utilized the works cited above, and Jeremy Black's *War for America. The Fight for Independence, 1775–1783* (Thrupp, Gloucestershire, 1998). The *London Courant's* mock-Horatian satire on Germain appeared on August 10, 1781. For Burke's letters, and life, see above. The anecdote from Philadelphia about the troops being Cornwallis's "physic" appeared in the *New Hampshire Gazette* on December 29, 1781. The lines from Shakespeare were quoted in *Gentleman's Magazine* in the February 1783 issue. The mock dialogue between the newly arrived Prince William Henry and Sir Henry Clinton first appeared in the *Pennsylvania Journal* and was reprinted on November 17, 1781, in the *New Hampshire Gazette*. The life of the prince, with his letters from New York to his father, the king, appears in Philip Ziegler's *King William IV* (New York, 1973). The ships' manifests of ammunition and provisions loaded in New York to succor Cornwallis's trapped troops, dated October 10, 1781, was offered for sale in the catalog of Joseph Rubinfine, a West Palm Beach, Florida, dealer, in his List 150, 2003.

There are many accounts of "The World turn'd Upside Down" played at the Yorktown surrender and at earlier capitulations, but the lyrics and possibly even the tune are in dispute. Various accounts—only a partial list—are in Harrison Bird, *March to Saratoga* (Oxford, 1963); Edward R. Riley, "St. George Tucker's Journal of the Siege of Yorktown," *William and Mary Quarterly,* July 1948; H. S. Commager and R. B. Morris, *The Spirit of 'Seventy-Six* (New York, 1958); Irwin Silber, *Songs of Independence* (Harrisburg, Penn.: 1973); Michael Pearson, *Those Damned Rebels* (see above); Burl Ives, *The Burl Ives Song Book* (New York, N.Y.: 1953); Keith and Rusty McNeil, *Colonial and Revolution Songbook* (Riverside, Calif., 1996); *Garden's Anecdotes of the Revolution* (Charleston, S.C., 1828); the International Anarchism web pages, undated; and Frank Luther, *The Americans and their Songs* (New York, N.Y.: 1943).

"State Cooks," published by W. Wells of 132 Fleet Street, is BM 5855. "The State Watchman" has been identified as both by Gillray and Rowlandson (BM 5850), but is more likely by Rowlandson, and published by W. Jones. Wraxall's *Historical Memoirs of My Own Time* (see above) describes the scene at Germain's residence when the news of Yorktown arrived, and his visit to North with the dread report. The mock sales offering was dated, from London, October 6, but did not reach the American press until December 29, 1781, the present text extracted from the *New Hampshire Gazette*. The tragedy of John Laurens's early death is told in Gregory D. Massey's *John Laurens and the American Revolution* (Columbia, S.C., 2001).

15 THE FAILURE OF FIRE AND SWORD:
   JANUARY 1782–JANUARY 1784

The scene with West and the king is based upon Alberts (see notes to the Preface). Alberts quotes Elkanah Watson from his *Memoirs. Men and Times of the Revolution* (New York, N.Y.: 1856). "The American Rattle Snake" cartoon issued by W. Humphrey, 227 Strand, on April 12, 1782 (BM 5973). Germain's final correspondence as American Secretary is in *Documents* for 1782–1783. "Fabricus" wrote in the *Chronicle* and *Morning Chronicle* for January 22, 1782, and is quoted by Solomon M. Lutnick in "The Defeat at Yorktown: A British View," in *The Virginia Magazine of History and Biography,* 72 (October 1964).

King George's abdication letter drafted for Parliament in March 1782 and never sent is in Fortescue's *Correspondence, V* (above) The king's second, and also never sent, abdication letter, March 1783, was quoted from the manuscript in *People in Politics.* The abdication cartoon by Rowlandson, printed by W. Humphrey, is BM 6384.

Valentine's life of Lord George concludes that "justice owes him a more balanced summary," yet the final chapter is a harsh indictment on his carrying resentments to the grave. Sackville's postministry letter to General Irwin is in the Stopford-Sackville MSS; his letter to Knox (June 21, 1783) is quoted by Valentine.

Colonel Ogden's plan to kidnap Prince William Henry for Washington is described in Philip Ziegler's *King William IV* (London, 1971). "Lord No— in the Suds" was drawn by Thomas Colley and printed by Thomas Evans of Oxford Street for sale on March 27, 1782 (BM 5968). "The State Cooks Making Peace-Porridge" is BM 6009. The cartoon of Britannia's offering to shake hands with America and be friends was issued by W. Humphrey on November 9, 1782 (BM 6162); "Reconciliation between Britannia and Daughter America" was drawn by Colley and printed by Humphrey in May 1782 (BM 5989). "Peace Soup" is BM 6172. The cartoon of hanged Tories (". . . the Cruel Fate of Loyalists") is BM 6529, February 1783.

Parson Woodforde's diary entries for Fast Day and for September 4, 1782, are from his published diary (above). John Jay's correspondence is in R. B. Morris, editor, *John Jay. The Winning of the Peace. Unpublished Papers, 1780–1784, II* (New York, 1980). Richard Oswald's prediction of the benefits to England of America's future growth and prosperity is from his journal in the Public Record Office, FO 95/511, quoted in Esmond Wright, *The Search for Liberty* (above). The thoughts of George III, in a similarly optimistic and undated memorandum, RA GEO/Add 32/20/10, are reproduced from the holograph manuscript in the Royal Archives by permission of Her Majesty Queen Elizabeth II. Josiah Tucker's *Four Letters on Important National Subjects* (London, 1783) was possibly seen by the king before he wrote his own notes. Walpole's letter to David Stewart Erskine, Earl of Buchan, September 23, 1783, on Uranus is in the *Correspondence, XV* (1951).

The rude postscript by Delancey and Watts to an Irish gentleman's intercepted letter of November 24, 1783, and dated from Cork January 7, 1784, is reproduced in the *New Hampshire* Gazette on May 22, 1784. The *Blessings of Peace,* an engraving of a London street scene marking the proclamation, was published in *Rambler's Magazine,* December 1, 1783.

Acknowledgments

Recognition of manuscript sources are in the text as well as in source notes above. Acknowledgments of illustration sources are included where relevant with the captions. (Many illustrations are from publications long out of print and out of copyright.)

I have been indebted to many individuals for resources utilized, often unidentifiable but valuable collaborators on both sides of the Atlantic. In addition, I am indebted to the generosity and often, too, hard work of Bruce A. Bailey, Pamela Clark, Robert C. Doyle, William Duncan, Thomas Fleming, Gladys Greenfield, Steven Greenfield, A. H. and Eileen Hanley-Browne, Robert Hume, Jürgen Kamm, John McLeod, Timothy D. Murray, William Pencak, Scott Pickett, Margaret Powell, Susan Reighard, L. G. Stopford Sackville, Sue Walker, David A. Weintraub, Mark B. Weintraub, Rodelle Weintraub, and Richard E. Winslow.

Index

About the Author

STANLEY WEINTRAUB is Evan Pugh Professor Emeritus of Arts and Humanities at Penn State University and the author of outstanding histories and biographies including *General Washington's Christmas Farewell: A Mount Vernon Homecoming, 1783; Silent Night: The Story of the 1914 Christmas Truce; MacArthur's War: Korea and the Undoing of an American Hero; Long Day's Journey Into War: Pearl Harbor and a World at War;* and *A Stillness Heard Round the World: The End of the Great War.* He lives in Newark, Delaware.